DALITS AND THE STATE

About the Editor

Ghanshyam Shah is an eminent political sociologist. He is Professor at Centre of Social Medicine and Community Health, Jawaharlal Nehru University, New Delhi. He held Dr. Ambedkar Chair at the Lal Bahadur Shastri National Academy of Administration, Mussoorie during 1996-97. He was Director of the Centre for Social Studies, Surat for many years. During his long carrier he has taught in various universities in India and abroad. Professor Shah is a receipt of Full Bright Award for 1984; VKRV Rao Prize in Political Science Research for 1979 and 1980, UGC National Lecturer for 1985-86 and UGC Swami Pranavanda Saraswati Award in Political Science in 1997. He has previously written, edited and co-authored twelve books including *Caste Association and Political Process in Gujarat; Economic Differentiations and Tribal Identity; Social Movements in India: A Review of Literature; Public Health and Urban Development; Social Transformation in India;* and *Dalit Identity and Politics.*

About the Centre for Rural Studies

The Centre for Rural Studies (formerly Land Reforms Unit) of the Lal Bahadur Shastri National Academy of Administration was set up in the year 1989 by the Ministry of Rural Development, Government of India, with a multifaceted agenda that included among others, the concurrent evaluation of the ever-unfolding ground realities pertaining to the implementation of the land reforms and Poverty Alleviation Programmes in India. Sensitizing the officer trainees of the Indian Administrative Service in the process of evaluating of land reforms and poverty alleviation programmes by exposing them to the ground realities; setting up a forum for regular exchange of views on land reforms and poverty alleviation between academicians, administrators, activists and concerned citizens and creating awareness amongst the public about the various programmes initiated by the Government of India through non-governmental organisations are also important objectives of the Centre for Rural Studies. The research excellencies of the Centre in the area of land reforms, poverty alleviation programmes evaluation, and issues related to rural labour, rural wages, migration pattern, gender issues and agrarian movements etc. are authentic and informative. Moreover, the Centre has been entrusted by the Department of Rural Development, Government of India to act as a think tank to suggest changes in policy measures and improvements in the delivery mechanism, to act in the capacity of an adviser to the different State governments on issues relating to land reforms and rural developments. A large number of books, reports related to land reforms, poverty alleviation programmes, rural socio-economic problems etc. published both externally and internally bears the testimony of research quality of the Centre.

DALITS AND THE STATE

Edited by

Ghanshyam Shah

Published for

CENTRE FOR RURAL STUDIES
Lal Bahadur Shastri National Academy of Administration,
Mussoorie

by

CONCEPT PUBLISHING COMPANY, NEW DELHI-110059

ISBN 81-7022-922-7

First Published 2002

Published and Printed by
Ashok Kumar Mittal
Concept Publishing Company
A/15-16, Commercial Block, Mohan Garden
NEW DELHI-110059 (India)

Phones : 5648039, 5649024
Fax : 091-11-5648053
E-mail : publishing@conceptpub.com

DEDICATION

For Valajibhai Patel, Rameshbhai Parmar, Martin Macwan and other social activist friends for their persistent struggle and search for human dignity and Just Social Order

PREFACE

We are celebrating the 50th anniversary of our Republic India. Half of century is not a short span in a nation's history. It is, therefore, an appropriate juncture to introspect and evaluate our achievements and failures. Are we on the correct path for fulfilling our objectives? What measures do we need to take in the coming years, as we have entered the 21st century, to build a just and egalitarian society? The authors of the present volume, civil servants and social scientists, ponder over these questions from the vantage point of the Dalits, who constitute the vast majority. The Dalits expect the State to improve their lot, to provide them economic opportunities, political power and dignity.

The Centre for Rural Studies (Formerly Land Reforms Unit) of the Lal Bahadur Shastri National Academy of Administration organised a seminar in Mussoorie on "Status of Dalits in Contemporary India", in March 1994. It was decided to publish a volume consisting of some of the papers presented at the seminar and also to invite other scholars to contribute to the volume. Mr. Harsh Mander, the then Chairman of the Centre for Rural Studies invited me in 1995 to edit the volume. At the time I was at the Centre for Social Studies, Surat, where I was looking after the project on "Social Justice". I accepted the invitation. Later, I joined the Academy where I began to read the papers presented in the seminar. Meanwhile, I edited the special issue of the *Administrator*, journal of the Academy, on Dalits, in which some of the papers, presented here were published. I thank Harsh Mander, and the former vice-chairman of the centre, Mr. B.K. Sinha, for providing an opportunity to undertake this assignment. I also acknowledge the Centre for Social Studies, Surat, for its support in bringing out this volume under its project on "Social Justice". I thank the staff of the Centre for Rural

Studies, which facilitated my work at the Academy. The paper "Untouchability and Atrocities" by P.S. Krishnan, presented in seminar has then published in *Social Action* (1993). We thankfully acknowledge the journal for granting permission to include the article in this volume. I dedicate this work to many friends to express my solidarity in their tireless struggle for social transformation—Just Social Order.

Jan. 26, 2001 GHANSHYAM SHAH

CONTENTS

THE CONTRIBUTORS

S.C. Behar
He is retired Officer of the Indian Civil Service from Madhya Pradesh cadre.

Susan E. Chaplin
Ph.D. Scholar at School of Politics, La Trobe University, Australia.

Gopal Guru
Professor of Political Science, Pune University, Pune. He is the author of *Dalit Culture and the Dialects of Dalit Politics*; *Theorising Dalit Movements in India*; and *Dr. Ambedkar's Critique of Hindu Nationalism* (in press).

Ramesh Kamble
Teaching Sociology at Dapartment of Sociology, Mumbai University, Mumbai. He is working on the theme : Dalit Diaspora in UK.

P.S. Krishnan
Former Secretary, Ministry of Welfare, Government of India. He was Member Secretary to the National Commission for Backward Classes and Member of National Commission for Scheduled Castes and Scheduled Tribes. He is the Chairman of the National Action Forum for Social Justice.

Vijay Kumar
He has retired as Government Officer from Gujarat. He is active on various issues affecting dalits in Gujarat. He is associated with Gujarat Vikas Sangh, Ahmedabad.

Harsh Mander
Civil Servant from Madhya Pradesh cadre. He was Professor at Lal Bahadur Shastri National Academy of Administration, Mussoorie. At present he is the Country Director, Action Aid India. His area of interest are: Development of the marginalised communities, and Human Rights. He is the author of *Unheard Voices: Stories of Forgotten Lives.*

Geetha B. Nambissan
Associate Professor in Zakir Hussain Centre for Educational Studies, Jawaharlal Nehru University, New Delhi where she is teaching Sociology of Education. Her research interests include the education of marginalised groups. She has been closely associated with a number of NGOs as a resource person in education.

Nandu Ram
Dr. Ambedkar Professor in Sociology, Centre for the Study of Social Systems, Jawaharlal Nehru University, New Delhi. He is the author of *Mobile Scheduled Castes: Rise of New Middle Class; Beyond Ambedkar: Essays on Dalits in India;* and *Encyclopaedia of Scheduled Castes—Five Volumes* (in Press).

P.V. Rathod
He served Government of Gujarat. He is associated with Gujarat Vikas Sangh, Ahmedabad.

G. Venkata Siva Reddy
He is teaching Political Science at the Government College, Anantapur, Andhra Pradesh. His areas of research interests are : Politics of Scheduled Castes, Human Rights etc.

Ghanshyam Shah
Professor in social sciences at Centre of Social Medicine and Community Health, Jawaharlal Nehru University, New Delhi. He is author of several books.

S.R. Sankaran
Former Chief Secretary, Tripura and Secretary Rural Development, Government of India. He is actively involved in movements for human rights; and associated with Committees of Concerned Citizens in Andhra Pradesh.

Takashi Shinoda
He is Professor of Economics at Daito Bunka University, Japan. The major areas of his interests are institutional change and caste mobility; entrepreneurial development among the weaker sections etc. He is the author of *A Study on the Status of Sweepers in India* (in Japanese); and has edited *Entrepreneurial Development in Developing Countries* (in Japanese) and co-edited *A Comparative Study on Irrigation Systems in Asia* (in Japanese); and edited *Other Gujarat* (in Press).

M. Thangaraj
Faculty Member, Madras Institute of Development Studies, Chennai.

1

DALITS AND THE STATE
An Overview

Ghanshyam Shah

Indian State in the post-colonial period has assumed a role of an interventionist to bring about social transformation. It aims at eradicating feudal hierarchical social order based on Brahminical ideology and building an egalitarian secular modern society guided by liberal values. In the preamble to the Indian Constitution, it is solemnly resolved to provide all its citizens: social, economic and political Justice; Liberty of thought, expressions, belief, faith and worship; Equality of opportunity and status; and Fraternity assuring of the dignity of the individual. These objectives are the result of the struggles of the masses not only against the foreign rule but also against an exploitative and overwhelmingly dominant feudal class. Dr. Baba Saheb Ambedkar, one of the chief architects of the Indian Constitution, and many other liberal members of the Constituent Assembly believed that the traditional established order in India was based on graded inequality. Justice in Indian social context, according to Ambedkar, as argued by Gopal Guru in the following essay, was served to validate societal stratification and perpetuate casteism. People of India in general and the deprived communities in particular looked upto the State not only to provide equal opportunities but also to create positive conditions for improving their socio-economic condition. The deprived communities perceived the State as a saviour to liberate them from the shackles of bondage and deprivation based on birth.

The authors of the volume, social scientists and civil servants, are committed to social transformation as envisaged in the Constitution. Hence, their concerns centre around policy and administrative measures. In this process they raise the very basic as pertinent questions relating to the status of the 'Dalits', such as : what changes have occurred in their socio-economic status during the past five decades and what role has the state played in this process? In this introductory Chapter, an attempt has been made to provide a historical overview of the condition of Dalits by generously using findings, conjectures, and theoretical propositions of other scholars. While doing so, it also highlights the arguments and findings of the contributors of this volume, and raises questions which may not have been answered here.

Who Are the Dalits?

The term "Dalit" is inclusive of all the oppressed and exploited sections of society. Etymologically the term is inclusive of meanings such as: downtrodden, disadvantaged, underprivileged, dispossessed, deprived, handicapped, abused, humble, prostrate, etc. It does not, however, confine merely to economic exploitation in terms of appropriation of surplus but also relates to suppression of culture—ways of life and value system—and more importantly the denial of dignity. It is not just one of the categories applied for analysing data. It is essentially a political category for assertion of identity and mobilization for collective action and connotes an ideology for fundamental change in social structure and relationships (Das and Massey, 1995).

Generally the term 'Dalit' includes, what is called in administrative parlance: Scheduled Castes (SCs), Scheduled Tribes (STs) and Other Backward Classes (OBCs). The present volume focuses mainly on the SCs. The term SC was first used by the British government in the Government of India Act, 1935. Prior to this, some of these castes were included within the Depressed Classes—a category which was used for the first time in the beginning of this century (Gupta, 1985: 7-35). Sociologically speaking SCs suffered the stigma of untouchability and were considered *Ati-Sudras* or *Avarna* in the Hindu caste-structure. However, all ex-untouchables do not find a place in this 'schedule' and all castes under the 'schedule' did not experience 'untouchability' to an equal degree in the recent or distant past.

According to the 1991 census, there were 138 million persons belonging to the SCs, constituting 15.8 per cent of the total population of the country. Though SCs are found in most states, they are largely concentrated in Uttar Pradesh and Bihar in the north, West Bengal in the east, Tamil Nadu and Andhra Pradesh in the south, Rajasthan and Maharashtra in western India.

Economic Status

The caste system, in which the SCs occupy the lowest position, perpetuates and maintains inequality. Discrimination which is the all pervading character of the caste system is not confined to production relations alone, but permeates the whole socio-economic sphere. This is evident from the land ownership pattern. A vast majority of the SCs, i.e., 84 per cent live in rural areas. They are agricultural labourers, sharecroppers or self-cultivators. Nearly 13 per cent of the SC households, as against 11 per cent of the others are landless. And among those who own land, a vast majority, nearly 86 per cent, are small and marginal farmers. Thangaraj in his essay presents a picture of land ownership, irrigation, crops grown, employment status, per capita consumption and expenditure etc. of SCs. In 1987-88 half of the SCs population was living below the poverty line. Though since the seventies, the State has launched number of poverty eradication programmes, they have not dent much in the situation. S.R. Sankaran, a retired civil servant tells us from his experiences that these programmes have not been conceived and implemented with competence, mission and imagination. The number of committed and compassionate civil servants are few and far-between.

Among bonded labourers, estimated at over twenty lakhs, SC labourers constitute a sizeable number if not a majority. They are bonded against the debt that they either incurred for marriage and/ or for day-to-day expenses. Some of these bonded labourers work for the same master for several years or, in a few cases, even for life. They live a wretched life. While bonded labour has been theoretically abolished under the Bonded Labour System Act, 1976, and every labour "shall stand freed and discharged from the obligation to render labour in lieu of loans", in practice, the system still prevails. Though one can cite isolated cases of bonded labourers who were 'freed' due to the efforts of some individual bureaucrats and activists, many such 'free' labourers reverted back to bonded labour sooner or later due to lack of infrastructural or institutional support.

Various land reforms related to ceilings and distribution of land have somewhat enhanced the SCs access to land, but these measures are not sufficient, as Thangaraj shows "to meet the vast needs of SCs for land." At the same time, it should also be noted that a small section of the SC cultivators, 4.5 per cent as against 10.5 per cent of the others, are middle or rich peasants owning 4 hectares or more land. Though they are not as better off as the caste Hindus of the same category, some of them, not all, have certainly improved their condition in comparison with their brethren who are poor peasants (Singh, 1980). They have taken advantage of the so-called development programmes in the last five decades and constitute a part of the 'creamy layer' of Dalits.

A section of Dalits, sometimes along with agriculture, pursue traditional caste occupations, such as leather work, weaving, fishing, scavenging, basket making etc. The market oriented economy and capitalist mode of production has certainly opened up avenues, which have economically improved the conditions of certain sections of Dalits. For instance, the Chamars of Agra are a case in point. But their social position has not changed (Lynch, 1969). They still suffer the stigma of untouchability. In urban areas, SCs are employed in the organised and unorganised industrial sectors, petty shopkeeper's, small entrepreneurs, scavengers, and white-collar occupations, mainly in public sectors.

Education

Formal education is one of the most important avenues to make the SCs aware of their rights and put them up for sustainable economic opportunities in different sectors. Article 45 of the Indian Constitution, enshrined under the Directive Principles of State Polices, urged the State to strive for universal free elementary education for all children in the age group between 6 and 14 years within ten years, i.e., by 1960. This was reiterated in 1968, by the resolution on the National Policy on Education. This has still remained an unfulfilled dream. According to the 1991 census, India has a literacy rate of only 52 per cent. But among the SCs, only 37 per cent are literate. After fifty years of Independence, all the children of school-going age do not enrol in schools. And all those who enrol do not pursue studies for more than two to three years. Every second enrolled child from the Dalits drops out before completing primary education till Vth standard; and is forced to sell his/her labour. The obvious reasons for non-attendance and high drop out rate are poverty, inadequate schooling facility and social discrimination. Though the state provides scholarships, hostel facilities and other incentives, their quantum is small—covering a small fraction of the SC population. Moreover, the funds earmarked for the purpose are managed with inefficiency, indifference and callousness. The Elayaperumal Committee, 1969, found that the governments of Andhra Pradesh, Bihar, Punjab, Rajasthan and West Bengal have allowed the amounts allocated for pre-matriculation scholarships to lapse, even as they denied scholarships to applicants on the ground that funds are not available.

Geetha Nambissan's essay examines in detail with historical perspective "Equity in Education: Schooling of Dalit Children in India". She draws our attention to "the distinct historical experience of Dalit communities in context of education" and asserts that equity in education is not consciously practised in formal schooling system. Usual stereotypes against Dalits such as they are mentally weak, dirty etc. are openly or subtly expressed by teachers and non-Dalit students. Dalit students are often discouraged access to "high status" knowledge. Nambissan questions the usefulness of the Non-Formal Education Programme (NFEP). On the basis of the available evaluation of the programmes, she argues that NFEP offers an inferior system of schooling that is vaguely formulated and difficult to monitor. She observes: "In the overall context of inadequate public resources for schooling, greater privatisation of 'quality' education for the elite, and the search for non-formal alternatives for the educationally backward, it is likely that socially and economically vulnerable groups will suffer greater neglect."

However, a small section of the Dalits has certainly benefited by the facilities—how so ever they are limited. Few belonging to relatively upper strata of Dalits have taken higher education (Chalam, 1988; Shah and Patel, 1977; Aggarwal, 1983; Visnadham and Reddy, 1985). Though seats reserved for SCs (14 per cent) in national level institutions, particularly in medicine and engineering, have not been fully utilised. And all those who succeed in getting admission are not able to complete the course in time. In order to improve the situation, various Committees and Commissions for SCs and STs have suggested that intensive coaching be provided for SC/ST students in medical colleges and various Indian Institutes of Technology. Coaching seems to have made some difference to their performance.

It is often argued that education often introduces 'bourgeois values' among SCs and inhibits the upsurge of radical consciousness about their oppression. The education system does not create 'new Ambedkars' (Isaac, 1965). It creates divisions between educated and uneducated SCs (Chitnis, 1977; Sinha, 1986). Several studies (Jayaram, 1983; Glass, 1982) point out that preferentially given educational opportunities are mere token, and an instrument for curbing disruption. Krishna Kumar on the other hand argues that "the experience of education, under prevailing curricular norms, can serve to assist SC and ST children to internalise the symbols of 'backward' behaviour. The claim that education introduces bourgeois values among the oppressed, and thereby curbs their potential for radical expression, is perhaps based on the impact of education on an extremely small minority perceived from the point of view of non-SC/ST educators; and both the tone and substance of the claim show a wrong choice" (1983:1572).

Causes for Untouchability : Some Conjectures

Dalits are poor and downtrodden. Particularly those belong to SCs suffer from social discrimination also. Untouchability a unique pan-Indian phenomenon, is the central problem affecting SCs. There are three schools of thought on the origin of untouchability. They are (a) racial and/or conquerors *vis-à-vis* natives; (b) religious; and (c) economic. According to the racial theory, the touchables (caste Hindus) and untouchables (*Ati-Sudras*) belong to two different races; differentiated by colour (Dutt, 1931). The lineage of the former can be traced to the Aryans who invaded India, while the latter have descended from the natives called the *Dasa* or *Dasyus*. The Aryans, a white race conquered the *Dasas*, dark-skinned inhabitants, and enslaved them (Risley, 1908; Dutt, 1931). According to Stanley Rice, the Untouchables were non-Aryan, non-Dravidian aboriginals who were conquered and subjugated by the Dravidians (Ambedkar, 1948). A religious sect of the Dalits like *Ad-Dharm* in Punjab advocates: "We are the original people of this country and our religion is *Ad-Dharm*. The Hindu *Quam* came from outside and enslaved us" (Juergensemeyer, 1982: 45).

The practice of untouchability developed in the course of time some argue (Bose, 1942; Fick, 1920; Oppert, 1972; Sharma, 1980; Mukherjee, 1988), as conflict between the Aryans and indigenous people became sharp. Prabhati Mukherjee argues that the practice of untouchability was preceded by a long history of social and cultural prejudice of the Vedic Aryans towards some groups of the indigenous population who posed a threat to their way of life, based on pastoral wealth and performance of religious rituals and sacrifices. In the early phase, till 800 BC, the Aryans made peace with groups which cooperated with them and allowed them to function at the peripheries of their social organisation. But those who continued to be hostile such as the *Dasa/Dasyu*, the Rakshasa, Asura, Pani, etc., were identified as enemies. With the exception of the *Dasas*, who probably were less aggressive than the others, they "were constantly being driven out of their homes and hearths". They were hated because "they spoke a different language and did not follow the religion of the Aryans" (Mukherjee, 1988:34). Cultural segregation increased as time passed by. Slowly, the habitational segregation and cultural-religious prejudice practised by the Aryans *vis-à-vis* certain groups identified as hostile and unassailable, resulted in the practice of untouchability. The Aryans could not bring them under their control. Some groups continued to rebel against the hegemony of the Aryans in economic as well as cultural spheres.

"It was the 'rebels' who suffered most, because the erstwhile enmity with and insubordination of the *Atavikas* in particular and of *Candalas* in general was neither forgotten nor forgiven. When they were brought under subjugation eventually, they were neither incorporated into the main economic activity prevailing at that time, that is, agriculture, nor into any other form of production in society. Only unskilled, unproductive, lowly and menial jobs were assigned to them. Thus, when they were forced to surrender it was not clemency they received. Instead, they were treated with utter contempt and were segregated as a residual category of people to be employed as and when necessary" (*Ibid.*: 104).

Among others, Ambedkar rejected the racial theory. He argued that "there is no evidence in the Vedas of any invasion of India by the Aryan race and its having conquered the *Dasas* and *Dasyus* supposed to be natives of India" (1946:57-82). According to him, there was no racial distinction between the Aryans and the *Dasa*. As far as physical characteristics were concerned there was hardly any difference, he argued, between the Brahmins and untouchables belonging to the same region.

B.R. Ambedkar was one of the leading proponents of the religious theory of untouchability. He held that during the Vedic period there was no separate *Sudra* varna. The *Sudras* ranked as part of the *Kshatriya* varna in the Indo-Aryan society. "There was a continuous feud between the *Sudra* kings and the Brahmins in which the Brahmins were subjected to many tyrannies and indignities. As a result of the hatred towards the *Shoetrees* generated by their tyrannies and oppression, the Brahmins refused to perform the *upanayana* of the *Shoetrees*. Owing to the denial of *upanayana*, fell below the rank of the *Vaishyas* and thus came to form the fourth varna" (1946, XIV-XV). In a later work (1948) he argued at length how Brahmanical Hindu religion, by evolving purity-pollution concepts, treated some sections of *Sudras* as untouchables who were competing with Brahmins. By the fourth century, as Brahmanical orthodoxy became firmly entrenched, killing of cows became a punishable offence. This was also a reaction against Buddhism. From killing of cows the Brahmins went a step further and declared eating beef a sin, although they ate it previously. Cows were now held to be sacred, and beef-eating was considered profane. Consequently, those who did eat beef came to be regarded with scorn in society. According to Ambedkar, hatred for Buddhism coupled with contempt for beef-eating were the reasons for making these people untouchables.

Caste System and Untouchability

Resurgence in Brahmanical Hinduism has been a recurrent phenomena, whenever it has faced challenges from the subjugated classes since the Vedic period. In the modern period, since the early 19th century various efforts have been made to redefine Hinduism with a view to reform it, so as to meet the challenges of the new era on the one hand, and counter Christianity and Islam on the other. Hindu reformers rejected caste system based on birth. They viewed it as a system of division of labour in society in which mobility by skill and virtue was permitted. In order to serve their vested interests and to perpetuate their dominance, the Brahmins, in the course of time, converted the caste system into a rigid, closed and hereditary one. For the reformers untouchability was a blot on humanity; a disgrace on Hinduism. Untouchability arose out of an aberration of the *varna-dharma*. What was needed was: to reform Hinduism (Vable, 1983; Jones, 1976; Weber, 1958). Even as they rejected the *jati* system, Hindu reformers continued to subscribe to the *varna* system. Gandhi was one of them. In recent times a prominent proponent of anti-untouchability, yet a champion of the *Chaturvarna* system, recipient of several international awards for his "new social movement", is Pandurang Athavale. According to him the *Chaturvarna* system created by Sri Krishna has no hierarchical differences of low and high. It is a materialist arrangement for distribution of occupations in society so that people need not have to worry about their bread and shelter. Rigid status differentiation of touchability and untouchability is a degeneration of the system. Athavale emphasises like many Bhakti saints that "no man born on this earth is lowly and degraded" (Shah, 1994). All are the children of the same Lord.

Communalist Hindus also subscribe to this theory. Their main thrust is to build Hindu unity and strengthen Hinduism. For them Hinduism and Indian nationalism are synonymous. Cooperation and unity of upper and lower castes for the protection of the Hindu dharma and Hindu samaj is called for. Hindutva consciousness and Hindu inspiration are the starting point for the realisation of the power necessary for the protection of Hindus. They reject the notion that *Sudras* occupy an inferior and degraded position. According to them, the low caste Hindus are the most hard working, strong and able to bear much suffering. "Because of their numerical strength, they are truly the spinal cord of Hindu *jat* (race). Lakhs and crores of these people are getting dissociated from Hindu samaj because they are humiliated and looked down upon. As a result Hindu *jat* is becoming weak and powerless." They are the real Kshatriyas, i.e., warriors who protected the Hindu samaj in the ancient period against all calamities, aggressions and shocks. The Hindu *jat*, it was argued, can become strong only by uplifting the lower castes and not without them. They could be brought forward by imparting knowledge to them in ethics, good behaviour, education and other fields. "They have to be made human beings in the true sense of the term" (*Ibid.*). In this discourse, one finds that the champions of Hindu unity do not place emphasis on equality and social justice, instead the stress is on improving, albeit sanskritising the behaviour of lower castes. Moreover, their approach is highly instrumentalist—as dilution of the high-low differentiation serves the purpose of strengthening Hinduism. The question arises: why should one have a project for strengthening a religion based community? And whose interests will it serve? Dalits have very little to gain from such an enterprise. Therefore, they regard with suspicion all those who plead for maintaining the *varna* system, irrespective of their political colour.

For many Marxist and liberal scholars wedded to modernisation untouchability is related to economic structure. It will disappear, they hope with 'capitalist' or 'socialist' economic development. The *Chaturvarna* division of society was a class division, based on the system of production, distribution and consumption. It became hereditary in course of time, which distorted and modified class formation and class relations. Morton Klass speculates that "egalitarian" social groups developed a stratified social system with rising population and the generation of surplus. He argues, "with the rapid dispersal of the new agricultural techniques to all favourable ecological areas of the subcontinent, contradictions inherent in a situation of 'absolute surplus' came to the fore equally rapidly, and throughout the subcontinent. Whatever, the total range of response, the solution that apparently achieved the greatest support and success was the one entailing the exchange of the services of non-food-producing corporate groups, for shares of crops of access of land controlled by food-producing corporate groups... This resulted in the full emergence of what—in all its social, economic, and ideological manifestations—we know as the South Asian caste system" (Klass, 1980:187-188).

Klass however does not speculate on how untouchability came into practice in this system. Soviet Indologist A.P. Kolontaav argues that the conditions of agricultural production in ancient India made it possible to reserve a considerable mass of labour which could exist only in the form of socially oppressed strata of society, used during the peak periods of agricultural work. Those oppressed classes were treated as untouchables (Yurlova, 1989).

Practice of Untouchability

The Indian Constitution gives cognisance to the problem of untouchability. The Constitution has made a number of provisions under various Articles—15(2), 17, 29(2)—considering the practice of untouchability as an offence. Article 35 provides that "Parliament shall have, and the legislature of a State shall not have, power to make laws... prescribing punishment for those acts which are declared to be offences under this part" (i.e. the fundamental rights section of the Constitution). The Parliament exercised its exclusive powers after five years and passed the Untouchability (Offences) Act in 1955. The Act outlaws the enforcement of disabilities "on the ground of untouchability" in public places. In practice it had very little teeth to take punitive action against the offenders. Thanks to the pressures built by various Dalit groups over several years, a bill aimed at amending the Untouchability (Offences) Act, 1955, was introduced in the Lok Sabha in April 1972. The Parliament took more than four years to pass the bill. The Untouchability (Offences) Amendment Bill, 1972, renamed as the Protection of Civil Rights (Amendment) Act, 1976, came into force on 19 November, 1976. The lone participating Congress MP, Sadhuram, was highly critical of government's attitude and its lack of seriousness in considering the bill as it was passed virtually without any discussion. This bill "was a victim of indifference, indecision and delay". The Act provides for enhanced and stringent punishment including collective fines for offences relating to untouchability. Later, a new Act, Scheduled Castes and Scheduled Tribes (Protection of Atrocities) Act, 1989, was also promulgated to revamp the previous Acts.

Notwithstanding the constitutional provisions and various legislations, untouchability continues, as Ghanshyam Shah finds in Gujarat, one of the more developed states of India. This is a restudy. I.P. Desai studied the problem in 1972. Shah visited the same villages to find out what changes have taken place in the practice of untouchability over a period of time. He observes that though untouchability is not visible in schools but it has not yet disappeared in village Panchayats. The elected members belonging to SCs experience discrimination in 30 per cent of the villages. It is still observed to some extent in public transport and postal services. There is no change in private spheres. It is still very high. In most of the villages they are not allowed to enter temples and private houses. On the basis of various studies, Harsh Mander finds that, "There is widest prevalence of untouchability in the cultural and domestic spheres. It is partial in occupational spheres. But in the public sphere, barring in Panchayats and occasional restrictions on dress and footwear, it is largely absent". A blatant display of untouchability is not discernible in urban areas but subtle discriminations in most walks of life have persisted. Krishnan observes that "In many metropolitan areas, 'untouchability' has seemingly attenuated, but is practised with sophisticated concealment in a variety of ingenious ways, revealing creativity worthy of a better cause. In many modern offices, Dalits have to suffer snide remarks and quiet and neat acts of discrimination". Ramesh Kamble substantiates the above observation in his study on "Untouchability in Urban Settings". Even in this cosmopolitan city, several educated middle-class Dalits perceive and experience discrimination and caste prejudice. The intensity of the experience however varies from situation to situation.

The *Bhangis*, scavangers who clean roads, remove carcass of animals from roads and carry night soil from the toilets, occupy the lowest position among the SCs. Studies on scavengers show that their condition has not much improved and their occupation is still looked down upon as polluting. Susan Chaplin observes that scavengers on the whole are "still marginalised" despite the several recommendations of various committees. At many places they still carry night soil on their heads. "This situation continues today", she argues, "because scavengers have not been able to apply enough political pressure on the three levels of government to ensure that they sustained an interest in improving their living and working conditions". However, compared to rural areas, scavengers of the cities employed in municipalities, are some what better off. But as Takashi Shinoda in his study of the sweepers in Ahmedabad district shows, that their occupational mobility remains extremely limited.

Atrocities

Though the visible practice of untouchability has declined, the incidents of atrocities against Dalits have not shown a similar trend. These continue unabated in post-Independent India in various forms —murder, grievous hurt, arson and rape. Annual reports by the Commissioner for Scheduled Castes and Scheduled Tribes give statistics on atrocities since 1974. These figures are mainly the cases registered in police records. The data between 1981 and 1986 show that there was a steady rise in the number of cases of murder of SC persons during this period. A similar rise was also found in the case of rape, except in 1985. One finds similar pattern during earlier years also. Cases of atrocities are found in all the states. Reasons for atrocities are many. The Commissioner for SCs and STs attributes three main causes. They are: (i) unresolved land disputes related to allotment of government land or distribution of surplus land to the landless SC/ST persons; (ii) tension and bitterness created on account of non-payment or underpayment of minimum wages prescribed by the State government, and (iii) resentment against the manifestation of awareness amongst the Scheduled Castes and Scheduled Tribes about their rights and privileges as enshrined in the Constitution and various legislative and executive measures. Caste prejudices too, often contribute to atrocities. Resentment against protective discrimination also accentuate conflict between caste Hindus and SCs/STs, leading to atrocities against the latter. Besides this, P.S. Krishnan notes two other causes for atrocities. One is lack of provision or access to essential facilities to Dalits; and their assertion for the facilities. Second is a new phenomena in which atrocities take place for no specific cause other than "Dalit assertion of self-respect". P.V. Rathod and Vijay Kumar critically examine the working of the Scheduled Castes and Scheduled Tribes (Prevention of Atrocities) Act, 1989 in Gujarat. They find that the Act is not yet implemented effectively. The authors make several suggestions to provide teeth to the Act.

Demand for Protective Measures

Over the years, the Dalits have increasingly felt that they have to depend on the state to get protection and equality in the social and economic spheres. By the turn of the 19th century different Dalit groups had started asserting their rights to get education, to enter temples, to dress like others, free movements on the public roads, economic opportunities in the non-traditional sectors etc. They pressurised the British rulers for creating space for them in public spheres, so as to protect their interests. They demanded for special representations in legislatures and government jobs. A number of struggles, culminated in 1932 in the Ambedkar-Gandhi Pact, known as the Communal Award or the Poona Pact. Ambedkar yielded to Gandhi's insistence and gave up his demand for a 'separate electorate'. Gandhi on his part conceded reservation of 148 seats for Depressed Classes for ten years. The Government of India Act of 1935 incorporated the agreement and guaranteed reservation to the Depressed Classes in various legislatures of India. It also provided for some safeguards against any discrimination on the basis of caste, religion, race etc. The Poona Pact had far-reaching impact on Dalit politics of post-independent India and in the making of the Indian Constitution.

On the eve of Independence, pressure from the Dalits—SCs and STs—mounted on the leading liberal members of the Constituent Assembly for providing special protective measures to SCs and STs. Dalit leaders asked: "What would be our place in Independent India?" There were a number of tribal upsurges demanding autonomous states for them within or outside the Indian Union. In such politically charged environment and along with the emotional turbulence because of the partition of the country, the main challenge before the Constituent Assembly was to assure Dalits of a better deal in Independent India (Shah, 1987). Hence, the Constitution directed the State to take positive measures for ameliorating the conditions of the weaker sections in general and the SCs and the STs in particular. In order to put Directive Principles into practice and thereby to reduce the deprivation of the SCs and the STs, the fathers of the Constitution made certain provisions known as 'protective discriminations'. They are related to political reservations (Articles 330 and 332); reservations of seats in educational institutions (Article 15(4) and 29) and reservation of government jobs (Articles 16(4), 320(4), 333 and 335). These provisions are variously known as 'protective discrimination', 'affirmative action' or 'reverse discrimination'. From the Dalit perspective, Nandu Ram observes that the provisions "may better be accepted as policies of compensation for discrimination of past as well as of present time".

The Constitution has authorised the President to identify these groups. The President promulgated an ordinance in 1950 which identified the SCs and the STs. It should be noted that the category 'SC' includes only those 'ex-untouchables' who call themselves Hindus and Sikhs. While moving the amendment to delete the Scheduled Castes from the list of minorities, K.M. Munshi, a champion of Hindu nationalism had said that "the Harijans are part and parcel of the Hindu community, and the safeguards are given to them to protect their rights only till they are completely absorbed in the Hindu Community". He further explained that "any safeguards as a minority, so far as the Scheduled Castes are concerned, is illogical and will possibly prevent their complete absorption in the Hindu fold" (quoted by Kananaikil, 1982). This explanation was not objected to by any member of the Constituent Assembly. Thus, it reflects that a large section amongst the framing of our Constitution were, consciously or unconsciously, affected by the logic of 'Hindu Nationalism'. Jose Kananaikil argues that:

> "as far as the Scheduled Castes were concerned, the Constituent Assembly made them like orphans adopted to a royal family. Those Scheduled Castes who paid allegiance to Hinduism became legally part of the great Hindu family. Those who refused to offer allegiance to it did not exist in the law. Yet the adoption was far from being a generous outpouring of the royal bounty to the Scheduled Castes. It did not make members of the royal family. The acceptance of the 'Hindu' Scheduled Castes as part of the Hindu community and the granting of special rights to them seem to have been more the results of a Hindu apprehension and a response to the growing disenchantment of the Scheduled Castes, and only to them, was one way to check the leakage from Hinduism" (1982:23).

However, reservation was extended to the SC converts to Sikhism, which according to Sardar Patel was, "a concession". This was done because, as Bhagwan Das argues "many among the Hindu political leaders believed that there was nothing to fear from Sikhism" (1995:43). Das further observes that the government of

India amended the Scheduled Caste Order in 1956 (*vide* Act 63 of 1956) to read as: "3. Notwithstanding anything contained in paragraph 2, no person who professes a religion different from the Hindu or the Sikh religion shall be deemed to be a member of Scheduled Caste". This was done to inhibit mass conversion of untouchables to Buddhism. In 1990, as a result of the struggle of Buddhist Dalits for two decades, the government amended the Schedule to include "the Buddhist of untouchable origin in the list".

Christian Dalits are still struggling to get themselves included in the Schedule. They argue that social discrimination is still maintained among the Indian Christians. Moreover, economic condition of the Dalit Christians is not different from that of the Hindu Dalits. But the demand is strongly opposed not only by the Hindu leaders and their parties, but also by many Hindu Dalits. The opposition not because they call themselves Hindus and would like to strengthen Hindu Community, but because they fear that they will have to share the cake which is already small.

White-Collar Jobs

Growth of higher education among a section of the Dalits on the one hand and reservation of 15 per cent of the jobs, under Article 16(4) and 333 of the Constitution at all levels in the Union as well as state governments and public sector undertakings, have facilitated their entry into middle class in general and government white collar jobs in particular. The formation of this 'new middle class' among the Dalits, Nandu Ram argues is "vivisected in its role of acting as catalytic agent of bringing social change and mobility among the Dalit masses and its efforts for getting structurally accommodated in the Indian middle class or classes as such".

Reservations have been accompanied by an array of other special provisions, designed to enhance the ability of the preferred groups to compete successfully for government posts. These include relaxation of the maximum age for entry into the service; the waiver or reduction of examination fees, reduction of the minimum qualifying marks in examinations and the lowering of a passing marks in *viva-voce* examinations; specific safeguards against retrenchment; and appointment of authorities to relax minimum standards, freedom for SC employees to register for better jobs while working for the government, travel allowance to reach the interviewing centre, pre-examination training, etc. (Galanter, 1984). Benefits of these provisions however are not received by a large number of SC students. The Twenty-Eighth report of the Commissioner for SCs and STs, shows that in the majority of the pre-examination training centres for SCs and STs, a considerable number of seats remain vacant. One of the reasons for inadequate utilisation of facilities is the low ceiling of income fixed for the parents of eligible candidates, i.e., Rs.1000 per month. The Commissioner observes, "today even the lowest paid employee gets a minimum salary of about Rs. 1000. This unrealistic ceiling makes the otherwise suitable candidates ineligible for admission, leading to non-availability of sufficient number of candidates and keeping a large number of seats vacant" (1988:487).

Reservation of jobs in the government however does not provide employment to all educated Dalits. It is partly because of rising overall unemployment in the country. And partly discrimination against Dalits also contributes keeping many of them out of white collar jobs. Often under one pretext or another reserved posts are not filled up and later they are declared unreserved and filled up by non-SC/ST candidates. Various reports of the Commissioner for SCs and STs note several instances, pointing out unsympathetic attitude of the upper caste officers. The SC candidates "are unfairly eliminated at the later stages of the selection process, particularly where there is scope for personal evaluation in the form of an interview or personality test. Scattered data on the selection process at the state level indicate very severe attrition at the interview stage" (Galanter, 1984:99). On the recommendations of various reports and under pressures from SC organisations, various devices have been adopted by Central and State governments "to offset the lack of zeal of appointing authorities; requirements that de-reservation be authorised by (or notified to) high ranking officers, requirements of periodic returns by appointing authorities and departments, creation of special grievance cells" etc. (*Ibid.*: 98).

There was no reservation of any promotion posts till 1957. It was introduced in 1957 and 'severely curtailed' in 1963 by the Ministry of Home Affairs. The orders were further modified in 1968 creating more scope for reservation in such posts. Some state governments have followed the Central government in extending reservation to the promotion stage. "It is promotions", Galanter observes, "rather than initial recruitment that have been the focus of the most controversy and the most adamant resistance from administrators and from other employees" (*Ibid.*: 101). On the whole implementation of the various provisions related to reservation of jobs is sluggish and there are a number of inherent contradictions built in them as they are differently interpreted and challenged in the court of law. There is a lack of political will, as Nandu Ram argues, on the part of the State.

Notwithstanding these limitations and prejudices and indifferent attitude of many caste Hindu officers towards SC candidates, there is a significant increase in the number of SC employees at various levels, thanks to pressures exerted by pro-Dalit political leaders and elite. As S.C. Behar shows, there were less than 1 per cent SC employees in class I services in 1953 and it has gone up to more than 8 per cent in 1987. A similar rise is also found in Class II, though they are far behind than their prescribed quota of 15 per cent. They lag behind in various public sectors, universities, and other such institutions. The states have uneven record in filling up the quota for the SCs at various levels. While Andhra Pradesh, Haryana, Madhya Pradesh, Orissa, Uttar Pradesh and West Bengal lag far behind than the prescribed reservation quota, Gujarat and Rajasthan have relatively better performance. On the whole, reservation has not been able to make, Behar argues, a significant dent in the stratified Indian social structure which seems to be resistant to change even though it has influenced the policy of reservation itself.

It is increasingly realised by many—particularly those who support the reservation policy—that though reservation is important, it is not a sufficient condition for social transformation. Moreover, contradictions of the reservation policy itself has come to surface.

Various Dalit castes compete with each other for a limited amount of benefits, and in the process Dalit unity suffers. The conflict between the Malas and the Madigas in Andhra Pradesh is a case in point. G. Venkata Siva Reddy, examines the protest of the Madigas against the Malas, demanding stratified reservation by sub-castes. The leaders of the movement believe that reservation should first be provided to those who are 'in lower stratum', so that the development from the below can be realised. Conflict is inevitable in a situation where jobs for educated persons are limited and overall economy is not growing at the expected rate. The net result is disunity and competition among the Dalits who struggle for the limited economic opportunities. How to resolve the emerging tension among the SCs is a challenging task before us.

Impasse?

The Indian Republic has completed half a century. Social and economic equality is still a distant dream. Sincere commitment to equality and fraternity is lacking: What we have is a lot of lip service and empty rhetoric as vote catching device. Moreover, Indian state is in a process of retreat from the public domain. And, Dalits have put lots of stake on the state intervention for improving their lot, as society on the whole is either indifferent or hostile to their plight. Though a large number of them—agricultural labourers, small and marginal farmers, workers in informal sector—often protest and occasionally launch militant struggles against the state and dominant sections of society, they are still too weak to make a decisive impact on the ruling classes.

It would be too simplistic and perhaps populist to say that nothing has changed in the last fifty years; that the condition of Dalits has remained the same as it was before Independence. However, the fact remains that the Dalit community has become politically more conscious of its rights and more determined to build a better future for itself and for other similarly oppressed groups, through social transformation. It has, at one level, become more unified and at the same time more stratified than the past. Various *jatis* from different regions and linguistic groups which suffered the stigma of untouchability in the past, have begun to identify themselves as one entity—the oppressed—and rally around the ideology of an egalitarian social order, with social justice and human dignity, as propounded by Phule and Ambedkar. They collectively challenge, at least at the theoretical level, Brahminical ideology of hierarchy, based on pollution and purity. It is their collective quest to usher in social transformation.

As far as Dalits are concerned two striking positive changes have taken place. First, crude and blatant forms of social discrimination, at least in the public sphere are practised far less frequently than before. Yet, they certainly have not disappeared. Second, a middle class within the community has emerged. Besides self-assertion by the Dalits, the following four factors have contributed in bringing about the changes.

First, there is an overall acceptance of equality as a desirable norm, thanks to the permeation of the liberal and radical philosophical discourse, capitalist development, and technological, including communications, changes in society. It is almost an outdated moral value to hold that inequality is desirable and necessary, or is the consequence of one's *karma* of the past birth. Even the most orthodox hesitate, at least publicly, to justify inequality as an ideal social order. Though social sanctions justifying social inequality and discrimination in the form of untouchability, not disappeared, they are certainly under attack. But there is always a gap between moral values and practice. Age-old prejudices and habits do not die that easily. It is more so when they are intertwined with material vested interests. The middle class among the upper and middle castes, notwithstanding its liberal education, has not yet shed off stereotypes against Dalits, not so much on moral ideological grounds, but more out of material considerations and the threat of loss of power. Treating Dalits on an equal footing and enabling them to avail of opportunities in the non-traditional sector, implies sharing the cake (of the country's resources) with them. And that cake is not big enough to meet the needs of every one. However, there is a microscopic minority among them which adheres to a liberal and/or radical ideology with decaste mental frame and behaviour and is supportive of the Dalit cause. The onus is on this group to pressurise through public action—protest, media, policy analysis and other forms—the middle class and the State, to respect the dignity of Dalits and protect their interests.

Second, capitalist development, nonetheless sluggish, has weakened the traditional functioning of the caste system. Though caste remains, its form and content are different from what prevailed in earlier societies. Caste is a limiting rather than the determining factor in choice of occupation (Gough, 1960). Occupational diversification, albeit to a limited extent, has taken place within the Dalit community. Those Dalits who have some assets for investment and/or marketable skills, have received university education, and have become professionals, entrepreneurs, white collar employees, professional politicians, etc. The recent agenda of the state of economic liberalisation and globalisation may to some extent accelerate the process of diversification of occupations in society, including among the Dalits. New non-traditional occupations, particularly in the informal sector, could increase, which may provide opportunities to Dalits for livelihood. But the present day capitalism is not the same as that of the last century with unlimited market and colonies. It is in crisis the world over. It will at the most continue to benefit a tiny section of Dalits. At the most it may reduce the number of Dalits living below poverty line. But the capitalist system has no potential for or pretension of ushering in social and economic equality. On the other hand, if new opportunities under economic reforms, do not percolate further, bloody competition as we witnessed in the 'eighties between Dalits and upper castes, Dalits and middle as well as OBCs, will increase. Such conflicts may redraw caste boundaries, reinforcing prejudices. This danger looms large.

Third, protective discrimination through reservations in government jobs and admission to educational institutions has paved the way for Dalits to enter the middle class. Upward mobility has created hope and given them confidence that there is scope for improving their condition and be at par with others. However, the recent process of retreat of the state has begun to affect them adversely. As such educated unemployment in general and among Dalits in particular is increasing by leaps and bounds. Most of the first generation educated Dalits seeking employment do not have the capital and/or skills to enter and survive in the market. Such a state of affairs leads to frustration among middle class Dalits. Nonetheless, middle class Dalits occupy an important position in the community by functioning as its vocal section. They articulate problems of the community and assert its identity.

Fourth, various legislations prescribing punitive action against the practice of untouchability, though not implemented very effectively, have checked to some extent, blatant discrimination against the Dalits. It is more so in public than private spheres.

Nonetheless, the condition of the vast majority of the Dalits who are agricultural labourers, small and marginal farmers, casual labourers in urban informal sector has not improved in the last fifty years despite a number of poverty eradication programmes. They still look towards the State—the bureaucracy—to improve their lot. Would the state positively respond to meet their expectation? Has the changes among the Dalits under the backward capitalist development have reached to a saturation point and cannot be multiplied in the given economic and political structure? If that happens, the Dalits would increasingly feel betrayed. Consequently, legitimacy of the State as the saviour of the deprived groups in the caste ridden society would decline. This is a major challenge before the State and the Parliamentary democracy.

REFERENCES

Aggarwal, Pratap C., *Halfway to Equality*, New Delhi: Manohar, 1983.

Ambedkar, B.R., *Who were the Sudras? How they Came to be the Fourth Varna in the Indo-Aryan Society*, Bombay: Thacker & Co., 1948.

Ambedkar, B.R., *Emancipation of the Untouchables*, Bombay: Thacker & Co., 1943.

Ambedkar, B.R., *Annihilation of Caste with a Reply to Mahatma Gandhi*, Bombay: Bharat Bhushan Printing Press, 1946.

Ambedkar, B.R., *What Congress and Gandhi Have Done to the Untouchables*, Bombay: Thacker & Co., 1946.

Briggs, G.W., *The Chamars*, Delhi: B.R. Publishing Corporation, 1920.

Chalam, K.S., *Education and Weaker Sections*, Delhi: Inter India Publications, 1988.

Chitnis, Suma, *A Long Way to Go: Report on a Survey of Scheduled Caste High School and College Students in Fifteen States of India*, Bombay: Allied, 1977.

Das, Bhagwan and Massey,(ed.), *Dalit Solidarity*, Delhi: ISPACK, 1995.

Dutta, Nripendra Kumar, *Origin of Growth of Caste in India*, Vol. 1, London: Kegan Paul, 1931.

Elayaperumal, L., *Committee on Untouchability, Economic and Educational Development of Scheduled Castes*, New Delhi: Government of India, 1969.

Fick, Richard, *The Social Organisations in North-East India in Buddha's Time*, Calcutta: University of Calcutta, 1920.

Galanter, Mark, *Competiting Equalities: Law and The Backward Classes in India*, Delhi: Oxford University Press, 1984.

Glass, R., "Divided and Degraded: The Downtrodden Peoples of India", *Monthly Review*, 34, July-August, 1982.

Gough, Kathleen, "Brahmin Kinship in a Tamil Village", *American Anthropologist*, 58, 1956.

Gupta, S.K., *The Scheduled Castes in Modern Indian Politics*, Delhi: Munshiram Manohar Lal Publishers, 1985.

Isaac, Harold, *India's Ex-Untouchables*, New York: Harper and Row, 1965.

Jayram, N., "Protective Discrimination and Education", *Mainstream*, Republic Day, 1983.

Jones, Kenneth W., *Arya Dharm: Hindu Consciousness in 19th Century Punjab*, Delhi: Manohar, 1976.

Joshi, Barbara R., *Democracy in Search of Equality: Untouchable Politics and Social Change*, Delhi: Hindustan Publishing, 1982.

Juergensemeyer, Mark, *Religions as Social Vision: The Movement Against Untouchability in 20th Century Punjab*, California: California Press, 1982.

Kamat, A.R., "Education and Social Change amongst the Scheduled Castes and Scheduled Tribes", *Economic and Political Weekly*, 16 (31), August 1, 1981.

Kananaikil, Jose, *Scheduled Castes in the Constituent Assembly*, Delhi: Indian Social Institute, 1982.

Keer, Dhananjay, *Dr. Ambedkar: Life and Mission*, Bombay: Popular Prakashan, 1962.

Kumar, Krishna, "Educational Experience of Scheduled Castes and Tribes", *Economic and Political Weekly*, 18 (36-37), September 3, 1983.

Lynch, Owen M., *The Politics of Untouchability*, New York: Columbia University Press, 1969.

Mencher, Joan, "The Caste System Upside Down to the Not-So-Mysterious East", *Current Antropology*, 15, 1975.

Mendelsohn, Oliver, "A Harijan Elite?' The Lives of Some Untouchable Politicians", *Economic and Political Weekly*, 21 (12), March 22, 1986.

Mukherjee, Prabhati, *Beyond the Four Varnas: The Untouchables in India*, Shimla: Indian Institute of Advanced Study, 1988.

Narayana, G., "Social Background of Scheduled Caste MPs in the Fifth Lok Sabha - A Comparative Study", *PUDR Digest*, 5 (2), 1972.

Narayana, R., "Social Background of Scheduled Caste Lok Sabha Members, 1963-71", *Economic and Political Weekly*, 13 (37), September 16, 1978.

Risley, Hebert, *The People of India*, London: Thacker & Co., 1902.

Shah, Ghanshyam, "Congress and the Deprived Communities", in Ram Hoshi and R.K. Hebsur (Eds.), *Congress in Indian Politics: A Centenary Perspective*, Bombay: Popular Prakashan, 1987.

Shah, Ghanshyam, "The BJP and Backward Castes in Gujarat", *South Asia Bulletin*, Vol. 14 (1), 1994.

Shah, Vimal and Tara Patel, *Who goes to College: Scheduled Caste/Tribe Post-Matric Scholars in Gujarat*, Ahmedabad: Rachana Prakashan, 1977.

Sharma, R.S., *Sudras in Ancient India*, Delhi: Motilal Banarsidas, 1980.

Singh, Soran, *The Socio-Economic Condition of the Scheduled Castes in India*, Allahabad: Programme Book Depot, 1980.

Sinha, R.H., *Alienation among Scheduled Castes*, New Delhi: Manas Publications, 1986.

Vable, D., *The Arya Samaj: Hindu without Hinduism*, Delhi: Vikas Publishing House, 1983.

Viswanadham, G. and K. Narasimha Reddy, *Scheduled Castes: A Study in Educational Achievement*, Hyderabad, 1985.

Weber, Max, *The Religion of India: The Sociology of Hinduism and Buddhism*, Glance, 1958.

Yurlova, Eugenia S., *Scheduled Castes in India*, New Delhi, 1989.

2

AMBEDKAR'S IDEA OF SOCIAL JUSTICE

GOPAL GURU

Anyone attempting to write on Ambedkar would agree that it is a tough job venturing into an analysis of his complex but important social ideas, particularly, his idea of social justice. To me, writing about Ambedkar is an enormous challenge for two reasons. First, Ambedkar did not systematically develop his concept of social justice in any of his writings and speeches, all of which are now available both in English and Marathi. Instead, his idea of social justice runs through his writings regarding equality, liberty, fraternity, human rights, socio-economic democracy, and the state and minorities. Secondly, Ambedkar's various theoretical positions with particular reference to social justice, are so close to each other that they often lead to misinterpretation. They have to be carefully understood through on dialectical unfolding of his works.

The purpose of this paper is twofold. First, to locate Ambedkar's idea of social justice on a more visible and systematic terrain. Second, to bring out the essence of his idea of social justice, developed through the dialectical negation of his earlier positions on this subject.

Before discussing Ambedkar's concept of justice, it would be useful to examine the various versions of social justice that thinkers in India have advocated from time to time, both in the pre- and post-Ambedkar periods.

Historically, justice in the Indian context was seen as an

important social value, as it consisted in the strict observance of enforcement of Hindu law, based on the four *varnas* and an elaborated caste system. According to Ambedkar:

> "Hindu Law is that law of the established order and was made by the touchables. The untouchables had nothing to do except to obey it and respect it. The untouchables have no right against the touchables. For them there is no equal right, no justice which is due to them and nothing is allowed to them. Nothing is due to them except what the touchables are prepared to grant. The untouchables must not insist on rights. They should pray for mercy and favour and rest content with what is offered."

Ambedkar further maintained that the established order was based on graded inequality and was legitimised by Hindu law which completely negated equality, fraternity, liberty, democracy and human rights (WSBRA, 1984:25). Ambedkar was of the view that the system of graded inequality was not notional but legal and penal (WSBRA, 1990:27). It could be argued that at the philosophical level, justice in ancient India had three characteristics: First, it gave preference to hierarchy over equality. Second, it underlined the importance of respecting traditional rights and performing traditional duties. Finally, Hindu law meant different things to different castes and people. The concept of justice contained no notion of equal treatment to all men. In other words, the function of justice in this kind of a society was to preserve the existing hierarchy rather than provide a criterion for social reforms. This concept has been used at the ideological level by the upper castes and classes to deny the deprived sections the essence of justice. Thus, in one sense justice in the Indian context served to validate societal stratification and perpetuate casteism.

Movements of Untouchables against this kind of injustice by the Hindu social order has a long history, particularly in Maharashtra. Dalit saints are found complaining to God about the injustice that was heaped on them by the exploitative social structure (BABBA, 1991). However, their idea of justice was chiefly concerned with equality only in relation to God and not elsewhere, and confined it to devotees and the common man. Ambedkar criticised this theologic-religious concept of justice on the ground that it was limited to devotees and failed to attack the "*Chaturvarna* system which was mainly responsible for perpetuating the structures of inequality" (*Ibid.*). He further argued that Dalit saints, individually speaking, might have achieved equality in the eyes of God and hence in the spiritual realm, but they failed to attack the social inequality that subverted the material life of millions of Untouchables for centuries (*Ibid.*).

In our time, we have come across the position taken by Walter. Kaufmann that the origin of justice has to be traced metaphysically to a kind of inherent moral sense in man, to his multiple emotive faculties (Dutta Gupta, 1979:2).

Ambedkar, like the overwhelming majority of liberal philosophers, has opposed this metaphysical concept of justice (*Ibid.*). He was of the opinion that it was absolutely futile to accept any compassion from Touchables, who were pledged to Brahminism (Ganvir, 1987:90). He said that Touchables lacked social conscience towards Untouchables and their sense of obligation was restricted to a limited class of people, mainly the members of their caste (WSBRA, 1989:99). It is because of this that the Untouchables could not be said to belong to the society of Hindus; the latter did not feel that they and the Untouchables belonged to one society. According to him, this is the reason why the conduct of the Hindus is marked by a moralistic unconcernedness (*Ibid.*). In his attack on this metaphysical theory of justice, Ambedkar says:

> "Not having conscience, the Hindu has no such thing in him as righteous indignation against the inequalities and injustices from which the untouchable has been suffering. He sees no wrong in these inequities and injustice and refuses to budge. By his absence of conscience the Hindu is a great obstacle in the path of the removal of untouchability (*Ibid.*)."

On yet another occasion, Ambedkar linked up this lack of

concern and the lack of righteous indignation to the spiritual and material interests of Touchables. He was of the opinion that Touchables are insensitive to the justice of untouchables due to the heavy influence of *Hindu Dharma* (BABBA, 1991). He argued that this impact is perpetuated by high-caste Hindus who would not like Untouchables to share their material comforts. Thus, Ambedkar, on very sound material grounds, rejects this metaphysical deduction of justice from the concept of self-consciousness. He contends that Touchables have become indifferent to Untouchables because of their material interests. Brahminial values are used by upper castes to deny Untouchables the social justice which otherwise directly threatens their material interests (*Ibid.*).

It is this caste consciousness among Touchables that makes Ambedkar suspicious about the validity of the legal concept of justice which involves punishment for wrong doing and the compensation of injury through the creation and enforcement of a public set of rules (Millan, 1979:277). In view of the fragmented and, therefore, discriminatory nature of Hindu law during the medieval period, however, Ambedkar seemed to welcome the legal intervention of the British. Their attempts to standardise the legal system in India gave effect to the concept of equality before law. For example, Ambedkar found British legal injunctions useful in declaring the practice of untouchability to be invalid (*Ibid.*). He said that it was possible under the rule of law to declare untouchability invalid on the ground that it was opposed to morality and public policy (*Ibid.*). But it would be of no use, Ambedkar lamented, unless it was declared to be so by a judicial tribunal. He was of the opinion that such a measure would be of great help to Untouchables in their fight for civil rights because it would seem illegal to import untouchability in civic matter (*Ibid.*).

However, Ambedkar maintained the view that legal justice at the formal or at the theoretical level would be ineffective at the practical level. As he said:

> "I might have been thought that the principle of equal justice would strike a death blow to the established order. As a matter of fact, far from suffering any damage, the established order has

continued to operate. It might be asked why the principle of equal justice has failed to have its effect. The answer to this is simple. To enunciate the principle of justice is one thing. To make it effective is another thing. Whether the principle of equal justice is effective or not must necessarily depend on the nature and character of the civil services who administer the principle. If the civil services are by reason of class bias, the friend of the established order and the enemy of the new order, the new order can never come into being. That a civil service in tune with the new order was essential for the success of the new order was recognised by Karl Marx in 1871 in the formation of the Paris Commune and was adopted by Lenin in the Constitution of Soviet Communism. Unfortunately, the British government never cared about the personnel in the civil service. Indeed, it opened the gates of the administration to those classes who believed in the old established order of the Hindus in which the principles of equality had no place. As a result of this fact, India has been ruled by the Britishers but administered by the Hindus (*Ibid.*)."

Ambedkar, while illustrating his point a little further said:

"From the capital of India down to the village the whole administration is rigged by the Hindus. The Hindus are like the omnipotent almighty pervading all over the administration in all its branches having authority in all its nooks and corners. There is no loophole for anyone opposed to the old order to escape. If the established order has continued to exist, it is because of the unfailing support it received from the Hindu officials of the state. The Hindu officials are not merely administrators administering the affairs on the merit, they are administrators with an eye to their parties. Their principle is not equal justice to all. Their motto is justice consistent with established order. This is inevitable. For they carry over into administration, the attitude towards different classes in society under the established order. This is well illustrated by the attitude of the

> state officials towards the untouchables in the field of administration. As every untouchable will be able to testify, if an untouchable goes to a police officer with a complaint against a caste Hindu, instead of receiving any protection he will receive plenty of abuses. Either he will be driven away without his complaint being recorded or if it is recorded it would be recorded quite falsely to provide a way of escape to the touchable aggressors. If he prosecutes his offenders before a Magistrate the fate of his proceeding could be foretold. The untouchables will never be able to get Hindus as witness because of the conspiracy of the villagers not to support the case of the untouchables however just it may be. If he brings witness from the untouchables, the Magistrate will not accept their testimony because he can easily say that they are interested and not independent witness, or, if they are independent witness the Magistrate has a easy way of acquitting the accused by simply saying that the untouchable's complaint did not strike him as a truthful witness. He can do this fearlessly knowing fully well that the higher tribunal will not reverse his finding because of the well established rule which says that an appellate court should not disturb the findings of the trial Magistrate based on the testimony of witness whose demeanour he had no opportunity to observe (Khairmode, 1989:265)."

Thus, according to Ambedkar, upper-caste administrators have a Hindu bias and an antipathy towards untouchables, which results in the denial of protection and justice to the latter.

During the Mahad conference, organised for establishing the right of Dalits to take water from the Chowder tank, Ambedkar proclaimed that untouchables wanted a complete overhauling of the Hindu social system. He further argued that this reconstruction must not have as its foundation the Hindu Shastra, but be consonant with justice and equality, which he later on found in the philosophy of Buddha. As is clear from the political practice of the Dalit movement, Ambedkar used all just forms of protest: from launching temple entry and boycott of Hindu practices to conversion to Buddhism for establishing social justice, and preferential treatment to Untouchables in the fields of bureaucracy and politics with the intention of protecting their interests. In this regard, it is essential to take into consideration Ambedkar's evidence before the South Borough Committee and later on in the first All India Depressed Classes Congress, held at Nagpur in 1930.

While advocating special treatment for Untouchables in the services, Ambedkar said:

> "The power to administer laws is not less important than the power to make laws. And the spirit of the legislators may easily be violated if not nullified by the machinery of the administrators. This is not the only reason why the depressed classes should show special concern for securing power of control over administration. Often times under pressure of work or under difficulties of circumstances one has to leave good deal of discretionary power in the hands of the heads of the administrative departments. The welfare of the people must greatly depend on how impartially this discretionary power is exercised. In a country like India where the public service is almost exclusively manned by people of one community, there is a great danger of this vast discretionary power being used for the personal aggrandisement of a class. The best antidote against it is to insist on a proper admixture of caste and creeds including the depressed classes and there will be no difficulty in guaranteeing this safeguard to us by a clause in the Constitution. Such protection you could have dispensed with if there was any chance of the depressed classes being represented in the future cabinets of the country. But there is not the remotest chance of this in view of the fact that the depressed classes will always remain in minority. This makes it all the more necessary why you should insist upon such a guarantee (WSBRA, 1979:265)."

Ambedkar, while stating the importance of political reservations for Untouchables, said:

> "The significance of suffrage or a political right consists in a

change for active and direct participation in the regulation of the term upon which associated life shall be sustained. Now the terms upon which the associated life between the touchables and untouchables is carried on today are the most ignominious to the former and highly detrimental to the latter. To make effective the capacities of a people, there must be the power to fix the social conditions of their exercise. If the conditions are too obdurate, it is in the interest of the untouchables as well as the touchables that the conditions should be revised. The untouchables must be in a position to influence the revision looking to the gravity of their interest. They should get their representation as proposed in proportion to their population (*Ibid.*)."

The mode of acquiring this political power in Ambedkar's scheme, however, has to be located in a pluralist framework where sharing of political power is the main assumption. Ambedkar's concept of political power aimed at enabling Dalits to secure social justice on a more equitable and honourable terms.

However, it is necessary to point out here the shift in Ambedkar's position. He started with a negation of the legal concept of justice on the ground that it cannot be realised because its implementation is in the hands of upper castes. On this occasion, however, he seems to be affirming this form of justice provided the implementation of the legal provisions is vested in the hands of untouchables. Therefore, in a way, Ambedkar's own concept of justice appears to be embedded within the liberal framework. In fact, Ambedkar's idea of social justice is tantamount to the concept of justice propounded by John Rawls, who includes in his theory of distributive justice an 'element of the difference' principle; in Ambedkar's case, it is the principle of special treatment. Both these principles of justice, require a distribution of resources that will most effectively satisfy the needs of the worst off (Millan, 1979:49). Distributive justice also involves the principle of equality. But in Ambedkar's case it involves prestige and honour along with equality principle.

The question that arises here is: Does Ambedkar's concept of justice remain fettered within the narrow contours of liberalism?

Does it imply the reconciliation of conflicting interests in society? Or does it expose the limits of both legal and political justice that Ambedkar was talking about earlier? Before answer to these questions can be given, it is essential to mention that Ambedkar's concept of justice is not an abstract or a static one; on the contrary, it is a concrete and dynamic concept to be understood in terms of the changing social reality. It keeps developing out of the negation of his earlier positions on justice. It moves in a direction away from the limits inherent in the liberal notion of social justice. Though his concept of social justice involves a normative element in as much as it aims at desirability or goodness in social life, yet he views rather objectively the limitations of the liberal concept of justice which does not see the contradictions between how one lives and how one can live.

Ambedkar very clearly saw the conflicting interests that severely baffled the Untouchables, bureaucrats and the legislators, who tried to meet out justice to their own caste people. Ambedkar was painfully aware that even if adequately represented, untouchables would not be able to meet out justice to their people, because they would be working under terrible pressures and conditions of socio-economic insecurity dictated by the dominant forces in this country (Guru, 1995). Regarding political leaders and the legislators, Ambekdar had little hope that they would be able to do any justice to their people without the permission of their political bosses in the Congress Party (*Ibid.*).

Therefore, it is clear that for Ambedkar political justice was not enough for the good of the Untouchables. In fact, he gave more importance to social and economic justice. Nay, he considered socio-economic justice as the precondition for redeeming political justice on the eve of the adoption of our Constitution he said:

> "We must not to be content with mere political democracy. We must make our political democracy a social democracy as well. Political democracy cannot last unless there lies at the base of it social democracy. What social democracy means? It means a way of life which recognises liberty, equality and fraternity as the principle of life. These principles are not to be treated as

separate items in trinity. They form a union of trinity, in the sense that to divorce one from the other is to defeat the very purpose of democracy. One the social plane, we have in India a society in which there are principles based on graded inequality, which means elevation of some and degradation for others. On the economic plane, we have a society in which there are principles based on graded inequality which means elevation of some and degradation for others. On the economic plane, we have a society in which there are some who have immense wealth as against many who live in abject poverty. On the 26th January 1950, we are going to enter into a life of contradictions. In political life we will have equality and in social and economic life, we shall by reason of our social and economic structure, continue to deny the principle of one man one vote one value. How long shall we continue to deny equality in our social and economic life? If we continue to deny it for long, we shall do so only by putting our political democracy in peril. We must remove this contradiction at the earliest possible movement or else those who suffer from inequality will blow up the structure of political democracy which this Assembly has so laboriously built up (Keer, 1954: 412)."

It is also clear from the above that unlike ethical philosophers who locate justice exclusively in moral terms, Ambedkar does not abstract the concept of social justice from its material base (that is the social base). His concept of justice is firmly rooted in the synthesis of social equality, involving freedom and liberty with economic equality. This is reflected in his understanding of the French and the Russian Revolution, Ambedkar considered the French Revolution as the first stage and the Russian Revolution as the second stage in human liberation (Khairmode, 1987:47-48).

REFERENCES

Babasaheb Ambedkaranche Bahishkruit Bharatatil Agralekh (BABBA) (Marathi), Bombay: Government of Maharashtra, 1991.

Dutta Gupta, Shobhan Lal, *Justice and the Political Order in India*, Calcutta: K.P. Bagchi & Co., 1979.

Ganvir, Ratnakar, *Ambedkaranche Bahishkruit Bharatatil Sfut Lekh* (Marathi), Bhusawal: Ratnamitra Publication, 1987.

Guru, Gopal, *Ambedkar's Concept of Political Power*, (unpublished) Pune: Deptt. of Political Science, University of Poona, Pune, 1995.

Millan, David, *Social Justice*, Oxford: Clarendon Press, 1979.

Keer, Dhananjay, *Life and Mission of Dr. Ambedkar*, Bombay: Popular Prakashan, 1954.

Khairmode, G.B., *Bhimrao Ramji Ambedkar* (Marathi), Pune: Sugawa Publications, 1989, Vol. 4, p. 265.

Khairmode, G.B., *B.R. Ambedkar* (Marathi), Bombay: Maharashtra Sahitya Sanskruti Mandal, 1987.

Writings and Speeches of Dr. B.R. Ambedkar, (WSBRA), Government of Maharashtra, Bombay: Government of Maharashtra, Vol. 4, 1989; Vol. 7, 1990.

3

ACCESS TO LAND BY SCHEDULED CASTES AND SCHEDULED TRIBES IN INDIA

M. THANGARAJ

Introduction

Ownership of land is closely associated with social stratification in India. An important historical characteristic of the Indian social and economic milieu is the overlap between caste and class. Some attempts have been made to study the access to land by Scheduled Castes (SCs) and Scheduled Tribes (STs), and compare their position with the rest of the population. An attempt has been made in this paper to study the access to land for SCs and STs at all India level. Data were collected from the population censuses of 1981 and 1991, and the *All India Report of Agricultural Census*, 1980-81 and 1985-86. Data on landholdings for the year 1990-91 were collected from the *Agricultural Situation in India* (GOI 1995), as the Agricultural Census Report for the year 1990-91 has not yet been published. A detailed analysis could not be carried out for 1990-91 as the *Agricultural Situation in India* provides data only on distribution of number and area of operational holdings by social groups and distribution of number and area of holdings of different size classes by social groups, i.e., we do not have the break-up of data on holdings for the "others" category, which constitutes several communities, such as Most Backward Castes, Backward Castes and

Forward Castes.

In this analysis, we have to bear in mind that the quality of land may not be the same in all parts of the country. The land cultivated by Scheduled Tribes may be barren, undulating and unirrigated. The quality of these lands is not comparable to those in the plains. Hence, the findings of an investigation pertaining to tribals may not be applicable to SCs and others. In almost all states in India, laws prohibiting the transfer of land owned by tribals to non-tribal have been enacted. But in practice alienation of land continues because of loopholes in the law. In many cases, the land is in the name of tribals but cultivation is carried out by non-tribal groups. Kaul's study shows that tribal lands are passing into hands of non-tribals in Andhra Pradesh, Assam, Bihar, Maharashtra, Orissa, Rajasthan, Uttar Pradesh and West Bengal (Kaul, 1977:185-186). Before attempting an analysis of the data, let us examine the pattern of land ownership evolved down the ages so as to provide a historical backdrop for this study.

In ancient India, the people now referred to as SCs and STs were the original inhabitants and sons of the soil, and naturally the land was cultivated by them. The Aryan invasion alienated these inhabitants from their traditional means of livelihood. Subsequently, "when the country was ruled by the kings, the ownership of land was vested with the peasantry, and kings received a share of the produce" (Vermani, 1983:58). When society was under the hegemony of Hindu religion, certain sections were despised and tormented and they subsequently became the Untouchables. When the caste system came into being, persons belonging to depressed communities were not permitted to acquire land. It was considered an offense for a member of the Untouchable community to acquire land and cattle in the villages (WSBRA, 1989: 21). In some parts of India, laws were enacted prohibiting Untouchables from purchasing land. For instance, in the province of Punjab, the Land Alienation Act specified the communities which could purchase land and the Untouchables were excluded from this category (*Ibid.*:23).

Prior to British rule, all the Pariahs, an Untouchable community, without exception, were slaves of the superior castes.

The British government freed them from the yoke of hereditary slavery (Tremenheere : 1). Harijans (SCs) and low-caste Sudra communities fell within the category of slaves. The Pariahs and Pallans (SCs) served superior non-Brahmin masters like Vellalas (Manickam, 1982:6). In some places, Pariahs were attached to the land as serfs, and in other instances they cultivated land, and for their labour, were provided with a share of the produce just enough to maintain themselves and their families (Iyer, 1974:505). Dharma Kumar indicates that the British government had shown some interest in removing slavery, but were reluctant to abolish it as it could have been dangerous to disturb the long-established relations between ryots and slaves (Kumar, 1965:69). Another view is that the class of landless labourers was created during the British period. An Untouchable leader, Gangadhara Siva, held the British government responsible for the landlessness of untouchables in India. He forcefully argued in the Madras Legislative Council in 1928 that the Untouchables were the real owners of the land. According to him:

> "The real owners of cultivable land in India were the depressed classes. In those days there were no boundary stones or anything of this sort as now exist. After the settlement of the East India Company in 1751, the British people adopted a system of lords, tenants and sub-tenants for the purpose of collection of revenues in India. The British, without enquiring into the grievances of the depressed classes, ascertained the opinion from caste Hindus who used to be in the centre of the village as to who is the owner of the cultivable lands whereas the depressed classes were shunted out of the villages on question. Caste Hindus said that the lands were their own and the British people made the pattas in their name and thus deprived the lands of the depressed classes (*Proc. Mad. Leg. Council*, Vol. XL:212)."

He also requested the British government to provide at least one acre of land for each depressed class family to lead an independent life without depending upon caste Hindus (*Ibid.*:213). M.J.

Walhouse had also shown that the deprived castes in South India once held far higher positions, and were the real masters of the land (Manickam, 1982). However, the British government in India which was primarily interested in generating revenue from land, did not yield to such pressure. Tremenheere's study shows that the untouchables had very little access to land in Chengleput district. During the early 1890s, the Depressed Class constituted 25 per cent of the population, but held only 2 per cent of the land (Tremenheere:8). The study further indicates that Pariahs were cultivating the land for rent as "subtenants" (*Ibid.*: 10). Further that the lands cultivated by Pariahs were forcefully and illegally occupied by caste Hindus (*Ibid.*: 54-56). This clearly shows the extremely low social status of Pariahs in the hierarchical caste society.

The British government, however, began to extend welfare schemes to the depressed classes to ameliorate their economic conditions. As a first step, the British administration issued an order in 1894 that untouchables should be freed from their serfdom by means of land grants and educational facilities (Rajagopal, 1985: 121). In 1918, the British government adopted special measures to assign lands to the Depressed Classes for cultivation and some lands for house sites. The labour department was created in 1920 to assign lands to the Depressed Classes. Total number of house sites provided by acquisition of land since the inception of the department was 36,530. Land assigned for cultivation rose from 19,251 acres in 1920-21 to 3,42,611 acres in 1931 (Boag, 1933: 131-32). When the freedom movement gained momentum in India, several leaders from the Depressed Classes fought against the social and economic oppression. They put pressure on the British government to initiate several welfare measures for the upliftment of the oppressed masses. The colonial authorities in India conceded their demands and introduced several welfare measures, such as the assignment of lands to SC families and provision of education for their children.

After independence, the Indian government started various welfare schemes to ameliorate the condition of SCs. Distribution of surplus land through land reforms and assignment of cultivable waste land were considered to be the crucial measures for their economic development and empowerment, since most of them worked as agricultural labourers. Despite the introduction of several welfare programmes, there has been no marked change in their socio-economic condition due to poor implementation of law and lack of political will.

However, there were changes in the tenurial relationships. It is important to note that Brahmins were interested in leasing out their land to Untouchables due to their submissive nature. Beteille's study indicates that in the South Indian villages, Brahmin landowners were replacing non-brahmin tenants with Adi Dravidars (SCs). As tenants, non-Brahmins became more demanding and aggressive, with the shift of political power in their favour, Brahmin landowners tended to show greater preference for Adi Dravida tenants who were on the whole less militant and more respectful (Beteille, 1971: 195-196).

Several micro-level studies have probed the question whether there has been any upward mobility in the distribution of land holdings by those who have been traditionally debarred from acquiring landed assets and whether land ownership has tended to get concentrated among the middle or dominant castes. A study conducted in a village in Andhra Pradesh based on data pertaining to four points in time, viz. 1930, 1948, 1965 and 1982, shows that the share of land owned by non-brahmins increased while that of brahmins decreased over time. The quantum of land owned by Scheduled Castes remained more or less the same (Namcharaiah, 1985). Another study in a Maharashtra village compares the position of the households in 1958-59 with those in 1942-43 and 1945 and shows that the area of land owned by higher castes decreased and that land held by middle castes increased over time. The land occupied by Buddhists (SCs) remained constant (Kamble, 1979). A village study in Tamil Nadu shows that land ownership is heavily concentrated among caste Hindu SCs, who constitute about 30 per cent of population altogether, own less than 3 per cent of the land. The holding among the 40 SCs who own some land add up to less than 2 acres (Guhan *et al.*, 1982). A study conducted by V.B. Athreya in 1983, compares the situations with those in 1916, 1936 and 1958. He found that the share of Scheduled Caste population in the total population in 1983 was 17 per cent, the share of land held by them was only about 3 per cent (1981). Another study conducted in Tamil Nadu village level shows that persons belonging to SCs and Backward Castes, who have been detached from the land for centuries, are in the process of wresting land from higher castes (Thangaraj, 1988). All these studies, by and large, show that the hitherto oppressed sections of society are beginning to acquire control over landed assets. In this context, it is worthwhile to examine the distribution of land holdings across social groups at the macro level.

Population

The censuses of India divide the Indian society into three distinct groups, viz., Scheduled Castes, Scheduled Tribes and others. Each group consists of numerous castes and sub-castes. The "others" category comprises of persons belonging to middle and higher castes. Table 3.1 shows that there was a slight increase in the percentage of SCs and STs between 1981 and 1991.

An access index of 1 indicates that there is a perfect equality between the proportion of the community i to the total population and proportion of land operated by community i to the total land operated. If the access index is less than 1 then it shows that the proportion of land operated by community i was less than the proportion of population of community i to total population. If the index is more than 1, then it indicates high access to land, i.e., the proportion of land operated by community i to total land operated was more than the proportion of population of the community i to the total population. By studying the magnitude and variation of i for SCs, STs and others for different types of land, certain broad generalisations may be derived regarding the extent and nature of access to land by these communities.

Land holdings by Social Groups

Distribution of number and area of operational holdings by social groups is shown at the all India level, in Table 3.2. It indicates that the percentage of area controlled by SCs and STs increased

TABLE 3.1 : Distribution of Population in India ... ocial Groups Between 1981 and 1991

Scheduled Castes			Scheduled Tribes			Other		
1981	1986	1991	1981	1986	1991	1981	1986	1991
104754623	119606422	138223277	51628638	57878056	67758380	508904588	559316347	632602331
(15.75)	(16.23)	(16.48)	(7.76)	(7.86)	(8.08)	(76.49)	(75.91)	(75.44)

1) a4 = 14 / p4   Where a4 = Access Index
14 = percentage of land operated by community I to total land operated
p4 = percentage of community I to total population

2) 14 = 14 / L   Where L4 = Amount of land operated by community i
L = Total amount of land operated by All communities

3) p4 where p4 / p = Population of community
P = P4 = Total Population

4) a4 = L4/L / P4/P

(Contd.)

TABLE 3.1 *(Contd.)*

Notes:

1. Figures in brackets indicate percentages.
2. Data for the year 1986 have been estimated from the 1981 and 1991 censuses by geometric growth rate for comparison purpose with the data on landholdings for 1985-86. A brief note on access index. The magnitude of access to land for SCs and STs has been examined in terms of simple index of access which is defined as follows:

Sources:

1. Census of India, 1981, Primary Census Abstract, General Population, Series-I, Part II-B (i) 1983.
2. Census of India, 1981, Primary Census Abstract, Scheduled Castes, Series-I, Part II-B (ii) 1983.
3. Census of India, 1981, Primary Census Abstract Scheduled Tribes, Series-I, Part II-B (iii) 1983.
4. Census of India, 1991, Final Population Totals: Brief analysis of Primary Census Abstract, Series I, paper of 1992.

marginally in 1985-86 and 1990-91 compared to 1980-81. Increase in the land operated by SCs may be partly due to the redistribution of land through Land Ceiling Acts. The share of land cultivated by others has come down slightly. Table 3.2 further shows that the per

TABLE 3.2: Distribution of Number and Area of Operational Holdings by Social Groups

Social Groups	Area Operated ('000 ha.)		
	1980-81	1985-86	1990-91
Scheduled Castes	11522	12639	13090
	(7.0)	(7.7)	(7.9)
PLA	0.11	0.11	0.99
Access Index	0.44	0.47	0.48
AAPH	1.15	1.05	1.00
Scheduled Tribes	16704	17234	17890
	(10.2)	(10.5)	(10.8)
PLA	0.32	0.30	0.26
Access Index	1.31	1.34	1.34
AAPH	2.44	2.25	2.09
Others	135571	134689	134650
	(82.8)	(81.8)	(81.3)
PLA	0.27	0.24	0.21
Access Index	1.082	1.082	1.078
AAPH	1.88	1.74	1.078
Total	163797	164562	165630
	(100.0)	(100.0)	(100.0)

Notes: 1. Figures in brackets represent percentage to total.
2. PLA—Per capita land availability.
3. AAPH—Average area per holding.

Sources: 1. All India report on Agricultural Census, 1980-81, Ministry of Agriculture, Government of India, New Delhi: 1987.
2. All India report on Agricultural Census, 1985-86, Ministry of Agriculture, Government of India, New Delhi: 1990.
3. Agricultural situation in India, Ministry of Agriculture, Government of India, New Delhi: 1995.

capita land availability and average size of holdings was lower for SCs compared to others and STs. This was true for access to land index as well.

Area Operated by Social Groups

Table 3.3 gives, the distribution of number of operational holdings and area by social groups, according to size classes. It shows that marginal and small holdings constituted 74.5 per cent of the total holdings and accounted for only 26.2 per cent of the area in 1980-81.

But, large size holdings to total holdings was minimal in the case of SCs. The concentration ratio (CR)* had declined in 1990-91 as compared to 1980-81, but the decline was greater in the case of STs than SCs and others. The CR continued to be higher even in 1990-91. Thus the data clearly indicate that persons belonging to SCs, by and large, operate relatively small size of holdings and the magnitude of land operated by them was also lower than the rest of the social groups.

Table 3.3 shows that access to land operated declines in the case of SCs as the size class of land increases. On the other hand, greater the size class, higher the access to land operated in the case of others. There was a marginal increase in the access to land in 1990-91 over 1980-81 for SCs. In case of SCs, the access to land was very low for all size classes, particularly in higher ones.

Irrigational Status

Irrigation is the most crucial input in any agricultural production. It is a scarce resource and hence its use has a tremendous impact on the economic condition of its users. It has been hypothesised that the less privileged sections of society, viz. SCs and STs, have limited access to irrigation facilities. Distribution of land by irrigational status is given in Table 3.4. It clearly shows that the share of area irrigated

---

* $CR=\{-P_{(i-1)} Q_i - P_i Q_{(i-1)}\}$ Where P_i refers to the $^{i-2}$ $^{i-2}$ cumulative percentage of households of the ith group and Q_i to the cumulative percentage of area owned by the ith group.

TABLE 3.3: Distribution of Holdings and Area Operated by Social Groups According to Size Classes

(Number in '000 and area in '000 ha.) (1980-81)

	Scheduled Castes		Scheduled Tribes		Others		All Social Groups	
Size Groups	No.	Area	No.	Area	No.	Area	No.	Area
1	2	3	4	5	6	7	8	9
Marginal	6923	2510	2728	1309	40471	15916	50122	19735
(Below 1 ha.)	(68.9)	(21.8)	(39.8)	(7.8)	(56.2)	(11.7)	(56.4)	(12.0)
Access Index	0.88	0.81	0.70	0.85	1.06	1.05		
Small	1644	2324	1551	2220	12877	18625	16072	23169
(1-2 Ha.)	(16.4)	(20.2)	(22.6)	(13.3)	(17.9)	(13.1)	(18.1)	(14.1)
Access Index	0.65	0.64	1.25	1.24	1.05	1.05		
Semi-Medium	952	2576	1405	3850	10098	28219	12455	34645
(2-4 ha.)	(9.5)	(22.4)	(20.5)	(23.1)	(14.0)	(20.8)	(14.0)	(21.2)
Access Index	0.48	0.47	1.46	1.43	1.06	1.07		
Medium	438	2554	936	5596	6694	40393	8068	48543
(4-10 ha.)	(4.4)	(22.2)	(13.7)	(33.5)	(9.3)	(29.8)	(9.1)	(29.6)
Access Index	0.34	0.34	1.49	1.48	1.09	1.09		

(Contd.)

TABLE 3.3 *(Contd.)*

1	2	3	4	5	6	7	8	9
Large (10 ha. and above)	95	1557	234	3729	1837	32419	2166	37705
	(0.9)	(13.4)	(3.4)	(22.3)	(2.6)	(23.8)	(2.4)	(23.0)
Access Index	0.28	0.26	1.39	1.28	1.11	1.12		
Total	10052	11521	6854	16704	71977	135572	88883	163797
	(100.0)	(100.0)	(100.0)	(100.0)	(100.0)	(100.0)	(100.0)	(100.0)
Concentration Ratio	0.5615	0.5624	0.6075	0.6037				

Notes: 1. Figures in brackets are percentages to total.
2. Totals may not tally due to rounding off in 1985-86.

Sources: 1. All India Report on Agricultural Census, 1980-81.
2. All India Report on Agricultural Census, 1985-86.
3. Agricultural Situation in India, August, 1995.

TABLE 3.3 *(Contd.)* (1985-86)

	Scheduled Castes		Scheduled Tribes		Others		All Social Groups	
Size Groups	No.	Area	No.	Area	No.	Area	No.	Area
Marginal	8508	3000	3161	1512	44478	17530	56147	22042
(Below 1 ha.)	(70.7)	(23.7)	(41.3)	(8.8)	(57.4)	(13.0)	(57.8)	(13.4)
Access Index	0.94	0.84	0.71	0.88	1.04	1.05		
Small	923	2713	1795	2563	14204	20432	17922	25708
(1-2 Ha.)	(16.0)	(21.5)	(23.5)	(14.9)	(18.3)	(15.2)	(18.4)	(15.6)
Access Index	0.66	0.65	1.27	1.27	1.04	1.05		
Semi-Medium	1067	2878	1545	4225	10640	29563	13252	36666
(2-4 ha.)	(8.9)	(22.8)	(20.2)	(24.5)	(13.7)	(21.9)	(13.6)	(22.3)
Access Index	0.50	0.48	1.49	1.46	1.06	1.06		
Medium	456	2636	936	55701	6524	38938	7916	47144
(4-10 ha.)	(3.8)	(20.9)	(12.2)	(32.3)	(8.4)	(28.9)	(8.1)	(28.6)
Access Index	0.36	0.35	1.50	1.50	1.09	1.09		
Large (10 ha.	87	1413	212	3365	1619	28224	1918	33002
and above)	(0.7)	(11.2)	(2.8)	(19.5)	(2.1)	(21.0)	(2.0)	(20.1)
Access Index	0.28	0.26	1.41	1.30	1.11	1.13		
Total	12041	12640	7648	17235	77465	134687	97155	164562
	(100.0)	(100.0)	(100.0)	(100.0)	(100.0)	(100.0)	(100.0)	(100.0)
Concentration ratio		0.5505	0.5330	0.5949	0.5913			

to net sown area has increased from 27 per cent in 1980-81 to 29 per cent in 1985-86 for all social groups.

The share of area irrigated to the net area sown has increased marginally for SCs and STs, and decreased for others in 1985-86 as compared to 1980-81, significantly, 3.3 per cent of the irrigated area to the total irrigated area was controlled by STs; 7 per cent by SCs and the rest, 89.7 per cent by Others in 1985-86. Further, the access index was less than 1 in the case of SCs and STs, while for others it exceeded 1.

TABLE 3.4: Distribution of Land by Irrigation Status

('000 ha)

	Net Area Sown		Net Area Irrigated	
Social Groups	1980-81	1985-86	1980-81	1985-86
Scheduled Castes	9631 (7.0)	10639 (7.7)	2201 (6.0)	2830 (7.0)
PLA	0.09	0.09	0.02	0.02
Access Index	0.44	0.47	0.38	0.43
Scheduled Tribes	12942 (9.5)	13606 (9.9)	1109 (3.0)	1333 (3.3)
PLA	0.25	0.24	0.02	0.02
Access Index	1.22	1.26	0.39	0.42
Others	114068 (83.5)	113183 (82.4)	33488 (91.0)	36298 (89.7)
PLA	0.22	0.20	0.07	0.06
Access Index	1.09	1.09	1.19	1.18
Total	136641 (100.0)	137428 (100.0)	36803 (100.0)	40461 (100.0)

Notes: Figures in brackets indicate percentages to the respective totals.

1. It is also clear from the table that the access indices have marginally increased for SCs and STs and decreased for Others in 1985-86 as compared to 1980-81. Access to both net area sown and net area irrigated was very low for SCs, while access to area irrigated was very low for STs.

Sources: 1. All India Report of Agricultural Census, 1980-81.
2. All India Report of Agricultural Census, 1985-86.

Area Irrigated by Different Sources

Theoretically, access to surface irrigation, viz., canals and tanks, is equal for all social groups. Sub-surface or ground-water irrigation, viz., through wells and tubewells requires heavy investment and hence it may not be equally accessible to all social groups. The distribution of area irrigated by different sources is presented in Table 3.4. It shows that there was a decline in the area of land irrigated by tanks and wells for others; there was also a marginal decline in the area irrigated by tanks for SCs; and there was an increase in the land irrigated by all sources of irrigation for SCs, STs and Others in 1985-86 over 1980-81.

Table 3.5 further shows that there was an increase in the area of irrigated land in the case of all sources of irrigation for SCs and STs. In the case of others, there was a marginal decline in the irrigated land by all sources in 1985-86 over 1980-81. The access to irrigated land was more than 1 by all sources of irrigation for others; while access was less than 1 for SCs and STs. In the case of SCs and STs, their access to irrigated land by all sources of irrigation taken together was, by and large, the same in both 1980-81 and 1985-86. It is important to note that access to irrigation by wells and tube-wells was low in comparison with canals and tanks for SCs. This clearly indicates that a majority of the farmers belonging to SCs largely depended upon surface irrigation, which is a free natural resource. While others had greater access to both surface and sub-surface irrigation.

Land-Use Pattern

Land is an important and scarce natural resource and its improper use leads to wastage. The land-use pattern is an important index of agricultural development. In the recent past, the per capita availability of land has been coming down because of the mounting pressure of population on land. The area under different land-use pattern, by social groups as given in Table 3.6 shows that the percentage of net sown area has marginally increased for SCs and STs and declined for others. The percentage of area under 'current'

TABLE 3.5: Distribution of Area Irrigated by Sources

(in '000 ha.)

	Scheduled Castes		Scheduled Tribes		Others		All Social Groups	
Source of Irrigation	1980-81	1985-86	1980-81	1985-86	1980-81	1985-86	1980-81	1985-86
Canals	920	1212	388	456	13065	13439	14373	15107
Access Index	0.41	0.49	0.35	0.38	1.19	1.19		
Tanks	253	252	124	128	2955	2404	3332	2784
Access Index	0.48	0.56	0.48	0.59	1.16	1.14		
Wells	380	433	320	367	6305	5943	7005	6743
Access Index	0.34	0.40	0.59	0.69	1.18	1.16		
Tube Wells	514	757	22	76	9111	12368	9647	13201
Access Index	0.34	0.35	0.03	0.07	1.23	1.23		
Other Sources	139	176	255	306	2052	2144	2446	2626
Access Index	0.36	0.41	1.34	1.48	1.10	1.08		
Total	2206	2830	1109	1333	33488	36298	36803	40461
Access Index	0.38	0.43	0.39	0.42	1.19	1.18		

Sources: 1. All India Report of Agricultural Census, 1980-81.
2. All India Report of Agricultural Census, 1985-86.

and 'other fallows' has declined for STs, whereas it has increased for SCs and others. The percentage of area of other uncultivated land has declined for SCs and STs, and increased for others. The percentage of land not available for cultivation has declined for SCs and others and increased for STs.

Table 3.6 also shows that the access indices were less than 1 for SCs in both 1980-81 and 1985-86. The access indices were more than 1 in the case of STs in both 1980-81 and 1985-86. But the access indices have declined for land under current fallows, other uncultivated land excluding the fallow land, and fallow land other than current fallow, for STs during this period. This is a positive development that STs have been able to reduce their access to uncultivated land. In the case of others, the access indices were more than 1 in all types of land use except fallow land other than current fallow. Although access to cultivable wasteland and land not available for cultivation declined in the case of others, there was an increase in the access to current fallow, other uncultivated land excluding the fallow land, and fallow land other than current fallow. It can be safely inferred from the data that others were not using the land efficiently.

Area Under Principal Crops

The cropping pattern is influenced, among other factors, by the farmers' preference for a particular type of crop. Farmers decisions about the cropping pattern vary from place to place, one social group to another, and with the size class of operational holdings. The rational farmer often tries to minimise the risks and uncertainties in agricultural production.

The area under principle crops by social groups is presented in Table 3.7. It shows that the percentage of area under all food crops to gross cropped area, has increased for SCs and STs, but declined for others in 1985-86 as compared to 1980-81. Conversely, the percentage of area under non-food crops to gross cropped area, has increased for others; while the percentage has declined for SCs and STs. The cropping intensity was highest in the case of others in both 1980-81 and 1985-86. The data clearly indicate that the share of land

TABLE 3.6 : Area Under Different Land Uses by Social Groups

Social Groups	Total Area 1980-81	Total Area 1985-86	Net Area Sown 1980-81	Net Area Sown 1985-86	Current Fallow 1980-81	Current Fallow 1985-86	Other Uncultivated Land Excluding Fallow 1980-81	Other Uncultivated Land Excluding Fallow 1985-86	Fallow Land other than Current Fallow 1980-81	Fallow Land other than Current Fallow 1985-86	Cultivable Land 1980-81	Cultivable Land 1985-86	Wasteland not Available for Cultivation 1980-81	Wasteland not Available for Cultivation 1985-86
1	2	3	4	5	6	7	8	9	10	11	12	13	14	15
Scheduled Castes	11521	12635	9631	10639	888	998	177	183	337	310	203	269	285	253
	(7.0)	(7.7)	(7.0)	(7.7)	(7.8)	(7.9)	(5.8)	(5.6)	(6.9)	(7.1)	(6.2)	(7.6)	(6.4)	(7.0)
	(100.0)	(100.0)	(83.6)	(84.2)	(7.7)	(7.9)	(1.5)	(1.4)	(2.9)	(2.5)	(1.8)	(2.1)	(2.5)	(1.8)
Access Index	0.44	0.47	0.44	0.47	0.50	0.49	0.37	0.35	0.44	0.44	0.39	0.47	0.40	0.43
Scheduled Tribes	16704	17233	12942	13606	1384	1319	498	494	1038	811	414	603	428	400
	(10.2)	(10.5)	(9.5)	(9.9)	(12.1)	(10.5)	(16.2)	(15.2)	(21.2)	(18.6)	(12.7)	(17.0)	(9.6)	(12.0)
	(100.0)	(100.0)	(77.5)	(79.0)	(8.3)	(7.7)	(3.0)	(2.9)	(6.2)	(4.7)	(2.5)	(3.5)	(2.6)	(2.3)
Access Index	1.31	1.33	1.22	1.26	1.56	1.34	2.09	1.93	2.73	2.36	1.64	2.16	1.24	1.53
Others	135567	134664	114068	113183	9174	10277	2399	2572	3531	3242	2648	2682	3747	2708
	(82.8)	(81.8)	(82.4)	(80.2)	(81.6)	(78.0)	(79.2)		(72.0)	(74.3)	(81.1)	(75.5)	(84.0)	(81.0)
	(100.0)	(100.0)	(84.1)	(84.0)	(6.8)	(7.6)	(1.8)	(1.9)	(2.6)	(2.4)	(2.0)	(2.0)	(2.8)	(2.0)

(Contd.)

TABLE 3.6 *(Contd.)*

1	2	3	4	5	6	7	8	9	10	11	12	13	14	15
Access Index	1.08	1.08	1.09	1.09	1.05	1.07	1.02	1.04	0.94	0.98	1.06	0.99	1.10	1.07
All Social	163792	164529	136641	137428	11446	12595	3074	3249	4906	4363	3265	3554	4460	3341
Groups	(100.0)	(100.0)	(100.0)	(100.0)	(100.0)	(100.0)	(100.0)	(100.0)	(100.0)	(100.0)	(100.0)	(100.0)	(100.0)	(100.0)
	(100.0)	(100.0)	(83.4)	(83.5)	(7.0)	(7.7)	(1.9)	(2.0)	(3.0)	(2.7)	(2.0)	(2.2)	(2.7)	(2.0)

Note: Figures in brackets indicate row and column percentage.

Sources: 1. All India Report of Agricultural Census, 1980-81.
2. All India Report of Agricultural Census, 1985-86.

TABLE 3.7: Area Under Principal Crops by Social Groups

(Area in '000 ha.)

Category	All Social Groups		Scheduled Castes		Scheduled Tribes		Others	
	1980-81	1985-86	1980-81	1985-86	1980-81	1985-86	1980-81	1985-86
All food crops	134221	137098	9668	10950	12268	13199	112285	122948
	(80.3)	(79.9)	(81.8)	(83.2)	(83.8)	(86.4)	(79.9)	(78.9)
Access Index			0.46	0.49	1.18	1.23	1.09	1.09
All Non-food Crops	32834	34533	2145	2204	2370	2075	28319	30254
	(19.7)	(20.1)	(18.2)	(16.8)	(16.2)	(13.6)	(20.1)	(21.1)
Access Index			0.41	0.39	0.93	0.76	1.13	1.15
Gross	167055	171631	11813	13155	14638	15274	140604	143202
Cropped Area			0.44	0.47	1.13	1.13	1.10	1.10
New Area Sown	136641	137428	9631	10639	12942	13606	114068	113183
Access Index			0.44	0.47	1.22	1.26	1.09	1.08
Cropping Intensity (3/4)	1.223	1.249	1.227	1.236	1.131	1.233	1.223	1.265

Note: Figures in brackets indicate percentages to gross cropped area total may not tally in 1985-86 due to rounding off.

Sources: 1. All India Report of Agricultural Census, 1980-81.

2. All India Report of Agricultural Census, 1985-86, STs, while the access had increased in the case others for all non-food crops.

under food crops to gross cropped area was higher in the case of STs, while the share of land under non-food crops to the total gross cropped area was higher in the case of others among all social groups.

Table 3.7 further shows that in the case of SCs the access was less than 1 for all food crops, non-food crops, gross cropped area and net area sown, and it marginally declined for all non-food crops in 1985-86 over 1980-81. In the case of STs, the access was more than 1 and increased in 1985-86 over 1980-81, in all categories except non-food crops. In the case of others, the access was more than 1 in all categories in both 1980-81 and 1985-86 and it marginally increased in all non-food crops in 1985-86 over 1980-81. It is clear from Table 3.7 that the access to food crops had increased in the case of SCs and STs, while the access had increased in the case of others for all non-food crops.

Tenurial Status

Tenurial status is an important index of the personal involvement of farmers in the production process. It is an established fact that the productivity of land cultivated by the owner is higher than that of land worked by tenants. In order to achieve social justice and to reduce inequality in the distribution of landholdings, some state governments abolished the tenancy system and tenants were made owners of the land. Distribution of the number of operational holdings by tenure and tenancy status, is given in Table 3.8, which indicates that there was not much difference between social groups with regard to the percentage of holdings and area with different tenurial status to total holdings and area. The percentage of owned and self-operated holding area has increased and the percentage of area and holdings of land wholly leased in declined in 1985-86 compared to 1980-81 among all social groups. The percentage of holdings and area of land wholly leased in was the highest for SCs and the lowest for others.

Access to landowned and self-operated was less than 1 both in terms of number and area for SCs and had increased marginally in

TABLE 3.8: Distribution of Number and Area of Operational Holdings by Tenurial Status by Social Groups in 1980-81 and 1985-86

(Number in 000 and area in 000 ha.)

Social Groups	Wholly Owned and Self-Operated		Partly Owned and Partly Lease-in		Wholly Leased-in		Wholly Otherwise Operated		Partly Owned and Partly Otherwise Operated		Partly Leased-in and Partly Otherwise Operated		Partly Owned & Partly Leased-in and Partly Otherwise Operated		Total	
	No.	Area	No.	Area	No.	Area	No.	Area	No.	Area	No.	Area	No.	Area	No.	Area
1980-81																
Scheduled Castes	9317	10677	302	352	143	134	91	83	119	243	5	5	24	27	10002	11522
	(93.2)	(92.7)	(3.0)	(3.1)	(1.4)	(1.2)	(0.9)	(0.7)	(1.2)	(2.1)	(0.1)	Neg.	(0.2)	(0.2)	(100.0)	(100.0)
Access index	0.71	0.44	0.97	0.60	1.15	0.91	0.97	0.75	0.58	0.41	0.33	0.29	0.36	0.31	0.72	0.45
Scheduled Tribes	6258	15340	131	299	73	120	147	184	222	680	7	29	13	52	6850	16704
	(91.4)	(91.8)	(1.9)	(1.8)	(1.1)	(0.7)	(2.1)	(1.1)	(3.2)	(4.1)	(0.1)	(0.2)	(0.2)	(0.3)	(100.0)	(100.0)
Access index	0.97	1.28	0.86	1.02	1.19	1.65	3.14	3.37	2.19	2.31	0.95	3.37	0.40	1.20	1.00	1.31
Others	67760	127924	1540	3096	574	683	364	436	965	2870	83	77	385	481	71672	135566
	(94.5)	(94.0)	(2.1)	(2.3)	(0.8)	(0.5)	(0.5)	(0.3)	(1.3)	(2.1)	(0.1)	(0.1)	(0.5)	(0.4)	(100.0)	(100.0)
Access index	1.06	1.09	1.02	1.08	0.95	0.95	0.79	0.81	0.97	0.96	1.14	0.91	1.19	1.12	1.06	1.08
All social groups in	83335	153941	1973	3747	790	937	603	703	1306	3793	95	111	422	560	88524	163792
	(94.1)	(94.0)	(2.2)	(2.3)	(0.9)	(0.6)	(0.7)	(0.4)	(1.5)	(2.3)	(0.1)	(0.1)	(0.5)	(0.3)	(100.0)	(100.0)

(Contd.)

TABLE 3.8: *(Contd.)*

Social Groups	Wholly Owned and Self Operated		Partly Owned and Partly Lease-in		Wholly Leased-in		Wholly Otherwise Operated		Partly Owned and Partly Otherwise Operated		Partly Leased-in and Partly Otherwise Operated		Partly Owned & Partly Leased-in and Partly Otherwise Operated		Total	
	No.	Area	No.	Area	No.	Area	No.	Area	No.	Area	No.	Area	No.	Area	No.	Area
1985-86																
Scheduled Castes	11008 (95.4)	12005 (95.0)			101 (0.9)	92 (0.7)	103 (0.9)	75 (0.7)					289 (2.5)	460 (3.6)	11501 (100.0)	12632 (100.0)
Access index	0.74	0.47			1.18	0.87	0.91	0.68					0.76	0.52	0.75	0.47
Scheduled Tribes	6971 (92.2)	15975 (92.7)			52 (0.7)	72 (0.4)	175 (2.3)	201 (1.2)					366 (4.8)	985 (5.7)	7564 (100.0)	17233 (100.0)
Access index	0.97	1.29			1.26	1.40	3.21	3.77					1.99	2.31	1.01	1.33
Others	73369 (96.8)	129780 (96.4)			373 (0.5)	490 (0.4)	416 (0.5)	402 (0.3)					1684 (2.2)	3992 (3.0)	15842 (100.0)	134664 (100.0)
Access index	1.06	1.08			0.93	0.99	0.79	0.78					0.95	0.97	1.05	1.08
All Social groups in	91348 (96.3)	157760 (95.9)			526 (0.6)	564 (0.4)	694 (0.7)	678 (0.4)					2339 (2.5)	5437 (3.3)	94907 (100.0)	164529 (100.0)

Note: Figures within brackets are percentages.

Sources: 1. All-India Report of Agricultural Census, 1980-81.

2. All-India Report of Agricultural Census, 1985-86.

1985-86 over 1980-81. For STs, the access to area was more than 1 and increased during this period. In the case of others, the access to both number and area, declined marginally during this period, but it was more than 1 in both 1980-81 and 1985-86. In the case of land wholly leased in, access to area was less than 1 for both SCs and Others, but during this period declined marginally for SCs and increased marginally for others; for STs the access was more than 1 but showed a decline. It is clear from the Table that access to wholly owned and self-operated was low, but the access was high in terms of land under wholly leased in, compared to other types of land for SCs.

Terms of Leasing

The leased in area by terms of leasing is also an important factor which decides productivity in agriculture. The area under "fixed money" and "fixed produce" is expected to encourage farmers to produce more. The implementation of land reform legislation is not uniform in India. Some states have abolished the tenancy system; others have regulated the rate of rent and protected tenants from eviction. The "share of produce" lease will not be beneficial to tenants as the rate of rent is proportionate to production. The land under this lease will not encourage tenants to strive for higher production. The break-up of land leased in according to terms of leasing and by social groups is given in Table 3.9. It is clear that the absolute area leased in for fixed money, fixed produce, and share of produce has declined for all social groups in 1985-86 as compared to 1980-81. The land under usufructuary mortgage has remained steady for SCs. It is also clear from the data that share of produce was the major leasing pattern which accounted for about 42 per cent of the total area leased in. Among all the social group the percentage of land under share of produce to total area lease in was highest for SCs, while that under fixed money, fixed produce, usufractuary mortgage, and other terms was the maximum for others.

Table 3.9 further shows that access declined in terms of 'fixed money', 'share of produce' and 'fixed produce', but increased in usufructuary mortgage and other terms for SCs in 1985-86, over 1980-81; access was more than 1 in terms of share of produce in both 1980-81 and 1985-86. In the case of STs, the access had declined in terms of fixed produce and usufructuary mortgage in 1985-86 over 1980-81, but the access was more than 1 in all categories of leases both in 1980-81 and 1985-86. In the case of others, access increased in terms of fixed produce and usufructuary mortgages in 1985-86 over 1980-81, it was more than 1 in all categories except share of produce and other terms both in 1980-81 and 1985-86. It is evident that access to land in terms of leasing in by fixed money was lower for SCs, compared to STs and others. In the case of fixed produce, access was highest by STs. For the share of produce category, access was lowest by others.

It is also important to examine the extent to which land redistribution through land ceiling legislation has contributed towards establishment of an egalitarian society. The land redistributed (Table 3.10) to SCs through the Ceiling on Land Holdings Act was only 2.64 per cent of the land operated. Though Land Ceiling Acts have played a positive role, they are not sufficient to meet the vast needs of land for SCs.

Access to land operated by SCs is relatively smaller in size as compared to STs and others. The access to wholly owned and self-operated land is low for SCs compared to STs and others. It is important to note that a small decline in the distribution of land among others will remarkably enhance the access by SCs and STs. The foregoing discussion clearly shows that the distribution of land is not equal.

The main reason for the low access to land by SCs is mainly their social and economic oppression. The existing distribution of landholdings is skewed in favour of higher and middle castes. Hence, there is need for state intervention to bring an equitable pattern of land distribution and provide land to the tillers and the landless. The government should lower the ceiling on landholdings and implement it more effectively so that surplus land can be assigned to the socially and economically vulnerable sections, particularly to the SCs, who form a major chunk of the landless agricultural labourers. Ceiling on

TABLE 3.9: Distribution of Leased in Area by Terms of Leasing by Social Groups

Social Groups	Fixed money 1980-81	Fixed Produce 1985-86	Share of Produce 1980-81	Usufructuary Mortgage 1985-86	Other Terms 1980-81	1985-86	1980-81	1985-86	1980-81	1985-86
Scheduled Castes	35 (11.8)	23 (11.9)	19 (6.4)	14 (7.2)	163 (55.1)	110 (56.7)	3 (1.0)	3 (1.5)	76 (25.7)	44 (22.7)
Access Index	0.47	0.39	0.62	0.61	1.22	1.17	0.43	0.54	0.70	1.00
Scheduled Tribes	38 (15.8)	37 (25.7)	21 (8.8)	13 (9.0)	72 (30.0)	58 (30.0)	6 (2.5)	3 (2.1)	103 (42.9)	38 (22.9)
Access Index	1.03	1.30	1.39	1.17	1.09	1.28	1.75	1.12	1.93	1.55
Others	401 (23.4)	302 (28.8)	154 (9.0)	114 (10.9)	614 (35.9)	409 (39.1)	35 (2.0)	28 (2.7)	507 (29.6)	194 (18.5)
Access Index	1.11	1.10	1.04	1.07	0.95	0.93	1.04	1.08	0.96	1.94
All Social Groups	474 (21.1)	362 (26.1)	194 (8.6)	141 (10.2)	849 (37.8)	577 (41.7)	44 (2.0)	34 (2.5)	686 (30.5)	27[illegible] (19.6)

Note: Figures in brackets represent row percentages.

Sources: 1. All-India Report of Agricultural Census, 1980-81.
2. All India Report of Agricultural Census, 1985-86.

TABLE 3.10: Distribution of Surplus Land by Social Groups – All India

	Scheduled Castes	Scheduled Tribes	Others	Total
1. Area distributed in acres	824551	325887	1110977	2261415
2. Percentage to total area	36.46	14.41	49.13	100.00
3. Number of beneficiaries	703690	223055	776308	1703053
4. Percentage to total	41.32	13.10	45.58	100.00

Source: Report of the Commission for Scheduled Castes and Scheduled Tribes (April 1983 – March 1984), Sixth Report, 1984, pp. 44-45.

land holdings should also be applied to institutions at par with individuals. It is instructive to recall here that the Karnataka government has fixed a ceiling, even on land held by religious institutions, unlike in Tamil Nadu, where there is no limit on the amount of land which religious and charitable institutions can own. Above all, those who do not engage in cultivation should not be allowed to own land. It is also necessary that the laws be enacted to protect the land owned or cultivated by SCs from being transferred to non-SCs.

REFERENCES

Athreya, V.B., "Vadamalaipuram: A Resurvey", Working Paper No. 50, Madras: Madras Institute of Development Studies, 1984.

Beteille, Andre, *Caste, Class and Power: Changing Pattern of Stratification in a Thanjore Village*, Delhi: Oxford University Press, 1971.

Boag, G.T., *The Madras Presidency: 1881-1931*, Madras: Government of India, 1933.

Dr. Babasaheb Ambedkar Writings and Speeches (WSBRA), Vol. 5, Bombay : Education Department, Government of Maharashtra, 1989.

GOI, *Agricultural Situation in India*, Delhi: Ministry of Agriculture, Government of India, 1995.

Guhan, S., and Mencher, Joan P. "Iruvelpattu : Revisited", Working Paper No. 28, Madras: Madras Institute of Development Studies, 1982.

Iyer, Ranam, *Rambles in Vedanta*, 1974.

Kaul, S.K., "A national picture", in S.N. Dubey and Ratna Murdia, (Eds.), *Land Alienation and Restoration in Tribal Communities in India*, 1977.

Kamble, N.D., *Poverty within poverty: A Study of weaker sections in a Deccan village*, 1979.

Kumar, Dharma, *Land and Caste in South India*, Cambridge University Press, 1965.

Manickam, S., *Slavery in the Tamil Nadu: A historical over-view*, Madras: Christian Literature Society, 1982.

Nancharaiah, "Caste and Land: A Study of Shift in Land Ownership in South India", unpublished Ph.D. thesis, Waltair, Andhra University, 1985.

Proceedings of Madras Legislative Council, vol. XL.

Rajagopal, Inda, *The Tyranny of Caste: The non-Brahman movement and political development in south India*, 1985.

Thangaraj, M., "Agricultural land transfers in Tamil Nadu", unpublished Ph.D. thesis, Mysore: Mysore University, 1988.

Tremenheere, H., "Note on the Pariahs of Chengleput", (year of the publication is not known).

Vermani, R.C., *British Colonialism in India*, Delhi, 1983.

4

EQUITY IN EDUCATION ?
The Schooling of Dalit Children in India

GEETHA B. NAMBISSAN

According to the 1991 Census of India, Dalit[1] (Scheduled Caste) communities are among the least literate social groups in the country. Barely 37.41 per cent of the population had acquired the most elementary skills in reading and writing, and in 1981 less than 30 per cent of rural Dalit children (5-14 years) were found to attend schools (India, 1993; India, 1989).

Explanations offered for the relatively poor spread of education among Dalit communities, mainly centre around factors that lie 'outside' the school system. Poverty and immiserization of majority of the Dalit population, their denigrated social status, illiterate home environments and apathetic attitudes towards education, are seen to be largely responsible for the poor response to schooling from these communities. Such arguments often tend to ignore the distinct historical experience of Dalit communities particularly in the context of education. These are the (ex) Untouchable communities that have traditionally been denied access to learning, specifically because of their position in the Indian caste structure. Though schooling was 'formally' open to all communities in the 1850s, the education of the 'Untouchables' proceeded at a snail's pace. Reports and studies have documented the social opposition to the early schooling of the 'Untouchables' as well as the social and economic constraints that impede their education even today.

The specific response, of the supposedly 'secular' and 'modern' formal, school to social discrimination and educational disadvantage has, however, received inadequate attention. An understanding of the role of the school is particularly critical given the growing realisation of the need for 'equity' in education, especially in the context of socially (and economically) vulnerable communities (Seceda, 1988). The term equity which has now become part of the language of education policy, incorporates the dimension of social justice along with equality of opportunity. It implies that communities which have suffered from an inequitous social structure cannot merely be given 'equal opportunity' in education but require affirmative action within the institution to remedy past injustice.

This paper draws attention to the nature of equity that prevails within schools. It focuses specifically on the experience of the (ex) Untouchables or Scheduled Castes in Indian schools and analyses three dimensions of equity in education:

- the access to schooling that is provided to Dalit communities;
- the social processes that influence 'treatment' of children within the institution and thereby their learning experiences; and
- the actual outcome that results from schooling.[2]

We attempt to show that equity in education is yet to be consciously practised within the formal school system and that this has impinged upon the learning opportunities for Dalit children. We argue that this issue must be urgently addressed especially when policy-makers, while setting targets for universalising elementary education, are voicing concern about the inability of 'Scheduled Caste' communities to avail of formal school opportunities and are advocating alternate systems of education for them.

The Historical Context

The status of communities as 'Untouchables', in the Hindu caste system, was the most serious impediment to their education. While stringent social taboos conscribed their behaviour, severe strictures were laid down to prevent their access to knowledge. It is said of some communities that they were prohibited from walking on the roads in daylight because even their shadow was considered polluting (Ghurye, 1957:166-167).

There is no record of Untouchable pupils, even in the nineteenth century indigenous schools, where the middle and some lower artisan castes were exposed to the '3 Rs'. Parulekar notes that 'the depressed (or Untouchable) classes had no access to schooling. They were, as a rule, not allowed to attend the indigenous schools whatever might be the caste or creed of the teacher. Tradition held them back with an iron hand allowing no exception under any circumstances whatsoever. In this prohibition, all castes joined hands and, the Brahmin was only one of them' (1945:LVI). Gough observes that "it was seen as improper, even ungodly for Adi Dravidas to read or write, and it was traditionally forbidden for both Adi-Dravida and non-Brahman castes even to hear the recitation of the Vedas" (Gough, 1981 in Saberwal, 1991:733).

Early efforts towards the education of the Untouchables are usually associated with British rule and the efforts of the Christian missionaries in India. The Caste Disabilities Removal Act of 1850 and subsequent establishment of schools are seen to have provided the first opportunities for education to the lowest of castes. What is relatively less known and acknowledged is the persistent struggle for access to schooling by the Untouchables themselves in the face of considerable opposition from caste Hindus.

British policy documents relating to the education of the Untouchables reveal a dualism, resulting from a liberal stance on the one hand and a tendency to compromise with dominant caste pressures on the other. This crucially affected the early educational opportunities of Untouchables and their experiences within schools. Thus, it was part of education policy to recommend that 'no boy be refused admission to a Government college or school merely on the ground of caste'. However, policy would simultaneously emphasise that '...this principle be applied with due caution....' (Hunter, 1882:516).

Institutionally, a number of options were made available by the administration. 'Special' government schools ensured 'separate' (and as will be shown later, unequal) education for Untouchables who would thereby not come into contact with upper caste children. Missionaries also were encouraged to run private (but aided) schools mainly for the lowest castes. Again, where other 'classes' (castes) objected to the association of their children with the Untouchables, the former were persuaded to set up their own special schools under the government grants-in-aid system. In other words, the rulers made little concerted attempt (despite their legal authority and control over funds) to enforce what was at that time a revolutionary principle of 'education for all' in common schools.

The reaction of caste Hindus was one of continuous opposition to the education of those who, in their eyes, were fated to a life of ignorance. Official reports in the late 19th and early 20th century are replete with accounts of the many trials and tribulations of Untouchable children, who persevered to receive an education even in the 'special' schools set up exclusively for them. For instance, it is reported that Cherumar (ancient slave caste) boys used to have their books snatched out of their hands as they went to schools established for them in Calicut (Hunter, 1882:514). In Kaira district, 'five or six large schools were closed down and the crops of the depressed people burnt' when they attempted to avail of education (Cotton, 1898:355). Hutton notes that in one case 'the depressed classes at Surat had to withdraw their children from the school as a result of indirect pressure exerted on them by higher castes' (Hutton, 1933:483). In the Multan division, it was reported that 'boys of low castes such as Chamars, Musalis and Sansis occasionally attend ordinary schools but are seated apart from the children of higher castes' (Richley, 1923:206). As late as 1931 the Kallar of Ramnad laid down a number of strictures on 'Exterior Castes'[3], which included one that emphasised that 'their children should not read and get themselves literate or educated' (Hutton, 1933:485).

The British government acknowledged that it was not religious sentiment, unclean habits and unpolished manners of low caste boys that drew objection to their education from the upper castes. 'They are also occasionally due to the desire of the upper castes to keep the low castes in a state of subjection and sovereignty' (Hunter, 1882:514). In their anxiety to refrain from antagonising caste Hindus, but yet retain a 'progressive' facade, the district education boards ingeniously evolved the principle that children of depressed castes shall be 'so placed as to have shelter from sun, rain and cold and that they shall receive a due share of teaching of the school' (Cotton, 1898:355). Thus Untouchable children who were allowed into ordinary schools were invariably seated on the verandah!

The Demand for Education

The early response to schooling from the Untouchable communities themselves was significant. In the 1850s itself, Elphinstone noted that '...the missionaries find the lowest classes the best pupils'. However, the official attitude towards the education of the Untouchables is reflected in Elphinstone's subsequent statement that 'we must be careful how we offer any special arrangement to men of that description... and it is to be feared that if our system of education first took root among them, it would never spread further, and we might find ourselves at the head of a new class superior to the rest in useful knowledge, but hated and despised by the castes to whom these new attainments would always induce us to prefer them' (quoted in Ambedkar, 1982:415).

It is significant that the refusal of admission to an Untouchable boy by the head of a government school was brought to the Bombay High Court as early as 1856 (Keer, 1971:4). In later years, reports refer to the 'constant pressure exercised to secure claims of low caste Hindus, to receive instruction'. Further that 'there is evidence that a few low caste boys of ability have already advanced beyond the elementary stage and are demanding an entrance into secondary schools' (Hunter, 1882:149).

Night schools were also extremely popular among the depressed classes despite the fact that they taught only the most elementary skills. The report of the Hunter Commission records that in Kaira, Gujarat, 'the night school is exclusively attended by low caste men and the towns people have frequently remonstrated against their education'. Further that 'notwithstanding the remonstrances of their neighbours, the Mahars of Bombay are in some places crowding into the night school' (Hunter, 1882:147).

Initiative was also taken by the first generation of educated Untouchables to press for greater learning opportunities for their communities. Ghokale refers to the informal process by which teachers emerged within the Untouchable Mahar community. Individuals with 'rudiments of an education in a Mahar primary school would undertake education of Mahar (and other Untouchable) children in the village' (1990:232). Retired Mahar military men were in the forefront of those who agitated for reforms in education. There are also scattered references to individuals who set up hostels and educational institutions for Untouchable youth (*Ibid.*, 229-32). Kamble also mentions that magazines and newspapers were published by enlightened Mahars to educate and politicise their people. One of these papers published at the turn of the century was aptly called *Vital Vidhushak* translated as 'Destroyer of Untouchability' (Kamble, 1983:42). Attention must also be drawn to the missionary zeal with which social reformers like Jotirao Phule and Bhavurao Patel took up the cause of the Untouchables in the second half of the 19th century. Enlightened rulers like Sahu Maharaj of Poona and the princes of Baroda and Travancore did much to bring education to the Untouchables (Kamble, 1983).

The singular role that Ambedkar played in the upliftment of the Untouchables in the early twentieth century and the importance that he gave to modern education for their betterment deserves special emphasis. In conferences, lectures and meetings, Ambedkar exhorted Untouchable youth to acquire education in order to raise their social status and image. As early as 1924, he established the 'Bahiskrit Hitkarini Sabha', which had among its objectives the opening of hostels, libraries, social centres and classrooms where the Untouchables could study. In 1928, Ambedkar established the Depressed Classes Education Society, 'to organize school education on a sound basis' (Keer, 1971). The People's Education Society that Ambedkar established in 1945 was in tune with his conviction regarding the role that education could play in the social and economic advancement of the Untouchables. As Thakkar observes, Ambedkar's ideal for the Untouchables was 'to raise their educational standards so that they may know their own conditions, have aspirations to rise to the level of the highest Hindu and be in a position to use political power as a means to that end' (Zelliot, 1972:77). This is best reflected in Ambedkar's famous slogan 'Educate, Agitate and Organize'.

The Quality of Schooling for the Untouchables

A significant proportion of Untouchable children who received formal education during British rule did so in missionary (aided) and special (government) schools meant exclusively for them. In Madras Presidency for instance, only 7 per cent of school going Untouchable children in 1931 studied in ordinary or common schools not reserved for the Exterior Castes (Hutton, 1933:487).

Schools for the Untouchables were mainly confined to the primary stage. Few children actually availed of further education for which they had to seek admission in common schools. For instance in Madras Presidency, while around 4 per cent of the Exterior Caste population was enrolled in schools in 1931 only 1 per cent of these school children went beyond the primary stage (Hutton, 1933:487).

The quality of schooling provided to the Untouchables appears to have been poor though adequate details are not available (Richley, 1923:206). The Report on Education in Bombay State (1855-1955) notes that separate schools provided for the Untouchables were inefficient and for the most part 'one-teacher' schools (1958:424).[4] Night schools as mentioned earlier were still popular. However, only the barest minimum of reading and writing skills were given to lower and labouring castes in such schools.

Recruiting suitable teachers for special schools was a particularly acute problem. Sharp commented on the 'unreadiness of teachers of better caste to take up the work and the paucity of qualified teachers among the depressed' (1918:207). Individuals from lower castes and Muslims formed the bulk of teachers in schools that catered to Untouchables (Nathan, 1904:393). The training of Untouchable youth as teachers was a slow and difficult process. The *Review of Education in Bombay State* (1855-1955) notes that 'segregation was generally allowed' in teacher training colleges 'in deference to the popular prejudice and with this compromise, the training of Scheduled Caste pupils as teachers of primary schools was pushed ahead'. However, public opposition to the Untouchables was so immense that even in 1921-22, 'it was next to impossible to appoint a Scheduled Caste teacher as the headmaster of a common school' (Bombay, 1958:417).

As mentioned earlier, missionary and 'special' schools for Untouchables offered mainly primary education. Where such schools were available, contact of Untouchable pupils with caste Hindu classmates (and often teachers) may have been postponed for a few years. At the middle stage, as well as where only common schools existed, Untouchable children faced virulent caste prejudice in the classroom. Some instances have already been touched upon in the discussion on the opposition of caste Hindus to the education of the Untouchables.

Official reports tend to ignore or gloss over the deleterious effects that segregation and discrimination within schools could have had for the learning experience of Untouchable children. Richley in his Report on the Progress of Education (1917-22) refers to the practice of seating Untouchable children apart from higher caste pupils in ordinary schools. He observed that 'such segregation, much as it is to be deprecated cannot seriously affect the children's education'. However, he concedes that 'there can be little advantage, except possibly in prestige gained by an Adi-Dravida child, who on admission to school is seated outside the building' (1923:206). *The Bombay State Review* (1855-1955) records that 'there were several orthodox teachers who refused to touch them (Untouchables) and corrected their exercises from a distance...'. They often have to sit apart sometimes on verandahs and sometimes on the window and thus *cannot, receive their due share of attention from the teacher'* (Bombay, 1958:416, emphasis mine).

The experience of the Untouchable child, often a first generation learner and frequently the only one from his community to go to school, must however have been traumatic. As Isaacs says, 'the lonely little boys who made their way to school in many scattered places in India during the first 30 years of this century had to accept the bluntest type of rejection and had to be able to persist in the face of it year after year to get through' (1965:75).

There are only few reminiscences of schooling in the early 20th century by the Untouchables themselves. Those that are available vividly sketch the humiliating experiences of children who were forced to sit on the dirt outside the classroom or on separate benches, and whose polluting presence was harshly brought home to them on several occasions (Isaacs, 1965; Aggarwal, 1983; Bombay, 1958). In this context, Bhim Rao Ambedkar's experience is revealing. Despite the advantage of birth in an educated family that was exposed to non-traditional employment, Ambedkar faced a hostile environment in school. Keer, his biographer relates how the child, Bhim, had to sit on gunny bags in a corner of the classroom along with his Untouchable classmates. He was not allowed to answer questions for fear of polluting the teacher. Caste Hindu pupils were afraid that if Ambedkar touched the blackboard he would pollute their lunch boxes kept behind it! In high school, Ambedkar was prevented from studying Sanskrit as the language was considered the key to the Vedas (Keer, 1971:12-19).

What emerges from such experiences is the crucial role of the 'significant other' in bringing the Untouchable child to school and motivating him to stay on in a system that provided little succour. An inspired father, an enlightened teacher or philanthropist were invariably crucial actors in the education of Untouchable children (Isaacs, 1965:69). In Ambedkar's case, his success in the high school examination publicly celebrated as an uncommon achievement, as well as his receiving the first ever doctorate by an Untouchable, may not have been possible but for the support received from his father, the encouragement given by a school teacher, as well as financial assistance made available by the Maharajah of Kolhapur (Keer, 1971).

Thus, while the institution of formal schooling provided opportunities for learning, in practice it offered few supports to communities like the Untouchables to whom society had denied human dignity. On the other hand, through the policy of segregation in separate schools and non-interference in classroom practices, the decision makers in education helped extend the practice of untouchability to the precincts of the school. In this context, the roles of the teacher or master were well defined—'it is not desirable for masters or inspectors to force on a social change which with judicious treatment will gradually be accepted by society' (Hunter, 1882:517).

The Spread of Schooling

The actual spread of schooling among the Untouchables was extremely slow in pre-independent India. In 1917, barely 1.01 per cent of the population of 'depressed classes' were at school (Sharp, 1918:204). The spread of schooling was uneven across the provinces. Madras had the highest percentage of its Untouchable population in school, 2.1 per cent, followed by Bombay 1.9 per cent. The United Provinces which had the largest number of people identified as belonging to the 'depressed classes' had the least number of persons in school, 0.1 per cent (*Ibid.*).

In 1931 the percentage of school going Exterior Caste population registered an increase over that in 1917. However this increase was marginal. It was only in Bengal that at least 5 per cent of the Exterior Caste population participated in schooling in the early thirties of this century. Literacy rates were hence abysmal. Less than 2 per cent of the total population categorised as 'Exterior castes' were literate in 1931 as can be seen from Table 4.1.

TABLE 4.1: Literacy and Participation of Exterior Castes in Schools in India, Provinces (1931)

	Population of E.C.*	E.C.% of total Population	% E.C. literate	% E.C.** in School	Literacy in General Population % ***
1	2	3	4	5	6
India	50,195,770	14	1.9	NA	9.5
Provinces (Total)	39,064,009	14	1.6	NA	9.9
Bengal	9,899,809	14	5.0	5.4	11.1
Bihar & Orissa	5,744,393	15	0.6	0.4	5.3

(Contd.)

TABLE 4.1 *(Contd.)*

1	2	3	4	5	6
Bombay	1,750,424	08	2.8	3.6	10.8
Madras	7,234,104	15	1.5	4.8	10.8
United Provinces of Agra and Oudh	11,322,281	23	0.5	1.1	5.5
Central Provinces and Berar	2,818,346	18	1.5	1.5	6.6

* E.C.—Exterior Castes. As mentioned earlier the term Exterior Caste was substituted for Depressed Class in the 1931 census.

** Figures are from the education department.

*** Literacy rates are based on the population of ages 5 and above.

Source: Hutton, 1933; *Census of India, 1931, Vol. I, India, Part I, Report.*

Literacy rates varied in the different provinces. As can be seen in Table 4.2, the Exterior Castes bear no comparison to the upper and middle castes where literacy was concerned. However, there were sharp variations in literacy among the Untouchables as well. Castes such as the Mahars of Bombay and Paraiyans of Madras Presidency were educationally relatively more advanced as compared to the Cherumars, Chamars and Bhangis.[5]

Early access to regular sources of income and opportunities for schooling, urbanisation, political mobilisation and enlightened leadership were among the socio-historical factors that were responsible for the initial though meagre spread of education among some sections of the Untouchables in pre-independent India (Chitnis, 1981; Patwardhan, 1974). The Mahars of the Bombay Presidency are an important example. The Mahars were an Untouchable community but were not among the most polluted of castes, such as the scavengers, upon whom fell the sub-human task of removal of 'night soil' (Zelliot, 1972:75). Mahars were the traditional 'general village servants' who were not tied to any specific occupation and were thereby spatially relatively more mobile than other Untouchable caste groups. They were hence in a better position to avail of new

TABLE 4.2 : Literacy Among Castes in the Provinces (1931)

Province	1931		1921	
	Male	Female	Male	Female
Bombay				
Brahman	78.8	23.1	65.2	14.4
Mahar, Dhed	6.3	0.5	2.3	0.1
Madras (Including Cochin and Travancore)				
Brahman	80.0	28.6	60.8	15.2
Nayar	60.4	27.6	49.1	21.5
Pallan, Paraiyan	5.6	0.6	3.7	0.3
Cherumar	1.3	0.3	0.8	0.1
Central Provinces and Behar				
Baniya	59.8	7.4	43.0	4.1
Brahman	58.1	12.2	38.6	6.3
Chamar	1.6	0.1	0.8	0.1
Bihar and Orissa				
Kayastha	60.5	11.8	59.1	8.4
Brahman	35.6	2.8	30.4	1.9
Dhobi	2.9	0.2	2.0	0.1
Dosadh	1.2	0.1	0.8	0.1
Chamar	1.0	0.1	0.8	—
United Provinces				
Kayastha	70.2	19.1	52.3	9.0
Brahmin	29.3	2.5	19.1	1.3
Bhangi	1.0	0.1	0.5	—
Chamar	0.6	—	0.2	—

Source: Hutton, 1933, *Census of India 1931, India Part-I Report.*

opportunities for regular income that came with the British rule. These included recruitment in the army, cotton mills, dock yards and so on, as well as domestic service in British homes. The 1921 census showed that only 13.5 per cent of the Mahar working force were employed in traditional caste based occupations (*Ibid.*, 74-75). Efforts by the Mahars themselves for the spread of education have already been highlighted. It is significant that political and social mobilisation among the Mahars was spearheaded by the early educated among them. These movements gave considerable importance to education as a tool for the betterment of the economic and social status of the community.

Ex-Untouchables in Independent India

Independent India offered to the Untouchables (now officially called Scheduled Castes) the promise of a life of dignity through a number of protective measures enshrined in its Constitution. The abolition of untouchability (Article 17), prohibition of 'begar' or forced labour (Article 23), positive discrimination in appointment to Government services and posts (Article 335) and so on. There is also a clear directive that the State shall promote the educational and economic interests of the Scheduled Castes and protect them from social injustice and all forms of exploitation (Article 46) (Radhakrishnan, 1991:1911). However, Scheduled Caste communities, or Dalits as they often prefer to call themselves are still plagued by both poverty and pollution.

Around 20 per cent of rural Dalit households possess no land. Of those who do, 85.5 per cent households possess 1 hectare or less land (NSSO, 1990). According to the 1991 census 55.1 per cent of the rural work force among Scheduled Castes were agricultural labour. Indebtedness and destitution (often bondage) is the lot of a large number of Dalit families. In 1976, a national survey estimated that there were around 26 lakh bonded labourers in agriculture, of which 62 per cent were ex-Untouchables (Joshi, 1986:2). Around 71 per cent of ex-Untouchable agricultural labourers surveyed in the Rural Labour Enquiry (1974-75) were found to be in debt, mostly to moneylenders, shopkeepers and landlords (*Ibid.*:2).

Only 18.7 per cent of the Dalit population live in urban India. Here again, except for a small section of workers, the majority are in the low income and least prestigious occupations. Scheduled

Castes are found predominantly in class IV positions in Government services, where reservation of posts is provided for them (India, 1986:482). Some ex-Untouchable communities, for instance the Bhangis, continue to perform their traditional occupation of sweeping and scavenging, even when employed in the Government sector. A study of *Bhangis* in Jodhpur city indicated that 75-85 per cent of those with employment were sweepers (Shyamlal, 1984:74).

While untouchability has been legally abolished, studies, reports and newspaper accounts suggest that this pernicious practice is still widespread, particularly in rural India. However, the magnitude of untouchability and its relative hold on different spheres of society today is yet to be fully understood. A survey conducted of 1,155 villages in 12 states found that 53 per cent of sample villages still barred members belonging to hereditary Untouchable castes from using village wells (India, 1980). A few years earlier, Desai's study revealed that 74 per cent of 69 villages surveyed in Gujarat practiced untouchability in relation to water facilities (1976:258). A more recent study of two districts in Rajasthan noted that 'clean' castes by and large do not accept water from utensils of Scheduled Castes (Lal and Nahar, 1990:65). Access to temples as well as to services of other occupational castes is still not common. Inter-dinning between the Untouchables and other castes is also rarely reported in studies (*Ibid.*: 65-66). Physical violence against Dalits is a common occurrence and finds frequent mention in newspaper reports even today. Very few atrocities are actually registered under the Protection of Civil Rights Act of 1955. Further, of the few that are reported only a negligible number of offenders are actually convicted. This is not surprising, given the vulnerability of both the victims and witnesses (Radhakrishnan, 1991:1918).

The relative anonymity that results from the nature of urban social organization accounts for the overt absence of untouchability in the city. However, residential segregation of Scheduled Caste families has been observed in many cities and house owners are often unwilling to have 'Untouchables' as tenants (Ram, 1988; Malik, 1979). In the context of interpersonal relations, it has been noted that 'even mobile Scheduled Castes do not get the same social status in society as is given to members of the higher castes as they are on the wrong side of the barrier of pollution' (Malik, 1979:51).

Schooling of the Ex-Untouchables

The spread of schooling among the 'ex-Untouchables' must be seen in the context of the state of education in post-independent India. Certain broad trends are visible, the neglect of education especially at the primary level, the gradual privatisation of 'quality' education and as will be discussed later, the expansion of non-formal learning programmes for the 'educationally backward'.

The proportion of plan resources initially allocated for the education sector was relatively meagre and it declined considerably over the years. From an allocation of 7.9 per cent in the first plan, the education sector received only 3.6 per cent of plan resources in the seventh. In the Eight plan outlay, allocation to education was raised to around 4.9 per cent.

Within the education sector, the share of primary education was drastically pruned from 40 per cent of total direct expenditure in 1950-51 to around 24 per cent in 1983-84. The proportion of expenditure on middle school education increased from 8.46 per cent to 17.13 per cent during the same period. The last few years have witnessed a shift in allocations towards elementary education. Figures from relevant budget documents reveal that the central plan outlay for elementary education increased from 284 crores in 1992 to 523 crores in 1994-95, an increase of around 84 per cent. During this period the magnitude of increase in allocation to secondary education was 44 per cent and to higher education was around 36 per cent (Varghese, 1994:9). It is estimated that the share of elementary education in total public expenditure on education is currently around 45 per cent (India, 1996). The extent to which apparent change in emphasis in favour of elementary education will benefit socially discriminated and educationally disadvantaged groups will depend not only upon the quantum of increase in budgetary allocations to this sector but also on the specific programmes that receive a larger share of resources.

The number of elementary schools in the country increased from 2.23 lakhs in 1950-51 to 7.28 lakhs in 1993-94. The rate of growth of schools has declined in each successive decade, especially at the primary stage. During 1950-51 to 1960-61 the number of primary schools increased by 5.8 per cent per year. In the seventies the increase was of the order of 2.1 per cent. Between 1980-81 and 1990-91 the rate of increase in primary schools fell to 1.3 per cent (India, 1993A: 11). The quality of physical facilities for education is poor especially in rural schools which receive an inadequate share of budgetary allocations.[6] This is reflected in the facilities available for elementary schooling especially at the primary stage. According to the *Fifth All India Educational Survey* (1986), 45.5 per cent of rural primary schools do not have a 'pucca building', 31.3 per cent are taught by a single teacher, 48.5 per cent are without usable blackboards and 17.2 per cent manage without adequate supply of chalks. As far as basic conveniences are concerned, around 96 per cent of schools have no lavatory and barely 45 per cent have drinking water facilities (NCERT, 1992:992). The state of rural middle schooling is only marginally better as can be seen in Table 4.3.

TABLE 4.3: Facilities for Elementary Schooling in Rural India (1986)

Facilities Available	Level of Schooling*	
	Primary (%)	Middle (%)
'Pucca' buildings	54.49	66.38
Single teacher only	31.27	NA
Adequate supply of chalks	82.78	92.38
Usable black boards	51.54	76.20
Lavatory	3.19	12.84
Drinking water within premises	44.50	63.39
Total No. of Schools**	475823	113087

* The percentage of rural schools with each facility is given separately for the primary and middle (upper primary) level.

** Facilities available relate to schools having primary/middle classes only except for 'black boards', data for which are given for primary schools as well as primary/middle sections in composite schools.

Source: NCERT, 1992: *Fifth All India Educational Survey*, Vol. I.

The management of schools at the elementary level vests mainly with the government and local bodies. In 1986, only 4.6 per cent of rural schools at the primary stage were privately managed—either aided or unaided by government (NCERT, 1992). Data from the NSSO (42nd round) also show that as many as 53.1 per cent of all students in general education in rural areas were in government primary schools, while only 7 per cent were in private primary educational institutions (NSSO, 1989). Private schools predominate in secondary and higher stages of schooling and particularly in urban areas. As many as 68.2 per cent of secondary and 60.4 per cent of higher secondary schools in urban areas are privately managed. (NCERT, 1992a). In recent years private unaided schools (which include elite public schools that are perceived to provide 'quality education') have expanded at the primary level as well. For instance in 1986, private unaided schools comprised 18.7 per cent of urban primary schools (*Ibid.*).

Access to Schooling

Schooling is not adequately available within easy access even at the primary stage. In rural areas 46.15 per cent of 'general' habitations (excluding predominantly Scheduled Caste and Scheduled Tribe habitations) do not have primary schools within them and only 86.15 per cent have this facility within a distance of 1 kilometre. The availability of schooling varies with the size of the habitation. The more densely populated habitations have better schooling facilities as compared to those that are relatively more sparsely populated. For instance, while 99.36 per cent of 'general' habitations with a population of 5,000 persons and above have primary schooling facilities within a kilometre's distance, this is so in 94.96 per cent of habitations with 500-999 persons and in only 63.07 per cent of those with less than 100 inhabitants (NCERT, 1992).

Data made available by the NCERT Survey (1986) reveal that Dalit (Scheduled Caste) communities have relatively poorer access to schooling when compared to the general population, in terms of the distance at which these facilities are available. There are for instance, primary schools/sections in only 37.67 per cent of predominantly Scheduled Caste habitations. For 81.59 per cent of these habitations schooling is available within a distance of 1 kilometre (Table 4.4). Smaller habitations (with less than 300 persons) account for 56 per cent of all predominantly Scheduled Caste habitations. Schooling is available within a kilometre for 73.70 per cent of these habitations. Scheduled Caste habitations are even more poorly served where middle schooling is concerned. As can be seen from Table 4.4 only 29.20 per cent habitations have middle schools within a kilometre, while 25.57 per cent of these habitations are unserved with middle or upper primary schooling even at a distance of 3 kilometres (NCERT, 1992).

TABLE 4.4: Availability of Elementary Schooling in Rural Habitations (1986)

Availability of Schools/Sections	General* Habitations % **		Scheduled Caste Habitations % **	
	Primary Schooling	Middle Schooling	Primary Schooling	Middle Schooling
Within the habitation	53.85	15.38	37.67	5.57
Within 1 km.	86.15	35.49	81.59	29.20
Within 2 km.	96.22	59.90	94.56	54.89
Within 3 km.	—	78.61	—	74.43
Beyond 3 km.	—	21.38	—	25.57

* 'General' habitations exclude predominantly Scheduled Caste and Scheduled Tribe habitations.

** These are percentages of habitations that have each schooling facility at the given distances.

Source: NCERT, 1992: *Fifth All India Education Survey*.

Facilities for primary schooling appear to be available within a kilometre to around 82 per cent of Scheduled Caste habitations. However, information on the physical accessibility of schools within a 'reasonable' distance gives no indication of how 'socially accessible' the institution actually is. Social accessibility becomes critical for communities that face discrimination and continue to live in relatively segregated habitations. For instance, Mencher in a study of Chinglepet district, Tamil Nadu, in the late sixties observed that a factor inhibiting the education of 'Pariyan' children was that 'students had to walk through the upper caste section of the village in order to reach the school' (Mencher, 1972:54). A more recent study notes that 'in the 28 Panchayats of Tikamgarh Block (Madhya Pradesh) where untouchability seems to persist more firmly, about 50 per cent of Harijan children have not been able to join schools'. It is mentioned that 'while there are a number of reasons for this, discrimination is certainly an important one' (Jalaludin, 1991:233).[7]

The relatively poor spread of middle (and high) schooling makes hostel facilities critical for post primary education of Dalit communities. What is the state of residential facilities made available to Dalit children to pursue their studies? Little is known on the subject except for a brief mention of Scheduled Caste hostels in a few studies. Chitnis refers to the comments of the *Basumatrai Committee Report* (1970) which listed serious shortcomings in the functioning of hostels for Scheduled Caste students. The Committee observed that 'some of the hostels are housed in totally unsuitable buildings and surroundings, and that the living conditions of inmates are far from satisfactory' (1981:115). A survey of the Scheduled Caste hostels in Andhra Pradesh in 1972, revealed that 'many hostels that were listed were non-existent; so were its inmates' (*Ibid.*: 116-117). The twenty-first report of the Commissioner for Scheduled Castes and Scheduled Tribes concludes that hostels in many states and Union Territories 'are generally overcrowded and admit more inmates than the sanctioned strength. The hostels are in small buildings leading to congestion, and unhygienic conditions' (India, 1974:62).

Participation in Schooling

What is the magnitude of participation of Dalits in elementary schools? Data from the Census (1981) reveal that only 32.21 per cent of Dalit children (aged 5-14 years) actually attend schools.[8] School participation data from the NSS (1987-88) shows that the proportion of 'out of school' Dalit children is far greater than those in the 'Other' (non-Scheduled Caste/Scheduled Tribe) population in both urban and rural areas (Table 4.5). What is also striking is the abysmal participation of rural girls in schools. Table 4.6 indicates that barely 31.1 per cent of Dalit girl children (aged 5-14 years) in rural areas participated in schooling in 1987-88. While the gender gap in schooling narrows down urban areas, it is still larger among Scheduled Castes, as compared to children from 'Other' social groups. A perusal of rural school enrolments indicates that girl children comprise 37.19 per cent of Dalit pupils enrolled in primary schools, 27.87 per cent of those in middle schools and only 23.64 per cent of those at the secondary stage (NCERT: 1992a).

TABLE 4.5: Participation in Schooling (1987-88)

	Children (5-14 Years) attending School%			
	Scheduled Castes		Others*	
	Male	Female	Male	Female
Rural	49.8	31.1	63.4	45.8
Urban	68.2	53.8	78.0	72.6

* Excludes Scheduled Castes, Scheduled Tribes and Neo Buddhists.

Source: National Sample Survey, 43rd Round, NSSO.

Dalit students mainly avail of schooling facilities provided by the government (and local bodies). Data from the NSSO (42nd Round) indicate that 82.89 per cent of all Scheduled Caste students in general education in rural areas are enrolled in government institutions. As many as 57.26 per cent of these students are enrolled in government primary schools, while only 6.79 per cent are in primary schools in the private sector (NSSO, 1989). School enrolment figures suggest that there is a relatively high degree of drop-out among Dalit pupils as they proceed through school. Table 4.6 reveals that 49.62 per cent of Scheduled Caste children leave school between Class I and V, 67.78 per cent between Class I and VIII and 79.68 per cent fail to reach class X. The percentage of drop-outs among female children considerably exceeds that among males.

TABLE 4.6: Drop-Out Rates of School Children (1988-89)

Classes	Scheduled Castes			All Students		
	Male	Female	Total	Male	Female	Total
I—V	47.24	53.39	49.62	46.74	49.69	47.93
I—VIII	64.37	73.60	67.78	59.38	68.31	65.40
I—X	76.52	85.62	79.68	72.68	79.46	75.36

Note: The following procedure is usually adopted to calculate drop-out rates:

$$\text{Drop-out between class I—V} : \frac{\text{Enrolment in class I during preceding 4 years-enrolment in class V during the year}}{\text{Enrolment in Class I during preceding 4 years}} \times 100$$

Source: India, 1993A *Education For All: The Indian Scene.*

There has been a tendency to emphasise economic factors such as poverty, participation of children in work and so on as largely contributing to the dropping out of Dalit children from school (Yadav, 1991:26). These factors are no doubt of importance in explaining the phenomenon of wastage in education and will be discussed in a later section. What is crucial is that a significant proportion of Dalit families are today ready to send their children to school and do so as reflected in class 1 enrolments. (In 1986 for instance, Dalit children comprised around 18 per cent of the 248 lakh pupils in class I). The fact that as many as 50 per cent of Dalit children who enter primary school should leave by class V (the majority of whom discontinue even before the end of class II) points to the need to also understand the extent to which schools fail to create conditions that encourage their retention.[9] Here, the learning environment that Dalit children experience in terms of education facilities provided, quality of instruction received, as well as the nature of school processes will be important.

Quality of Schooling for Dalit Children

As discussed in an earlier section, the general quality of schooling especially at the primary stage is extremely poor. Table 4.3 showed that the basic infrastructure associated with education as well as minimum civic amenities are absent in a significant proportion of schools, especially in rural areas. Official data on the quality of schools that cater predominantly to Scheduled Caste children (by virtue of being located in their habitations) is not separately available. However, it has been observed that the 'quality of inputs and the functioning of schools especially those which had a large percentage of Scheduled Caste and Scheduled Tribe students have left much to be desired' (India, 1988:303). A study of school drop-out among Harijan children in Uttar Pradesh stresses that the physical conditions of the schools are of deplorably low standards and are partly responsible for their inability to retain Dalit pupils (CIRTPC, 1975:79,115). A report by an advocate of the Cochin High Court on a school catering to Dalit girls in Idukki district (Kerala), is revealing. The study which finds a special mention in the SC and ST Commissioner's Report (1986-87) notes that there were 4000 students for whom only 25 benches and 25 desks were available. Most of the students were forced to sit on the cold damp cement floor. There was no toilet, latrine or urinals available for the use of the pupils. The supply of text-books and note books was quite inadequate. There were 12 sanctioned posts for the school whereas only 5 had been filled up and at the time of the enquiry two teachers were on leave... 'The environment of this institution was reported to be very dirty as the ground was swampy and there were cow-dung heaps and firewood stocked all over the area' (India: 1988:303).

In the absence of adequate data it is not possible to make generalisations regarding the facilities available in 'predominantly Dalit' schools. However, it is obvious that if the quality of inputs in schools is poor, the learning environment that is provided, particularly for first generation learners, will be adversely affected.

Learning in Schools

How well are school children equipped with scholastic competencies, at least those usually associated with early education? Data is relatively scanty in this respect. However, a study of more than 8,000 children in the Hindi speaking states, conducted between 1969-71, suggests that achievement levels of children in general are poor even in basic skills of reading and comprehension (Kurrien, 1983).

More recent findings of studies on the achievement of children at the primary stage of education give cause for concern. Schools in 46 districts, in 8 states, were surveyed as part of the baseline studies conducted by the District Primary Education Programme (DPEP) of the Ministry of Human Resources Development. The learning levels of around 50,000 students from 1817 schools were assessed. It was found that in none of the 46 districts surveyed did primary school students achieve an average score of 80 per cent in the basic letter and word reading tests that were administered to assess their learning levels. In many districts students could barely read 5 to 8 words correctly. Children also fared poorly in basic numerical skills (*Times of India*, 1994). The DPEP base line studies reveal that 'low achieving schools' are to be found in all states. Even in Kerala, 38.3 per cent of surveyed schools had an average score of less that 40 per cent in Mathematics. Though the performance of schools in Language is relatively better than that in Mathematics, here again 73 per cent of schools in Madhya Pradesh and 56.3 per cent in Maharashtra averaged scores of less than 40 per cent (India, 1996:10).

Lamenting that 'virtually every child suffers for want of an imaginative curriculum and pedagogy', Kurrien underlines in particular the detrimental effect that deficiencies in schooling have on 'early learning' of children from poor and illiterate backgrounds (1983:179-80). An intensive study of 120 grade I pupils of a Bombay Municipal School, 80 per cent of whom were from Scheduled Castes, Scheduled Tribes and Backward Classes, bears Kurrien's point out. He notes that a majority of children were found to have deficiencies in each of the eight dimensions of language ability, with a sizeable number having 'serious inadequacies' (Kurrien, 1989:2). Similar results were observed in language abilities of children in grades II and III of a Municipal Corporation School in a 'backward area' of Baroda. It was found that 'the majority of children could not read at all including simple two letter words' (*Ibid.*:3). Again, a study of 60 schools in selected districts of

Maharashtra, found that in only 9 schools did all students pass standard I. The Commissioner for SC and ST who incorporated the results of the study in his report, noted that the problem of failure was 'more in single teacher schools and schools having a large percentage of Scheduled Caste and Scheduled Tribe students on their registers'. These schools had a low percentage of students passing standard I and a still lower percentage of those passing standard IV. 'In 9 of the schools having a vast majority of students belonging to Scheduled Castes and Scheduled Tribes, there was not a single student who passed standard IV' (India, 1988:299).

Inadequate inputs (including teaching) and consequently the poor quality of education has meant that 'the vast potential for children to benefit from early learning is barely tapped' (Kurrien, 1983:179). This is likely to hold true for Dalit children who may be less able to compensate (through educated parents, paid tuitions and so on) for deficiencies in the quality of schooling. On the other hand, it has been shown that the performance of children can be improved through conscious efforts at pedagogy (Jalaludin, 1991; Kurrien 1983). For instance, a short-term programme initiated to improve the language skills of children in the earlier mentioned Baroda Municipal School study showed 'quite dramatic results'. At the end of the programme, 'a majority of children were not only recognising most letters, but were also able to read words and simple paragraphs' (Jalaludin, 1991:199). Kurrien quotes a study referring to the field experiences of the Homi Baba Centre for Science Education (HBCSE), Bombay, which observed that 'when teachers were aware of the linguistic difficulties of first generation students and were given specific guidance to overcome disabilities, the performance and participation of students in the classroom improved' (Kurrien, 1983:137).

The HBCSE also carried out a two-year programme to improve the performance of SC/ST children in the Secondary School Certificate Examination. For the project, 33 students who averaged 40 per cent till class VIII were selected from the Bombay Municipal Corporation Schools. With pedagogic input of only two and a half hours every week for about 30 Saturdays in a year, the performance of the students improved to an average of 80 per cent in the SSC examination! (Jalaludin, 1991: 190).

Thus, when Dalit and other 'educationally backward' pupils are provided with learning opportunities as well as effective pedagogic supports to acquire specific language, numerical and other competencies, they are likely to be better able to academically cope with the rigours of the formal school. Sarup's remarks in relation to the poor achievement of Blacks in schools could be related to the Scheduled Caste children as well—'This does not mean that Black children (read Scheduled Castes) are culturally deprived, or that they are deficient in some way. It is just that they have fewer opportunities to develop the specific skills and knowledge demanded by the school' (1986:5).

The Processes of Schooling

Knowledge and skills transmitted within schools are part of the 'official curriculum' that children are exposed to. On the other hand, a crucial dimension of school experience is the nature of social relations (influenced by the norms, values, attitudes and expectations of pupils, teachers, administrators and so on) that influence the daily routine of teaching, learning and peer interaction. This is the all pervasive 'hidden curriculum'[10] that powerfully affects learning experiences, particularly of socially discriminated communities. What is the experience of schooling for an ex-Untouchable child? Is social prejudice and opposition to the schooling of these children an aberration of the past?

The official curriculum of 'legitimate' school knowledge appears relatively silent about Dalit communities and their experience of untouchability. Kumar made a study of text books of classes IV, V and VI in Government schools in the State of Madhya Pradesh, where ex-Untouchable communities comprise 14 per cent of the population. He found that none of the characters in the 77 story lessons in the text-books could be identified as coming from Scheduled Caste backgrounds (Kumar, 1985). Khosla also makes a similar observation in his intensive study of untouchability in Indaur Panchayat in Madhya Pradesh. He notes that untouchability is mentioned perfunctorily in a few sentences in officially approved school text-books and only in the context of discussions on Gandhi. Further, no book except a social studies text used in high school, mentioned the fact of the legal abolition of untouchability (1987: 149). Teachers who were interviewed by Khosla could not recall ever having a classroom discussion on the issue of untouchability, even while discussing Gandhi and his contribution to the social philosophy of contemporary India (1987:149).

(Ex) Untouchable adults who reflect on their experience of education refer not to the lack of their visibility in text books, but to the 'hidden curriculum' that underlies school processes—i.e., the distinct message of social inferiority that is often quite clearly conveyed to them by teachers and peers.[11] Personal narratives of Dalits, educated just three decades ago, offer glimpses of untouchability blatantly practised in schools—Scheduled Caste students being asked to sit separately from their classmates, refused drinking water or served in broken cups, made to dine separately and so on (India, 1969; Joshi, 1986; Roy and Singh, 1987). For instance, as many as 80 per cent of the 1030 students from Milind College, Aurangabad who were surveyed in 1971-72, said that they were made to sit outside the classroom during primary schooling because of the practice of untouchability (Chitnis, 1986:45). A school teacher respondent in Roy and Singh's study of 'Harijan elites' in Azamgarh, recalled that 'we were asked to sit separately. Our copy or slates were not touched by the teachers' (1987: 46). Others referred to the fact that they were even spared physical punishment for fear of pollution (*Ibid.*). Aggarwal and Ashraf's educated respondents while recalling their experiences in school, poignantly revealed that they longed to be physically punished if only to be treated as the other children in class and not kept at a distance (1976:10).

According to Jalaludin, in some villages of Hoshangabad, Madhya Pradesh, it was observed that Scheduled Caste children were required to sit separately in one corner of the classroom. In a few villages they were made to sit at the door outside the classroom. He contended that 'while dramatic manifestation of untouchability in educational institutions may be rare, the existence of social discrimination is a reality' (1991:233). Another study mentions the routine exclusion of 'Untouchable' students from singing songs of worship to Goddess Saraswati or in specific instances asking only non-Untouchable students to serve food at picnics (Khosla, 1987:150). Lal and Nahar's study of Scheduled Castes in Ganganagar and Jodhpur districts, as well as Desai's exploration of Untouchability in rural Gujarat, caution against complacency regarding the prevalence of social discrimination in schools. The former report that a 'small minority' (12.9 per cent) of their rural Scheduled Caste respondents with school going children 'categorically said that no common arrangement of drinking water exists in schools where their children are studying'. In some cases, 'there are different pots/utensils'. However, they note that in urban centres, schools were reported to have common arrangements for drinking water (1990:90). Desai found that 'in about 14 per cent of villages (i.e. 59 surveyed that had schools) untouchability was practised in regard to the use of facilities for drinking water in schools' (1976:227).

The above discussion points mainly to the more obvious and easily observable instances of the practice of social discrimination in schools. However, what are less tangible are the attitudes, expectations and norms of 'school actors', i.e. teachers, administrators, pupils and so on. These pervade interpersonal relations and are reflected in the use of language, gestures, and subtle nuances with which individuals and groups give meaning to the social world within the school and classroom. Teachers' attitudes and expectations of their Dalit pupils are particularly important.

Teachers' perceptions about the 'mental' abilities of Dalit pupils as well as the stereotypes they hold about these communities are likely to crucially affect the pedagogic supports offered to children. It has been often noted that non-tribal and high caste Hindu teachers look down upon tribal and Scheduled Caste students. Some of them even regard these students as uneducable[12] (Sachidananda 1974:199). Radhakrishnan and Ranjana note that perhaps the most serious problem that Dalits have to face in school is discrimination. They emphasise that the experience of discrimination 'can discourage young students from further education' (1989:47). Their study of Scheduled Caste youth in Bihar and Madhya Pradesh notes that a significant proportion of student respondents found their teachers unhelpful (*Ibid.*). Recalling their school experiences, Scheduled Caste professionals in Aggarwal and Ashraf's study speak of being made to feel 'unintelligent' and 'inferior' by teachers and of being deliberately ignored by them during lessons (1976:29). On the other hand, there is Kumar's example of a teacher consciously drawing attention to a 'Harijan boy' during a civics lesson to point out an exception to a popular stereotype—the 'dirty' (ex) Untouchable. 'Look how neat and clean Chandu appears today. We should not hate him'[13] (Kumar, 1985:338).

Are Dalit children allowed easy access to 'high status' knowledge areas? Does social prejudice act as a constraint in this regard? A few instances referred to in passing point to the need for systematic research in this area. In Aggarwal's study mentioned earlier a Dalit respondent notes that the teacher discouraged him from opting for composite Maths as he thought 'we were not capable enough' (1983:144). The report of the Committee on Untouchability cites the case of a head master refusing to give Science as a subject to an Untouchable boy despite his request for it (1969:1909). An extreme case mentioned is the murder of a Scheduled Caste student by two Brahmin boys in New Delhi as 'they could not tolerate a lower caste student studying a Sanskrit course (Acharya) along with them' (India, 1988: 224).

The dimension of caste appears to powerfully constrain interpersonal relationships of Dalit children within schools. In the Milind college study referred to earlier, 51 per cent of Dalit students who were interviewed said that they had experienced discriminatory treatment from fellow classmates. That they had to face opposition 'whenever they sought to exercise their natural right to receive education on an equal footing' (Chitnis, 1986:45). A few studies suggest that children often tend to confine friendships in school to those who fall within the pollution boundary. An all India study conducted in the mid-seventies explored the nature of friendship patterns of Scheduled Caste high school students. Around 57 per cent of Dalit high school students who were surveyed revealed that their three best friends belonged to their own caste or another Scheduled Caste. The author concluded that 'at least as far as Scheduled Castes are concerned, school and college have not functioned effectively as melting pots for caste boundaries in the matter of friendships' (Chitnis, 1981:102).

Do interpersonal relationships that cross the purity-pollution boundary among children, confront social norms and prejudices especially in rural areas? Khosla in his study of Indaur Panchayat, Madhya Pradesh, refers to the few 'dyadic relationships' between Scheduled Caste and higher caste students that were brought to his notice as 'accidents'. He clarifies that such friendships occurred between the least polluted of the (ex) Untouchable castes, e.g., Dhobi and a higher caste individual. The inevitable severing of bonds as a result of social pressures caused 'extreme emotional hurt and pain' (1986:158).

The 'deep structure' of schooling particularly in the context of social discrimination is yet to become the focus of systematic research. However, personal experiences of educated Dalits and references in a number of studies suggest that social prejudices and negative stereotypes regarding Dalits, often held by the school community, prove to be traumatic for those at the receiving end.

Poverty and Schooling of the Dalit Child

The discussion thus far has focused largely on the context and processes of schooling in relation to the education of Dalit children. This was deliberately done in order to draw attention to the concrete experience of schooling for children coming from socially discriminated and educationally backward communities. It is however important to emphasise the serious impediments to schooling posed by poverty of the average Dalit family as reflected in their relatively low income, poor consumption expenditure and high degree of indebtedness.

In the context of schooling, economic constraints are translated into the inability of families to provide adequate resources to meet the direct and indirect costs of educating children. For instance they may be unable to meet the expenses that have to be directly incurred on uniforms, books, transport, hostels (when required) and so on (Yadav, 1991:261). In addition schooling represents an indirect cost to families where children are involved in economic (including household) activities both within and outside the home. Children may be required to participate in such activities full-time, part-time or seasonally. This usually leads to non-enrolment, irregular attendance and drop-out of school. For instance it has been observed that at the time of harvesting, children of landless labourers are required to assist their families in the fields (*Ibid.*:27). During conditions of famine and extreme scarcity in Maharashtra in the early seventies, Dalit students were forced to leave their studies and participate in relief work (Chitnis and Kamble, 1973). A study of pre-university students in Milind college, Aurangabad, revealed that out of 686 Dalit students enrolled in 1973, as many as 606 had been involved in relief work during vacations. Parents of 444 students had asked them to leave their studies and contribute to family income through participation in relief work (*Ibid.*).

The earlier quoted ICSSR sponsored studies on Scheduled Caste students in 15 states (in the mid-seventies) also highlight the poor economic status of majority of Dalit high school pupils. Of the 3,644 Scheduled Caste high school pupils surveyed across the country, only 12 per cent said they came from 'financially comfortable' backgrounds. Around 46 per cent perceived their economic status to be 'difficult' (Chitnis, 1981:35).[14] The Milind college study (1971-72) revealed that 73 per cent of students surveyed came from families belonging to the category of 'landless worker' (Chitnis, 1986:44). Chitnis comments that 'parents of Scheduled Caste students have to carry a financial burden for the education of their wards', and are 'continually haunted by the spectre of poverty' (*Ibid.*:35).

Schemes that offer financial assistance for education are both limited in their coverage of Scheduled Caste pupils and inadequate in terms of the amount that is extended as scholarship. Data collected by the NSSO (42nd round) indicate that only around 15 per cent of Scheduled Caste students in institutions of general education receive scholarships. To what extent do school children benefit by these schemes? As can be seen in Table 4.7 only 2.36 per cent of all rural and 1.32 per cent of all urban primary school students receive scholarships. Around 40-45 per cent of those who receive such financial assistance are beneficiaries because they belong to

Scheduled Castes (NSSO, 1989). A special scheme of 'attendance scholarships' has also been instituted to encourage schooling among girl children. Table 4.8 indicates that barely 4.65 per cent of primary and 10.83 per cent of middle schools are covered by this scheme (NCERT:1992). Only 1.71 per cent of Scheduled Caste girls in primary schools and 6.46 per cent of those in middle schools in 1986 received attendance scholarships (*Ibid.*).

TABLE 4.7: Scholarships for Students in General Education (1986-87)

Region/Level at which Enrolled	Students receiving scholarships %*	Average Amt. per student (Rs.)	Beneficiaries from Scheduled Castes** %
RURAL			
Primary	2.36	90	40.42
Secondary	9.93	167	39.99
Others	12.59	539	51.76
N.R.	9.80	137	25.86
All	5.51	183	41.28
URBAN			
Primary	1.32	115	45.03
Secondary	6.91	217	45.49
Others	7.05	653	38.85
N.R.	8.87	131	73.07
All	4.20	294	44.20

* Gives percentage of students who receive scholarships in each category of schools.

** Gives percentage of all scholarship receiving students who belong to the Scheduled Castes.

Source: NSSO, 1989, *Participation in Education, (Forty Second Round).*

The actual amount that is received as financial assistance is meagre. Barely Rs.90 per annum on an average is received as scholarship at the primary level in rural areas and this increases to around Rs.167 at the secondary stage (NSSO, 1989). Free uniforms and text-books (which can subsidise some of the direct 'costs' of schooling for individual families) are also not available to all Dalit pupils. As can be seen in Table 4.8 only 46.83 per cent primary and 34.56 per cent middle schools are covered by the 'free uniform' scheme. Around 26 per cent of Scheduled Caste students in primary schools and 27 per cent of those at the middle school stage are covered by this scheme. Free text books are given to a larger number of students. Information on the number of beneficiaries from these schemes has been obtained from official records. In concrete terms, the implementation and monitoring of incentive schemes are so deeply pervaded by bureaucratic delay, corruption and apathy that they often prove to be relatively ineffective.

TABLE 4.8: Schooling Incentives for Dalit Children (1986)

Incentive Scheme	Schools Covered by Scheme %		Scheduled Caste Beneficiaries %*	
	Primary	Middle	Primary	Middle
Free Uniforms	46.83	34.56	25.67	26.67
Free Text Books	59.62	50.98	35.08	47.14
Attendance Scholarship (for girls)	4.65	10.83	1.71	6.46

* The percentage of Scheduled Caste students who are beneficiaries of each scheme.

Source: NCERT, 1992 *Fifth All India Education Survey.*

What is noteworthy but little acknowledged is the extent of support, material and moral, that Dalit parents (and relatives) extend to their children despite poverty, 'lack of educational exposure' and the quality of schooling they experience. In the ICSSR study mentioned earlier, 89 per cent of Scheduled Caste high school respondents stated that they had to depend on parents and relatives for financial support (Chitnis, 1981:34). This is despite the fact that only 12 per cent of students came from financially 'comfortable' homes. Only 5 per cent of pupils interviewed in the study said that the entire cost of their education was covered by freeships etc. (*Ibid.*:34). The Milind college study reveals that the parents of 52 per cent of the Scheduled Caste students had to raise loans from village money lenders at exorbitant rates of interest, to finance the education of their wards (Chitnis, 1986:44). Parents of only 46 per cent of students were actually able to provide them with the necessary text books for their studies. As many as 54 per cent of students had to make do with the notes dictated in class by their teachers or had to borrow books from their classmates (*Ibid.*:46).

The high degree of illiteracy among Dalit communities implies that Scheduled Caste school students are often first generation learners. It is hence not unusual for scholars to assume that Dalits 'come from backgrounds disadvantaged for education' because of the 'inability of uneducated parents to appreciate the advantages of education and to understand the educational needs of their children' (Chitnis, 1981:32).

A careful reading of some of the findings suggests that support and encouragement for education may not be lacking in Dalit families even where parents are poorly educated. The financial support extended by parents to children for the pursuit of studies even under adverse conditions is a concrete indication of their positive attitudes to education. Further when high school students in the ICSSR studies were questioned as to who had encouraged them most in their education, 76 per cent mentioned their parents, while 17 per cent named a close relative. It is significant that 48 per cent of fathers and 63 per cent of mothers of these students were illiterate. The percentage of those with more than primary school education was negligible (*Ibid.*:33). Around 85 per cent of students surveyed in the Milind college study had illiterate parents. Yet only 25 per cent of them mentioned that their parents were indifferent to their education. Around 75 per cent of students noted that 'their parents very often made enquiries about their progress in their studies' (Chitnis, 1986:46).

The form that parental encouragement takes and the extent to which it facilitates the child's 'preparedness' for the formal school and ability to cope with the academic programme is important. Where elders are illiterate or poorly educated, children are likely to be forced to grapple with the day to day exigencies of school life entirely on their own. A study of 'Harijan Elites' in Azamgarh, Uttar Pradesh, observes that 'respondents had themselves to overcome any difficulty that they may have encountered in their education without an educationally salubrious family' (Roy and Singh, 1987:40). It is in this context that pedagogic support and encouragement to Dalit children from within the formal school becomes critical. This can assume the form of specific academic programmes to facilitate development of language, conceptual and other skills, that are required within the classroom. In addition teachers can be made more sensitive to the difficulties that first generation learners encounter in their studies and be suitably equipped to cope with them in the classroom. This is a sphere where the formal school can positively intervene in favour of the socially discriminated and educationally disadvantaged. A review of relevant research as well as policy programmes indicates that (with few noted exceptions) a beginning is yet to be made in this direction.

Outcomes from Schooling

The large number of drop-outs from schools and their relatively low achievement levels has meant that very few Dalit children actually reach high school. Table 4.9 indicates that for every 100 Dalit pupils in class I in 1986 there were barely 4 pupils in class XII.

TABLE 4.9: Scheduled Caste Students in Each Class as a Percentage of Enrolment in Class I (1986)

Class	Rural Schools			All Schools		
	Boys	Girls	Total	Boys	Girls	Total
Class I	100.00	100.00	100.00	100.00	100.00	100.00
Class V	44.87	33.49	40.37	47.98	37.84	43.88
Class VIII	25.95	13.92	21.19	30.68	18.79	25.86
Class X	14.00	8.83	10.96	18.60	9.50	14.95
Class XII	2.43	0.88	1.82	4.69	2.20	3.69

Source: NCERT 1992, *Fifth All India Education Survey, Vol.II*

In rural schools only around 2 children entered class XII for every 100 who enrolled in class I in the same year. Table 4.9 suggests that the number of girl children who complete high school is likely to be much smaller than the number of boys who do so. For every 100 rural girls in class I in 1986, there was possibly not even one in class XII. A direct consequence of the large number of drop-outs from school, is the relatively high percentage of illiteracy among Dalit communities. As mentioned earlier only 37.41 per cent of Dalits were returned as literate in 1991. The particularly low enrolment of Dalit girls in schools and the high rate of drop-outs among them is reflected in the fact that only 23.76 per cent of the female population is able to read and write (India, 1993a).[15] A considerable volume of research today emphasises the positive role that literacy plays in raising the status of women and quality of life of children.

Subject options made towards the end of schooling are likely to influence the range of opportunities that are available to students, both within the sphere of higher learning and the job market. Choice of subjects made by pupils in the first year of higher secondary schooling is reflected in the pattern of enrolments in class XI. The majority of Scheduled Caste students in class XI appear to opt for Arts rather than Science or Commerce. In 1987-88 around 60 per cent of Dalit pupils in class XI were enrolled in the Arts stream, while 20 per cent had opted for Science. Commerce had still fewer takers—14.8 per cent of class XI enrolments. The 'Vocational' stream comprised only 3.7 per cent of all Dalit pupils in class XI (India, 1993b). The overcrowding of Scheduled Caste pupils in the Arts stream is likely to restrict the range of future options that are available to them.

How do Dalit students fare in high school examinations? Available data reveal that there is a relatively high degree of failure among students, i.e., around 54 per cent of pupils who appeared in their examinations in 1984, failed to clear them. However, the magnitude of failure is significantly higher among Dalit students. Barely 34.1 per cent of SC pupils who appeared for high school examination in 1981 passed. In 1984 the percentage of those who passed fell to 32.8 per cent. It is interesting that while girls in general tend to have an edge in the examinations as compared to boys, this is relatively less striking among Dalit girls. A study of Scheduled Caste students enrolled in fifteen degree colleges in Bombay in 1972, suggests that their performance in school leaving examinations is relatively poor as compared to the general category of pupils. 'As many as 22 per cent of Scheduled Caste respondents as compared to only 3 per cent of non-Scheduled Caste peers have failed during the last two years in school' (Chitnis, 1975:173).

TABLE 4.10: Pass Percentage of Students Appearing for the Annual High School Examinations* (1981-84)

(Percentage **)

Year	All Students ***			Scheduled Caste Students		
	Male	Female	Total	Male	Female	Total
1981	46.2	52.2	47.2	35.5	30.5	34.1
1982	47.6	48.8	48.2	34.4	33.3	35.0
1983	44.7	50.2	46.3	33.1	36.6	33.9
1984	44.8	51.6	46.4	32.5	33.8	32.8

* Results are of 24 Boards of Secondary Education in India .

** Percentages are of those students who passed (from among those who appeared) in the High School Examination.

*** All Students include SC and ST Students.

Source: Board of Secondary Education in India—*Results of High School and Higher Secondary Examinations* 1983-84, 1981-82, Ministry of HRD, Deptt. of Education, 1986 & 1988.

Poor performance at the end of school has serious implications for the participation of Dalit students in higher education. While Dalits comprise only around 7 per cent of enrolment in graduate and post-graduate institutions, they are found overwhelmingly in Arts as compared to the more prestigious professional courses (India, 1990).

An outcome of education that is often emphasised is that it allows for relatively easy entry of Dalits (through the policy of reservations) into jobs in the Government and public sector undertakings (PSU). Data on the representation of Scheduled Castes in government services and PSUs indicate that they comprise only a relatively small proportion of those employed in this sector and that they are mostly in the lower level, less prestigious class III and IV posts. Only 8.23 per cent of group A posts in the Government sector and 4.86 per cent of those in PSUs in 1987 were occupied by members of the Scheduled Castes. On the other hand 20.09 per cent of the lower paying and less prestigious group D posts in government services and 22.53 per cent of those in the PSUs had Scheduled Castes on their rolls (India, 1988:482-491). What is important is that even the lowest paid government job today usually requires a minimum of metric or high school education. The poor enrolment of Dalit children in school and large magnitude of dropout imply that the majority of them are unlikely to be in a position where they are even able to compete for jobs that are 'reserved' for them.

The Perspective of Policy - Equity in Education?

One of the major objectives of education policy in India has been the equalisation of education opportunity among different social groups. This is reflected in the National Policy on Education (1986) which reiterates that the 'central focus in the educational development of Scheduled Castes has been their equalisation with the non-Scheduled Caste population at all stages and levels of education' (India, 1986). The strategy laid down for this is, the expansion of schooling facilities including hostels, provision of financial assistance, especially to indigent groups, as well as incentives such as free books, uniforms and so on (India, 1986a: 112-114).

As has already been discussed, incentives for the education of Dalit children are inadequate in terms of both value and coverage especially at the elementary level, where the bulk of children drop-out with the first two years of schooling. According to the Commissioner for Scheduled Castes and Scheduled Tribes, '...the little assistance which pupils receive at the primary, middle and secondary level also comes too late' (1988:301). Streamlining of lengthy procedures that have been evolved to receive scholarships, text books, uniforms and so on are necessary to motivate parents of educationally backward social groups to send their children to school. The earlier reference to the condition of hostels for Dalit pupils, also points to the tendency of apathy and indifference, where the education of poor and deprived groups is concerned.

The national education policy seems by and large oblivious of the special context of education of the Scheduled Castes, arising not only because of poverty but because of their position in the social hierarchy. Further, there is a tendency to treat the 'Scheduled Castes' as a homogeneous group being insouciant to their varied historical experiences and present day economic, social and educational situation.

Issues relating to social accessibility of schooling and discriminatory attitudes towards children within schools are not adequately addressed. As Dushkin says, this appears to be in accordance with the general policy of the government to improve the 'secular conditions of Scheduled Castes' (Dushkin, 1972: 176). However, discrimination within educational institutions, to the extent that it occurs, can have debilitating implications for learning experiences of children. In fact the relatively poor learning environment made available to children is closely linked to the social and economic circumstances in which their families live.

A crash programme to recruit teachers from among the Scheduled Caste communities has been emphasised in policy documents (1986a:113). It has also been recommended that qualifications be relaxed while recruiting teachers belonging to Scheduled Caste communities. However, the policy does not see the need for specific kinds of training to sensitise the teaching community to the vulnerability of Dalit and other social groups and create an awareness of the special role that they, as teachers, can play in this context.

What is disturbing on the other hand is the impression that the State seeks to absolve itself of the ills of the formal system by creating new 'non-formal' structures for educationally backward groups. While laying down the objective of universalization of enrolment and retention of SC and ST children at the primary stage, the NPE (1986) clearly states that this goal will be achieved by 1990, through the formal school or *'its equivalent through the non-formal stream*' (1986a:111; emphasis mine). In a later document, 'Education for All by 2000', it is estimated that 'nearly one-third of the children in the 6-11 age group will be served by non-formal education programmes (NFE) up to 1995' (India, 1990a). This perspective of government policy is highlighted in a number of subsequent official documents. The statement that the National Policy on Education, 1986, envisages 'a large and systematic programme of NFE to achieve universal elementary education', finds repeated mention in the Annual Reports of the Ministry of Human Resources Development (India, 1992a: 1993). The section of children who are to be covered by NFE are those 'who for various reasons cannot attend formal schools', 'who live in smaller habitations', 'who cannot benefit from the school system' and so on (India, 1992b:37). The recently begun District Primary Education Programme (DPEP) which aims at 'the reconstruction of primary education' has as one of its tasks, 'the provision of alternative systems of comparable standards to the disadvantaged groups...' (*Ibid.*:37).

The increasing 'non-formal' component of the Central Elementary Education Budget (Plan) is a clear indication of the shift in government policy in the last few years.[16] An analysis of budget documents indicates that the 'actuals' in plan expenditure on NFE, by the Department of Education of the Central Government, rose from Rs.2627 lakhs in 1989-90 to Rs.3489 lakhs in 1990-91. The plan estimates under the item NFE, which was Rs.7,500 lakhs in 1991-92, rose to Rs.10,627 lakhs in 1994-95. As can be seen in Table 4.11, the NFE component was as high as 25.54 per cent of estimated central plan expenditure in 1992-93. Though 1994-95 was the year when high profile programmes in elementary education like the DPEP, Bihar Education Project and so on received considerable official attention, NFE continued to receive a significant 20 per cent of the Central Revenue Budget (Plan). In fact policy documents of programmes like the Lok Jumbish, Bihar Education Project and other externally funded programmes indicate that they envisage a sizeable non-formal component for educationally backward sections in rural areas.

TABLE 4.11: Central Revenue Budget (Plan) for Elementary Education (1989-90 to 1994-95)

(Rs. in lakhs)

Years	Elementary Education Budget*	Allocation for NFE**	
	Total	Total	%***
1989-90a	21633	2627	12.14
1990-91a	22473	3489	15.53
1991-92b	27880	7500	26.90
1992-93b	27750	6810	25.54
1994-95b	52236	10627	20.34

a — Actuals

b — Budget estimates

* This is the revenue budget (plan) for elementary education of the Department of Education of the Central Government.

** These appear to be allocations specifically for government run NFE Centres, general as well as those set up for girls. Grants to voluntary organisations involved with NFE have not been included.

*** Gives the percentage of the total elementary education budget allocated to NFE.

Source: India 1993 *Analysis of Budgeted Expenditure on Education (1989-90 to 1990-91 and 1992-93 to 1994-95).*

The number of NFE centres has grown rapidly over the years. From 1.09 lakh centres in 1986, the number of NFE centres increased to 2.74 lakhs in 1992. Around 33 lakh children were covered by the NFE programme in 1986. By 1992 their number rose to 68 lakhs. If recent government pronouncements are to be taken seriously, NFE is to be assigned the stupendous task of covering 'all out of school children in educationally advanced states and *50 per cent of out-of-school children in educationally backward states*' (India, 1996:18; emphasis mine). Critical questions that fail to be addressed are—has the NFE programme been adequately and realistically conceptualised? Do those entrusted with the programme have the necessary expertise to provide the kind of education envisaged? Are the funds made available commensurate with the tasks expected of the programme? And most important, has the concrete experience of the programme been documented and are there any lessons that can be learnt? According to policy-makers, the NFE scheme has been visualised as a 'child centred, environment oriented, flexible system to meet the educational needs of the comparatively deprived geographical areas and socio-economic sections of society' (1993:25). One of the main objectives of NFE is to encapsulate the five year primary schooling programme into a flexible two-year one, offering education of comparable standards and thereby facilitating entry of children into formal schools. There is as yet little concrete evidence that this objective is being accomplished. Subramanian and Paliwal, who work with Ekalavya's school education programme in Madhya Pradesh, comment upon the dismal performance of NFE Programmes. 'Vast majority of the non-formal centres are either fictitious or function erratically. There is no mechanism to ensure that they work. An instructor is expected to be motivated enough to work on a pittance.... Under such conditions turning over the working children to the non-formal sector is as good as washing ones hands of them' (1989:74). One of the few evaluations of NFE for tribal students in 5 states tellingly sums up the programme thus:

> One of the objectives is to complete the five-year course of primary education in two to three years through a condensed course. Howsoever poor the facilities in primary schools may be, they are definitely better than those in the non-formal centres. Teaching in the former takes place for four to five hours as compared to two hours in the latter. Primary schools have at least one full-time teacher, a set of prescribed textbooks, teaching aids and other equipments. Non-formal education centres lack most of these. There teaching is listless, the instructor comes to the centres at his own convenience; reading materials are conspicuous by their absence; to inflate the attendance even regular students of primary school are allowed to sit in the classroom and their names entered in the attendance register. With all these drawbacks of the non-formal centres, it is not clear as to how a five-year course can be completed in two/three years, and how students who go through such

condensed course would compete with regular primary school students who studied for five years (Srivastava and Gupta, 1986: 17).

Non-formal Education Programmes (NFE) appear to offer an inferior system of schooling, that is vaguely formulated and difficult to monitor. The so-called strengths of the NFE are flexibility in curriculum and textual materials (which in reality may mean that anything can go in the name of education), dependence on local people (often unprofessional and poorly paid) and the absence of rigidly organised teaching and learning (likely to make evaluation of either teaching or learning problematic). These features of the NFE are likely to be its major weaknesses particularly because it is meant for people who are vulnerable and do not have the power or the resources to demand an education that compares with what the more advantaged sections receive.[17]

Today a significantly larger number of children from lower caste groups attend schools as compared to the situation that prevailed five decades ago. However, the forgoing discussion suggests that the formal school has failed to consciously intervene in favour of socially discriminated and educationally backward groups such as the Dalits. On the one hand it is yet to be seized of the need to 'create and sustain a consciousness against social discrimination' (Kamat, 1985:281). On the other hand the institution does not appear to significantly provide the academic supports that children from these social groups clearly need if they are to successfully chart the educational mainstream. In other words schools are yet to ensure equity in education to Dalit children.

In the overall context of inadequate public resources for schooling, greater privatisation of 'quality' education for the elite, and the search for non-formal alternatives for the educationally backward, it is likely that socially and economically vulnerable groups will suffer greater neglect. Unless the present state of formal education is brought centre stage and the issue of equity in education is squarely addressed, we will continue to witness the abdication by the State of its social responsibility in education.

NOTES

[This has appeared as Discussion Paper No. 15 of the Studies on "Human Development in India" Project of the United Nations Development Programme, 1996.]

1. The term 'Dalit' is today increasingly being used by the vocal and activist sections of the former 'Untouchables' in preference to 'Harijan' and 'Scheduled Caste'. Joshi notes that the term 'Dalit' was popularized by Untouchable protest movements since the early 1970s. The word itself means 'oppressed', but the term 'Dalit' has become a 'positive, assertive expression of pride in Untouchable heritage and a rejection of oppression' (1986:2). According to Zelliot, there is in the word 'Dalit' itself 'an inherent denial of pollution, karma and justified caste hierarchy' (Zelliot, 1978:77). In the discussion that follows, the term 'Untouchables' is often used to refer to Dalits in the pre-independent period because it starkly draws attention to the social situation of the majority (not all) of these communities in Indian society of that time.
2. The concepts of 'access', 'treatment' and 'outcome' have been used to compare the opportunities that ethnic minorities receive in education *vis-a-vis* 'majority' groups (Open University, 1982:11). In this paper these concepts are used in the context of 'equity' or the practice of social justice in education for the socially discriminated Dalit communities.
3. The Untouchables were first officially called 'Depressed Classes'. The Census of India, 1931, substituted the term 'Exterior' castes for 'Depressed Classes' as it was felt that the latter was an 'unfortunate and depressing label' (Hutton, 1933:471).
4. The Starte Committee recommended the closure of 'separate' schools for the Depressed classes. While the Bombay Municipality closed all special schools between 1922-27, they were officially abolished all over the country only in 1946-47 (Bombay, 1958:424).
5. Most of the discussions has pertained to the education of the Untouchables or Exterior Castes in British India. Mention must be made of the significant advances made in the education of the Untouchables in some of the Indian States in the pre-independence period. Baroda, Travancore and Assam registered relatively high literacy rates among the Exterior Castes. According to the 1931 Census, 14.9 per cent of the Exterior Castes in Travancore State, 10.3 per cent in Baroda and 12.9 per cent in Assam were literate. In contrast literacy rates among Exterior Castes were dismal in Central India Agency 0.3 per cent, the Punjab state 0.3 per cent and Rajputana Agency 0.4 per cent (Hutton, 1933:494).
6. Expenditure on education is not available separately for rural areas. Ahmed referring to Jalaludin (1991), notes that '... rural schools receive as little as one quarter of the per student urban allocations' (1991:147).
7. Details of the study referred to by Jalaludin were reported in the *Times of India* (January 14, 1991). The report mentions that 47.9 per cent of Scheduled Caste

and Scheduled Tribe children surveyed by Rusia in the Tikamgarh block of Jhansi district did not even enrol in school because they feared that 'they will not be allowed to sit with upper castes or the elite'. The report also mentions factors such as poverty, migration and so on as being serious deterrents to the schooling of Scheduled Caste children.

8. The 1981 Census figures and NSSO (1987-88) data on school participation may appear outdated as we are presently well into the 1990s. Though enrollment data from school records is available for more recent years it is grossly inflated as can be seen in official reports and documents. In 1980-81 for instance, the gross enrollment ratio (GER) of Scheduled Castes 6-11 years in Class I-V was calculated to be as much as 82.2. In 1991-92 the G.E.R. of Dalit Children in primary school was found to be as high as 103.01! (India, 1993:28).
9. The findings of the NSS (42nd round) regarding reasons why Dalit children discontinue their studies are of interest. While around 46 per cent of Dalit drop-out in rural areas is attributed to 'economic reasons' (including participation in domestic work), a significant 30 per cent of children discontinue their education because of lack of interest in studies/further studies. A further 16 per cent leave the educational mainstream as a result of failure (NSSO, 1989). While lack of interest in studies and failure are often seen as a consequence of parental and community attitudes as well as poor academic abilities, the quality of education that children (especially first generation learners) are exposed to, surely needs critical attention.
10. Chapman defines the hidden curriculum as 'all those things that are learned in schools, other than what is officially time-tabled. The hidden curriculum includes, attitudes, values, notions of 'normal' and 'not normal' (1986:113).
11. Experiences of social discrimination within schools are yet to be systematically documented. Part of the difficulty lies in the tacit assumption made by scholars that untouchability is no longer practised, and if it does occur, it remains confined to the private sphere governed by social norms and customs. The other problem is the sensitivity of the issue concerned. The methodology used in conducting research relating to discrimination is also crucial. For instance, a researcher conducting a rapid impersonal survey is unlikely to establish the rapport that is necessary for Dalits to share experiences that may often be painful. On the other hand, a sensitive researcher, using a more humane methodology may be in a better position to understand what it means to be a Dalit child in an Indian school.
12. School teachers belong predominantly to the middle and upper caste groups. Data from the earlier mentioned NCERT Survey (1986) indicate that only around 15 per cent of teachers in elementary schools in the country belong to Scheduled Caste and Scheduled Tribe communities.
13. The process of 'labelling' of 'ex-Untouchable' children in school is reflective of stereotypes that prevail in wider society about these communities. Freeman in a study of the 'Untouchable' Muli (belonging to the Bauri sub-caste) refers to the 'low regard for the personal character and

integrity, intelligence and morality of Untouchables' that high caste individuals usually hold. They are 'spoken to in familiar terms' and with abuse - 'uncivilized', 'famished ones', 'wife's brother' and so on. In fact, the very term 'Bauri' had become a word of abuse (Freeman, 1979:54). Aggarwal and Ashraf also observe that 'Harijans' are seen as 'dirty and immoral, lacking in intrinsic worth... they are never regarded as adults' (1976:5).

Freeman suggests that the Untouchables tend to reject the high caste derogatory view of them, frequently show their resentment and make attempts to raise their status (1979). Mencher also argues that there has always been a large amount of hostility and resentment among 'Harijans' towards those higher in the social hierarchy (1972). The magnitude of such resentment and the forms that it can take, for instance forging of a positive sense of identity and 'community', (facilitating social and political mobilization) would depend upon the dynamics of specific contexts—the nature of social groups, their interests, strategies evolved and so on. Dalit children who encounter the often harsh structure of schooling as young and defenseless individuals are likely to be in a particularly vulnerable position. We know practically nothing of Dalit children's daily experience of schooling, the manner in which they confront different situations and the strategies they may evolve to cope with the system. This is an area which requires research attention.

14. It is to be remembered that by the time a cohort of class I students enters high school the majority of them have already 'dropped-out' leaving a relatively 'more select' group to complete school. This would be increasingly so as one moves from school to higher levels of education.

15. The dimension of gender and its interplay with poverty, caste discrimination and school processes is crucial if we are to understand the dismal spread of schooling among Dalit girls. However it has not been possible to undertake such an analysis in this paper which focuses on Dalit children in general.

16. Central assistance is provided for the NFE Programmes - 60 per cent funding for co-ed centres, 90 per cent for girl centres and 100 per cent assistance is given to centres run by voluntary groups.

17. There may of course be non-formal programmes that are well run. It is possible that a new orientation has been given to NFE in some areas in recent years. However, such programmes remain largely undocumented. Unless there is adequate information on 'success stories' in NFE, there does not appear to be much grounds for optimism regarding the non-formal alternative in education.

REFERENCES

Aggarwal, Pratap C., *Halfway to Equality*. New Delhi: Manohar, 1983.

Aggarwal, Pratap C. and Mohommad Siddiq Ashraf, *Equality through Privilege—A study of special privileges of Scheduled Castes in Haryana*. New Delhi: SRC for Industrial Relations and Human Resources, 1976.

Ahmed, Manzoor (with Ming *et al.*), *Basic Education and National Development*. New York: UNICEF, 1991.

Aikara Jacob, 1980, *Scheduled Castes and Higher Education: A Study of College Students in Bombay*. Poona: Dastane, 1980.

Ambedkar, B.R., *Dr.Babasaheb Ambedkar—Writings and Speeches*, Vol. 2. Bombay: Government of Maharasthra, 1982.

Bombay, *A Review of Education in Bombay State, 1855-1955*. Bombay: Government of Bombay, 1958.

Chapman Karen, *Sociology of Schools*. London: Tavistock, 1986.

Chitnis, M.B, 'An Educational, Social and Economic Survey of Milind College Students' Joshi, Barbara ed. *Untouchable! Voices of the Dalit Liberation Movement*. New Delhi: Select Services Syndicte, 1986.

Chitnis, M.B. and D.D. Kamble, 'Survey of Impact of Scarcity Conditions on Milind College Students' *Milind College Annual, Vol.X*. [reprinted in Joshi, (ed.) *op.cit.* 1986], 1973.

Chitnis, Suma, 'Education of the Scheduled Castes', *Journal of Higher Education* (2), 1975.

Chitnis, Suma, *A long Way to Go*. New Delhi: Allied Publishers, 1981.

Chitnis, Suma, 'Education and Social Stratification - An Illustration from a Metropolitan City' in Ghosh, R. and Zachariah, M. (ed.), *Education and the Process of Change*. New Delhi: Sage Publications, 1987.

CIRTPC, *School Drop-outs among Harijan Children - Causes and Cure*. New Delhi: Central Institute of Research and Training, 1975.

Cotton, J.S., Progress of Education in India 1892-93 to 1896-97. Calcutta: Office of the Superintendent of Govt. Printing, 1898.

Desai, I.P, *Untouchability in Rural Gujarat*. Bombay: Popular Prakashan, 1976.

Dushkin, L., 'Scheduled Caste Politics' in Mahar, J.M.(ed) *The Untouchables in Contemporary India*. Tuscon: The University of Arizona Press, 1972.

Freeman, James M., *Untouchable: An Indian Life History*. London: George Allen and Unwin, 1979.

Ghokale, B. Jayashree, 'The Evolution of a Counter Ideology: Dalit Consciousness in Maharashtra,' in Frankel Francine R. and M.S.A. Rao (ed.) *Dominance and State Power in India. Vol.II Decline of a Social Order*. Delhi: Oxford University Press, 1990.

Ghurye, G.S., *Caste and Class in India*. Bombay: Popular Book Depot, 1957.

Gough, Kathleen, *Rural Society in Southeast India*. Cambridge: Cambridge University Press, 1981.

Hunter, *Indian Education Commission*, 1882.

Hutton, J.H., *Census of India, 1931. Vol. 1. Part 1 Report.* Delhi: Manager of Publications, 1933.

India, *Report of the Committee on Untouchability, Economic and Educational Development of the Scheduled Castes and Connected Documents.* New Delhi: Government of India, Department of Social Welfare, 1969.

India, *Report of the Commissioner for Scheduled Castes and Scheduled Tribes' 1971-72 and 1972-73* (Twenty-First Report). New Delhi: Govt. of India, 1974.

India, *Report of the Scheduled Castes and Scheduled Tribes Commission 1978-79.* New Delhi: Govt. of India, 1980.

India, *National Policy on Education 1986.* New Delhi: Govt. of India, Ministry of HRD, Deptt. of Education, 1986.

India, *Programme of Action: National Policy on Education 1986.* New Delhi: Govt. of India, Ministry of HRD, Deptt. of Education, 1986a.

India, *Report of the Commissioner for Scheduled Castes and Scheduled Tribes.* New Delhi: Govt. of India, 1988.

India, Census of India 1981. Series-1 India Part-IV A (VII) (SC/ST) *Social and Cultural Tables (Table C-4 SC/ST).* Delhi: Controller of Publications, 1989.

India, *Selected Education Statistics (1988-89):* Ministry of HRD. New Delhi: Government of India, 1990.

India, *Education for All by 2000.* New Delhi: NIEPA, 1990a.

India, *Towards an Enlightened and Humane Society.* (Ramamurti Report). New Delhi: Govt. of India, 1991.

India, *Statistical Abstrate India 1990.* Ministry of Planning. New Delhi: Govt. of India, 1992.

India, *Annual Report 1990-91,* New Delhi: Govt. of India, Ministry of Human Resource Development, 1992a.

India, *Programme of Action 1992.* New Delhi: University Grants Commission, 1992b.

India, *Report of the Working Group on Early Childhood Education, Non-Formal Education, Elementary Edudation and Teacher Education for the Ninth Five Year Plan.* New Delhi: Govt. of India, 1996.

India, *Education for All The Indian Scene* (Second Edition). New Delhi: Govt. of India, Ministry of Human Resource Development, Deptt. of Education, 1993.

India, *Selected Educational Statistics.* (As on 30 Sept. 1992) New Delhi: Govt. of India, Ministry of Human Resource Development, Deptt. of Education, 1993a.

India, *Education of Scheduled Castes and Scheduled Tribes 1988-89.* Deptt. of Education. New Delhi: Govt. of India, 1993b.

India, *Analysis of Budgeted Expenditure on Education (1989-90 to 1994-95).* New Delhi: Govt. of India, 1993c.

India, *Annual Report 1991-92.* New Delhi: Govt. of India, Ministry of

Human Resource Development, 1993d.

Isaacs, Harold R., 1965, *India's Ex-Untouchables*. New Delhi: Asia Publishing House, 1965.

Jalaludin, A.K., 1991, *Basic Education and National Development*. (mimeo).

Joshi, B.R., *Democracy in Search of Equality: Untouchable Politics and Indian Social Change*. Delhi: Hindustan Publishing Corporation, 1982.

Joshi, B.R., *Untouchable! Voices of the Dalit Liberation Movement*. New Delhi: Select Book Service Syndicate, 1986.

Kamat, A.R., *Education and Social Change in India*. Poona: Somaiya, 1985.

Kamble, N.D., *Deprived Castes and Their Struggle for Equality*. New Delhi: Ashish Publishing House, 1983.

Keer, Dhananjay, *Dr.Ambedkar: Life and Mission*. Bombay: Popular Prakashan. (first published in 1954), 1971.

Khosla, Dinesh, *Myth and Reality of the Protection of Civil Rights Law: A Case of Untouchability in Rural India*. New Delhi: Hindustan Publishing Corporation, 1987.

Kumar, Krishna, 'Educational Experiences of Scheduled Castes and Tribes' in Shukla, S.C and Krishna Kumar (ed.) *Sociological Perspectives in Education*. New Delhi: Chanakya, 1985.

Kurrien, John, *Elementary Education in India: Myth, Reality, Alternative*. Delhi: Vikas Publishing House, 1983.

Kurrien, John, *Levels of Attainment in Primary Schools in Language and Mathematics*. Pune: Centre for Learning Resource, (unpublished), 1989.

Lal, S.K, and Nahar, U.R., *Extent of Untouchability and Pattern of Discrimination*. New Delhi: Mittal Publications, 1990.

Lynch, O.M., *Politics of Untouchability, Social Mobility and Social Change in a City of India*. New York: Colombia University Press, 1969.

Mahar, Michael, (ed.) *Untouchables in Contemporary India*. Tuscon: University of Arizona Press, 1972.

Malik, Suneila, *Social Integration of Scheduled Castes*. New Delhi: Abhinav Publications, 1979.

Mencher, Joan, 'Continuity and Change in an Ex-Untouchable Community of South India' in Mahar (ed.) *op.cit.*, 1972.

Nathan, R., *Progress of Education in India 1897-98 — 1901-2*. Calcutta: Office of the Superintendent of Govt. Printing, 1904.

NCERT, *Fourth All India Education Survey*. New Delhi: NCERT, 1978.

NCERT, *Fifth All India Education Survey Vol. 1*. New Delhi: NCERT, 1992.

NCERT, *Fifth All India Education Survey Vol.II*. New Delhi: NCERT, 1992a.

NSSO, *Participation in Education Forty Second Round — July 1986-87. Part 1: All India*. New Delhi: Dept. of Statistics. Govt. of India, 1989.

NSSO, *Employment Unemployment Situation of Scheduled Caste and Scheduled Tribe Population During Late Eighties, Forty Second Round, 1987-88.* New Delhi: Deptt. of Statistics, Govt. of India, 1990.

Open University, *Ethnic Minorities and Education*. Milton Keynes: The Open University Press, 1992.

Orange, H.W., *Progress of Education in India 1902-1907*. Calcutta: Superintendent of Govt. Printing, 1909.

Parulekar, R.V., *Survey of Indigenous Education in the Province of Bombay (1820-1830).* Bombay: Asia Publishing House, (1951 reprint), 1945.

Parvathamma, C., *Scheduled Castes at the Cross Roads*. New Delhi: Ashish Publishing House, 1989.

Parvathamma, C., and Satya Narayana, *New Horizons and the Scheduled Castes*. New Delhi: Ashish Publishing House, 1984.

Patwardhan, Sunanda, 'Aspects of Social Mobility Among the Scheduled Castes in Poona' in Rao M.S.A. (ed.) *Urban Sociology in India*. Delhi: Orient Longmans, 1974.

Radhakrishnan, P., 'Ambedkar's Legacy to Dalits. Has the Nation Regard on its Promises?' *Economic and Political Weekly*, August 17, 1991.

Radhakrishnan, S. and Ranjana Kumari, *Impact of Education on Scheduled Caste Youth in India. A Study of Social Transformation in Bihar and Madhya Pradesh*. New Delhi: Radiant Publishers, 1989.

Ram, Nandu, *Mobile Scheduled Castes: Rise of a New Middle Class*. New Delhi: Hindustan Publishing, 1988.

Ramaswamy, Uma, 'Preference, and Progress: The Scheduled Castes' *Economic and Political Weekly*. Vol.XIX No.30, 1984.

Richley, J.A., *Progress of Education in India. Eighth Quinquinnial Review. 1917-1922*. Vol.1, 1923.

Roy, Ramashray and Singh, V.B., *Between Two Worlds: A Study of Harijan Elites*. Delhi: Discovery Publishing House, 1987.

Saberwal, Satish, 'Segmentation and Literacy' in *Economic and Political Weekly*. Vol XXVI Nos. 11 and 12, 1991.

Sachchidananda, *Education among the Scheduled Castes and Scheduled Tribes in Bihar*. Patna: A.N. Institute of Social Studies, 1974.

Sarup, Madan, *The Politics of Multi-Racial Education*. London: Routledge and Kegan Paul, 1986.

Seceda, Walter G., *Equity in Education*. The Falmer Press: New York.

Sharp, H., 1918, *Progress of Education in India 1912-1917*. Calcutta: Superintendent of Govt. Printing, 1988.

Shyamlal, *The Bhangis in Transition*. New Delhi: Inter-India, 1984.

Singh, Madhu, *Social Origins, Educational Attainments and Occupational Mobility among Scheduled Castes in Delhi*. New Delhi: JNU, (unpublished Ph.D. thesis), 1980.

Srivastava, L.R.N., *Hostel Facilities for Scheduled Castes*. New Delhi: NCERT, 1979.

Srivastava, L.R.N. and Gupta, B.S., *A Study of Methods, Processes and*

Practices of Non-Formal Education Programme for Tribal Students. New Delhi: NCERT, 1986.

Subramanian, N., and Paliwal, R., 'The New Dispensation and School Education—The Limits of Development without Democratisation'. *Social Scientist* Vol.17, Nos.9-10, 1989.

TOI, 'Report on Rusia's Survey'. *Times of India*, Jan.14, 1991.

TOI, 'Studies Confirm Low Levels of Learning in Primary Schools Report', *Times of India*, Aug. 28, 1994.

Tuinmin, Hans, *The Political Economy of Untouchability* (unpublished thesis). Sydney: University of New Southwales, 1984.

Varghese, N.V., *Economic Reforms and Prospects for the Educational Sector*. New Delhi: NIEPA, 1994.

Yadav, S.K., *Educational Schemes for Scheduled Castes*. Delhi: Shree Publishing House, 1985.

Yadav, S.K., *Education of Scheduled Castes*. New Delhi: Common Wealth Publishers, 1991.

Zelliot, Eleanor, 'Gandhi and Ambedkar - A Study in Leadership', in Mahar, M.J. (ed.) *Untouchables in Contemporary India*. Tuscon: University of Arizona Press, 1972.

Zelliot, Eleanor, 'Dalit, New Cultural Context for an Old Marathi World' in *Contributions to Asian Sociology* (11), 1978.

5

UNTOUCHABILITY IN RURAL GUJARAT Revisited

GHANSHYAM SHAH

Untouchability is the worst form inequality. It is just not inequality of income and economic status. It is social inequality coupled with discrimination. It has religious sanction to back up. Mindset in terms of values, attitudes and behaviour for observing and legitimising discrimination in private and public spheres begins to form since childhood among the Indians, both of the untouchables and non-untouchables.

The Indian State does not legitimise discrimination of any form. In fact the Constitution has made a number of provisions under various Articles to categorise the practice of untouchability—the stigma from which the Scheduled Castes suffer—as an offence. Article 15(2) of the Constitution proclaims :

> No citizen shall, on grounds not only of religion, race, caste, place of birth or any of them, be subject to any disability, liability, restriction or condition with regard to:
> (a) access to shops, public restaurants, hotels;
> (b) the use of wells, tanks, bathing ghats, roads and places of public resort maintained wholly or partly out of state funds or dedicated to the use of the general public.

Further, Article 17 deals with specifically the issue of

untouchability as an offence. It declares:

> "Untouchability" is abolished and its practice in any form is forbidden. The enforcement of any disability arising out of "untouchability" shall be an offence punishable with law.

The State follows two approaches for annihilation of discrimination. One is overall economic development in general and the other of Scheduled Castes and other deprived groups though special measures. It had been more or less assumed in the fifties that economic development would create the condition and generate the forces which would resolve social and cultural problems including untouchability (Nehru, 1942; Desai, A.R., 1948; Ranadive, 1979; and Mukherjee, 1991). Intervening to resolve social problems was not a priority of the State. Since Independence, the government has followed various strategies for economic development. Yet, the State took nearly eight years after Independence in enacting legislation for punitive action against those who observe discrimination in general and untouchability in particular. The Parliament passed the Untouchability (Offences) Act in 1955. The Act outlaws the enforcement of disabilities "on the ground of untouchability" in regard to, *inter alia*, the entrance and worship at temples, access to shops and restaurants, the practice of occupations and traders, the use of water sources, places of public resort and accommodation, public conveyances, hospitals, educational institutions, construction and occupation of residential premises, holding of religious ceremonies and processions, use of jewellery and finery. The imposition of disabilities is made a crime, punishable by a fine of upto Rs. 500 and imprisonment for upto six months, cancellation or suspension of licences and of public grants. But, as the Elaya Perumal Committee observed in 1969, the Untouchability (Offences) Act, 1955, had failed to make any impact on the eradication of untouchability. The Committee recommended that the penal provisions of the Act should be made more stringent. Consequently, after three years, a bill aimed at amending the Untouchability (Offences) Act, 1955, was introduced in the Lok Sabha in April 1972. The Parliament took more than four years to pass the bill. The

Untouchability (Offences) Amendment Bill, 1972, renamed as the Protection of Civil Rights (Amendment) Act, came into force in 1976. The Act provided for enhanced and stringent punishment including collective fines for offences relating to untouchability. Some salient features of the amended Act were:

1. All untouchability offences continued to be cognizable. Hitherto, untouchability offences could be compounded, but they were made non-compoundable;
2. The punishment for untouchability offences were considerably enhanced, and both imprisonment and fine were to be simultaneously awarded for such offences; and
3. Direct or indirect preaching of untouchability or its justification on historical, philosophical, religious or traditional grounds was made an offence under the Act.

The State governments were directed to introduce separate measures to fight against untouchability, notably, to appoint officers and special courts to deal with offenders, to provide legal aid to victims, and to take strong steps to identify and remedy problems in areas with a particularly high incidence of untouchability. Later, Scheduled Castes and Scheduled Tribes (Protection of Atrocities) Act, 1989, was enacted. Our intention is to see what impact these Acts and other measures have had on the practice of untouchability. To what extent untouchability has been abolished and in which spheres it is still observed?

Twenty-five years back late Professor I.P. Desai inquired into these questions in rural Gujarat (1976). The study was sponsored by the Indian Council of Social Science Research in 1971. It was a pilot project and in the light of experiences gained from the study, the ICSSR, then "proposed" to undertake similar studies in other parts of the country. However, this has not been done so far. It is important both for theoretical and policy purposes to find out what changes have taken place in regard to untouchability in Gujarat, one of the developed states of India. The present study is a restudy of the inquiry carried out by Prof. Desai.

The 1971 study covered 69 villages for observation. The

villages were selected randomly according to their size from each district and non-tribal talukas. We obviously, selected the same villages for the restudy. Three investigators were trained in observation and interview method. They read the earlier village reports and the book. The sample villages were distributed among them for fieldwork. They visited the villages and stayed for five to seven days in each of them. During the stay, the investigators talked to members of the SCs and non-SCs, who are called *Savarnas*, in villages, panchayat office etc. Report of each village was written before starting the study of the next village. The study was carried out in eight months in 1996.

Untouchability in Public and Private Spheres

The population of Gujarat has nearly doubled in the last twenty-five years. It was 266.97 lakh in 1971, and has reached 411.74 lakh in 1991. During this period the urban population has increased from 28.08 per cent to 34.40 per cent. The literacy rate (of the above seven years age) has increased from 35.79 per cent to 60.91 per cent. Gujarat ranked eighth in industrial production in 1960. Now it occupies the position of a close second in the country. Industrial growth rate has increased from 3.4 per cent in the 1960s to 8 per cent in the 1980s. With the spread of irrigation and infrastructure facilities, agricultural production, particularly commercial crops, has nearly doubled.

The Scheduled Castes constitute seven per cent of the total population of Gujarat. They are scattered all over the State. 51 per cent of the SC population is literate, but less than 1.15 per cent have acquired higher education. According to a recent survey (Navsarjan, 1997) of seven districts of the state, nearly 50 per cent of the SC workforce is agricultural labourers, who on an average get 200 days' work in a year. Three out of four SC households have less than Rs. 2000 income per month. 82 per cent of the SC live in *kachha* dwellings.

On the whole, the population of the villages under study had registered an increase of over a hundred per cent between 1971 and 1991. However, demographic figures of a few villages had not changed much, as many of them had migrated to urban areas in search of livelihood. Except one, all villages were multi-caste, varying from three to sixteen castes. One village had predominantly Muslim population.

The study did not intend to address the question, in a dichotomy, whether untouchability exists or not. Instead the initial study looks into the practice of untouchability in seventeen spheres of village life, which includes private and public domain was divided into two spheres—those institutions and places which were managed through the funds provided by the State and/or local community from common resources like land, forest, pond or river and those managed by market, in which relationship was contractual of buying and selling commodities and/or services. The former included public transport, public roads, schools, postal services, Panchayat, common source of water and temples. The latter included shops selling goods, services such as hair cutting, tailoring, and paying wages. A few of the traditional occupational activities such as hair cutting, pottering etc. were still caste based. The private sphere was confined to one's house where one had the power of allowing or not allowing the SC to enter the premises without discrimination. There was some quasi-public spheres, which involved personal preference in public places. Interaction between labourers while carrying out the work in farm or other places was one such sphere.

Table 5.1 reports our observation regarding the practice of untouchability in different spheres. Though we have tried to present the observations in an objective manner, an element of subjectivity still cannot be ruled out. Bias of the respondents, who narrated their views on untouchability and bias of the investigators, may still have left their impressions. Moreover, when we were told that some members of the village did observe untouchability and some did not, we treated them as practice of untouchability in the village. Similarly, when we found that though untouchability was not overtly observed, the members of the SCs were made to feel that they were not supposed to touch the *Savarnas* and should keep distance. (This was particularly so in the case of movements on roads and travelling in public transport). We treated them as the practice of untouchability. In this we have relied more on the opinion of the SCs than those of the non-SCs. The "nebulous" category indicates that untouchability is openly not practised. We have classified those villages in this category, where there is no uniform practice by all—some castes observe untouchability and some do not.

TABLE 5.1: Observance and Non-Observance of Untouchability in Different Behavioural Situations in 1996 and 1971

(N = 69)

Behaviour	1996			1971		
	Untouchability observed	Nebulous	Untouchability not observed	Untouchability observed	Nebulous	Untouchability not observed
1	2	3	4	5	6	7
Public Transport	1 (1)	4 (6)	64 (93)	3 (4)	—	65 (96)
School	—	—	69 (100)	4 (6)	1 (2)	57 (92)
Post-office, while buying stamps	2 (4)	2 (4)	47 (92)	1 (4)	—	24 (96)
Delivery of letters by postman	4 (6)	2 (3)	62 (91)	10 (17)	—	49 (83)
Panchayat sitting arrangement	12 (18)	8 (12)	46 (70)	23 (47)	—	26 (53)
Savarna and untouchable workers in the field	17 (26)	11 (17)	38 (57)	23 (42)	—	32 (58)
Paying wages to untouchable workers	20 (29)	9 (13)	40 (58)	38 (69)	—	17 (31)
Giving things and receiving money in shop	14 (22)	4 (6)	47 (71)	35 (67)	—	17 (33)

(Contd.)

TABLE 5.1 *(Contd.)*

1	2	3	4	5	6	7
Entry into private shop	14 (21)	5 (8)	46 (71)	46 (85)	—	8 (15)
Entry into private house	55 (80)	10 (14)	4 (6)	62 (90)	—	7 (10)
Entry into temple	44 (69)	4 (6)	16 (25)	57 (89)	2 (3)	5 (8)
Barber serving SCs	39 (68)	5 (9)	13 (23)	48 (94)	—	3 (6)
Potter selling pots to SCs	10 (22)	5 (11)	31 (67)	26 (72)	—	10 (27)
Tailor giving service to SCs	1 (2)	— —	42 (98)	11 (31)	2 (5)	23 (64)
Restrictions on roads	3 (4)	13 (19)	53 (77)	41 (60)	—	27 (40)
Common source of water	14 (61)	6 (26)	3 (13)	7 (28)	13 (52)	5 (20)

The practice of untouchability in sitting arrangement of the students was negligible in 1971. It has disappeared completely in 1996. The SC and non-SC students intermingled in school freely. But in many villages, their friendship did not extend beyond the school hours. They hardly visited each others place. Non-SC teachers did not discriminate against SC students, but they were not easily accessible to SC students outside the school boundary. Though all the schools did not have the facility for drinking water for students, but wherever the facility existed, there was no discrimination. From our observation and talking to a few students, we could say that neither SC students nor their parents had any complaints of discrimination by *savarna* teachers. There was no conspicuous discrimination in sitting arrangements while distributing mid-day meal. However, in a few villages some of the *savarna* students did not take meal in the school. This was so partly because the parents of these students did not wish their children to take cooked food along with SC students in school, and also because they came from well-off families who could afford it.

Nearly ten per cent of village schools have teachers belonging to SCs. None of them complained that their colleagues discriminate against them in school. They take water from the same source in the school and also occasionally take snacks and tea together. However, except in the south Gujarat, these teachers do not get accommodation in *savarna* locality of the village. They either commute from their village or from nearby town or they get house on rent in Dalit locality. "They do not say that they would not give house on rent to us, but they would give excuses giving signal that we were not wanted in the *savarna* locality. Even if we get, we would not prefer to live there, because we fear that neighbours would not help when we need them, in sickness and other crisis. Moreover, we fear that they may insult us if something goes wrong", a teacher from north Gujarat village said. Another teacher said that "our relatives from villages visit us. They are not well clothed and do not know etiquette of upper caste, hence we get embarrassed if we live in Patidar or Baniya locality. It is better to live with one's own caste fellows. You get intimacy with them, whereas in the *savarna* locality you are treated like an alien; and live in fear that you may be humiliated."

All villages are now more or less covered by the state transport bus in fair season. Except in seven per cent of the villages, untouchability is not observed while boarding and sitting in the bus. Crude discrimination against SCs is observed in one per cent of the villages, where he/she is almost prohibited from sharing seats with *savarnas* while travelling. In as many as six per cent of the villages, practice of untouchability is in nebulous form. That is, a member of SC passenger is expected to stand up and give seat to a *savarna* passenger. Or the later is allowed to board first in the bus. Some instances of quarrel have taken place in Gujarat between SC and *Savarna* passengers, when the former did not vacate the seat for the later. "They (SCs), particularly youths, have become arrogant and do not show respect to us and do not give seat", a member from upper caste complained.

The 1971 study found that there were certain restrictions on the free movement of the SCs on some roads, in as many as 60 per cent of the villages. Now, the number of villages having restriction on the movement on public roads have declined considerably. But still the SCs encounter some restrictions on their movement in 23 per cent of the villages. Though, as such there is no bar on the SCs using village roads. But they do become victim of wrath varying from abuse to physical assault, if they enter certain *Khadaki,* i.e., streets of the upper castes. They have to stop and give way to the members of the upper castes, particularly Brahmins and Rajputs, in general and elderly persons of the dominant upper castes in particular. An elderly Dalit from Sarangpur village in the Panchmahals district reported, "*Savarnas* do not free touch us, we also observe our *maryada,* i.e., boundary, and accordingly use the road for our movement". The SCs do not take out *Varghoda,* i.e., marriage procession on the main roads of these villages. If they do, they fear that they would be ridiculed by the dominant caste.

Even in many villages, where the SCs do not face any restriction in their day to day movements, a few of them once in a while do hear a mortifying comments from members of the upper castes, which remind them of their "Untouchable" status. R.K. Hazari, one of the leading economists, recalled a humiliating experience of his younger days: "One morning, as I was going through this very narrow street, I saw a few high caste Hindu children coming towards me; but, as soon as they saw me, they stood up against the wall, and one of them shouted to the others to keep clear of the "Untouchable". This distressed me deeply, perhaps because I was weak from illness, and, for the first time, I became aware of real anger within myself" (Hazari, 1969:91). Though Dalits of all villages do not encounter such experience everyday, once in a while, they do experience such offending situations. And, many urban, educated Dalits do recall similar experiences.

Most of the village post offices and the postmen do not practice untouchability while giving stamps and taking money as well as delivering mails. The postmen go to the Dalit localities and hand over the mails to the person concerned. But there are few exceptions. There are still 8 per cent villages, where postal employees observe untouchability. They do not give postal stationary and mails in hand of the SC person. Though there is a slight decline in practice of untouchability during the last twenty-five years in delivering mails. But there is no change so far as selling of stamps is concerned. In fact the proportion of villages in this category has increased since 1971. Such rise, one may argue is due to the expansion of postal facility, from 24 to 51 villages and in many villages, selling of postal stationary is carried out from the residence of the postal employee.

Open or subtle untouchability is practice in Panchayat meetings in 30 per cent of the villages. It was 47 per cent in 1971. There is not only reservation of seats for the SCs, but since 1976, the Government of Gujarat introduced a Social Justice Committee in Panchayat institutions, comprising the SC and ST members, to protect the interests of the deprived communities. However, SJC is either not formed or remained on paper in as many as 60 per cent of the villages. And wherever they exist, they hardly function. The sitting arrangement in Panchayat offices, thanks to legal provisions, is common for all the members. But there is tacit convention whereby certain seats are marked for SC members. One SC member from the village in Sabarkantha district reported: "The sitting arrangement is the same for all the members, but the SC ('Untouchable' expression used by the respondent) member knows his boundary and occupies a seat accordingly. Though tea and snacks are served to everyone, but SC member is given in separate plate and cup meant for them. Water is also served to them in a glass meant for them. Cup, glass and plate meant for the SCs are kept separately in cupboard. In the past the members used to wash their used utensils. Now, thank God, it is not done. They are washed by the Panchayat peon." In another village in the Ahmedabad district, one SC youth reported that, "Though, as such there is no discrimination against the members in the sitting arrangement in Panchayat meetings, but tea, water and snacks are not offered to Jagdish Parmar, the SC member. Whenever, eatables are to be served, the upper caste members see to it that Parmar leaves the Panchayat office."

In most of the village, three out of four, the SCs are not allowed to enter beyond the threshold of the village temples. At the most, they can have *darshan*, i.e., worship from a distance. There are variations within some of the villages, so that one temple is open for the SCs and restrictions are observed in another temple. For instance, in the village Kothamba Pella, in Panchamahals district, the SCs are not allowed to enter the *Mahadeo* temple, but can enter the temple of Goddess *Kodiyar*, who is considered to be the Goddess of the lower castes. Because of the restriction in temple entry, the Dalits in many villages, where they are in a large number, have constructed their own temples, in their localities to avoid confrontation. In three villages, the SCs youths insisted on temple entry. There was initial resistance, but they were not stopped. But in one case, Dalit youths were beaten up for violating the custom. They were told that they should maintain their *maryada*. "Law cannot help them in the village", a person from the upper caste told us. While we were in the village Eklera, Junagadh district, for the field work, we witnessed that Dalit girls were not allowed by the temple priest to perform *puja*, i.e., worship Lord Mahadeo, which was a part of *Shankar-Parvati Vrata*. While the investigator was talking to the girls, a Dalit leader of the locality prevented the girls from discussing the matter. He said, "Let us not discuss and precipitate the conflict. After all we have to live in the village and we cannot afford to have conflict with the upper castes. If the conflict accentuates, we would not get work. We depend on them for our livelihood". In the village Sokhada, Vadodara district, the Dalits were not allowed to light the *Holika* in 1995, by the upper caste youths, who asserted that the land on which it was to be done did not belong to the SCs. It was a village common land. The Dalits in two cases, had to seek protection of the Police.

In 1971, 44 villages had separate water facility for the SCs near their localities. Two villages have been added during the last twenty-five years in providing this separate facility to the Dalits. In normal times the problem of untouchability does not arise because there is separate water facility in different localities. But in a situation when taps are not working or there is a scarcity of water, the SCs experience difficulties in getting water from other localities. From the remaining 23 villages in which the SCs take water from the common source, untouchability is practised in 61 per cent of the villages. In most of such villages the women from SCs take water after the upper caste women; or their tap or position on the well is separately marked so they do not touch the SCs. But in seven villages, the SC women cannot fetch water from the well. They have to wait till the *Savarna* women pour water in their pots. The Dalit women are constantly shouted at by the upper caste women "keep distance, do not pollute us!" In response to our question, "why the SCs women are not allowed to fetch water from the village well?", a caste Hindu leader in one such village in Kheda district replied, "there is no one in the country who is more *sukhi* (happy) than them (SCs). When they asked the villagers for *rotalo* (bread), when they ask for other eatable and food grain, they get. If I go in their place, I would not get even a single piece of the food grain. When they go to well to get water, our women folk pour water in their pots, they do not have to do anything. What a great life they have! Are they not happier than you and me?"

If there is any sphere where the practice of untouchability has strikingly declined during the last twenty-five years, it is in the occupational activities—in buying and selling commodities. In 1971, shops in as many as 85 per cent of the villages, shop proprietors used to restrict admission of the SCs. Such restriction has been reduced to 30 per cent villages. Similarly, practice of untouchability in giving things and receiving money, has been reduced from 67 per cent to 28 per cent. A Baniya grocer said, "we do not observe untouchability in shop. Like other clients they too enter in the shop. We do not mind giving things in their hands. If we observe untouchability we would not get SC customers and our income will go down. We cannot afford that." However the shop owners in one-fourth of the villages still do not feel a need to adopt such pragmatic approach. They know that, as one of them bluntly put, "where else they would go"? Moreover, all those shop owners who do not discriminate against SC clients, they do not always treat them at par with the non-SC customers. The bargain power of the farmer is limited. In Kadi, Mehsana district, when a Dalit bargained with shop owner over the price of battery cell, not only was he, but other Dalits of the village were severely beaten up by the members of the dominant caste in 1995 (Desai and Parmar, 1995). A Dalit teacher in village Nigala, Sabarkantha district, narrated his experience: "Last year (1995) there was scarcity of kerosene, hence whenever the supply of kerosene used to come to the village, there was a queue to get it. I was in queue. When my turn came, the seller , Vaghari by caste, asked me to get out of the queue. I ask him why? He replied, 'Don't you feel ashamed for physically touching others. These *dhedas* (derogative word for untouchables) are shameless'. Other caste Hindus supported him and I was watching the scene helplessly... The *Savarnas* have no respect for Harijans, howsoever important position he is occupying. They maintain relationship so long they need you..." In this case the shop owner had no need of a client.

Status of being untouchable comes in the way of SC entrepreneurs to start a shop in a village. They fear that upper caste members would not buy from their shop, or they might get harassed by them. In a village in Ahmedabad district, a Dalit auto-rickshaw driver was severely beaten when he asked for the fair from a *Sarpanch* belonging to middle caste ... Though such cases do not occur everyday, they are not rare. More important, such incidents haunt Dalits and prevents them from exploring an occupation which might put him in a competitive state with the dominant castes.

Most of the tailors do not observe untouchability. They touch the SC client to take measurement. However, in most of the cases they do not repair used clothes of the Dalits. Nearly one-third of the potters observe untouchability, while selling pots to the SC clients. The case of the barbers is different. Most of them—nearly 70 per cent—refuse to cut hair of the SC males. The barbers belonging to Muslim community do not practice untouchability. Traditional patron-client relationship still continues, though the client pays in cash against service. A few barbers in a large village have set-up shops for hair cut. Many but not all, do not mind cutting hair of SC client. But in Kalamazoo, Kheda district, the barber shop owner refused to give service to Dalits. Nagindas and other Dalits complained to the Collector in 1985 that the barbers were not cutting their hair. The Police came and sealed the shops. The barbers then gave in writing to the government that they would cut hair of SC members. But since then the barbers do not open their shops and serve to non-SC by visiting their homes, as they used to do earlier.

I.P. Desai observed that "there may be less untouchability between the *savarnas* and the untouchable workers engaged in the activity of similar or the same social status and working in the same or the common situation" (1976:261). However, it was not found to be so. Untouchability between the SC and non-SC workers is observed in as many as 58 per cent villages. The situation was almost the same before twenty-five years. During the last two decades conflict between SC and other backward castes have increased in Gujarat. And, we observed that members of the OBCs, particularly in Central and North Gujarat and Saurashtra, practice untouchability relatively in more spheres than *Baniyas* and *Brahmins*. These are the castes, who have not much improved their economic condition. There is limited diversification in occupations within these communities. Moreover they follow the path of sanskritisation for upward mobility.

Untouchability has almost remained intact in the sphere of house entry. Except a few villages, SC members of village society do not get entry beyond the outer room of the *savarnas*. Even in the villages where younger persons do not believe in physical untouchability, and who serve tea to SC guests in their houses, entry in dining room is generally not encouraged. "I do not believe in untouchability. I have good friendship with SC members. We eat and drink together. But in the house we have to be somewhat careful because of elderly persons", a Patidar youth said.

Atrocities against Dalits

Though overt practice of untouchability in public spheres have declined, the cases of atrocities against the Dalits have increased during the last twenty-five years. Wherever the SCs asserted their self-respect and freedom of movement and occupation, they experienced the wrath of the *Savarnas*. As mentioned above, when they asked for temple entry or celebration of certain festivals, they were beaten up. The cases of murder and rape are not rare. During the anti-reservation riots in the mid-eighties, their houses were set on fire in a number of villages. When Dalits in a village in Ahmedabad district, cultivated land which they received from the government, their leader was hanged in the Panchayat building. The Dalits, not only are abused but also occasionally physically assaulted, when they make little hurry in trying to get water from common source of water. Table 5.2 depicts the registered cases with the police on atrocities against the SCs. The Prevention of Atrocities Act of 1989 has not been very effective in all these cases, in protecting the SC victims.

TABLE 5.2: Atrocities against SCs in Gujarat

Year	Murder	Serious Injury	Rape	Fire	Others	Total
1981	14	75	3	142	420	654
1982	13	66	6	25	345	455
1983	20	48	8	22	378	476
1984	13	63	10	12	484	582
1985	22	64	7	51	603	747
1986	18	61	9	17	558	663
1987	12	76	18	16	604	726
1988	14	50	21	10	570	665
1989	14	64	16	12	488	594
1990	18	71	14	16	841	960
1991	22	97	15	24	1138	1296
1992	29	72	11	17	1537	1666
1993	27	63	21	17	1623	1751
1994	15	73	34	21	1773	1916
1995	24	78	20	23	1631	1776

Source: Compendium on Scheduled Castes and Scheduled Tribes of Gujarat and Dadra Nagar Haveli, Ahmedabad: Office of the Director General and Inspector General of Police, 1996.

Overview

The problem of untouchability is a complex one. It is essentially a social issue, though its economic dimension is not unimportant. Traditionally it was related to economic status and occupation. In course of time, religious ideology and culture—value system, life style, inter-personal relationship etc.—not only did reinforce the economic and social divisions, but have formed the material base of segregation of residence, economic dependence, rituals camouflaging economic returns. Therefore, theoretically, has become difficult to isolate the structure from the superstructure, which has very much become a part of the material structure.

There is no striking change in occupation and economic condition of the SCs in the sample villages since 1971. A majority of them still work as agriculture labourers. A few received land from the government under various land reform Acts. But the land that they received is small in size without much infrastructure facilities. They do not produce marketable surplus. They continue to pursue traditional occupations such as removing dead animals and night soils, scavenging, sweeping, tanning, selling skins and bones etc. In few villages, they continue the practice of collecting *varu* (left over food) from *Savarnas*. However, a tiny number from SCs—varying from four to seventeen in most of the villages have taken high school and college education. A few have got employment in government and government sector. Such occupational diversity however has marginal impact on their social status in rural society.

Legal punitive measures, economic development, both of the SCs and the rest of the population, in terms of diversity of occupations; competitive polity and liberal secular values, have certainly affected inter-caste relationship in general and SCs and *Savarna* relationship in particular. The *Savarnas* who believe in the principles of purity—pollution as necessary but do not openly practice it in public spheres out of fear from punitive action are many. Consequently, practice of untouchability has been considerably reduced in some of the public spheres which are directly managed by the state laws and which have relatively non-traditional character, such as school, postal services and elected Panchayats. A number of villages observing untouchability on public roads, restricting free movements of the SCs, has considerably declined from 60 per cent in 1971 to 23 per cent in 1996. But we cannot say what I.P. Desai observed in 1972 that "it is nearly the established practice that the untouchable is not discriminated against in the public sphere" (1976:259). They are certainly not discriminated in all villages, but as many as 30 per cent of the village Panchayats still observe open or subtle discrimination with their elected members belonging to SCs. One would have expected by now, complete disappearance of untouchability in public transport and post offices as it was not widespread in 1971. But it has not happened. The proportion of the villages observing untouchability in these spheres have, in fact slightly increased.

Days are gone, when some untouchables imbibed the Brhaminical values of *dharma* and *karma* and accepted their station in life. We have not come across even an old man who would say: "you may have given up your religion, ... but we have not given up ours" (Hazari, 1969:153-154). Though there might be such a thing what Barrington Moore (1978) puts a, "pride in resignation", in the past, but it is hardly found now. They do revolt occasionally. Many of them assert their rights and that is the reason why the cases of atrocities against them are increasing. But at the same time all of them do not confront the dominant castes everyday out of the fear of failure. Some of them accept the situation as *fait accompli*—that after all "we have to live in the village and we are dependent on them". But they have not resigned to their fate and still come up with innovative tactics, as weapons that the weak use when they cannot openly revolt.

Acknowledgement

The study was sponsored by the Centre for Social Studies, Surat, under the project "Social Justice". The fieldwork was carried out by Rasik Parmar, Ramesh Vasava and M.D. Rathod, under the supervision of Kiran Desai. Satyakam Joshi helped me at the coding stage. I thank all of them for their assistance.

REFERENCES

Desai, A.R., *Social Background of Indian Nationalism*. Bombay: Popular Prakashan, 1948.

Desai, I.P., *Untouchability in Rural Gujarat*. Bombay: Popular Prakasan, 1976.

Desai, Kiran and Parmar Rasik, "Kadi: Signs of Dalit Assertation", *Economic and Political Weekly*, 15(26) July 1, 1995.

Hazari, R.K., *Untouchable : The Autobiography of an Indian Outcaste*. New York, 1969.

Isaacs, Harold, *India's Ex-Untouchables*. Bombay: Asia Publishing House, 1965.

Moore, Barrington, *Injustice: The Social Basis of Obedience and Revolt*. New York: M.E. Shape, 1978.

Mukherjee, Ramkrisna, *Society, Culture, Development*. Delhi: Sage, 1991.

Navsarjan, *Gujarat Dalit, Garib Hak Rakshak Samiti*. Ahmedabad: Navsarjan, 1997.

Nehru, J.L., *What India Wants*. London: India League, 1942.

Ranadive, B.T., "Caste, Class and Property Relations", *Economic and Political Weekly*, Annual Number, February, 1979.

6

STATUS OF DALITS AND AGENDA FOR STATE INTERVENTION

HARSH MANDER

Dalits in contemporary India bear the anguished burden of a long, unbroken legacy of the deepest social degradation. Whereas they usually fall at the bottom of almost any parameter relating to economic well-being or quality of life, the distinct burden that only they bear, among all underprivileged groups in India, is the degradation of centuries old tradition of untouchability. Unlike tribals, who have lived until recently in almost complete (but never total) isolation from mainstream civilisation, society and economy, Dalits have always been an integral part of these, but placed determinedly right at the bottom, below the ritually sanctioned "line" of pollution.

The word "Dalit" literally means poor and oppressed persons. But it has acquired a new cultural connotation implying "those who have been broken, ground down by those above them in deliberate and active way" (Zelliot, 1978). The term has been used chiefly to refer to ex-Untouchables, although more recently it has sometimes been extended to include other oppressed groups, such as tribals, women, bonded labour, minorities and so on. But for the purpose of this paper we will confine our usage to the popular interpretation of the term, that is, to ex-untouchables or the Scheduled Castes.

It is important at the outset to understand that the central problem and paramount aspiration of the Dalit is not only economic emancipation and improvement in conventional quality-of-life indices, although these are extremely critical, but equality and dignity within the traditional social order which has denied them justice and self-respect for centuries.

This is by no means to deny that the "pollution line" and the "poverty line" do very substantially overlap. The 1981 census indicated that 84 per cent of SCs reside in rural areas, against the all-India figure of 76.3 per cent. As many as 48.2 per cent of those employed are agricultural workers, as against an all India average of 25.2 per cent. In fact, 33 per cent of all agricultural workers are SCs. The next largest category among SCs is that of share-croppers and small peasants (28.2 per cent against an all India Share of 41.5 per cent). SCs form only 11.3 per cent of all farming households. Of these, 68.8 per cent have land below 1 hectare and 85 per cent below 2 hectares.

The picture is no different in the case of urban areas. Eighty-four per cent of urban SCs work as unskilled labour in the unorganised service sector, e.g., as loaders, porters, cycle rickshaw pullers, sanitary workers, brick-kiln, quarry workers, etc.

The situation is equally dismal with regard to literacy levels, as can be seen from Table 6.1.

TABLE 6.1: Literacy Rates Among Scheduled Castes and Rest of the Population

Year	Rest of the Population	Scheduled Castes
1961	27.86	10.27
	(16.59)	(3.29)
1971	33.80	14.67
	(17.11)	(6.44)
1981	41.22	21.38
	(29.51)	(10.93)

Note: Figures in brackets represent female literacy percentages.

Source: VII Plan Document. Delhi : Government of India Press.

It is clear from the above Table that SC literacy in 1981 had not even reached the position of the rest of the population in 1961. Even more regrettable is the fact that the disparity between the literacy of SCs and the rest of the population instead of diminishing from one Five Year Plan to another, has in fact been increasing. The gap between female literacy among SCs and in the general population is greater and the rate of increase in literacy among female SCs is particularly slow.

Thus poverty and lack of economic resources and literacy, both in rural and urban contexts, remain central to the Dalit existential reality. Therefore, state intervention for poverty alleviation, rural development, wage employment schemes, food security, implementation of laws relating to minimum wages, bondage, etc., must consciously focus most significantly on Dalits.

But in addition to this, special intervention, exclusively for Dalits relating to the practice to untouchability, is required. To what extent is untouchability still a major dimension of the life of Dalits in contemporary India is a question to which the following discussion is devoted.

Status of Practice of Untouchability

By the practice of untouchability, we mean the avoidance of physical contact with persons and things because of beliefs relating to pollution.

There are many empirical studies which indicate that untouchability continues to be an important component of the experience of dalithood in contemporary India, especially the countryside. We shall summarise the findings of only three studies in this regard. The first is the report of the National Commissioner for Scheduled Castes and Scheduled Tribes, April 1990. The Commission undertook a sample study in seven states of Bihar, Madhya Pradesh, Maharashtra, Rajasthan, Andhra Pradesh, Tamil Nadu, Karnataka and Kerala, and found that untouchability was prevalent in the following forms:

(i) Scheduled Castes did not have access to temples and other places of public worship to a large extent in UP, Tamil

Nadu, Kerala, Rajasthan and Karnataka.

(ii) A sizeable section of Scheduled Castes in Tamil Nadu did not have access to drinking water resources. A similar situation existed in UP, Rajasthan and Kerala.

(iii) Untouchability in the form of non-access to tea stalls and hotels was still found in UP, Tamil Nadu, Rajasthan and Kerala.

(iv) Barber services were not available to a section of Scheduled Castes in Tamil Nadu and to a lesser degree in UP, Rajasthan, Maharashtra, Karnataka and Kerala.

(v) Washermen services were not found to be available to a section of Scheduled Castes in Tamil Nadu. To some extent this disability existed in UP, as well.

(vi) In Tamil Nadu, Bihar, UP, Kerala and Karnataka, Scheduled Castes were found to be discriminated against in the matter of participation in social ceremonies.

(vii) Discrimination in matter of participation in sittings at village *Chaupals* and gram sabhas existed in Tamil Nadu and UP, and to a lesser extent in Rajasthan.

(viii) In Rajasthan a section of Scheduled Castes were discriminated against in educational institutions, public health centres, etc.

(ix) Discrimination in respect of use of utensils meant for the general public existed in UP, Tamil Nadu, Rajasthan and Maharashtra.

(x) Forced practice of occupations like removal of carcasses, etc., by Scheduled Castes was found prevalent in Tamil Nadu, and to a lesser extent in UP.

(xi) Scheduled Castes were discriminated against in the use of public cremation/burial grounds, public passages, etc., in Tamil Nadu, and to a lesser extent in Maharashtra and UP. Scheduled Castes were at a disadvantage in the matter of construction/acquiring occupational residential premises in Tamil Nadu, and to a lesser extent in UP. This includes access to *dharmshalas/sarais*.

The second is a study of untouchability in rural Gujarat by

Desai (1976).

According to the study, (see above Shah) barring untouchability in the village Panchayat, in all other matters in the public sphere, untouchability in the sense of (avoidance of) physical contact is no longer a problem.

In the private sphere, there is not that uniformity either, in regard to observance or non-observance of untouchability. If we further divided the private sphere into religious or cultural, domestic and occupational we might yet be able to discern a pattern. While it is true that in the private sphere untouchability is widely prevalent there are differences between certain groups of matters. For example, untouchability is very widely prevalent in regard to religious matters such as temple entry. It is equally widely prevalent in regard to what we have temporarily termed as domestic sphere and in which we have also included the shop of a *Savarna* Hindu along with his house.

The third sphere could be distinguished as the occupational sphere. It can be observed that significant changes are occurring in this sphere.

In the public sphere, except in the Panchayat, untouchability is no longer a overtly practiced phenomena. So far as the Panchayat is concerned the status acquired by the untouchable member due to the political position is nullified largely by his illiteracy, economic dependence and numerical weakness. However, in 53 per cent of villages these weaknesses are not effective as far as avoidance of physical contact is concerned.

The upshot of the inquiry is that, untouchability is strong in the religious and domestic sphere. It is less so in the occupational sphere and it is not a problem in the public sphere.

Similarly, in 1990, the Ambedkar Centenary Celebration Committee of Chittoor district of Andhra Pradesh, conducted an elaborate door-to-door survey over four *padayatras* to 249 villages to assess the prevalence of untouchability (Frontier, 1991). The following are some of their findings:

Throughout the district, as a rule, members of SC communities were not allowed into the houses of non-SCs. Even major towns like Chittoor, Tirupathi, etc., are exceptions to the extent that the rule does not apply to unknown persons. If a person belongs to an SC community from the same (or nearby) village as the resident of the house he is visiting, he cannot enter the house.

It is also not at all easy for members of Scheduled Castes to get accommodation in areas where non-SCs live either in the town or the village.

The *Padayatra* team came across 122 tea shops in 249 villages including 3 mandal headquarters where tea is served in separate glasses for SCs, and in most cases members of SC communities have to wash the tumblers themselves, both before and after drinking tea and hold the glass when the tea shop owner pours tea from a height.

Members of SC communities are not allowed entry in as many as 80 temples in 249 villages. This does not mean that there is free entry into temples in the rest of the villages. In most cases the temples are not enclosed by a wall. The deity is either placed on a raised platform or kept inside a small temple with space not sufficient to allow anyone inside. So there is no scope for either entry or preventing people from worshipping.

As a rule no barber in any village cuts the hair or shaves an SC. The SCs shave and cut their hair themselves or some of them turn into barbers to serve the rest.

What came as a shock to the *Padayatra* team was the fact that in at least 16 of the 249 villages visited, till date SCs are not allowed to walk through the streets with any type of footwear (Frontier, 1991).

Untouchability continues to be practised in many parts of rural India. But the situation is different in urban areas. There is in towns and cities far greater anonymity and occupational mobility, which enables blurring of caste identities. It has been revealed through studies that urban migration of Dalits, is often impelled not only by economic compulsions, but also to escape the social degradation of untouchability. But untouchability continues to be practised widely in cities in the domestic sphere (marriage, inter-dining, and social intercourse). As M.N. Srinivas puts it, "when the urban Indian puts on his shirt, he takes off his caste, but when he takes off his shirt, he puts on his caste". The study of Chittoor district referred to above reinforces this contention.

The situation is most acute for those Dalits in cities, who are still engaged in traditional occupations, such as scavenging. This author found in city after city of Madhya Pradesh that urban scavengers continued to be victims of untouchability, precisely because they were denied caste anonymity as a result of their continued adherence to their traditional "unclean" occupations.

Atrocities against Dalits

A related issue is that of atrocities against Dalits. The National Commissioner for Scheduled Castes and Scheduled Tribes (April, 1990) made a detailed study of atrocities such as murder, grievous hurt, rape, arson and crimes involving substantial loss of property of Dalits during the period 1983 to 1987, in five states: Bihar, Rajasthan, Madhya Pradesh and Tamil Nadu.

The Commission found an alarming increase in crimes against SCs (an 8 per cent rise between 1981 and 1986), especially murder and rape. There was an apparent link between atrocities, both of caste prejudice and untouchability, and political and economic issues regarding land, wages, indebtedness, bondage, etc. Disputes related to land were identified as the single most important cause, including disputes regarding implementation of land reforms, and allotment of cultivable land and house-sites, other conflicts centred around envy of a good crop raised by Dalits, use of community land, etc. Likewise, any attempt by Dalit agricultural labourers to agitate for reasonable wages were usually met with violence at the hands of the landowning classes.

Vulnerability of Dalits

The relative dissonance between economic and social parameters of deprivation is most acutely visible in relation to the status of Dalits engaged in traditionally "unclean" occupations, such as scavenging, disposal of human and animal carcasses, flaying and tanning, and prostitution. We have already noted that such adherence remains the primary reason for the survival of the practice of untouchability in the public sphere in urban areas.

These socially most disadvantaged Dalits are continuously confronted with a most tragic dilemma. Because of their continued adherence to occupations such as scavenging, which are indispensable for society but which no other caste group is willing to perform, their monopoly status ensures that they are economically more secure than almost any other underprivileged, under-resourced category. But this economic security is at the brutal price of the greatest social degradation, including being victims of untouchability in an environment of anonymity and economic mobility in cities. Yet, if they seek to escape this social degradation to achieve dignity, they have to abandon the economic security of their traditional occupations and join the vast ranks of the proletariat. This then is the core of their dilemma: If they seek economic security, they must, accept the lowest depths of social degradation; but if they aspire for social dignity, they must accept the price of economic insecurity and deprivation.

Caste in Non-Hindu Religions

The strength of the institution of caste in Indian tradition could also be understood by the manner in which it has permeated even the most professedly egalitarian religions, such as Christianity and Islam.

Traditional scavenging communities which sought social dignity through conversion to Islam, for instance, the Helas of the Malva and Nimar regions of Madhya Pradesh, have achieved no change in status except the right to read *Namaaz* in the mosques alongside their co-religionists. Otherwise nothing has changed, they remain scavengers, other Muslims deny them all forms of social intercourse except community prayers, and there are no inter-dining or marital bonds between them. In fact, along with untouchability, they also carry the newer burden of communal battering, because it is usually their *basti* the Hindu mob attacks first and most brutally, during the outbreak of any communal violence. The experience of the Pulaya Christians of Kerala, formerly untouchable Hindus, they continue to be treated as Untouchables even by the Syrian Christians, who enjoy high social and economic status.

Dalit Cultural and Political Assertion

A brief overview of Dalit status would be incomplete without a reference to the process of Dalit cultural and political assertion. This is reflected during the present century in the evolution of the designation by which Dalits have described themselves. From the *achhut* (untouchable) and *ati-shudra* at the turn of the century, the large majority in the community initially accepted with gratitude Gandhiji's new coinage "Harijan" (children of god) to escape the indignity of their earlier appellations. However, in the decades after Independence, to many within the community there appeared to be a flavour of patronising condescension in the term, and they preferred the neutral usage of Scheduled Castes found in the Indian Constitution. But after the 70s, the term "Dalit" has become increasingly popular, with its connotations of active anger, assertion and pride. "There is in the word itself an inherent denial of pollution, *karma* and justified caste hierarchy" (Zelliot, 1978). And more recently, the ambit of the term "Dalit" has been widened to embrace other oppressed categories, possibly as part of a growing consciousness to build a larger alliance of all disenfranchised and exploited groups.

However, Dalit assertion is not a phenomenon of the present century. The Bhakti movement, between the 10th and the 16th centuries, was at its core, a revolt against caste identities, untouchability, and especially restrictions on worship. It asserted equality before God (Shah, 1990). Such revolts against restrictions on worship continued sporadically through the centuries. More recently, the Arya Samaj, as also Gandhiji, sought to reinforce the traditional identity of Dalits as Hindus, but without the stigma of untouchability. Gandhiji during the freedom movement rallied public opinion against untouchability and sought to restore their dignity by gestures, such as living in scavenger *bastis*, adopting a Harijan girl, and cleaning his own toilet.

Baba Saheb Ambedkar was far more radical in his opposition to the caste system. He was convinced that untouchability was an integral element of the caste system and the former could not be overcome without destroying the latter. In his seminal address during the agitation by Dalits to draw water from Chavandar Lake at Mahad, access to which they had always been denied, he said, "It is not as if drinking the water of Chavandar Lake will make us immortal. We have survived well enough all these days without drinking it. We are going to the Lake to assert that we too are human beings like others". Towards the end of his life, Ambedkar was totally disenchanted with Hinduism, and felt that the path of dignity of Dalits lay in abandoning their Hindu identity. Along with many of his followers he chose to convert to an alternate "indigenous" faith, of Buddhism.

In independent India, the Left parties have neglected, even opposed, caste as a legitimate basis for forging the identity of and organising the oppressed. It was in 1972 that a radical group in Maharashtra constituted the Dalit Panthers, patterned after radical Black groups in America. The emphasis was on cultural assertion, pride and self-respect, with a central role for protest Dalit literature.

Organised political assertion by Dalits as a separate power group in North India is a comparatively recent phenomenon, sysmbolised most dramatically in the rise to power of the Bahujan Samaj Party, in the winter elections of 1993, to the Uttar Pradesh assembly. Coming as it did less than a year after the demolition of the Babri Masjid in Ayodhya, these results seem to suggest a new consciousness imbibed by Dalits. They seem to have come to understand that, so far they have been used by major political parties of the centre and the right, mainly the Congress and the BJP, to attain political power; the real agendas of both the parties are perceived to have had no real relationship with the problems and welfare of Dalits. The new assertion by Dalits, as a separate self-conscious political entity, is based on a shared perception of caste discrimination and oppression. This new-found militant and aggressive caste consciousness is in some way parallel to classical marxist "class consciousness", because it signifies an awareness of oppression and the consequent need for organised mass action to fight it. But it simultaneously runs fundamentally counter to Marxian class consciousness because the basis of a shared identity is not ones position in the mode of production, but in the ritual caste hierarchy of the society.

These are, of course, preliminary observations, which need to be empirically examined. What also remains to be seen is the extent to which this new dalit political assertion will in practice articulate and address the problems of the "lower depths" among Dalits, the scavengers and others in traditional "unclean" occupations, Dalit women, landless labourers, bonded labourers, unorganised unskilled workers in urban slums, etc. This experience will have important implications not only for future modes of political organisation and assertion by Dalits, but also for the nature of effective state intervention to be adopted for Dalits in future.

Strategies of State Intervention

The state has intervened in favour of Dalits in a variety of ways. These include: an array of constitutional and legal provisions; positive discrimination in government employment as well as in elected representative bodies, through reservations; budgetary support through the Special Component Plan (SCP) approach; special programmes of health and education; priority to SCs in all rural development, slum improvement and anti-poverty programmes, and technological changes such as conversion of dry latrines to flush latrines for release of persons engaged in traditional occupations.

These wide ranging measures have succeeded to some extent in restoring the balance of social, economic and political power in favour of Dalits. Yet, as we have seen in the earlier sections, not only does the poverty line substantially overlap with the pollution line, but Dalits do continue to suffer from caste prejudice, untouchability, and atrocities in large parts of the country. In the following sections some existing strategies, as well new measures which can make state intervention in support of Dalits more effective, have been examined. The attempt is only to indicate some possible directions for state action and initiate a debate on these issues, without staking a claim for comprehensiveness.

Let us first look at the existing constitutional and legal provisions. The Constitution of India contains a number of provisions for the removal of disabilities and discrimination against

SCs. These relate to prohibition of restriction of any access to public places (Article 15.2); reservation of appointments or posts in favour of any backward classes of citizens not adequately represented in the services under the state (Article 16.4); abolition of untouchability (Article 17); restriction of traffic in human beings and forced labour (Article 23); protection of right to admission to educational institutions (Article 29.2); special care for promotion of educational and economic interests of Scheduled Castes (Article 46), reservation in seats and special representation in Parliament and State legislatures (Article 334), reservation in services (Article 335); and appointment of a Special Officer for Scheduled Castes and Scheduled Tribes (Article 338).

The Prevention of Civil Rights Act, 1955, prohibits and provides penalties for enforcement of any religious disability in any religious place like a temple; social disability in public places like shops/ restaurants, hospitals, etc.; refusal to sell goods or render services because of considerations of untouchability, and demand of compulsory labour relating to untouchability; like scavenging, sweeping, removal of carcasses, flaying animals, etc. It contains provisions for all offenses to be cognizable, for minimum punishment and summary trials. The Scheduled Castes and Scheduled Tribes (Prevention of Atrocities) Act, 1989, specifies the atrocities which are liable to attract penalties under the Act. These are, forcing the eating of noxious substances, dumping waste matter on land, denudation, wrongful occupation of land, dispossession, bonded labour, intimidation during voting, mischievous litigation, false information, public humiliation, outrage of modesty, sexual exploitation, fouling of water source, obstruction of entry to a public resort, eviction from habitation, mischief with explosives, destruction ofbuildings, and suppression of evidence. These offences under the Prevention of Atrocious Act, carry heavier penalties than similar offences under the Indian Penal Code. The Act also provides for forfeiture of property, externment and collective fine.

In addition to these special enactments, there are other protective measures of special relevance to SCs because they, along with the STs, constitute a substantial proportion of the disadvantaged persons whom these enactments are meant to benefit. These are the Bonded Labour System (Abolition) Act, 1976, the Minimum Wages Act, 1984, and the Child Labour (Prohibition and Regulation) Act, 1986.

Despite this impressive range of protective legislations, the record of implementation of these measures has been dismal. Social, economic, administrative, and judicial arrangements are heavily weighted against the poor with regard to the response of the law and order machinery to atrocities against Dalits. Both the National Commission for SCs and STs and the National Police Commission documents reveal recurring pathologies, such as delays in reporting, refusal to register complaints, delayed arrival on scene, half-hearted investigation, failure to cite relevant provisions of the law, brutality in dealing with accused persons of the weaker sections, soft treatment of accused persons from influential sections, and failing to make arrest on consideration of modification. Poor quality of prosecution, protracted pendency and procedural delays before courts, and high percentage of acquittals were some of the other common maladies documented by these bodies.

Among specific examples, the National Commission for SCs and STs found that investigating officers visited the place of crime after a lapse of more than 12 hours in a very large number of cases, even when the crimes committed were murder, rape, grievous hurt, and arson. Such delays would naturally result in the destruction and suppression of evidence. The Commission also found an abnormal delay (beyond 60 days) in the filing of charge-sheets in as many as 72 per cent cases involving SCs in Bihar, and 50 per cent in AP. The percentages for MP, Rajasthan and Tamil Nadu were 27 and 42 per cent, respectively. The study has shown that even in cases where the provisions of other enactments like the Bonded Labour System Abolition Act, 1976, get attracted, police officers, at the station house level, continue to cite only the IPC provisions in the charge sheets.

These various pathologies are also reflected in the high rate of acquittals in atrocities cases against SCs. In Tamil Nadu, acquittals were as high as 88 per cent of the cases disposed of. The percentages in Andhra Pradesh and Rajasthan were 62 and 71 per cent, respectively. In cases of atrocities against Scheduled Tribes, the corresponding figures for Tamil Nadu, Andhra Pradesh and Rajasthan are 75, 74 and 42 per cent, respectively.

In several states, special police stations for SCs and STs have been set up, but unwieldy jurisdiction and demotivated staff have caused only further hardships to the victims of untouchability and atrocities. The same tokenism is also reflected in the setting up of special courts for speedy trial of atrocity cases for which there is provision in the Atrocities Act, 1989. Most states have resorted to designating the existing district sessions courts as special courts, which in practice contributes little to the speedy implementation of these cases.

The situation is further complicated because of the uncomfortable reality which is usually not confronted, is that in a large number of cases involving SCs and STs, the opposite party is actually the state. Thus the Dalit litigant does not only have to cope with the extreme inequity of the legal system and the economic strength of the opponents, but also with the power and majesty of the State itself as adversary.

What are the measures that can be adopted to remedy the intrinsic imbalance of our legal system? A few suggestions are outlined below:

Legal Aid Guarantee Programme

One of the most important measures proposed is the enforcement of a legal aid guarantee programme in every case, criminal, civil, forest, excise, etc., where one party belongs to the SC/ST community and the other is a non-SC/ST, even if the opposite party is the state itself. In fact, it is suggested that the law be suitably amended to ensure that the presiding officer of any court is legally debarred from processing any case of such a nature until satisfactory legal aid has been provided to the Dalit litigant.

It may be argued that since in most states some kind of a legal aid programme is in existence, such measures would be superfluous.

However, legal aid is at present implemented in a highly token form, with lowly paid, briefless, demotivated lawyers who are offered cases in only a few of the wide range of suits involving the weaker sections. Barring the local patronage they enjoy, they are at a distinct disadvantage.

What is being proposed here is a guarantee programme. Legal aid should no longer remain a matter of discretion in a small proportion of cases involving weaker sections. It should be recognised as the obligation of the state to provide adequate and effective legal aid to every case where a Dalit is confronted with an unequal adversary, including the state.

Secondly, the lawyers must be paid at the prevailing market rate, and should be freely selected by the Dalit litigant himself or herself. This will ensure that Dalit litigants are not given the services of rejects; instead they can avail of the best locally available legal talent. The involvement of the legal aid lawyer should further be reinforced by an incentive scheme of additional payment to the lawyer in all such cases in which the judgment in the concerned court goes in favour of Dalits.

In atrocity cases, it is often the experience that because of overwork and lack of social orientation, public prosecutors often do not ensure a high and rigorous quality of prosecution. Here again, what is proposed is the setting up of an extensive panel of senior and experienced lawyers, and the selection of special public prosecutors in each atrocity case with the consent of the concerned victims of atrocities.

It is believed that only such a legal aid guarantee programme, in which the operational words are guarantee and consent of the litigants, will ensure that Dalit litigants have any real access to the legal system to redress the many injustices heaped upon them.

Other Legal Support

Such a legal aid guarantee programme should also cover, all cases in which a Dalit is pitted against a non-Dalit or the state, travel expenses and daily allowance for the litigant and witnesses for journeys to the police stations and courts, and photo copying fees, etc.

Support of Public Interest Litigation and Voluntary Organisation

In the highly unequal fight between Dalits and their adversaries, activist voluntary organisations, wherever they exist, have been found to provide valuable legal and moral support to the victims. They give legal guidance, ensure that cases are registered, the victims and witnesses are not pressurised, investigations are not deliberately delayed, and so on. The state should provide financial and administrative support to such NGO groups, and may even take the initiative for motivating such NGOs to come up where they do not exist, especially in atrocity-prone areas.

Side by side, it is now a well-established principle that persons who are disadvantaged because of social or economic disabilities may not themselves seek redress against injustices. This has been evocatively brought out by social activist, Nandita Haksar, who has said in the context of bonded labourers:

> "It is hardly likely that a bonded labourer working in a stone quarry will even think of moving the Supreme Court. Bonded labourers are non-beings, exiles of civilisation. The bonded labourer has no hope. A human being without hope cannot dream of going to the Supreme Court. It is only a socially committed individual or a politically aware organisation that can speak on his behalf (RNCSCST, 1990)."

Therefore the law now recognises the right of any public-spirited individual or social action group to move through a writ petition for enforcement of the legal rights of a disadvantaged group. In consonance with this our legal aid programmes should also now broaden the ambit of their agenda to support such public interest litigation.

Measures for Improving Response of Law and Order Machinery

We have already noted how a highly demotivated, overburdened, and often deeply prejudiced law and order machinery results in difficulties in registration of complaints, poor quality of investigation, and high rate of acquittal in atrocity cases. A series of measures are proposed to make some dent in this problem.

The police administration already has a well-developed system of monetary rewards and medals as tokens of recognition for good work done. It is necessary to only consciously extend this reward system to accord high priority to and encourage prompt, impartial, and effective investigations in atrocity cases. For instance, for investigations in such atrocity cases which end in conviction, attractive rewards may be instituted for the investigating officer. Medals may also be awarded for consistently high quality of investigation in cases involving the weaker sections.

Postings to special police stations for weaker sections, as also to Scheduled Castes cells, etc., are normally considered a matter of punishment at all levels. It is suggested that a substantial special allowance be given for postings to these police stations and cells, and that at least one year's posting in Scheduled Caste sections be made mandatory for qualifying for every level of promotion.

It is also necessary to consciously reduce the mechanical reliance on crime statistics. A higher rate of registration of cases of atrocities, for instance, may reflect not a declining security environment for Dalits, as it may superficially appear, but on the contrary a more responsive police administration now registering atrocity complaints, where earlier they were simply not being registered.

In the manner that gender sensitisation programmes are being organised for government official at all levels, a similar package of training programmes should be regularly organised at all levels of the regulatory, police and development state machinery, as also the judiciary, in an effort to sensitise them and influence their attitude towards the weaker sections.

Vigilance Committees should also be established at *thana* and district levels, comprising on the one hand members of the executive and judicial magistracy and the police, and on the other, elected and NGO's representatives, and representatives of educated local youth and weaker sections to oversee registration of complaints, investigation and progress of cases. For instance, if a Dalit is unable to register an atrocity complaint in the police station, he or she should have access to appeal to the committee, which in turn should be suitably empowered to make necessary recommendations to the Station House Officer.

Other Recommendations to Fight Atrocities

The National Commission for SCs and STs has made a number of other recommendations in relation to atrocities, which include:

(a) Revocation and suspension of gun licences in places where atrocities have occurred;
(b) liberal invocation of provisions of Bonded Labour System (Abolition) Act, 1976 and other such measures, vesting of powers with executive magistrates wherever such provisions exist, and resort to summary trials;
(c) review of debt relief legislation on an all-India basis and framing of guidelines incorporating salutary features of various state enactments;
(d) instead of opening special police station for SCs/STs, special police officers or head constables be posted in all police stations for such cases; and
(e) establishment of special courts exclusively for atrocity cases.

Mass Legal Literacy and Mobilisation for Legal Action

Strong protective laws for weaker sections, even when backed by a legal aid guarantee programme of the kind proposed above, are necessary, but not sufficient to ensure that the weaker sections do actually avail of these legislative measures to secure protection and justice. These are enabling conditions, but there is no substitute for mass legal literacy and mobilisation for legal action.

In the absence of adequate public action, it is necessary for a humane State, committed to social justice, to intervene effectively to ensure such legal literacy and mobilisation. This is a relatively unmapped territory, and such strategies require imagination, creativity and social sensitivity.

For instance, texts may be prepared in simple local languages, elaborating all the relevant provisions and laws as well as practical details such as rights, legal aid facilities, who should apply in what circumstances and in what format, etc. Volunteer resource persons in government run SC and ST hostels, both form within and outside the government, may be first educated with regard to the relevant legal provisions and procedures. These young persons, equipped with their new found legal literacy and texts, may be encouraged in their holidays to educate in turn their own communities, as well as to initiate legal action in the event of atrocities, untouchability, bondage, and injustice in issues relating to land, wages etc. It should be clear that such mobilisation for legal action would be fragile in the absence of a legal aid guarantee programme.

Alternately, wherever total literacy campaigns are in progress or have been successfully completed, legal literacy and mobilisation for legal action can be effectively integrated into both the learning and post-literacy phases.

Restructuring of SCP Strategy

The device of the Special Component Plan (SCP) was introduced in the budgetary mechanism to ensure the earmarking of separate plan outlays for the development of SCs. This has ensured the allotment of substantial plan funds for SCs yet the share of SCP in the total plan budget is still well below the percentage of SCs in the total population of most states.

However, what is far more serious is the grave distortions in the implementation of the SCP strategy. One common problem is the widespread tendency to lapse SCP funds. Even more problematic is the propensity of the large majority of departments to mechanically book under SCP, programmes which are not even remotely connected with the welfare of SCs. Such diversions can be achieved with even greater impunity than in the case of TSP, because Dalits do not live in geographically contiguous areas. Instead, their settlements are highly dispersed in most regions. Therefore, it is possible to portray almost any general infrastructural programme as one whose benefits accrue to SCs. This ensures only a mechanical adherence to form, with a complete subversion of the content.

The State has been somewhat more successful in ensuring diversion of a significant share of poverty alleviation programmes to SCs. A review by the Department of Rural Development, Government of India, during 1988-89, found that 28 per cent of beneficiaries belonged to SCs in Integrated Rural Development Programme (IRDP), 38 per cent in NREP and 40 per cent RLEGP. A mid-term appraisal of the Seventh Plan recommended a greater share for SCs. It must be kept in mind that government statistics in these programmes often distort and hide the real impact of these programmes on beneficiaries. The limitations of self-employment strategies such as IRDP, apply even more acutely to the most economically and socially deprived categories, but the significance of wage employment programmes, especially with a food-for-work component, for these groups cannot be underrated.

However, there is no doubt that the SCP strategy needs fundamental restructuring. The SCP component of the plan budget, in proportion to the SC population in the state, should be separated at the outset from the general budgetary mechanism and taken out of the purview of various government departments. The SCP should instead be almost completely delegated to the districts in proportion to their respective SC populations. Here, they should be used exclusively for programmes which meet the genuine, direct and felt needs of SCs. In particular, the highest priority needs to be accorded to identifying SC settlements, both in villages and towns, and ensuring that there minimum needs are met and basic facilities are systematically provided. As we saw in an earlier section, Dalits continue to be victims of untouchability and abject poverty in large regions of the Indian countryside. They continue to reside mostly in hamlets separated from the caste Hindu settlements. These SCs settlements are still denied access to water, primary schools, health facilities, approach roads, internal drainage, electrification, etc., although many of these may have been created out of SCP funds. Therefore, after careful identification, SCP funds should be utilised exclusively for time-bound project aimed at meeting the basic needs of these settlements by the turn of the century. The same approach needs to be extended to urban slums, which usually have a high proportion of Dalits, but which are totally deprived of even minimal human facilities.

Health and Education Strategies

As we saw at the outset, literacy levels among Dalits, especially the women, are abysmally low. A major component of state intervention strategies for Dalits has therefore been for raising literacy and educational standards among SCs. The principal strategies have been providing incentives like scholarships, freeships, mid-day meals, uniforms, books, stationery, establishing SC hostels, reservation of seats and relaxation of standards for admission to institutes of higher learning, remedial coaching and special coaching for competitive examinations, etc.

Whereas one endorses almost all these strategies with the provision that far greater stress has to be placed on quality and also on the magnitude of efforts required, there is one specific strategy with which there is fundamental disagreement. This is the establishment of separate SC hostels. Whereas separate hostels make enormous sense for tribals, because of the remoteness and extreme dispersal of their settlements as well as their distinct cultural identity, a mindless and mechanical duplication of this strategy for SCs can be counter-productive. As we saw at the beginning, the central aspiration of the Dalit is reintegration into the social order on a basis of social equality and dignity. Separate hostels only provide state sanction to their segregation. Instead, the state should sponsor general hostels for indigent and meritorious students, with substantial reservation of seats for SC boys and girls.

Existing educational and literacy programmes also need to be restructured in line with the new approaches in this sector for all sections of the rural poor, with stress on mass mobilisation and participation, voluntary support, flexibility, and innovation.

This applies also to public health systems, assuming that SC settlements have even less access to whatever minimal health infrastructure is available than the general population. By and large, the same remedial measures would apply as in the case of the general rural and slum populations, except that even more careful targeting of these services would naturally be required for specially disadvantaged categories. The strategies would include greater stress on prevention, health education, upgradation of skills of traditional health workers like *dais*, and development of the basic health skills of village workers.

Liberation from Traditional 'Unclean' Occupations

As we have already seen, the anguish of the socially oppressed Dalit is most acutely centred in those still trapped in traditional "unclean" occupations, such as sweeping, scavenging, tanning and flaying, disposal of carcasses, prostitution, etc. We have also noted that the practice of untouchability in the public sphere in cities continues mainly because specific communities continue to be engaged in scavenging of dry latrines, carrying of night-soil on their heads, cleaning of drains and streets, etc.

There is no doubt that the beginning of the end of untouchability is possible only when these castes are liberated from these professions. So far, what has been done to liberate them has mainly be conversion of dry latrines into flush latrines, and supplying scavengers with wheelbarrows, handcarts and implements such as gumboots, gloves, buckets, etc. The progress even in these measures has been negligible and these anyway do not go to the heart of the problem. Only recently in 1991, a centrally sponsored scheme has been launched to systematically survey and release scavengers from their traditional occupations.

We have already noted the tragic trap in which the scavengers are caught: If they seek social dignity they have to accept economic insecurity by abandoning a profession over which they have monopoly rights. Whereas, if they cling to economic security, they remain victims of untouchability even in the otherwise anonymous and mobile socio-economic environment of cities.

Therefore, it is simplistic to suggest that routine loans for alternative economic activities will be adequate intervention for liberating scavengers. The cruel trap can be broken only by a major programme of mobilisation of scavengers to accept the risks of breaking free from their traditional occupations. The next step would be a careful selection of alternatives, and ensuring that these are completely caste neutral and dignified, economically secure and viable, and preferably part of the modern economy. In every other kind of self-employment programmes, an unemployed impoverished family is being assisted to improve its economic status by entering the informal sector. Here a person, already securely entrenched in the formal sector is being motivated and assisted to enter the informal sector. Therefore the state has a special responsibility to carefully nurture these new ventures and ensure that they do not fail.

Given the will, this is not an insurmountable task because the number of persons engaged in "unclean" occupations is not large. According to the Report of the National Commissioner for SCs and STs (1979-81), India had a scavenger fleet of about 6.5 lakhs, distributed over 3,119 towns. There is also a widespread belief, even among policy-makers, that traditional scavengers do not want to be released. The experience of this author, based on fieldwork in scavenger *basties* throughout the state of Madhya Pradesh, has been to the contrary. Especially, the younger generation, including women (who even within scavenger families alone actually handle night-soil) are eager to take the plunge to liberate themselves from their traditional occupations, provided they are convinced about the credibility of alternatives and of the implementing machinery. They are eager to labour to acquire dignified new skills and willing to accept some risk and even lower remuneration. Educated scavenger youths have developed skills in computers and electronics, and women have been trained in handicrafts such as hand printing and dyeing for which the state handicrafts corporation guaranteed marketing support. The extraordinary pride and speed with which they acquired these alternative skills should set at rest all misgivings about their motivation, or of the feasibility of the paramount task of liberation.

REFERENCES

Desai, I.P., *Untouchability in Rural Gujarat*, Bombay: Popular Prakashan, 1976.

Frontier, "*Untouchable Still*", Vol. 23; no. 47, 6 July, 1991.

Report of the National Commission for SCs and STs (RNCSCST), Delhi: Government of India (different years).

Shah, Ghanshyam, "Dalit Movements and the Search for Identity", *Social Action*, October-December, 1990.

Zelliot, E. Dalit: "Dalit: New Cultural Context for an old Marathi Word", in Contributions to *Asian and African Studies*, 1-2.1.1978.

7

UNTOUCHABILITY IN URBAN SETTING
Everyday Social Experience of Ex-Untouchables in Bombay

RAMESH KAMBLE

In the Introduction to his edited volume on *Dalit Movements and Meanings of Labour,* Peter Robb observed that the powerful and intrusive forces such as colonialism, capitalism, communications or English law influencing the Indian society and economy, have coexisted with the force of specific cultural memory in India (Robb, 1993:66). The practice of untouchability, notion of segregation, imposed inferior status and socio-economic marginalization, as one of the most oppressive and traumatic aspects of India's cultural memory, continue to characterize lives of ex-untouchables in Indian society. Designated in the traditional society as polluting to other castes, they were made to settle outside the village without any access to basic civic necessities. Their physical contact, even their shadow, was considered polluting. The practice took a pervert and inhuman form when untouchables were made to tie earthen pots around their necks and broom behind, so that the earth should not be polluted by their sputum and footprints. Of course this polluting designation of untouchables did not desist high castes from using them as menial slave labourers, paying them a pittance as a constant reminder of the masters benevolence. Thus, we are confronted with a peculiar form of slavery, in which the slave labourer was kept inhumanely segregated and inferior; and the high caste master extracted maximum labour without taking an adequate responsibility of his slave labourer. Moreover, the Brahminical *dharma*, through the religious code *Manusmriti*, systematized perennial slavery in the lives of untouchables, by closing all avenues of social and economic prosperity.

Indeed, over the last two hundred years this scenario has changed and factors such as industrialization and urbanization have effected unprecedented changes in the lives of ex-untouchables. These forces have provided the basis for their independence from enslaving, oppressive and exploitative rural social situation and acted as an impetus for their struggle against this oppressive social condition. Further, in the post independence era, along with the adoption of the Constitution, we have witnessed measures such as abolition of untouchability, protective discrimination etc. for the community.

However, despite legislative initiatives and various policy efforts, the ex-untouchables continue to remain abjectly poor, subject to forced labour, discrimination, economic exploitation and brutal socio-religious atrocities. Though, there have been some gains, particularly in the areas of education and employment in governmental services, the condition of bulk of the people, as the Commissioner for Scheduled Castes and Scheduled Tribes points out, has not improved and in many cases it has further deteriorated (Commissioner, 1989:2).

In everyday life situations ex-untouchables are subjected to segregation, insult, humiliation and frustrations. In this regard earlier studies such as, J.M. Freeman's study of Bauris in a Orissa village, reveals that in everyday social life Bauris are suppressed, cheated, insulted and used by the so called high castes[1]. Even the recent volume on caste by Searle-Chatterjee, which argues that western anthropologists have 'epitomized' Indian society in terms of caste and that there is a need to 'put caste in its place', does not deny the centrality of caste as lived, and performed reality in Indian social life and its oppressive and inescapable character (even in diaspora) in the untouchable's everyday social experience (Searle-Chatterjee and Sharma, 1994 :9).

This paper attempts to understand notions of discrimination, imposed inferior status and marginalization experienced by ex-untouchables in urban situation, through the case study of three ex-untouchable castes from Maharashtra, namely, Buddhists (formerly Mahars), Matangs and Charmkars (leather craftsmen). I would seek to understand how do the life situations and work situations reiterate their identity as ex-untouchables in the urban context; and how do they perceive themselves and react to this imposed inferior identity in the urban context; are these perceptions and reactions generally identical or necessarily complex, diverse, varied, situated and conflicting in nature. What are thc factors and forces which generate diverse—sometimes contradictory—actions and reactions about commonly experienced segregation and marginalization by these three castes. Finally, do these castes feel a need for cooperative efforts to fight their subordination and marginalization.

The paper draws on informal interview sessions with and observations of these individuals in concrete settings, such as places of dwelling and work. Accordingly I would deal with ex-untouchables in BIT *Chawl* (Mazgaon), Ramabai Nagar (Ghatkopar), Dharavi, cooperative housing colonies at Kandivili[2] as places of dwelling and government, public sector offices and academic institutions, as places of work.

Bombay: Context of Change, Contestation and Subordination

Since Bombay city has been an important context for socio-economic changes in the lives of Buddhists, Matangs and Charmkars, it would be pertinent to review their social experience in this city.

However, before plunging into this discussion, it is useful to briefly touch upon their historical background in the rural society of Maharashtra. The 1991 Census of India enlists 59 Scheduled Castes in Maharashtra (Census, Statement 8, 1991:38). And their total population is 87,57,842 (Handbook, 1994:26). Among these, Buddhists, Matangs and Charmkars are (in that order) most in number.[3] In the traditional society Mahars were the major field labouring caste and within *balutedari* (jajmani) division of labour, were general village servants responsible for removing dead cattle, sweeping village roads, serving as guides and messengers for government officials, escorting the government treasury, assisting in arbitration of boundary disputes over land claims, acting as village watchmen and so on. As village servants they had claims on *watan/ inam* lands (Omvedt, 1994:68)[4]. In Vidarbha region, they were also weavers of coarse cloth, and had a strong military tradition in Maharashtra (*Ibid.*:70). The Matangs also provided general field labour. Their traditional caste duty in the *balutedari* organization of labour involved rope making (*Ibid.*). They also made brooms and baskets, and played drums at village ceremonies. Whereas the Charmkars were engaged in leather craft which involved making of chappals (shoes) and other items needed in the agricultural economy—muzzles, blinkers, belts for cattle, and *pakhals* (water carrying pots) used for irrigation. The association with leather craft had two important implications for Charmkars: it made the village dependent on them, ensuring greater access to the village in terms of intermingling with other castes; and better economic position compared to other untouchable castes. This situation made Charmkars claim higher status than other untouchable castes in the caste hierarchy.

With the arrival of the British, specially their presence in Bombay presidency, new opportunities were opened up for the untouchables in Maharashtra. Mahar's employment as soldiers in the company's army, and as cooks and butlers in British homes, sowed the seeds of awareness in them. The rise of Bombay as an urban centre of commercial, and subsequently, industrial activity, offered still further possibilities for gainful employment for the untouchables.

In 1661, when Bombay was ceded to the British, population of the island was 100,000 and by 1864 it rose to 816,522 (Morris, 1965:11,13). The increase in trade and industrial activity provided impetus for construction of port facilities and improvement of internal communication systems such as, railways and post and telegraph. This contributed to a steady increase in population of Bombay in the form of weavers, goldsmiths, iron smith, traders, construction workers, coolies and so on. This migration to the city, however, as Chandavarkar points out, 'occurred within the framework of caste, kinship and village connections and migrants to the city lived with their co-villagers, caste fellows, and relatives and sought work with their assistance...' (Chandavarkar, 1994:10,11). This meant that caste and kinship groups' competition for labour opportunities and the urban space in the city, helped invigorating the rural caste divisions in the city's life. Thus in textile mills, which had become the mainstay of Bombay's industrial activity, vast majority of the working class population belonged to Kunbi/Maratha castes from Konkan and deccan plateau. These groups also dominated the better paid weaving sheds and resisted entry of any other group, mainly Mahars, in them.

For the untouchables, labour options were available in the form of coolies in railways, docks and in construction work, and subsequently in the ring-spinning departments of textile mills. Their population in 1864 was 3.92 per cent of Bombay's total population and in 1921 it rose to 11.53 per cent (*Ibid*.:72). The Mahars worked as coolies in building trade and in the docks, railways, factories and companies (Chandavarkar, 1994:223,226; Pradhan, 1938:54,56). In the Port Trust, the Mahars were predominantly *mathadis* (head loaders) hired to shift cargo on shore. Indeed they monopolized the Mathadi gangs in the Port Trust and resisted entry of any other group. Here we should note that though both Maratha/Kunbis and Mahars tended to dominate certain labour opportunities in the city, the Marathas/Kunbis monopolized high paid (weaving) section, whereas Mahars dominated the low paid coolie jobs. Moreover, despite their dominant position in the *Mathadi* work, Chandavarkar points out that they were made to shift the most offensive (difficult to carry) cargo (Chandavarkar, 1994:224). Later they gained employment in textile mills, mainly in the ring-spinning departments where in the late nineteen-thirties their percentage was around 70 to 80 per cent (Morris, 1965:75, Pradhan, 1938:55). However, any attempt for their entry in weaving sheds was resisted by the Kunbis/Marathas. For instance, in the years following the general strike of 1928, the Bombay Millowners Association's attempt to recruit untouchables in the weaving sheds was resisted by the Maratha weavers on the grounds that working with untouchables would defile their (Marathas) ritual status. Because, 'whenever a weft bobbin was replaced, yarn had to be sucked into the shuttle. If untouchables were employed, other groups working with the same shuttle would have been ritually defiled and polluted' (Morris, 1965:79). This was an expression of untouchability in the urban setting, as it involved both the notion of pollution and an attempt to marginalize untouchables from skilled and better paying labour options.

For Charmkars, with their traditional role as leather craftsmen, the rise of Bombay as an urban and industrial centre, provided labour opportunities in shoe-making and other articles of day to day use. *Daboro* (jars made from leather), leather scales, saddles and bags were popular items among residents of Bombay in the late nineteenth century (Gazetteers, 1909:481). However, the real boost to leather production came from the textile industry, which needed bands and belts made from leather for pulleys and machines (Chandavarkar, 1994:76). Similarly, the Second World War, apart from setting the city's looms in motion, also gave rise to the production of boots, army bags and so on (*Ibid.*:120).

Though Matangs were part of the untouchable groups in Bombay, their number was relatively less. The reasons for their small number (till the nineteen-sixties) could be located in their acceptance of the *balutedari jati* duties of Mahars in villages, who had either migrated to city or refused to carry out the caste duties as a protest against the imposed inferior status and treatment.[5] Nonetheless, during the thirties, we witness a spirit of awakening among Matangs in Bombay, where they were part of the unskilled labour force.[6]

Thus, not only in villages but even in the city, untouchable's segregation in employment continued.

If the experience of employment was segregatory, the experience of settlement too was not without it. Even in the city untouchables were forced to live in separate ghettos in extremely unhygienic conditions. The untouchable workers were often excluded from working class *chawls* by its landlords or residents, and were forced to live in huts and sheds called *zavlis* made of corrugated iron and wood. Dr. Burnett-Hirst observed that 'persons from depressed and Backward Classes frequently find great difficulty in obtaining accommodation, as no other community will stay near them. When they cannot find room in the *chawls* set apart for them, they live in huts or sheds' (cited in Chandavarkar, 1994:181). These sheds, Dr. Burnett-Hirst pointed out:

> "are level with the street and are not high enough for a person to stand erect. The tins are fitted together with stones etc. and men, children, chicken and goats are herded together as one family. Each big shed is divided by cloth droppings into four or six rooms, occupied by four to six families. There is no light, or ventilation, and such huts are absolutely unsuited for any human habitation....There are no taps, latrines, no water supply....(*Ibid.*)."

Indeed, accommodation in some *chawls*, mainly in those constructed by the Bombay District Development Board (BDDB) and Bombay Improvement Trust (BIT) became available to the untouchables. However, settlement in these *chawls* too tended to be organised on caste lines. If untouchables came to be concentrated in some *chawls*, the caste Hindu labourers generally preferred those in which untoucahbles were absent. This pattern continue to exist even today in many of these *chawls*, maintaining the caste character of urban space in Bombay. Though, it could be argued that caste and region based character of urban space occurred because of the reasons of security and as a basis for seeking employment, the caste Hindu settlers' aloofness in terms of everyday social interactions with untouchables in the 'untouchable *chawls*' seem to suggest that caste organization of urban space was—and is—mainly due to caste bias.

Despite the segregatory experience both in employment and settlement and the fact that they remained labourers engaged in impure and menial, and unskilled jobs, the possibility of wage employment meant relative freedom from the servile social relations of work in the rural set up. This independence from exploitative and oppressive rural milieu provided an impetus for their movement for self-dignity and struggle against the caste system.

Thus the emergence of Mahars as urban working class (their percentage in textile mills was 9.05 in the 1911, which increased to 11.91 per cent in 192: Morris, 1965:74), created a ground for their movement against the unequal status and treatment. The nineteen-twenties witnessed an independent self-assertion of untouchables for equal rights and self-dignity in the form of Mahad tank satyagraha and burning of the *Manusmriti*, as this religious law code sanctified iniquitous caste structure and violated the basic human rights of the untouchables. However, since these movements did not bring in the desired change in the caste Hindu's attitude towards the untouchables, the untouchables' struggle, led by Dr. Ambedkar, focused on the economic, educational and social improvement rather than temple entry and inter-dining (Source Material, 1982:102). It is important to note that in the struggles of Chavdar tank and *Manusmriti* episode and in the later radical economic and political struggles, the untouchable workers of Bombay played the leading role. Further the spirit of awakening and revolt, as Gail Omvedt points out, did not remain limited to the city but was 'transferred back and forth from city to villages, back and fourth from an emerging educated section to the working class and poor peasant masses' (Omvedt, 1994:142).

The attempts for political representation during the early thirties under the leadership of Dr. Ambedkar made the untouchables an important force in Indian politics. This political assertion of untouchables created a situation of confrontation between Gandhiji and Dr. Ambedkar whereas, Gandhiji argued for moral and social reforms and protection from above, Dr. Ambedkar was convinced that without political rights and economic measures the slavery of untouchables could not be removed. Moreover, disturbed by Dr. Ambedkar's representative status, the Indian National Congress 'sought to organize meetings of the untouchables, manoeuver Dalit spokesmen...who took a line opposing Ambedkar... to show that untouchables are denouncing Ambedkar' (Omvedt, 1994:172). It is necessary to see that these attempts on the part of the Congress further added to social divisions among the untouchables and sowed the seeds of political rift, mainly between the Mahars and Charmkars, which continue to haunt Dalit social and political life in Maharashtra even today.

Amidst the challenges of 'Gandhian paternalism' and the communist's indifference towards the problems of untouchable workers in textile mills, dismissal of the problem of caste and untouchability as 'bourgeois divisiveness' and treating untouchables' struggle as 'separatist' and 'pro-British', the Untouchables' economic and political struggles did not only contest the issues of marginalization and discrimination suffered by them, but essentially, as the experience of Ambedkar's Indian Labour Party (ILP) reveals, the larger issues affecting the working class and peasantry. Thus Ambedkar's Independent Labour Party in its programme stressed on the workers in the unorganized sector, offered land resettlement and public works to aid the unemployed and landless. It promised measures to save peasants from the clutches of money-lenders, put up a strong opposition to land revenue, and campaigned for legislation for a more equitable system of tax as well as the establishment of land mortgage banks and agricultural producers' cooperatives and marketing societies. It also promised protection to tenants of *khot* landlords. Later the ILP also led the struggle to abolish the *khoti* system (Omvedt, 1994:193). Thus right from the nineteen-twenties onwards Bombay had become an important context of untouchable assertion and movement as the city was the centre for many important conferences of the Depressed classes and their political organizations in the Bombay presidency.

However, despite the ongoing social, economic and political struggle; and various legal and policy initiatives in Independent India, the ex-untouchables continue to suffer social segregation and marginalization. In the Bombay city bulk of them continue to reside either in the separate *chawls* in overcrowded condition or in separate slums at the outskirts of the city, where the living condition continue to resemble Dr. Burnett-Hirst's description during the nineteen-thirties. According to an informal survey conducted in the year 1991-92 by a voluntary organization—Bombay Urban Dwellers Federation—around 70 to 75 per cent of ex-untouchable population in the city stays in slums.[7]

As regards employment, large section of ex-untouchable population in the city is either unemployed or forms part of the unorganized labour force. Indeed since the early decades of the present century, ex-untouchables have received opportunity of wage labour in the organized sector in the city. Though options were still available in the same menial, 'impure' and unskilled work, wage employment meant relative independence from servile social relations of work in the villages and possibility of a guarantee of minimum rights. Later employment in governmental services, though generally in class four category, also ensured independence from servile relations of work and contributed to the spirit of awakening. However, in recent times the paucity of labour options in the organized sector has reintroduced servility in the lives of Dalits. This has negative implications for their self-perceptions, social consciousness and the movement for changing the social order.

Since there is a lack of systematic data on the present socio-economic condition of the ex-untouchables in Bombay, I would use the case study approach to understand these issues. I intend to examine experiences in three localities, namely, BIT *chawl* at Mazgaon (mainly inhabited by Buddhists), Mata Ramabai Nagar at Ghatkopar (Buddhists and Matangs) and Dharavi (Charmkars).

Inscription on the BIT buildings at Mazgaon reveals that these buildings were constructed in the year 1924. There are three buildings in this chawl-cluster. One witnesses castewise settlement in these buildings. Thus No. 1 is populated by the OBCs/Kunbis/Marathas. No. 2 is occupied by the Buddhists and in No. 3 there are Christians (majority) and Buddhists.

Since nineteen-thirties three to four generations of Buddhists have been staying in this locality and it has been a strong centre of Ambedkarite movement since that time. From the accounts of older residents it is clear that many of them have been brought up here. That their parents, generally illiterate, worked mainly as *Safai kamgars* in the Municipality, and as *coolies* in Railways and Port Trust, and in textile mills. The present old generation, i.e., the second generation, were absorbed, due to the policy of employing one son of the family in various organizations, in their fathers' work places. Since this policy was generally limited only to one member of the family, others went through various occupations before settling into specific jobs. Their ability to read and write, apart from helping them in upward occupational mobility later in their service, also made them active members of the Ambedkarite movement. Some of them took initiatives in organizing districtwise or regionwise organizations for social and educational upliftment, and became important local activists of the Republican Party of India.

With awareness about education as an important source of upliftment and social status, the upcoming generation, both boys and girls, were sent to schools. Through the avenue of the Municipal schools, boys and girls were educated upto seventh standard. Some of them could reach college education (through the Siddharth Collage, 'our college', as they put it). Like their fathers, many even now work in the municipality class four jobs. But the nature of their work participation has changed. Many now work in different departments such as maintenance (maintenance of the BMC buildings: schools, hospitals, offices, residential quarters etc.), water department (on pumping operations), public health departments and hospitals (as ward boys). Those with slightly higher educational background have secured class four or class three category employment in Government and semi-government organisations. This generation is sensitive to social and political issues and provided the main support base of the Dalit Panther movement. However, it should be noted that those who were pursuing higher studies, rather careers, generally kept themselves aloof from such activities.

The large part of the present generation, which is between the age group of 18 to 25 years, is frustrated, confused and indifferent to social issues. For though educated upto the 10th standard (many of them have not been able to clear the tenth standards despite repeated attempts) they have been either jobless or are engaged in contractual or unorganized sector on daily wages with remunerations which rarely cross Rs. 1000 a month. My inquiries with this group revealed that some of them now work in the same professions as their forefathers, i.e., on the *kachara gadi* (garbage carrying lorries).

However, unlike their forefathers who worked as organized sector workers, these boys work as casual labourers on the contract basis. Still others are engaged in unskilled work, as helpers in various works such as painting, plumbing, in automobile garages or as watchmen for private security agencies. Moreover, I came across some who told me that they are working in 'private' and 'industry', which means in small manufacturing units in unorganized sector. Recently, slightly better educated (upto 12th standard) among them have found jobs in courier services and as sales men for new consumer products manufactured in small units on a commission basis. However, since all these employment opportunities are in informal sector or on contract basis, it involves absence of the guarantees of stable employment, of minimum and stable wages, of fixed and regular working hours or basic minimum right, such as right to health insurance, compensation against injuries and provident fund. Thus such a vulnerable position has reintroduced servile social relations of work in their life. Of course the large chunk of the present generation do not have possibility of employment even in the unorganized sector. Without any role in productive processes or in service sector, we witness the process of lumpenization gradually entering in their lives. My interaction with them suggested that they are aimless, unsure, even unconcerned, about what they would do in future. For them 'passing time' today is the immediate concern. I observed them standing whole day at the gates of their building. With 'nothing to do' and lack of financial resources, some of them have become totally indifferent to the issues of atrocities, injustice and marginalization. I also witnessed that some of them are taking lead roles in organizing the 'Hindu' cultural festivals in the locality which was known for its vibrant *dalit consciousness*. Moreover, as opposed to the earlier generation, this generation of Buddhist was more communal in outlook.

Many in these buildings live in inhuman conditions. Rooms of 12/15 ft. size is generally shared by 6 to 10 members where it is difficult to carry out even the day-to-day chores. Many, because of the ever growing family size (by marriages of sons), have left their rooms. Those with relatively stable economic condition have attempted to secure houses in cooperative housing schemes in the suburbs, whereas the poor have ended up selling the room, and shifting to the slums in the suburbs. This throws up the tempting parallel of the village life of the untouchables, where too they reside outside the village space.

Compared to the BIT *chawl*, the settlement at the Mata Ramabai Nagar, a slum settlement near Ghatkopar, is of recent origin. The local social activist informed me that it came into being in 1964. It has various small hutment-clusters known by different names, for instance, Bouddha Rahiwashi Sangh, Dadasaheb Gaikwad Nagar, Nalanda Chawl Committee, Annabhau Sathe Nagar, Magasvargiya Jhopadpatti Vikas Sangh and so on. The settlement is largely populated by the Buddhist and Matangs, who have been either later migrants to the city or those who had to sell their one room dwellings in the heart of the city due to growing family size or indebtedness. The Buddhist here exhibit similar awareness about education. Some of them are graduates and few post-graduates too. However large number of the youths have either gone upto SSC or, because of repeated failures, have given up education at this level. Hence occupationally, though there are some doctors, teachers in Municipal schools, class four and class three employees in government and other services, sizeable number of them is either unemployed or employed in 'private', i.e., informal sector. Some of them self-employed, such as Auto-rickshaw drivers, wiremen (electricians), *Benjo party* (music party for marriage and other purposes). However since this type of employment does not have any security or stability in terms of work or wages, here too we witness servile relations of work being introduced in the city. Compared to Buddhists, Matangs are less conscious towards education. However, as they observe change in general awrareness, better self-esteem and life style among the Buddhists, Matangs too have become aware about the need for education as an important source of self-development. As a result one witnesses insistence on enrolling children in schools and pursuing higher studies. Among Matangs too there are teachers, clerks, peons in government services and in banks, but their number is remarkably low.

If the experience in BIT *chawl* and Ramabai Nagar exhibits exploitation and marginalization, the reality in Dharavi where the Charmkars have settled is also not without it. Some worked in the tanning factories, whereas many others came in to cater to the demands of growing urban population. One old charmkar in Dharavi described to me how his father used to make chappals, shoes and sell them by moving from place to place. Since then many changes have taken place. Leather activity has grown into an important business with high returns and with it the charmkars have been either ousted from the trade or exist as leather labourers. Today many charmkars in the city work as *Gatai kamgars* (workers repairing leather goods) at the street corners. However, here too getting licensed place has become extremely difficult. Thus though a *Gatai kamgar* makes Rs. 50 to 100 a day, there is no surety of such earnings.

In Dharavi many charmkars work as skilled craftsmen in small leather goods manufacturing units where bags, belts and other fancy items are produced. Earlier these craftsmen used to manufacture limited quantity of goods for the retail markets. However, since prices of raw materials have gone beyond their reach, these craftsmen have become leather workers. Here too they are in a vulnerable position. Though they earn around Rs. 3500 to 4000 per month, these returns are not stable. They fluctuate as per the fluctuating market for leather goods and there are irregularities in receiving wages too. The owner of the units would pay them only when they (owners) get their payments from distributors. The principle of fluctuation also apply to the number of working hours. If the orders are large and urgent they could easily stretch upto 10 to 12 hours a day. And sometimes, because of non-availability of orders, there are lean periods of no work. In these situations the craftsmen generally are paid in advance by the unit holders who in turn borrows from the agents. The system of advance payments binds the worker to the unit holder even if he does not have work at the unit. The unit holder has paid him through his lean periods and if he joins other unit it would ruin the possibility of work in future. Thus these conditions have introduced servility in Charmkar's life in the urban centre. In addition to the *karigars* (craftsmen), there is a growing class of unskilled labour force among the Charmkars in Dharavi, who neither have learned skills in leather nor have they succeeded in education. In absence of any other work, they now work as sole pasters. And as unskilled labourers they receive only around Rs. 800 to 1000 a month.

Of course, as a result of years of urban experience there has emerged a class of educated Charmkars in the city. They are employed in government services and other public undertakings. Among Charmkars too (atleast the educated ones) there is an awareness about the need for social and economic development. However, as many Charmkars in Dharavi told me, concerns of these educated Charmkars are generally limited and centred around their personal gain and they have been indifferent towards the issues of exploitation and marginalization experienced by their brethren.

Both in terms of employment and physical settlement in Bombay, we witness that the members of these three ex-untouchable castes continue to experience exploitation, marginalization and servile social relations of work.

The question that arises is if their social and economic experience is more or less identical, are their self and social perceptions identical too? In other words, enmeshed in similar plight, do they respond to it in similar manner? Answer to this question is at one level, one finds realization of the need for united action, whereas at another, they are sharply divided and tend to see each other as causes of their deprivation. Various factors have contributed to their disunity in perceiving the similar plight. Before we go into this, let me point out some specific experiences from the case studies.

For a long time, the settlement at the BIT *chawl* has been a strong support base of Ambedkarite movements. Many old Buddhists here, even today, recall the vibrant and charged days of the movement. Further this place has also been a strong centre of political mobilization of Republican Party of India and later of the Dalit Panther movement. However this consciousness is, atleast in the younger generation, gradually warning. The youths of this generation, which are largely unemployed or engaged in casual daily wage labour, are either frustrated or so embroiled in the problems of day-to-day existence, that often they are indifferent towards the larger issues of the movement. In contrast, the Buddhists at the Ramabai colony exhibit keen political consciousness and readiness to revolt against the caste hierarchies. One witnesses charged atmosphere at the *chowk* in the evenings, with people always ready to join a *morcha* or other forms of protest concerning the issues of atrocities and injustice. However, this social and political consciousness does not have an ability (or even awareness) to transform structures which reiterate such servility.

Matangs at Ramabai colony have become aware of their need to assert themselves. However, though some of them have been closely associated with Buddhists in the ideological struggle against the caste system, many have remained aloof or, following some Matang leaders and casteist Hindus, have become antagonistic towards the Buddhists. They now consider the Buddhists as responsible for their deprived conditions. As a result, one finds them now as strong supporters of *Hindutvavadi* (Hindu communal) parties. Indeed there is a group of college going students and activists among Matangs, who feel the need for remaining away from the *Hindutvavadi* parties. However, this voice is extremely weak and feeble. One Matang youth told me that in the villages, Mahars and Matangs have stayed together, in cities too they share this pattern. But, as they were ideologically divided in the villages, they are divided here too. That the political forces have been dividing them intentionally because if united they would disturb various political equations in Maharashtra. Some Buddhists and Matangs, who are not 'Ambedkarites', do not join the struggle against the hierarchical Hindu social order, lack Dalit consciousness and hence are of little importance to them. Of course, some of them (Buddhists) now realize that it was a mistake to have distanced themselves from Matangs in the post-Ambedkarian phase of Dalit movement.

As regards Charmkars in Dharavi, we find that some of the old generation still have sympathy with Congress, whereas the youth have become active workers and convinced supporters of the *Hindutvavadi* parties. They are quite aloof from Buddhists and anti-caste, anti-*Hindutvavadi* ideology. They tend to view both Buddhists and Matangs as lower than themselves in the traditional caste hierarchy. My interaction with Charmkars revealed that they too are treated as low caste by the caste Hindus. However, this does not bind them with other ex-untouchable castes in the struggle for an egalitarian social order. The reasons for Charmkar's social distance from other ex-untouchable caste could be located in their (Charmkar's) rural and urban experience. In the rural society, the village needed their services for agricultural and consumer purposes. Thus the Charmkars had greater possibility of intermingling with the village and also relatively better economic condition than other lower castes in Hindu caste hierarchy. Compared to them the Buddhists and Matangs were agricultural labourers or menial village servants, who were treated as slaves by the village community. Thus in an atmosphere of clearly spelt out and rigidly followed social hierarchies, Charmkars' access to village community has made them perceive themselves as superior than other lower castes in the caste hierarchy. Though marginalized and exploited, even in the urban setting, their concerns are social and economic development and not the change in caste structure. As a result Charmkars and Buddhists are sharply divided, even hateful towards each other, in Bombay.

As pointed out earlier, various factors have contributed to the disunity among the Dalits. The reasons for this indifference towards each other are rooted in their internalization of the principle of caste hierarchy (even by the Buddhists), past experiences and current politics.

These members (class four employees, informal sector and daily wage labourers) of ex-untouchable communities do feel that they experience caste discrimination in everyday social life. Both at places dwellings and work they feel there is no caste prejudice. However, my observations of their work environment, for instance in Municipality, suggest that the supervisors and clerks of high caste (also of backward castes) often harass them in delaying their leave forms, in transfers from one department to another, neglect their queries and so on. Of course, the supervisors would act differently, i.e., with affinity and respect with the non-Dalit members of the class four employees. Among the class four category employees of ex-untouchable castes working in public undertaking's offices, we encounter a complex process of accommodation and resistance against caste prejudice. The Buddhists, for instance, would participate in *Satyanarayan Puja* (which otherwise they would criticize as irrational) organized in the office, for maintaining better relations and ensuring cooperation in the office. This does not mean that they do not resist such a situation but their resistance depends on their strength and awareness in the particular office. Thus one witnesses that their responses are essentially situated and varied. Nevertheless, compared to the educated ex-untouchables, the class four employees experience caste prejudice in lesser intensity. However, this is because of their settlement patterns and the occupational status. Since the urban space in Bombay is organized on caste basis, the ex-untouchables too are settled in the caste specific dwellings. In such dwellings there is no possibility of caste prejudice, atleast in the immediate neighbourhood. Of course, even in the immediate neighbourhood, the caste Hindus, however less they may be in number, tend to practice social distance towards the ex-untouchables. The feeling one encounters at a deeper level is clearly that of '*us* and *them*', and these divides do not only characterize the social relations among the caste Hindus and ex-untouchables, but exists even within the three ex-untouchable castes. Moreover, the occupational status of ex-untouchables as unskilled unorganized sector labourers and class four employees in government services make them more vulnerable and dependent. Thus even in the urban centre, in case of the majority of ex-untouchables, the nature of their work has not changed. As a result they are not in a position to pose challenges to the traditional social hierarchies. The experiences of caste prejudices in the changing socio-economic situation are more prominently prevalent, as we shall see later, in the everyday social lives of educated and occupationally well placed ex-untouchables, because by the virtue of their occupational mobility, they are in a position to challenge the traditional hierarchies. In the following pages we would try to understand quotidian experience and resistance of the better of ex-untouchability.

II

I intend to present representative case studies of better placed ex-untouchables such as class three government servants, students pursuing higher education and a class of professionals and bureaucrats from amongst the Buddhist, Matang and Charmkar communities.

Case I : Clerk

Raju Bansode, a Buddhist, works as a clerk in a public undertaking. He is educated upto twelfth standard and hopes to continue his studies further. He joined this office seven years back as a peon and now been promoted to the level of a clerk. When I approached him, he was trying to make sense of some purchase correspondence in a bunch of files. I noticed that his office is a context for various Hindu Gods and Goddesses. Framed photographs of various Gods and Goddesses were hung all over the office, I also noticed Dr. Ambedkar's photograph under the glass top of his table. When I told him the reason for my visit, to know about the new forms of untouchability, he asked me to wait in the canteen fearing that people might get suspicious. In the canteen we started the conversation about his work. He told me that he is new at the purchase department table and it is really difficult to understand things as no one is willing to teach him the basics. He recalled his days as a peon. Being a young enthusiastic boy, ever ready to do any work, he was greatly appreciated and liked by his caste Hindu colleagues. They took him for tea, shared lunch with him. Of course there were times when food of his lunch box was refused on the plea of dislike for that particular item or on the pretext of observing 'fast'. However, the happy days were over the moment he ceased to be a peon. As a clerk he had his own table and chair, and was no more a service boy-helper in getting files, opening cupboards, fetching glass of water for clerks and so on. Thus his becoming a clerk, becoming one of them, equal to them was disliked and scorned at by his 'friends' from Hindu community. His regular trips to the canteen along with them became less frequent or stopped and he often found himself either alone at the lunch table or with his earlier peon colleagues. His minor mistakes were blown out of proportion and linked to his caste background. Raju also narrated experiences of his fellow ex-untouchable colleagues to me. 'The non-SC superior in the office would not give us *important desks,* so that we would not get to know the important areas of administration. In case we are assigned these duties, non-cooperation is always the fate'. Further, 'our direct recruitment as senior clerk is hated by most, because that would make us 'superiors' in the office and many non-SCs will have to work under us'. Raju told me that the photograph of Dr. Ambedkar he has, suggests that he does not identify with the Hindu culture, however such assertion also means isolation and harassment if Ambedkarites in that department are few in number. Some of his 'Ambedkarite' colleagues, who, though proclaim radical consciousness, talk about struggle, are more concerned with their promotions than the issues of exploitation, atrocities experienced by the common Dalits.

Prashant Dabholkar, a Charmkar, works as a clerk in a nationalized Bank. He has been working for the last five years. With *tilak* on forehead he appeared quite at ease with his colleagues. To my query about the new forms of untouchability, he responded by saying that these things do not exist now and in the urban context it has died out. He introduced me to a colleague from caste Hindu community and said that we treat everybody as equal here. As a strong supporter of Shiv Sena he maintains that everybody who stays in Hindustan is a Hindu. He was a active member of the *Satyanarayan Pooja* Committee. When I asked him how did he get this job, his reply was: "through the reservation policy". However whenever his friends expressed their anger and hatred towards the policy of reservation, he either kept aloof or reacted by saying that people from the 'quota' are often weak in their work and should prove their merit. His bank has a unit of SC/ST Employees Union. However, his participation in its activities is limited only to the demands of implementation of reservation policy in promotions. In private he told me 'these Buddhists, though educated now, are lower than us in the hierarchy'. Prashant, though claims to be a Hindu, does not form a part of the core group of high caste Hindus—Marathas and Brahmins in his bank.

Nivruti Sakpal, from Matang community, is a junior clerk in a government office. He too was a peon before getting promoted to this post. Minor mistakes on his part are treated with the remark that 'a promoted peon is bound to make such mistakes'. He shares a complex relationship with both Hindus and Buddhists. His attempt is to get assimilated into the group of Maratha caste colleagues, though he resents the way they treat him. As regards his relationship with Buddhists, one witnesses that he tends to consider them as responsible for his community's lack of property. In his opinion, highly educated Buddhists have captured all the jobs, hence his community is left with nothing. However, his experiences of caste prejudice and feeling of resentment towards it sometimes provides the ground for the associative action between him and his Buddhist colleagues. Here too, his not being a Buddhist, i.e., not being converted to Buddhism, creates social distance between them.

Case II : Students

Tushar Londhe, a Buddhist, is a student at an institute for higher level professional course. He stays in the institute's hostel. Right at the time of his entry in the institute his lower caste background was known to everyone as his name in the list of the admitted students was placed in a separate list for the Scheduled Castes. In addition to this his hostel mess card and the library card too mentioned his Scheduled Caste background. Though this is an administrative necessity, it also serves as a source of greater discrimination. The non-SC/ST students generally feel that "these lower caste students have impinged on our rights for higher education". Tushar told me that despite the hard work and sincerity in pursuing their studies, the SC boys, because of years of imposed inferior status, still are not free from a feeling of inferiority and lack of self-confidence, especially when amidst the non-SC colleagues. Hence, there is always a hidden urge on the part of SC students to share their achievements with the so called high caste colleagues and receive their appreciation. This is an attempt to prove that 'I am no less' in anything, but it also speaks about the perennial inner turmoil and desperation of having to prove their worth. Of course, Tushar also told me that 'there are numerous examples of our students who feel that only upper caste people can appreciate their achievements as our people are not educated. These students gradually come to feel that they are different from other SC students and get alienated from them. They even tend to believe that 'our students are worthless'. Thus we see that an SC student himself becomes a instrument of discrimination.

Though in the everyday interactions on the campus and in the hostel, discrimination is rare, the Scheduled Caste students do not form part of the core groups of caste Hindu students. Further in hostel the resentment against 'Reservation Policy' is so acute that the Scheduled Caste students fear disclosing their identity and shy away from openly arguing in favour of the policy. Though there are some who openly declare their identity as SCs and assert themselves, they suffer isolation from other students, sometimes also from Scheduled Caste students. Another interesting aspect of campus life is the interpersonal relationships among boys and girls. Though the group life of boys and girls do not exhibit caste discrimination, the intimate relationships (which result in marriage) are undoubtedly formed on caste lines. The high caste girls, Tushar told me, definitely share our company, but keep away from getting into serious relationships. Even if they get into such a relationship, it mostly depends on the future prospects of the boy. The bright Scheduled Caste boy who gets into intimate relationship with a high caste girl is also pleased with himself. That a upper caste girl (who is mostly from upper middle or middle class) has chosen him. Hence, he is always insecure that he should not loose her. As a result he gets completely isolated from 'our' boys, from the community and commitment towards Dalit consciousness. Loses sensitivity towards the issues of injustice, atrocities etc. He starts complaining about the lack of hard work, sincerity and motivation on the part of 'our' students. He says "see I have come up with hard work. Now they are changing. Absorbing us. Feeling of caste is dying now." Now he talks about *economic basis*, the '*creamy layer*' and becomes scathingly critical about the movement. Thus in the process he becomes a self-centred middle class person. Such relationships resulting in inter-caste marriages, one of Tushar's friends told me, "have created middle class Dalit Brahmins. Their children have been socialized not into the Ambedkarian ideology of change and struggle, but encultured with the cultural traditions of the enslaving ideology." Hence, this "pillars of future change" are changed completely. With better socio-economic background, they have an edge over other Dalit students in availing benefits of the Reservation Policy. This is not unique to the children of inter-caste marriages, but also true in case of children born in the Dalit middle class background. Moreover, even those who constantly harp on caste discrimination, injustice, etc. are quite detached from their own less fortunate brothers. They treat less educated people in an unequal manner or even with contempt. Never get really disturbed with news of atrocities or participate in students or people's protests. For, it is below their 'dignity'.

Samir Shinde, from Charmkar community, is an engineering student. He comes from an educated family and is bright and sincere in pursuit of his career. In his everyday interactions I found him always in the company of the so called high caste/class friends. He does not experience any discrimination in everyday life. His upper class friends from different region, (who are generally unaware about the lower castes here) think of him as a Maharashtrian Hindu. Even his Maharashtrian Hindu friends are not really sure about his caste as his surname does not clearly indicate his caste, though some of them have found it out when he went to collect his Government of India Scholarship given to the SC/ST students. Since then some of them have become resentful towards him. He is a devout Hindu, sometimes even shares socio-political and cultural ideology of *Hindutwa*, and at the same time is quite detached from and critical of Ambedkarian movement. He is accepted by his upper caste friends. However the recent Cobbler's Scam has disturbed him. Though he does not know what *he* could do about this. He does not think of protesting against it. In future he has plans to help starting educational institutes for Charmkars. He thinks they should get educated and come out of the leather activity because it has made them low in the social hierarchy.

Case III : Professionals

Siddarth Gaikwad is a lecturer at a prime academic institute. He was born in an agricultural labourer's family from one of the remote villages of Maharashtra, where he had his early education. He has come a long way. Working as *saldar* [working for land owning master on a yearly contract basis in return of two meals a day (of course he never got the same meal eaten by the owner's family), two dresses (of cheap variety), some grain at the harvest times and Rs. 100 per year] he supported himself while completing his matriculation. While in college he has worked as ironing boy in a laundry. Though a teacher himself, Siddarth does not have much to share about his school teachers. "I hate the teacher community, for I do not remember any teacher who has helped me during my school days". While in the fourth standard when he received a merit scholarship, his teacher was surprised and commented "how come you (a Mahar) got this". His note books never got good remarks, but those who had copied it were always appreciated and encouraged. Siddarth and other students from untouchable community were severely beaten for small mistakes. Despite this Siddarth could clear his SSC examination. It was only in the College that he realized the importance of a teacher's role in life. For teachers here made him aware about the social issues.

Right at the time of his appointment in the present job, he was confronted with caste prejudice and preconceived notions of his 'incompetence'. Though they did not express anything openly, the prejudice was clearly expressed through their indifferent and sarcastic looks. This experience was extremely painful as he was being judged as inefficient without experiencing him as a teacher and scholar. It was more painful because he could not do anything immediately to change this perception. Of course despite this experiences of 'imposed incompetence', he tried to overcome this feeling of unwanted 'outsider' through hardwork and diligence. The change in his image could happen only with those students who came in his contact. His colleagues always speak with him politely and in respectful manner. However, with their common students they 'casually' mention his background by remarks such as, 'though from Scheduled Caste background he is a good scholar'. Siddarth feels that this new form of untouchability is basically a power struggle. "Now that (despite all odds) we have achieved things in life , have become aware about our rights, the Hindus feel that we should not challenge their supremacy, in everyday social life or in the field of scholarship." If this was his experience with learned colleagues, how did the less learned, i.e., the supportive and clerical staff react to him? For them the dilemma was that in the institute he is higher in the hierarchy, whereas by his caste background he is lower than them. Hence, their reactions were quite complex. Sometimes they would address him as 'Sir', at other they call him by his Surname (caste name). These experiences have made Siddarth more sensitive to the problems faced by his fellow Dalit colleagues, students and the large mass of marginalized in the city. However, these concerns are not necessarily shared by the majority of his Dalit colleagues in the institute. Many of them, though well read in Ambedkarian thought, are driven more by their immediate personal interests of promotions (even conceive their interests as that of the community's) than the marginalization and servility experienced by ex-untouchables in the city. Contrary to their claims that 'Ambedkarian movement has introduced self-respect in our lives', many of them would not mind making compromises, even assume servile postures before the authorities, if it suits their self-interests. Thus the notion of Patron-Client relationship survives in the urban context due to the narrow self-orientations of some of the better placed ex-untouchables. The notion of 'imposed inferiority' has been internalized by some of the better placed ex-untouchables, as they tend to value the comments and judgments of the so called upper caste colleagues more than their fellow brothers and accept their 'constructed images' of the fellow Scheduled Caste brothers.

Siddarth often visits his village, as his parents still stay there. Now as an highly educated person from the village, the villagers, caste Hindus, treat him with respect. They invite him for tea in their houses. Further though the basic structure of the villages has remained the same, i.e., ex-untouchables continue to stay at the outskirts, they now stay in pucca houses. The 'villagers' now invite them for their marriage ceremonies and feasts. However, they continue to be positioned in the gathering, in a segregatory manner. With the government's efforts, village wells have been constructed closer to the ex-untouchable's *Bastis,* so that their segregation is minimized. However, these attempts created a new situation. The caste Hindus fetch the water from western side whereas ex-untouchables are asked to use the eastern one. With processes of modernization wells have been replaced by taps. Even here too we find that at the common water sources ex-untouchables are asked to take water after everybody has finished or if the person is already at the tap, the taps are cleaned very carefully by the caste Hindu before fetching water. With the policy of 'Reservations', in some cases the post of *Talathis* (village level administrator) have gone to ex-untouchables, and in politics, ex-untouchables have become members of village Panchayats. However, Siddarth told me that 'these positions have been used by the dominant landowing masters for their own political equations. Moreover, the Panchayat has also been used to create rifts among the ex-untouchables in villages. Matangs are now told by the villagers that your rights have been appropriated by these educated Buddhists. That you people have remained loyal to the village, have provided your services when the village was in need (when Buddhists refused to carry out the imposed degrading caste duty) and the villagers have provided for you, therefore you should not join the Buddhist who have left our ancestral religion and distanced themselves from the village. The larger political forces have also taken advantage of the situation and divided Buddhists and Matangs for their interests.' This process, says Siddarth, 'has been accentuated since the Sena-BJP forces have come to power in Maharashtra'.

Bhau Gaikwad, from Matang community, is also a teacher/scholar working in an academic institution. His experiences of 'imposed inferiority', and 'incompetence' are similar to that of Siddarth's. He is well read in Ambedkarian thought and convinced that it was only due to the struggles and movements led by Dr. Ambedkar that the ex-untouchables are experiencing liberation and socio-economic development. However, 'the mentality of caste', Bhau says, 'has delimited the scope of Dr. Ambedkar's struggle. Despite all his (Ambedkar's) efforts the Matangs have perceived him as leader of the Mahars, whereas even the Mahars have perceived him in the same casteist terms. As a result, the attempts of caste Hindus to divide these two exploited and oppressed communities, have been successful. Despite his known ideological orientations, he feels, the Buddhist colleagues still exhibit invisible distance from him. That despite being an Ambedkarite and 'Buddhist', in the sense of rational world-view, his not undergoing 'ritualistic conversion' sometimes creates hurdles in their common concerns. He says that 'if the Buddhists and Matangs are to be united in the common struggle, the Buddhists should pay attention also to the oppression suffered by Matangs'. That 'if this is not achieved immediately, the Sena-BJP forces will further divide them to the point of closing all the possibilities of a broad based struggle'.

If the notion of 'imposed inferiority' pervades social experiences of ex-untouchables in academic institutions, it assumes its worst contours in bureaucracy, where the notions of power and authority override the social life. The ex-untouchables' exposure to positions of power and authority, due to the 'reservation policy', has been conceived as a challenge to the traditional identities and hierarchies. This has created a complex situation of accommodation and resentment on the part of both SCs and others. That is, in everyday interactions SCs and others 'mask their real feelings (to use Freeman's phrase) towards each other. Even among the SCs, one also witnesses both sharp divisions and cooperation, in terms of sharing of power and authority. Our next case study focuses on the experiences in bureaucracy.

Surendra Meshram is a senior bureaucrat. To my inquiries about the new forms of untouchability, he said, 'now you can't be directly discriminated in the service, however, there are indirect forms which are more effective and dangerous'. One's surname is an important aspect of social interaction in the office. Based on this other codes of identity and interactions are formed. That the people from the 'quota' are incompetent, is the confirmed truth shared by the non-SCs, in the administration. The constant hammering of this 'imposed incompetence', he says further, 'sometimes really contributes to our incompetence as in the mentally disturbed state of mind we are prone to commit mistakes. The non-SC higher ups are quick in acting upon these small mistakes so that we get warning "memos", chargesheets or even suspension orders. This is more so if the person concerned is assertive and believes in Ambedkarian ideology. Some phrases seem to be reserved for us. "Gross neglect", it is "unbecoming of any respectable officer", are some forms of harassment in working life which are also used by the so called upper castes officers to halt our promotions and to ensure that we never become the supreme authority'. 'There are many examples of our officers facing suspensions and Departmental inquiries on "cooked up" cases which years later have been proved baseless'. Direct confrontation is not the only strategy used in the bureaucracy. The strategy of cooption has also been a powerful tactic used to alienate the dashing, self-assured, ex-untouchable officers. The non-SC colleagues often praise such a person for his competence with the remark that 'you are very good, almost like us. But this is very rare in your community. Now that they have come into the service, they should improve themselves'. The concerned SC officer feels extremely elated that 'he is accepted by his upper caste colleagues and at the same time start sharing their notions about his brothers in service. Now his time is mostly spent in 'their' company. Since he occupies an important position, many of these 'colleagues' get their work done through him. At the same time they belittle his efforts, by saying that "we have managed to get this work done, for who listens to this SC officer at the higher levels". Moreover, once cordial relations are established with him, he could also be "fixed" in some problem or other. Through these manipulations designed by the upper castes, the other backward castes act as the instruments in actualizing them. That the other backward castes people exhibit blatant forms of caste prejudice in the offices now.'

Surendra stays in a cooperative housing society's building in

Kandivili. In his building eighty per cent of the occupants are from SC background and remaining twenty per cent are non-SC. This, he told me, was due to the government's policy to achieve intermingling in the dwelling places. Government recommends that the cooperative housing society proposed by the Scheduled Castes should reserve twenty per cent of the flats to the other communities. Similarly the non-Scheduled Caste's housing society should have 20 per cent for the Scheduled Castes. Surendra stays in the building of the first type. He points out that the upper caste apartment holders rarely come and occupy the house. For they see it as an investment which could be encashed later on for a higher price or could be rented out. Even if they have to stay in 'our' building, they maintain aloofness in terms of day to day interaction. Functions in their family are always meant for their relatives and though we are invited, it is a mere ritual. Surendra's friend who stays in the other type of building says that 'you have to adapt to the Hindu culture, i.e., you have to take part in Hindu festivals even if you do not believe in them. If we refuse we are isolated'.

My observation of the better placed Buddhists at the working places suggests that though they generally assert themselves and contest caste discrimination, it also depends on their number in the specific department. In the departments where their number is relatively less, they tend to 'adjust' with the dominant groups. Further, though, they face caste discrimination at the working places, it does not necessarily make them sensitive to the problems of socio-economically marginalized Buddhists.

Sunil Devrukhakar is an officer belonging to the Charmkar community. My repeated requests to meet him regarding this inquiry had to be postponed many a times as he was busy or engaged in some important meeting. When I actually met him I found him rather unwilling to speak on this issue. To my persistent efforts he responded by saying 'everything now depends on your merit'. All along he was a meritorious student and even in the service, his ability is counted more than anything else. He has not received any negative remarks so far in his service. Further, he told me look at my appearance, do I, by any chance look like a lower caste man? 'Yes indeed he looked quite polished, spoke 'standard' Marathi and was consciously self assured. Yet to my question, 'how did he get his promotions', his spontaneous answer was 'of course through the reservation policy. How else we will get our promotions'? However, my further probe revealed that his getting quick promotions (due to the reservation policy) was quite a irritation to many of his close upper caste friends. They reacted by saying 'he is lucky! look at us! We are slogging for so many years without any breakthrough'. Despite this the everyday interaction between him and his Hindu colleagues is not affected. For, he not only accepts their supremacy, but tends to look at them as his role model. He regularly brings *Ganapati* home, i.e., celebrates the Ganapati festival. His children attend the English medium school managed by the 'Indian' (Hindu) management. For 'they must inculcate "our" Indian (Hindu) culture'. However, my probes suggested that despite his attempts at assimilating into the 'Hindu' culture, his everyday social experience is not without caste prejudice, though its intensity differs from that of the assertive Buddhists. Thus we see a complex picture. That on the one hand he is generally isolated from the Buddhists in the office (they also think of him as belonging to the 'other' side) and at the same time not fully accepted by his upper caste friend. Further, though aware of the plight of Charmkars, I found him rather indifferent. He does see the need to work to bring economic changes in Charmkars' life but that he thinks 'depends on your own development first'. He accepts that the common Charmkars experience caste discrimination but thinks that the 'end of caste system is possible only with economic changes in their lives'.

III

We have seen that caste prejudice and discrimination continue to pervade the everyday social experience of ex-untouchables in the city. In case of the better placed ex-untouchables, it assumes an indirect yet more effective and traumatic form. As one member of the ex-untouchable community told me, 'when we were uneducated we thought it was our fate, but now after taking education and realizing that given the opportunity we can prove our worth, it is painful to accept the imposed inferior status'. However, our case studies also revealed that though caste discrimination is generally experienced by all three ex-untouchable castes in some form or other, the intensity of this experience differs and the responses towards it are necessarily varied, diverse, contextual and complex. Though the better placed Buddhists (because of their rejection of Hinduism, constant attempts of contesting the caste hierarchies) generally experience caste discrimination more acutely and in greater intensity than the Matangs or Charmkars, their responses exhibit a more complex process of (to use Freeman's expression) 'accommodation to and rebellion against' the caste oppression. That is, their experiences and perceptions of discrimination varies as per the situations.

In case of the better placed Charmkars we find that despite experiencing caste discrimination, their reactions to it, unlike their counter parts in Agra (Jatavs), exhibit an attempt to get assimilated into the upper castes. Their attempt of identifying themselves with *Hindutvavadis* though does not end the caste prejudice, certainly reduces its intensity. As regard the better placed Matangs, we witness that they identify themselves with the legend of brave unfearing Mang rebellion against oppression, they exhibit resentment against the imposed inferior status. That this brings them closer to the Buddhists and provides ground for the united action against caste oppression. However, their not being Buddhists distances them form Buddhists and also makes them more prone to be used by the upper castes as instruments of counter actions against the Buddhists. Hence among the better placed Matangs there are convinced supporters of the upper castes' constructed notion that the Buddhists are the cause of their non-development.

We witness that the ex-untouchable castes in Bombay tend to perceive each other in terms of 'us' and 'they'. This process of social and ideological distance exists, apart from the internalization of 'mentality of caste', because of the competition for sharing the ever shrinking prospects for socio-economic development and political power. The Matangs and Charmkars, who were traditional vote bank of the Congress party have felt disenchanted with it and the politically ambitious among them, have chosen the path of *Hindutvavadi* parties and in the process have become ideological and political opponents of the Dalit consciousness and politics. As a result, this disunity in perception is resulting, instead of fighting the state for achieving radical changes in policy orientations, in greater dependency on it. And in retaining the patron-client relationship between them and the state, and thereby hampering the possibility of any meaningful change in their lives.

In contemporary times, the challenges posed by the Shiv Sena-BJP government has created a need to arrive at the broader unity among Dalits. This government's decisions of distributing different school uniforms for scheduled caste and scheduled tribe students, scrapping of the 1100 cases filed under the 'Atrocities Act', and introduction of an Act to ban the slaughter of cow and its progeny (which has marginalized Charmkars from their traditional source of livelihood), have posed disturbing problems before the Dalits. Many people from the Buddhist community I met, now think that it was a mistake to have remained aloof from Matangs and Charmkars. That without forging a broader unity of Dalit forces it is not possible to challenge the *Hindutvavadi* forces. Even among the Matang community, a section of educated youth, following Annabhau Sathe, thinks that ideologically they are more close to the Dalit movement than to the *Hindutvavadi* parties. Reading of Annabhau's literary works, especially, the famous line in his poem *Jag Badal Ghaluni Ghau Sangun Gele Bhimrao* (change this world through a decisive blow, this is what Bhimrao Ambedkar has taught us), is bringing the youth from Matang community ideologically closer to the Dalit movement. Moreover, some Charmkar youths who are disillusioned with their community's apathy towards the recent *Cobbler's Scam*, affecting the common Charmkars, have sought to protest against it through the activists of the Republican Party of India. Though these are extremely rare instances of attempts of some united action, they atleast provide some scope for sharing the consciousness about their marginalization.

NOTES

Case studies bear pseudo names.

1. Though suppressed and cheated in life, Bauris did not merely rejected the high castes' ranking of society, and high caste view of them, but also showed resentment towards the ways high caste people treated them.
2. These places of dwellings have been selected to understand the diverse nature of ex-untouchables' social experience. Thus the BIT chawl, built in 1924, provides understanding of various generation's experience in the city; Mata Ramabai Nagar for experiences at slums at the outskirts; Dharavi for understanding Charmkar's life situations; and Housing colonies at Kandivili, Charkop, to understand the experiences of educationally and socio-economically better placed ex-untouchables.
3. Total number of Buddhists (Mahars) in Maharashtra is 1,648,269 (1981, Census), Matangs, 1,211,335 (1981, Census), whereas the Charmkars rank third in the list. We should note that Matangs are totally absent from the Konkan region.
4. Though Mahars and Matangs had *Watan/Inam* land rights, these land entitlements were generally inadequate for the family's needs and these lands were also instruments aimed at maintaining their untouchable's their loyalties towards the village.
5. For Matangs, possibility of getting employment in villages was extremely important as they were poor. However, it also led to the caste Hindu's attempts of creating rifts between them and Mahars.
6. During the nineteen-thirties and forties Matangs along with Mahars were active workers of Ambedkarian movement and politics. See *Source Material On Dr. Babasaheb Ambedkar and The Movement of Untouchables,* Bombay: Government of Maharashtra Press, pp. 163, 205, 235.
7. The informal survey conducted by Mr. Magar for the Bombay Slum Dweller's Federation. This survey also points out that 10 per cent of the total slum population stays there because accommodation in buildings is not affordable, as regards work experience in Bombay's slums, 40 per cent work in informal sector, 20 per cent in organized activity and 40 per cent are unemployed.

REFERENCES

Census of India 1991. Final Population Tables. Brief Analysis of Primary Census Abstract Paper 2 of 1992. Delhi: General Census Commissioner of India. 1992.

Chandavarkar, R., *The Origin of Industrial Capitalism in India, Business and the Working Classes in Bombay: 1900-1940*. New Delhi: Cambridge University Press. 1994.

Freeman, J.M., *Untouchable: An Indian Life History*. London: George Allen and Unwin. 1965.

Morris, M.D., *The Emergence of An Industrial Labour Force in India: A Study of the Bombay Cotton Mill, 1854-1947*. Bombay: Oxford University Press. 1965.

Omvedt, Gail, *Dalits and the Democratic Revolution*. New Delhi: Sage Publications. 1994.

Pradhan, G.R., *Untouhable Workers of Bombay City*. Bombay: Karnatak Publishing House. 1938.

Searle-Chatterjee, M., and Ursula Sharma (eds.), *Contexualizing Caste*, The Sociological Review. Oxford: Blackwell Publishers. 1994.

Sharma, B.D., *Report of the Commissioner for the Scheduled Castes and Scheduled Tribes*, Twenty-ninth Report, 1987-89. Delhi: Government of India Press. 1989.

8

SCAVENGERS
Still Marginalised

SUSAN E. CHAPLIN[1]

In India today, scavengers and sweepers still carry out the basic sanitary services in cities and towns. While many are employed by local urban authorities to clean the sewers and sweep the streets, a significant number still work in their traditional occupation. This means that scavengers are still cleaning latrines by hand and carrying night soil in baskets on their heads. As their occupation renders them permanently polluted, according to Hindu society, scavengers are treated as untouchable, even by other untouchable castes. This discrimination also means that scavengers have extremely limited job opportunities other than sanitary work, that they live in acute poverty in segregated communities, and have extremely low levels of literacy and job mobility. Such socio-economic conditions for scavengers still persist despite various articles in the Indian Constitution, which stipulate that the state should promote the economic and educational interests of Scheduled Castes and protect them from discrimination and exploitation.

Since Independence, the three levels of government have lacked a sustained interest in implementing these provisions of the Constitution.[2] This has been demonstrated by the fact that several enquiries have been conducted into scavenging conditions throughout India, which resulted in comprehensive recommendations, but no substantial implementation. There has also been a very limited attempt to gather sufficient information about scavengers and sweepers, so that an adequate understanding of their socio-economic circumstances can be constructed. In the census of 1971, their occupation was not even listed in a separate category, and in the 1990s there are varying estimates of the actual number of people involved in scavenging. Governments at all levels have generally relied on rhetoric while addressing these issues, setting dates for the abolition of scavenging (the latest being 1997), but generally neglecting to discuss alternatives and failing to provide adequate resources for the retraining of scavengers.

During the independence struggle, attempts to improve the inhuman working conditions of scavengers and to eliminate untouchability within Indian society became part of the campaign by Gandhi. Scavengers themselves attempted to improve their wages and living conditions by forming trade unions and taking industrial action. In the immediate aftermath of independence, the Government of India began to instigate efforts to improve the working conditions of scavengers by seeking to abolish the practice of carrying night soil as a headload. These attempts were formalised in several government enquiries. The first was conducted by the Government of Bombay in 1949. This was followed by the Scavengers Conditions Enquiry Committee of 1960, which was established by the Ministry of Home Affairs, Government of India.

The Report of the Scavengers Conditions Enquiry Committee will be examined in detail as it provides graphic details of the working conditions of scavengers, many of which are still prevalent in the 1990s. Basically, the report censured local governments for the callous disregard shown towards the working conditions of scavengers, and their misappropriation of centrally financed programmes aimed at alleviating this problem. It was critical of the customary rights inherited by scavenger families, and implied that the scavengers themselves were the cause of some of the unsanitary conditions in many Indian cities and towns. The report failed to provide workable alternatives. It simply recommended that the majority of scavengers should become municipal employees and be given a minimum wage.

The outcome of the Scavengers Committee Report was more

committees because sanitation is a local government subject, and the Government of India cannot legislate on local government issues without the concurrence of at least two state governments. Initially, the Government of India attempted to improve scavenging conditions by using a top-down developmental approach of making grants to state government to be distributed for the recommended sanitation reforms. Such attempts were under resourced and encountered indifference by local governments. They also failed to address the discrimination and exploitation suffered by scavenger and sweeper communities.

Scavenging Castes

Scavenging are predominantly found in cities and towns as the need for a special caste to remove night soil and clean latrines is minimal in rural areas, where villagers prefer to defecate in the fields. Officials in the 20th century have tended to use the term *Bhangi* as a label for scavengers, and sweepers, throughout the country. This name is now used for a widespread jati in Hindi-speaking areas of Northern India. Thus, when the term Bhangi is used in this article it will be used as an occupational description, as is the case when citing census statistics. The term "scavenger" will generally be applied to persons employed to clean latrines and remove night soil. But such a distinction frequently becomes blurred, because even within one family, several members may be employed as municipal sweepers who clean roads and remove garbage, while others work as scavengers cleaning public and private latrines. Hence, the family may be called scavengers or sweepers depending on the inclination of the author.

Bhangis have an occupation that has remained hereditary, because their tasks are dirty and they have to work in appalling conditions, especially during the monsoon season. The removal of night soil and refuse is viewed by the Hindu society as a very degrading occupation which constitutes a permanent state of pollution. As a consequence, scavenger and sweeper communities have been treated as untouchable, unapproachable and unseeable. This permanent state of pollution applies to the entire community and is hereditary. This untouchability has resulted in scavenger, and sweeper communities being physically segregated into overcrowded slums which are generally located in the centre, or older sections, of cities and towns. They are characterised by filth and squalor, with pigs roaming around. Families are frequently forced to live next to the night soil dumping grounds or on top of garbage collection sites in these slums. Rama Sharma, in her study of 300 scavenger families in Delhi, describes one such garbage dump:

> "Overflowing with refuse, they attract pigs and dogs. It is not unusual to see them receiving their load until filled to their capacity. Foul matter adheres to their walls which smells awfully... An outsider feels dizzy after inhaling two breathfuls of [the] stench hanging in the atmosphere affecting the nighbourhood."[3]

Such ostracisation by society has made scavenger and sweeper communities fearful and distrustful of outsiders. They are also reluctant to provide information about their socio-economic conditions because it may be used to increase their exploitation, rather than bring benefits. Such reactions are described in studies of scavengers and sweepers done by Shyamlal[4] in Rajasthan and Mary Searle-Chatterjee in Varanasi.[5] This distrustfulness is further entrenched by the fact that even amongst the number of occupational groups in Indian society who have been considered untouchable, scavenger have the lowest status of any group. This outcaste status was illustrated in the late 1950s, when the Rajasthan Government offered financial inducements in the form of a special allowance, representing 100 per cent of the wage paid to a Bhangi, for any unemployed other caste person to take up the occupation. The offer was totally ignored.[6]

Bhangis also faced isolation from other low caste groups. Owen Lynch, in his study of the low-caste Jatavs in Agra,[7] noted that there was a definite opposition to marriage with Bhangis, which was only qualified by such provisos as the boy being well-educated or having other qualifications. For Jatavs, it was a case of "marrying down" to associate with Bhangis. In Uttar Pradesh, the Chamars (leather workers) avoid social contact with the Bhangis.[8] In the old quarter of Jaipur, neighbourhoods can be found that are split down the middle. On one side of the road are the Meenas (a herdsmen tribe), low-caste Hindus and Muslims, and on the other are the scavengers. The tension that exists between the two can erupt easily. A seemingly minor incident, such as a scavenger boy brushing against a drunken Meena in the street, was viewed as such an affront by an "untouchable" that the Meenas responded by bloodying the boy's face. A group of nearby unemployed scavenger men retaliated by throwing bricks through shop windows. The ensuing riot needed police intervention.[9]

Their occupation, ironically, also brings envy from some low caste groups, because one of the traditional rights has been the leaving of left over food and old clothing by households for their scavenger. In circumstances of acute poverty, such a "privilege" is viewed as a reason for excluding them from the benefits offered by the state, such as job reservation.[10] Within the Bhangi caste, there is also a hierarchy. Sweepers consider themselves superior to scavengers because they do not carry night soil. Also, those scavengers who are employed by municipal corporations, consider themselves to be higher than those who are self-employed and clean private houses. This division has mainly occurred due to the pensions that are payable to municipal employees. This division is also largely gender based. It is women who are predominantly employed to do the scavenging for private households, as they are not strong enough to do the heavy lifting associate with mechanisation or the work at the dumping grounds or collections points.[11]

Abolition of Untouchability

State efforts to remove the social disability, economic inequality, and religious inferiority suffered by scavengers and sweepers have concentrated on the abolition of untouchability itself, by the use of Article 17 of the Constitution and a system of reservations in employment, educational institutions, and political bodies. While religious preachers and social reformers upto the beginning of the 20th century had made some efforts to abolish untouchability, it was

Mahatma Gandhi who gave the movement momentum. In 1915, when he established his ashram at Ahmedabad, he recommended that a Harijan family be admitted. He also encouraged all the members to routinely undertake sweeping and scavenging: "No sin or shame is involved in cleaning for others even as it is sin for a mother to clean her baby or for a nurse to clean his or her patients."[12]

After the 1920 Calcutta session of the Indian National Congress, it became the responsibility of Congress members to do everything possible to eradicate untouchability. But it was Gandhi's clash with Ambedkar over the issue of separate electorates for the Depressed Classes, his ensuing fast in 1932, and the resulting Poona Pact,[13] which eventually focused attention on untouchability throughout India.

Concurrent with these actions by Gandhi was the establishment in 1933 of the Harijan Sevak Sangh (Service Society for the Children of God). The aim of the Sangh was the eradication of untouchability by non-violent and truthful means, and the eventual absorption of Harijans into the caste system. But significantly, the Harijan Sevak Sangh was to be non-political in nature. Hence, the Sangh concentrated its efforts on education, vocational training, and welfare work. In particular, scavengers were trained in advanced sanitation methods, and caste Hindus were encouraged to clean latrines. More recently, the Sangh has campaigned for the abolition of the practice of head loading night soil, as well as demanded better wages and conditions for scavengers. Schools have also been established to train Bhangi children in various crafts so that they can leave this traditional occupation.[14]

Since independence, Article 17 of the Constitution, which says that untouchability is abolished and its practice in any form forbidden, has been implemented the form of the Untouchability (Offences) Act, 1955. It was not until its amendment in November 1976, to the Protection of Civil Rights Act, 1955, that this anti-discrimination policy was applied to private sector employment. However, the implementation of these measures has been largely ineffective as is shown by the studies, of the atrocities committed against Scheduled Castes, conducted by the Commissioner has not really been able to fulfil the "watchdog" role that was envisaged for it by article 338 of the Constitution because it has faced shortages in the necessary personnel and resources that are needed to cope with the enormity of the problem. As a consequence, its role has become one of making recommendations.[15]

Attempts at Improving Scavenging Conditions

In 1949, the Government of Bombay, on the recommendation of the Backward Classes Board, made one of the first formal attempts to improve the social and economic inequality suffered by scavengers. It appointed a committee to enquire into their living and working conditions. The Living Conditions Inquiry Committee submitted its report in 1952. It recommended that scavengers should be given a prescribed minimum wage of between Rs. 25-30 per month, and that they only work a maximum of five hours a day. The Committee also recommended that suitable measures should be taken to awaken the sanitary conscience and civic sense of the public in the manner of abolition of the process of removal of night soil by hand by Bhangis, and to raise the culture of the Bhangi caste and make them fit to take their due share in the public life of the society.[16]

Other issues addressed included the recommendation that the system of customary right of scavenging be abolished in the interests of Bhangis and of public sanitation; the provision of housing in healthy locations and water for washing and drinking; that local authorities should construct new latrines to avoid the process of hand removal and finally that the carrying of night soil as head loads be prohibited.[17] These recommendations were also supported by the Commissioner for Scheduled Castes and Scheduled Tribes in his report for 1956-57, which stated that the head loading of night soil should be immediately stopped because such practices were responsible "for the spread of the evil of untouchability", and were an inhuman and very unsanitary method of disposal.[18] The Ministry of Health, Government of India, responded to the recommendations in 1955 by suggesting that they should be adopted by all states.[19]

In an attempt to encourage local government bodies to improve the living and working conditions of scavengers in their employ, the first centrally sponsored programme was implemented in 1957-58.

A sum of Rs. 984,000 was allocated as a grant-in-aid for local bodies to provide scavengers with wheelbarrows or hand carts. This funding was to meet 50 per cent of the expenditure for those local bodies, who agreed to immediately stop the practice of night soil head loading. The scheme received a very limited response, with only 600 out of nearly 126,000 local bodies participating. The Commissioner for Scheduled Castes and Scheduled Tribes, in his report for 1957-58, suggested that this poor participation rate may have been the consequence of financial difficulties facing such bodies.[20] It is against this background of faltering attempts to abolish the practice of carrying or head loading of night soil that the Central Advisory Board for Harijan Welfare established the Scavenging Conditions Enquiry Committee in October 1957. The Committee was under the chairmanship of N.R. Malkani, a Gandhian social worker, who had been involved with the Harijan Sevak Sangh and was a member of the Rajya Sabha and of the Central Advisory Board for Harijan Welfare.

Scavenging Conditions Enquiry Committee

The Committee was established to prepare "a scheme to put an end to the degrading practice of having to carry night soil in buckets and baskets". As the Committee found these terms of reference to be very narrow, the enquiry was broadened to include suggestions of how the living and working conditions of scavengers could be improved. The Committee studied the whole process, from the cleaning of latrines, to the collection and removal of night soil and its transportation to dumping grounds and other places of disposal. The Committee also addressed such issues as the housing and other welfare amenities provided for scavenger communities.

Initially, the Committee proposed to collect all the necessary information from questionnaires which the Ministry of Home Affairs has sent to all state governments, members of Parliament, and local government bodies. As the initial responses to the questionnaires were very slow the Committee decide instead to visit the states of Andhra Pradesh, Bihar, Gujarat, Kerala, Madhya Pradesh, Madras, Maharashtra, Mysore, Orissa, Punjab, Rajasthan, Uttar Pradesh,

West Bengal, and the union territories of Delhi and Himachal Pradesh, to gather the necessary information. These visits involved observing the methods of scavenging used in various localities, the condition of public and private latrines, and the tools and equipment used to remove and transport night soil to dumping grounds and sewage plants. The Committee also consulted with the government officials in charge of scavenging work, with non-government organisations interested in scavenger welfare, and with scavengers themselves.[21] It found that scavenging conditions varied immensely from state to state, but that in general they were, appallingly unsanitary. In fact, the Committee members found:

> The conditions at some of the places seen were so nauseating that a few of the members, in spite of having been accustomed to visiting the filthiest spots in the towns, had vomitings. A few of the towns in the country were so filthy that they could well be called 'Big Latrines'.[22]

As a result of such observations, the Committee felt that the only way in which the conditions of scavenging could be improved, was by introducing new methods for carrying out the removal and disposal of night soil. They felt that the problem would continue to exist as long as dry latrines existed. Installation of underground sewers for all towns and cities was viewed as a very distant possibility.

Latrines and Night Soil Removal

The Scavenging Enquiry Committee found that the very design of latrines meant that scavengers always came into direct contact with night soil and therefore constantly had soiled hands. This applied to about 80 to 90 per cent of cases because latrines did not have any receptacles and the human excreta was deposited on the ground. The unsanitary nature of such latrines was compounded by the fact that they were frequently not scavenged for days at a time. The Committee, therefore, recommended that receptacles, and scrapers for cleaning the latrines, should be supplied periodically by the local body, and that it should be the duty of the scavenger to report or sanitary inspector of breakages or damage. An emphatic note was added that unless proper scrapers were introduced, there was no hope of improving the unsanitary nature of night soil removal. The report contained several designs for such receptacles and scrapers.[23]

Addressing the "heinous practice" of carrying baskets of night soil on the head, the Committee found that the best system must be a mechanical one. In those situations where the street or lane was too narrow for a wheelbarrow, scavengers should be issued with buckets that could be carried. The bamboo baskets that were found to be in common use were generally only lined with leaves, and had no lids or covers. The consequence was that leaking night soil covered the body of the scavengers. The other area of "human ill use of scavengers" was the cesspool, in which small drains deposited an accumulation of urine, ablution water, and night soil. Such cesspools were emptied by scavengers standing in the effluent and using buckets to remove it to a municipal van by a human chain. The Committee urgently recommended the abolition of such cesspools where possible or the use of mechanical means such as suction pumps to empty them.[24]

The continuing use of traditional types of service latrines was thus found to be the greatest impediment to improving scavenging conditions. The Committee found that people seemed unwilling to construct latrines at all in their houses because of sentimental reasons. That is, they preferred to defecate in open fields or squate by the roadside or open drains. In urban and semi-urban areas, only 25 per cent of households were found to have private latrines, and the number of public latrines was totally inadequate to meet the massive demand. The end result was that the entire locality became filthy and insanitary. The Committee, therefore, concluded that:

> It is evident that the dimensions of the problem are prodigious. Even in advanced cities like Delhi, children make use of surface drains for the purpose..... The Committee suggests that people must be educated and persuaded to construct latrines in their houses.[25]

This attitude to the problem of defecation and use of latrines very much reflects the Gandhian notion that clean and sanitised localities are the hallmark of a modern nation. Hence, the Committee recommended that local bodies should give serious attention to remodelling public latrines. This should preferably involve installing water borne arrangements which are within easy reach of the public.

Wheelbarrows

Addressing the issue of the centrally sponsored scheme for the purchase of wheelbarrows by municipalities/local bodies, the Scavenging Enquiry Committee found that the scheme had not been taken seriously. During their visits to various municipalities, the members discovered that in many instances, State Governments had not even informed the local bodies about the scheme and therefore had not utilised any of the funding available. Even in those instances where wheelbarrows were introduced, the results were unsatisfactory. The problem which besets many top-down development projects was also prevalent here, i.e., no consultation with the scavengers about the design of such wheelbarrows. As scavenging work is primarily undertaken by women, the wheelbarrows introduced were simply too heavy for them to use and were discarded. In other instances, as in Andhra Pradesh, the wheelbarrows were repeatedly stolen and sold as scrap iron. In summary, the Committee found that "many of the State Governments have not studied the scheme properly and there have been many misunderstandings. There is as yet no standardised wheelbarrow with the result that the amounts spent so far, have virtually gone to waste".[26]

The Committee was not moved by the argument put forward by a few municipalities that since they intended to lay underground sewers in the near future, there was no need to introduce wheelbarrows. This attitude was regarded as wishful thinking. Instead, the Committee felt that one of the reasons the municipalities had failed to implement the wheelbarrow scheme was that other items like the development of water supply schemes (which provided a financial return to the municipality), the installation of street lights, and the construction of roads were considered to be more important. Such activities directly enhanced the appearance of localities, while spending money on public health issues and improving the working conditions of scavengers showed little immediate return.[27]

Depots and Disposal of Night Soil

After collection from houses and public latrines, night soil is deposited by scavengers at depots for transportation to the dumping grounds or other place of disposals. The Scavenging Enquiry Committee found depots to be very few in number, which meant that scavengers were often forced to carry loads of night soil for up to half a kilometre. The consequence of this was that "scavengers accumulate the night soil in a corner of the street or stealthily dispose (of it) into the open drain wherever such a drain exists. This makes the entire area filthy and also there is a waste of night soil which can be very well converted into manure".[28]

The process of loading and unloading night soil was found to be extremely dirty, especially when scavengers had to wade through ankle-deep night soil diluted with water, to physically unclog the hole in the centre of the floor of the depots which connects it to the underground sewer. Besides recommending that all workers at the depots be provided with gum boots, gloves, aprons and waterproof headgear, the committee suggested that these depots be better designed to permit the use of trailers and tankers. The depots were also found to have insufficient quantities of water to either clean the vehicles in use, or to allow scavengers to wash themselves. Hence, scavengers were usually forced to return home in filthy clothes.[29]

While the depots were extremely dirty and poorly maintained, the condition of the dumping grounds where night soil was brought for final disposal was found to be even worse. The Committee found that:

> The conditions of the dumping grounds and the workers there as seen by the Committee have been found horrible. The Surat and Karnal dumping grounds may perhaps be considered some of the worst in the country. Most of the dumping grounds are

stinking and full of flies and it is a tough job to visit them. The conditions at a few were so nauseating that one member or the other of the Committee invariably felt sick during the visit.[30]

Most of these dumping grounds were also found to be too close to habitation and too small to cope with the needs of the towns.

Customary Rights

Probably the most controversial section of the report was the one relating to the hereditary customary rights of private scavengers. These rights are of two kinds. One gives scavengers the exclusive right to clean a certain number of private latrines or localities. The other relates to rights for the sale and disposal of collected night soil. These customary rights are possessed by either a family or a Jagirdar,[31] until they decide to sell or mortgage these rights, as would be done with property. The Scavenging Enquiry Committee found that because of the rigid enforcement of caste rules upon scavengers, the profession had become monopolistic. Thus over time, scavengers had come to consider particular streets and localities to be their own private properties, with the consequence that night soil was disposed of in whatever manner they decided. The Committee reported that the problem,

> .... is worst in (the) Punjab and (the) Western parts of Uttar Pradesh where the local bodies are not allowed to collect even the night soil left over in the street corners by private scavengers. The night soil collected by private scavengers is considered to be their property. We cannot expect any improvement in the methods of scavenging or think in terms of putting an end to the practice of carrying night soil as head loads or improve sanitary conditions of the towns as long as such rights continue in a larger part of the country. Proper maintenance of the conditions of sanitation and keeping an eye over the health hygiene of the towns is a primary responsibility of the local bodies, and a few private scavengers and their '*Jagirdars*' should not hold the community to ransom.[32]

Private scavengers responded to these suggestions by making representations to the Committee that if customary rights were abolished, and scavenging became a municipal concern, they would not only lose their income, but also the food and old clothes that they received from households. The Committee replied by recommending that scavengers should become full-time, not part-time, municipal employees and receive wages according to the Minimum Wages Act. They should also be provided with uniforms, and those who could not get municipal employment should be compensated in cash. A further suggestion was also made that Government of India grants for the welfare of Scheduled Castes could be utilised in vocational training for those Bhangis who remained unemployed. The cooperation of non-government organisations and social workers could also be sought by local governments in tackling this problem.[33]

Local Government's Responsibility

In general, the Scavenging Enquiry Committee found that since independence, "progress" had been made in every walk of life except in the working conditions of scavengers.[34] Even the Planning Commission was found to have ignored this problem in the first two five-year plans. Somewhat in exasperation, the Committee wrote:

> The problem of scavenging is a complicated socio-economic problem. There seems to be a deep rooted prejudice in the minds of several caste 'Hindus' with regard to the disposal of night soil. People are opposed even to the construction of latrines in their houses and prefer to go out in the fields or squat in open spaces within their easy reach. The question is not of finances alone but needs a radical change of mental outlook and habits arising therefrom.[35]

The Committee expressed similar frustration with local government bodies, who lacked the initiative "for one or other reason" to implement many of their schemes for improving scavenging conditions. The failure of these local government bodies to even abide by their own by-laws was viewed as selling an extremely poor example to the rest of the community. The Committee observed that state governments should be more actively involved in guiding local bodies on ways to improve scavenging conditions.

On the issue of housing for scavengers, the general observation was that their hovels, were not fit for human habitation, and were often located in the filthiest parts of towns. Hence, the first priority of local bodies should be to house them away from the dumping grounds and nearer to the actual place of employment of municipal workers. The Committee also noted that in the provision of quarters for municipal employees, sweepers had been given preference over scavengers. To facilitate these improvements, it was suggested that the slum clearance schemes should be utilised to help with the construction of public latrines, and housing, which scavengers could buy through a hire-purchase scheme. As scavenging is predominantly a female occupation, the establishment of creches in scavenger colonies was recommended, so that the children could be taken care of and taught cleaner habits. Such improvements in living conditions, the Committee felt, would help address some of the scavengeres' grievances and thereby reduce the number of strikes, and would "create a new sense of self-respect in them and particularly their children".[36]

Comments on the Report

Overall, the Report of the Scavenging Conditions Enquiry documented the working conditions of scavengers, and the somewhat indifferent attitudes of state and local governments to centrally funded schemes. Underlying many of the report's observations was the tendency to blame the scavengers for their main failure to adopt new technology because of their "passive attitude" to change. This attitude was seen to stem from entrenched habits and prejudice, implying that scavengers find it more convenient to carry loads on their heads. Unfortunately, no research was conducted into the actual reasons that scavengers have for carrying night soil as headloads and what they would actually prefer. Similarly, it was noted that in Delhi, West Bengal and Rajasthan, some women had already changed their attitude and were using small pushcarts to carry away night soil.[37]

Again, no attempt was made to find out why these women had adopted the new technology.

A major shortcoming of this report was that no statistical data was collected on who employed scavengers and where they worked. How can the socio-economic conditions of these large urban communities be improved if there is no accurate or reliable information available? Also, to conclude that scavenging had become "monopolistic" and that scavengers and Jagirdars "should not hold the community to ransom", demonstrated a considerable lack of understanding of the conditions of poverty in which scavengers live. Customary rights represent the only "job security" that manual scavengers (unlike municipal workers who receive a minimum wage) possess—their only bargaining power for increasing their incomes. The committee also appeared to lack an awareness about the stigma suffered by scavengers from working in an "unclean occupation" and how this affected their job opportunities.

In April 1965, another committee, once again under N.R. Malkani's chairmanship, was established to examine the abolition of customary rights. The Committee found that the existence of such rights was disputable and that in practice there was an agreement, a mutual understanding among Bhangis as to two would scavenge certain households. These findings provoked and agitation by Bhangis in Delhi, who vigorously questioned the integrity of the committee. At a public assembly on 3 July, 1966, Bhangis were invited to bring along their documents relating to hereditary scavenging. They voiced their opposition by putting up posters in Delhi stating that the Malkani Committee had completely failed to interview any Bhangis during its hearings. These posters also claimed that since the times of the Muslim kings, scavenging had been the legal right of scavengers. The outcome of this strong protest was that efforts to abolish customary rights of scavengers were put aside by the Delhi Corporation.[38]

Responses to the Report of the Scavenging Conditions Enquiry

While the recommendations for liberalising the funding for the wheelbarrow schemes were implemented, the general response by the Central and State governments seems to have been setting up of more committees. The Government of India established an advisory committee, under the chairmanship of N.R. Malkani, to provide suggestions on how to mobilise efforts to abolish the practice of headloading night soil throughout the country. The Punjab government appointed a committee to enquire into scavenging conditions in that state, while the Rajasthan government established a committee to look into the recommendations of the Report of the Scavenging Conditions Enquiry Committee. This particular Committee was asked to visit all the state's municipal boards and obtain their views before even considering any action to abolish the practice of headloading night soil.[39]

In 1967, the National Commission on Labour (which had been appointed by the Government of India to review how labour conditions had changed since Independence) established a working group to look into the working and service conditions of scavengers and sweepers, with the intention of providing practical suggestions of how improvements could be achieved. This committee pointed out that despite numerous efforts, the practice of headloading night soil was still very much in existence. It also felt scavengers and sweepers had been denied the benefits that progressive labour legislation had achieved for other sectors of the working class. Hence, it urged the Government of India to enact legislation which would create adequate enforcement and inspections machinery for improving their living and working conditions. The Committee also addressed the continuing demands by scavengers and sweepers for minimum pay, working hours, and supply of uniforms.[40] An enquiry conducted into the working and living conditions of Scheduled Castes in Agra in 1976-77, found that the carrying of night soil as a headload was still prevalent among sweepers and scavengers, especially those engaged in servicing private households. Once again, customary rights were seen as an obstacle to the municipalisation of scavenging. In contrast to the vehement protests by scavengers in Delhi over the issue of customary rights, this enquiry found that about 56 per cent of the families engaged in scavenging were willing to forgo these rights if offered alternative employment.[41]

Comments by Commissioner for Scheduled Castes and Scheduled Tribes

In the yearly reports after 1961, the Commissioner for Scheduled Castes and Scheduled Tribes consistently criticised the performance of local government bodies in implementing the Third Plan funded scheme for providing wheelbarrows to scavengers. In 1963-64, the Commissioners in fact, doubted that the scheme should be continued at all due to the apathy of various local bodies, the reluctance by scavengers to participate, and poor acceptance by the public of the scheme. One of the major defects in the scheme was found to be the misappropriation of funds. For instance, the Lucknow Corporation was found to have used Rs. 5,00,000 to purchase 644 handcarts, when it was reported that only 90 scavengers were in the corporation's employ! The wheelbarrows were instead used by sweepers to carry garbage. In West Bengal, the Murshidabad district authorities purchased 151 handcarts and 44 wheelbarrows for a staff of 50 sweepers and scavengers. The municipality also failed to replace these wheelbarrows when they became unserviceable, so that the scavengers were forced to resort to carrying night soil as a headload again.[42] In 1963-64, the commissioner proposed that as the results of the scheme were "not commensurate with the money spent", the funding should instead be used to educate the children of the scavenger communities and improve their living conditions:

> The environments in which a child is brought up and his education have a bearing on the mental facilities of the child. When he lives under hygienic conditions and is given proper education, he is bound to develop aversion towards insanitary conditions of work.[43]

In 1967-68, the Commissioner 'sincerely hoped' that during the Fourth Plan, state governments would adequately fund the conversion of dry latrines to water-flush ones, as 15 million urban households did not have the necessary sanitary conveniences.[44] But as these recommendations and suggestions went largely unheeded, the commissioner observed in 1974-75 that the Government of India should attempt to solve the problem of carrying night soil as a headload by abolishing scavenging as a caste profession.[45] The subsequent reports of various commissioners have reiterated these recommendations along with appeals to local governments to regularly examine the working and living conditions of scavengers and sweepers, and to take steps to rectify the shortcomings.[46]

Education and Occupational Change

The lack of socio-economic advancement for Bhangis since independence is shown by low levels of increase in literacy and job mobility during this period. This poor progress is even more significant because the Bhangis are a predominantly urban class, with greater exposure to the growing variety of jobs and occupations that cities offer. Opportunities for education should also have increased as schools, colleges and universities are physically more accessible. The evidence from the census of 1961, 1971 and 1981 do not support this trend, despite the existence of reservation policies for jobs and education. As the census statistics for Scheduled Castes cannot be aggregated on an all-India basis, because the lists for Scheduled Castes are notified for individual states and hence are only valued within the concerned state the comparison will be based on the Bhangis in Maharashtra, Delhi and Rajasthan. These states and territory have been chosen because they represent the regional variations in economic development within India, with Maharashtra at the top, Delhi somewhere in the middle, and Rajasthan languishing at the lower end of the scale.

Literacy

In Maharashtra, the literacy rates for Bhangis have slowly improved, from 26 per cent in 1961, to 34 per cent in 1974, and 41 per cent in 1981. The all-India rate in 1981 was 43.6. But these figures only apply to a "person who can read and write with understanding in any language" and do not reflect the poor representation of Bhangis in higher education. In 1981, the Bhangis had a total population of

1,33,386 in Maharashtra of which 89.62 per cent lived in urban areas. Only 3,026 people had reached the matriculation/secondary level, while only 77 had a technical diploma or certificate not equal to a degree. Furthermore only 2 males had engineering degree, while 6 had medicine, along with 11 who were qualified teachers. Of the teachers, only 4 were women.[47] In Delhi, the literacy rate in 1961 was 16.6 per cent, the share of males stood at 28.6 and of females at only 3.97 per cent. By 1981, out of a total population of 21,752, almost 32 per cent were literate, with the rate for males at 43.5 per cent and for females at 17.9 per cent.

In Rajasthan, this educational backwardness is extremely pronounced. In 1961, the total literacy rate for 182,933 Bhangis was only 7.6 per cent. For females, it was 1.5 per cent. In 1981, when the population had grown to 263,565, the total rate was only 15.3 per cent. The female rate was still a dismal 3.92 per cent. That is out of 1,26,878 females in the state, only 4,977 had basic reading and writing skills.[48] In his study of Bhangis in Jodhpur, Shyamlal analysed the literacy of 1,189 families and found that in 939 families not a single member was literate. Only 3 of the families (0.25 per cent) had a member who was a graduate, and in the entire study group only 2 had completed a Master of Arts.[49] In Jaipur in 1996, only 3 children from a slum of 700 scavenger families have attended college. For those Bhangi children, who do manage to attend school or college, the uppermost issue is still discrimination. "Untouchable" students are generally ignored/shunned by high-caste students and this tend to stick together.[50]

These figures thus portray the continuing failure of the state to provide a reasonable level of literacy for Bhangis, which is the first step in obtaining the education necessary for job mobility and entering mainstream society. Illiteracy has another socio-economic fallout, in that families have no idea of how to record family expenses or create a budget, hence they are a regular income from municipalities. In a study of scavengers in Himachal Pradesh, it was observed that because of the high levels of illiteracy, they are still bound to the customs of their caste, like joint families and the dowry system. When combined with large number of dependents and the tendency of men to spend up to 9 per cent of their income on liquor, high levels of debt repayment become the norm. This also means that limited money is allocated to education. In this study only 3.5 per cent of the income was used in this manner.[51]

Job Mobility

In Maharashtra in 1961, out of the total of employed Bhangis (21,028) 29.4 per cent were employed as scavengers. Other services (which include cleaning, ironing, etc.) was the main area of employment (52.6%), with other occupations, that require higher levels of literacy, such as manufacturing (6.6%), transport (9.4%), trade/commerce (0.7%) and construction (0.44%) making up the balance. By 1981 there were a total of 77,387 employed Bhangis, out of a total population of 1,33,386 of which 32,984 were listed as scavengers (43%). Thus while urbanisation may provide more job opportunities, it also means more scavenging until dry latrines are replaced and municipal toilets and sewers are properly maintained. As Sharma has pointed out, if there is a shortage of urban scavengers, then migrant scavengers from rural areas meet the shortfall especially in rapidly growing cities like Bombay.[52] Hence, between 1961 and 1981, the Bhangi population in Bombay grew from 16,526 to 58,862.[53]

In this study of Bhangis in Jodhpur, Rajasthan, in 1973, Shyamlal showed that while Bhangis found employment in 70 different occupations, 80.29 per cent of the 2,856 cases he surveyed were still dependent on sweeping and scavenging for their incomes. Of the reminder, 121 were labourers, 6 were teachers, 6 in small business, 16 clerks, and only 1 lecturer and 1 physician. Such figures indicate that even horizontal occupational mobility is fairly limited in Jodhpur, despite the scope offered by the urban environment.[54] Sharma's study of Bhangis in Delhi in the eighties presents a similar picture of traditional employment. Of 300 families interviewed, 224 (74.7%) were employed as sweepers and scavengers, while there were 17 skilled manual labourers, 15 sanitary inspectors, 6 clerks, 9 drivers and 1 lawyer. When studied on a generational basis, there was a tendency among the younger people to move into more diverse occupations. Some of these changes Sharma attributed to the reservation policy of the government.[55]

Women and Scavenging

Scavenging as an occupation for women is still predominant among the Bhangis, and as the Delhi survey showed, their occupational mobility has not really improved over three generations. Of the 300 women interviewed, 175 (58.33%) were in private scavenging, while 104 (34.67%) worked for the Municipal Corporation of Delhi. In three generations the percentage involved in private scavenging had only dropped from 60 to 53.3 per cent, and the percentage as municipal scavengers and sweepers had remained around 34-35.[56] Besides the fact that the degrading and unclean nature of the work affect women's health, there is also an adverse impact on the children of these families. A survey of 90 female scavengers in Patna in the late 80s found that 66 of these women faced many difficulties in taking care of their children. While babies often have to accompany their mothers and be exposed to the filth of the occupation, and sleep by the roadside, the older children are left at home to be supervised by relatives. These problems are compounded by the fact that women also have to get up as early as 4 am to do domestic chores, or work night shifts.[57] In a survey of sweeper/scavenger women in rural Punjab, the frequent response was that nobody was looking after their children.[58] In such a situation children get a neglected appearance, which in a society that places great emphasis on dressing and grooming, further distinguishes scavenger and sweeper children and increases the possibility of discrimination at school.

Scavenger and sweeper women, due to their extremely low status in society, and the fact that they are often working for the survival of their families, are frequently subjected to harassment and sexual exploitation by fellow male workers and employers. The Patna women reported that male workers would often compel them to do more work, and subjected them to obscene jokes and suggestions. In rural Punjab, while the sexual exploitation of Scheduled Caste women was found to be a wretched reality, it was worst among scavengers and sweepers. There is also the problem of having to pay bribes to officials to obtain a permanent municipal position, which in one instant cost Rs. 2000 (a monthly salary being between Rs. 300-600). In another case, a woman had to provide free work at the official's home.[59]

Trade Unionism

Despite the numerous government schemes that have been implemented to improve their working and living conditions, the most beneficial efforts have come from collective action by scavengers and sweepers. As Bhangis live and work together, they have been able to rely on rapid mobilisation. Searle Chatterjee, in her study of scavengers and sweepers in Varanasi, argues that they have been able to make effective use of trade unionism because no other caste is interested in challenging their monopoly of this low status occupation.[60] Scavengers obviously have a very potent weapon when they strike, creating stinking latrines and sewers, especially in the summer months. But such industrial action is only taken in extreme cases, because people who live in such poverty and have high levels of indebtedness, cannot afford to jeopardise a weekly wage. Trade union demands have generally centred around such basic claims as better wages, improved working conditions, provision of uniforms, allegations of bribery, and improvement in housing conditions. But, of course, any benefits that result from such industrial actions only apply to those scavengers and sweepers employed in the formal sector. The predominantly female private scavengers are excluded from such pay increases and still work in filthy conditions.

Strikes by Bhangis have been sporadic since the turn of the century. Between 1924-1940 there were five strikes in Calcutta by municipal employees. Generally, the response by the Calcutta Corporation was the establishment of a committee to sympathetically consider the strikers' demands. While such offers generally ensured the cessation of the strike, the resulting reports usually only brought a provision of housing and a promise to stop graft. Nothing was done to actually improve the working conditions of Bhangis.[61] The April 1946 sweepers' strike in Bombay was of significance because

Mahatma Gandhi voiced his opposition to the use of 'coercive methods' by the Bhangis:

> Coercion cannot but result in the end in chaos. An impartial tribunal for setting disputes should always be accepted. A Bhangi may not give up his work even for a day. And there are many other ways open to him for securing justice.[62]

After independence there were strikes by scavengers and sweepers in Delhi in 1949, 1953, and 1957, under the leadership of their union, the Delhi Prantiya Mazdoor Sangh. The July 1957 strike was violent confrontation, and the Prime Minister, Jawaharlal Nehru was persuaded to mediate by the New Delhi Municipal Corporation. This strike, in the middle of the monsoon season, saw rubbish and night soil dumped on the middle of roads. When the police intervened, four sweepers were injured and the leader of the protest killed. This conflict between Bhangis and the municipal corporation continued throughout the 60s and into the 70s. In May 1972, a nine-day strike occurred in Delhi, which was followed by one of 45 days during November and December. The strike was declared illegal under the Essential Services Maintenance Act, [63] on the grounds that it could lead to an outbreak of epidemic diseases due to the hot weather. This pronouncement meant that many scavengers and sweepers were arrested, and the services of casual and temporary workers were terminated.[64] Sweepers and scavengers in Varanasi went on strike in 1960, and conducted a three-month campaign of weekly procession in 1972, in support of their demand that the municipal administration implement the provision already granted to them.[65] In Rajasthan, Bhangis have also resorted to industrial actions over similar demands, and strikes took place in Jodhpur during 1946 and 1950, and in Bikaner in 1958.[66]

Attempts to Abolish Scavenging

By the early 80s it was obvious that attempts to improve working conditions of scavengers and sweepers had been basically confined to widespread municipalisation of the workforce. Thus, the

Government of India was forced to change its tactics on improving the sanitary conditions in Indian cities and towns. Instead of seeking to improve the working conditions of scavengers, the Government of India sought amendments to the Municipal Act in May 1981, to "prohibit the construction of new latrines requiring the carriage of night soil manually. As regards the existing latrines, the State government were requested to adopt a phased programme to convert them into sanitary ones".[67]

At a conference of state representative in February 1982, it was resolved that a programme to construct low cost pour-flush latrines in urban area would be implemented "as expeditiously as possible". This programme, which was to be financed by the Housing and Urban Development Corporation, a Government of India undertaking, was thus the first formal attempt by the state to eradicate scavenging.[68]

In 1992, Prime Minister Narasimha Rao, during his Independence Day address, promised to abolish scavenging by the end of the Eighth Plan. This intent was finally formalised in the Employment of Manual Scavengers and Construction of Dry Latrines (Prohibition) Act, 1993. By obtaining the support of the states of West Bengal, Tripura, Karnataka, Maharashtra and Goa, the Government of India was able to legislate on a local Government Issue. But the implementation of this legislation has so far been limited to those five states that supported the Act, thereby ensuring that the dehumanising practice still continues in 2,587 towns, involving 7,00,000 scavengers.[69]

What Type of Sanitation System?

Unfortunately, government attempts to abolish scavenging to date have relied largely on the rhetoric of politicians[70], with little attention being paid to four major problems confronting such efforts. First, little consideration seems to have been given to the question of what is the most appropriate and affordable sanitation system for India's rapidly growing cities and towns. Currently, it is estimated that only 29 per cent of the population (70 per cent in urban areas and 14 per cent in rural areas) have access to adequate sanitation facilities. This means that over 700 million people are still reliant on dry latrines or defecation in the open. To rectify this sanitation problem will cost an estimated minimum of Rs. 728 billion, if a water borne system were to be adopted, Rs. 416 billion for a septic system and Rs. 250 billion for a twin-pit-pour-flush system. These are only capital costs and hence do not include maintenance, depreciation and operational costs.[71]

The second problem is: How does the government persuade people living in old or rented housing in Patna asking people why they had not converted to the twin-pour-flush system, the most important reason cited was the lack of adequate funds.[72] Even in situations where the local government has issued notices asking people to convert their latrines, scavenging is not necessarily abolished. In Ajmer, Rajasthan, such conversions have taken place, but houses now have gutters which drain into *nalas*. As water is scarce in Ajmer, these *nalas* frequently get blocked, hence scavengers are required to clean them out by hand.[73] A similar study of two towns in Madhya Pradesh (Satna and Khandwa), where various agencies like the UNDP/World Bank, the Ministry of Urban Development, Housing and Urban Development Corporation, and the State Government have been implementing low cost sanitation schemes for at least a decade, found that significant problems with maintenance were due to lack of water, low levels of literacy, lack of mechanical knowledge of the pour-flush latrine, blockage of outlets, and the collapse of the brick drains.[74]

Local Government

The third problem is the role of local government in any attempts to abolish scavenging. Previous attempts to improve the working and living conditions of scavengers have been ineffective because sanitation is a local government concern, with substantial amounts of the funding being supplied by the Government of India and distributed by State Governments. Hence none of the recommendations made by Government of India appointed committees about improving scavenging conditions and removal of the practice of headloading night soil have been mandatory, because the Central

Government cannot legislate on local government problems without the concurrence of at least two State Governments. Therefore, the various committees sponsored by the Government of India lack any statutory force, and the implementation of most of the recommendations is not uniform throughout the country.

This relationship between the three tiers of government has basically remained unchanged since the Government of India Act of 1935, and arrangement which meant that local bodies had to acquire their authority and the bulk of their finances from the provincial legislatures.[75] This situation of financial and political dependence has continued since Independence, with the result that:

> During the last few years many of the local governments were superseded; bureaucratic elements dominate them; most of them are financially anemic and politically subservient to certain dominant classes and narrow sections of the population. The quality and volume of civic services deteriorated during this period in several places and localities.[76]

This political subservience to "certain dominant classes" has meant that local governments have generally made very poor attempts to collect or raise taxes such as octroi. In his study of Surat, Ghanshyam Shah found that while the problem of direct taxation has existed since the earliest days of local government, the "evasion of taxes has been blatant in the last three decades".[77] The extent of these financial problems is demonstrated, for instance, by the municipal corporation in Ahmedabad, which in 1994 had an accumulated deficit of Rs. 30 crore and debts amounting Rs. 250 crore. Even to implement a proper maintenance system for its sanitation system would require Rs. 72 crore.[78]

Local governments, which are regarded as non-plan non-development bodies, have also been weakened by the constitution of single purpose institutions to handle the emerging housing, land development, water supply and sewage needs of the rapidly expanding urban populations.[79] Financial constraints, lack of bargaining power due to political subservience loss of functions, and exclusion from the planning process have meant a growing apathy towards local government institutions. This public apathy has accentuated the internal struggles within municipal bodies and frequently seen the executive gain the upper hand, with the result that elections become infrequent.[80] When such public apathy combines with the general lack of accountability by local governments to the electorate, it is little wonder that attempts to improve scavenging conditions have shown limited success since Independence.

It was only in 1989 that efforts were made to accord constitutional status to the local governments. This process was formalised by the 73rd and 74th Amendments to the Constitution in 1992. These amendments were designed to make local governments, both rural and urban, more participatory and accountable. They stipulated the holding of regular elections and increasing political representation by the reservation of seats for Scheduled Castes, Scheduled Tribes, women, and increased reservations for other Backward Classes. They are also intended to decentralise various powers and functions to local governments and ensure the implementation of arrangements that will provide adequate finance.[81]

Sulabh International

The fourth problem is that the 'liberation' of the estimated 7,00,000 scavengers from the task of manually removing night soil is fraught with difficulties. Even if they are provided with alternative jobs, they continue to face discrimination and exploitation because of their low status, their untouchability. One of the recommendations of the Scavenging Conditions Enquiry Committee, was that scavenging was a very complicated socio-economic problem and that "the question is not [one] of finances alone but needs a radical change of metal out look and habits arising therefrom". A frequent response by scavengers to the proposal that their profession be abolished is that "I hate scavenging, but what else can I do?" Rameshwari, who has worked as a scanvenger for 15 years in Ajmer, Rajasthan, responded as follows when it was suggested that she could do dish washing or laundry for a living:

> Who will let me do these jobs? Every house here has a separate entrance to the latrine. I am not even allowed to cross the threshold of a house. When we are born, our caste is not stamped on our foreheads. Only the very big people who stay in bungalows, and the Christians treat us like human beings. Even the government does not do so, for it would have thought of the repercussions on us before deciding to end scavenging.[82]

One successful approach to the liberation of scavengers has been the one adopted by Sulabh International, a non-government organisation that was registered by Dr. Bindeshwar Pathak in 1970, with the declared objective of converting dry, household latrines to hand-flush waterseal-latrines (Sulabh Shauchalaya System). The Sulabh sanitation system, which was designed by Dr. Pathak, is low cost, requires little space for construction, one in which the night soil decomposes to become manure. Hence, there is no need for scavengers to remove the waste. The initial Sulabh complexes were built in Patna and the liberated scavengers were given alternative jobs such as sweeping, cleaning and garbage removal by the local municipalities. By 1978, Sulabh International had converted some 10,000 latrines, and the project's success drew attention from the World Health Organisation, which subsequently impressed its findings upon the Government of India. Since then Sulabh International has moved into a second phase by constructing pay and use public toilets which employ the liberated scavengers as caretakers.[83]

Today Sulabh International maintains about 3,000 toilet-cum-bath complexes in nearly 650 towns and cities across India, and manufactures some of the component parts. Such complexes are generally only constructed after it has been approached by municipalities on request from local communities. The local governments then provide the land on which the complexes are constructed. Former scavengers in that community are given training in various vocations, such as driving, tailoring, typing, carpentry, leatherwork, and the maintenance of sanitary latrines. While such occupations may not actually improve monthly earnings, "liberated" scavengers surveyed in Patna admitted of changes in their interactions with other low and high caste people. Sulabh claims to have found new jobs for more than 40,000 scavengers and has established a school for their children in New Delhi.[84]

Sulabh has also implemented a somewhat novel approach to overcoming the discrimination those scavenger communities suffer. A programme called "adopt a scavenger family" has been established to help them integrate into the mainstream of Indian society. This programme has been targeted at Delhiites from different professions, with the intention of establishing social interaction between the two families and helping the scavengers find employment and access government benefits. Critics have viewed this scheme as mere tokenism, which fails to provide the educational and economic inputs that will bring equality for scavengers. Still, Sulabh International is the only organisation that has made a significant contribution to the national goal of eradicating scavenging.[85]

Conclusion

Scavengers remain marginalised in Indian society today despite the constitutional provisions which direct the state to promote their educational and economic interests. They remained marginalised because their communities are still predominantly employed to carry out the country's basic sanitary services. Lacking the necessary literacy skills to take advantage of government reservations in education and employment, scavengers have not been able to participate in the job mobility associated with living in a rapidly growing urban environment. While these economic and social problems are shared by other Scheduled Castes, it is the 'unclean and polluting nature' of their sanitary work that marginalises scavengers. The nature of their employment causes even other Untouchables to discriminate against them.

This situation continues today because scavengers have not been able to apply enough political pressure on the three levels of government to ensure that they sustained an interest in improving their living and working conditions. Scavengers lack effective political representation and influence because they are a minority group amongst the Scheduled Castes. In Maharashtra for instance, the 1981 census shows that Bhangis comprised only 2.96 per cent of the total Scheduled Caste population of 44,79,776.[86] This lack of political representation is compounded by the reservation of constituencies which force the various castes to compete among themselves to get elected to legislative seats. Finally, there is little possibility of scavengers establishing political alliances because of their isolation from other low caste groups.

Since independence some attempts have been made by the state to abolish untouchability and the discrimination that it causes. These have mainly centred on the passing of progressive legislation such as the Untouchability (Offences) Act. But such measures have been largely ineffective as shown by the annual reports of the Commissioner for Scheduled Castes and Scheduled Tribes. The Commissioner's efforts have also proved to be inadequate because it has been understaffed and underresourced and thus unable to play the "watchdog" role envisaged for it in the Constitution. In the 60s and 70s a whole chapter in the annual reports was frequently devoted to comments and recommendations on the centrally funded programmes devised to improve the living and working conditions of scavengers. But these comments and recommendations went unheeded. This was true of the Report of the Scavenging Conditions Enquiry Committee as well. The response of local government to centrally funded schemes for purchase of wheelbarrows was either a misuse of funds or apathy towards the entire scheme.

In the 80s and 90s governments have changed the focus to the abolition of scavenging as in occupation, rather than attempts to improve the socio-economic conditions of scavengers and sweepers. But the scenario has merely repeated itself. Pronouncements have been made by Prime Ministers that scavenging will be abolished by a specific date, but they have failed to detail how all the dry latrines will be replaced. This is a critical decision because dry latrines are the very source of scavenging. Adequate attention has not been paid as to how scavengers will become "liberated" from manually removing night soil. There is a lack of information about the actual number of people involved is the occupation, considering their low levels of literacy. Perhaps, it is indicative of the lack of interest by the state that the most substantial work today to "liberate" scavengers is being carried out by one of the few non-government organisations concerned about their welfare, Sulabh International notably.

Scavenging remains a complicated socio-economic problem, which not only requires adequate funding for its redressed, but needs a "radical change of mental outlook" by Indian society as was pointed out by the Report of the Scavenging Conditions Enquiry Committee in 1960. Since it appears highly improbable that the inadequacies of India's sanitation systems will be rectified in the near future, given of the huge costs and the logistics of the problem, the likelihood of scavenging as a profession disappearing is remote. The prospect of changing social attitudes to scavenging, which is seen as "unclean and polluting", also appears distant. It appears that the only way in which scavengers can be brought forward from the margins of Indian society is by providing them with the skills to take advantage of government reservations in education and employment. This is something that the state can do. But unfortunately, scavengers do not have the necessary political representation or support from the non-government sector to be able to apply enough pressure to ensure that such reservations are implemented. Therefore, it has to be concluded that the best hope that scavengers have of lessening their marginalisation resides with the slowly increasing political awareness of the younger members of their communities.

NOTES

1. The author would like to thank Robin Jeffery for his comments and suggestions.
2. For example, Article 46 of the Indian Constitution says, "The state shall promote with special care the educational and economic interests of the weaker sections of the people, and in particular of the Scheduled Castes and Scheduled Tribes and shall protect them from social injustice and all forms of expolitation".
3. Lannoy Richard, *The Speaking Tree: A study of Indian Culture and Society*, London: Oxford University Press, 1971, pp. 145-47, Rama Sharma, *Bhangi: Scavenger in Indian Society - Marginality, Identity and Politicization of the Community*, New Delhi: M.D. Publications, 1995, pp. 43-45.

4. Shyamlal, *Caste and Political Mobilisation*, The Bhangis, Jaipur: Panchsheel Prakashan, 1981.
5. Mary, Searle Chatterjee, *Reversible Sex Roles: The Speical Case of Benares Sweepers*, Oxford: Pergamon Press, 1988, pp. 7-8.
6. Sharma, *op.cit.*, p. 51.
7. Owen M., Lynch, *The Politics of Untouchability: Social Mobility and Social Change in a City of India*, New York: Columbia University Press, 1969, pp. 180-81.
8. Barbara Joshi, *Democracy in Search of Equality: Untouchable Politics and Indian Social Change*, Delhi: Hindustan Publishing Corporation, 1982, p. 10.
9. Peter, Waldman, "Reforms bring Little Change for India's 'Untouchables' ", *Wall Street Journal*, 20 June, 1996, pp. 1 & 7. This article was posted on the India News Network Digest, 20 June, 1996, Vol. 2, No. 916; e-mail address: India-L@Indnet.BGSU.edu.
10. S.P. Punalekar, "Prison Without Walls: Social Situation of Sweepers and Scavengers in Western India", *Social Change*, 1990, Vol. 9, Nos. 1 & 2, p. 155.
11. Sharma, *op.cit.*, pp. 52 & 56. It is interesting to note that when Stephen Fuchs describes the Bhangis in *At the Bottom of Indian Society*, Delhi: Munshiram Manoharlal, 1981, pp. 236-41, this division within the Bhangi caste was reversed.
12. Quoted in Sachchidananda, *Congress and the Harijans*, New Delhi: Congress Centenary Celebrations Committee, 1985, p. 36.
13. The Poona Pact increased the number of separate electorates for the Depressed Classes. But as Eleanor Zelliot pointed out in "Learning the Use of Political Means", in Rajni Kothari (ed.), *Caste in Indian Politics*, New York: Gordon and Breach, 1970, the conflict between Ambedkar and Gandhi over the advancement of untouchables, was one between using political power to achieve social and economic equality and the cleansing of untouchability from the *Varna* system whereby Untouchables would become *Shudras*.
14. Sachchidananda, *op.cit.*, pp. 39-45, and Mark Thomson, *Gandhi and His Ashrams*, London: Sangam Books, 1993, p. 177.
15. P. Radhakrishnan, "Ambedkar's Legacy to Dalits: Has the Nation Reneged on its Promises?" *Economic and Political Weekly*, 17 August, 1991, pp. 1914-20.
16. Scavenging Conditions Enquiry Committee, *Report of the Scavenging Conditions Enquiry Committee*, New Delhi: Central Advisory Board for Harijan Welfare, Ministry of Home Affairs, Government of India, 1961, Appendix 1, p. 140.
17. *Ibid.*, pp. 140-42.
18. L.M. Shrikant, *Report of the Commissioner for Scheduled Castes and Scheduled Tribes*, hereafter RC/ST/C for the Year 1956-57, Faridabad: Government of India Press, 1957, p. 16.

19. Scavenging Enquiry Committee, *op.cit.*, p. 139.
20. Shrikant, *op.cit.*, 1957-58, New Delhi: Government of India Press, 1958, p. 16.
21. Scavenging Conditions Enquiry Committee, *op.cit.*, pp. 3-6.
22. *Ibid.*, p. 5.
23. *Ibid.*, pp. 8-14.
24. *Ibid.*, pp. 19-22.
25. *Ibid*, pp. 68-69.
26. *Ibid.*, p. 37.
27. *Ibid*, pp. 46-48.
28. *Ibid*, p. 52.
29. *Ibid.*, pp. 53-55.
30. *Ibid.*, pp. 57-58.
31. A Jagirdar is a man who employs others to clean latrines, to whom he pays an agreed nominal amount. These middle men frequently enjoy a very good standard of living from this provision of labour.
32. Scavenging Conditions Enquiry Committee, *op.cit.*, pp. 79-80.
33. *Ibid.*, pp. 80-84.
34. The Committee included a chapter containing reports on methods of scavenging in 18 developing countries (which were compiled by the Ministry of External Affairs from Indian Missions abroad) in an attempt to demonstrate that 'progress' had been made in improving scavenging conditions in many countries (Chapter 12, *Ibid.*).
35. *Ibid.*, p. 92.
36. *Ibid.*, pp. 97-102.
37. *Ibid.*, p. 46.
38. Sharma, *op.cit.*, pp. 83-87.
39. Shrikant, RC/SC/T, 1960-61, Part I, pp. 306-7.
40. N.K. Bose, RC/SC/T, 1969-70, p. 62 and Sharma, *op.cit.*, p. 185.
41. Shishir Kumar, RC/SC/T 1978-79, Part I, p. 121.
42. Anil Chanda, RC/SC/T, 1963-64, p. 144.
43. *Ibid.*
44. Bose, RC/SC/T, 1967-68, p. 98.
45. Kumar, RC/SC/T, 1978-79, Part I, p. 123.
46. Kumar, RC/SC/T, 1984-85, p. 9.
47. Census of India 1981, *Maharashtra Part-IX* (ii), Special Tables for Scheduled Castes, Tables 4 to 6, pp. 960-83 and 1284-87.
48. O.P. Sharma, *Scheduled Castes: Population and Literates*, New Delhi, Kar Kripa Publishers, 1991, pp. 245 and 338.
49. Shyamlal, 1992, *op.cit.*, pp. 42-44. These figures were largely based on the 1971 census.
50. Waldman, *op.cit.*
51. K.C. Sharma, D.S. Thakar, and Jasminder Kaur, "Socio-economic Conditions of Scavengers in Himachal Pradesh", *Social Change*, 19/3, September 1989, pp. 49-53.

52. Sharma, *op.cit.*, p. 96.
53. Census of India 1961, *Volume X Maharashtra Part X (I-B)*, p. 304 and Census of India 1981, *Maharashtra, Part-IX(I), Special Tables for Scheduled Castes* (Table 4 to 6), p. 978.
54. Shyamlal, 1992, *op.cit.*, pp. 120-3.
55. Sharma, *op.cit.*, pp. 96-97.
56. *Ibid.*, pp. 102-3.
57. Pratima Chaudhury, "Problems of Female scavengers of Patna" in S.N. Chaudhury, (ed.), *Changing Status of Depressed Castes in Contemporary India*, Delhi: Daya Publishing House, 1988, pp. 152-3.
58. Parmajit Judge S., *Scheduled Caste Women in the Workforce in Rural Punjab*, Surat: Centre for Social Studies, Occassional Paper No. 9, October, 1990, pp. 30-31.
59. *Ibid.*, pp. 36-37 and Chaudhury, *op.cit.*, pp. 153-45.
60. Searle Chatterjee, *op.cit.*, p. 82.
61. Mohinder Singh, *The Depressed Classes: Their Economic and Social Conditions* Bombay: Hind Kitabs Ltd. 1947, pp. 102-5.
62. M.K. Gandhi, *Collected Works*, *op.cit.*, Volume 84, pp. 8-9.
63. The Essential Services Maintenance Act prohibits strikes in essential services such as sanitation and water supply, along with the railways, post and telegraph, etc.
64. S.M. Banerjee raised this issue in the Lok Sabha on 12 December, 1972, *Lok Sabha Debates*, Fifth Series, Vol. 22, 12-22 December, 1972, pp. 215-6, and Rama Sharma *op.cit.*, pp. 219-47.
65. Searle Chatterjee, *op.cit.*, pp. 81-2.
66. Shyamlal, *op.cit.*, pp. 48-49, and 58-61.
67. Bhishma Narain Singh, Minister of Parliamentary Affairs and Works and Housing, 22 March, 1982, *Lok Sabha Debates*, Vol. XXVI, 19-25 March, 1982, pp. 89-91.
68. Buta Singh, Minister of Parliamentary Affairs, Sports and Works and Housing, 21 February, 1983, *Lok Sabha Debates*, Vol. XXXIV, 16-24 February, 1983, pp. 319-23.
69. C. Jayanthi, "The Sewage Problem", *The Pioneer*, 14 December, 1995, p. 9.
70. These pledges were even included in the election manifestoes of the Congress (I) and the Bharatiya Janata Dal Parties for the 1996 general election.
71. Anon, "Sanitation Facilities for All, An Uphill Task:, *The Hindu Daily*, On-line Edition, 14 August, 1996, Section, National (http:/www.webpage.com/hindu/today).
72. Bindeshwar Pathak, *Road to Freedom: A Social Study on the Abolition of Scavenging in India*, Delhi, Motilal Banarsidass Publishers, 1991, p. 149.
73. Amit Mitra, "I hate scavenging, but what else can I do?" *Down to Earth*, 30 November, 1992, p. 51.
74. Sabir Ali, "The Sanitation Situation: A Case Study", *Yojana*, 15 October, 1996, pp. 23-5.

75. M.J.K. Thavaraj, "Finances of Local Government in India" *Indian Journal of Public Administration*, 24/3, July-September 1978, p. 620, and Faraz Ahmed, "Scavengers' Lot Worst in Uttar Pradesh", *Pioneer*, 17 May, 1993.
76. Thavaraj, "Finance of Local Government", *IJPA*, p. 621.
77. Ghanshyam Shah, "Economy and Civic Authority in Surat", *Economic and Political Weekly*, 8 October, 1994, p. 2675.
78. Anon, """Our Filthy Cicities: Can We clean up the mess?" *India Today*, 31 October, 1996, p. 43.
79. Examples of such single purpose bodies are the Delhi Development Authority, the Calcutta Metropolitan Development Corporation, Housing Boards and Urban Improvement Trusts.
80. Iqubal Narain and P.C. Mathur, "Urban Development and re-vitalisation of local Self government institutions: A conceptual analysis in the Context of Some Lessons from anti-poverty rural development programme and policies in India", *Indian Journal of Public Administration*, 30/4, October-December 1984, p. 948.
81. Abhijit Dutta, "Municipal Reform in India: Comparative Models and Processes", *Economic and Political Weekly*, 30/38, 23 September, 1995, pp. 2395-96.
82. Amit Mitra, "I have scavenging", *Down to Earth*, p. 51.
83. National Institute of Urban Affairs, *A Revolution in Low Cost Sanitation: Sulabh International*, New Delhi, NIUA for the Mega-Cities Project, New York University, 1990, pp. 3-8.
84. Pathak, *Road to Freedom*, pp. 131-32.
85. National Institute of Urban Affairs, Revolution in Low Cost Sanitations, p. 12, and Anon, "Scavengers Interact with Delhi's Elite", *Times of India*, 13 March, 1995, p. 5.
86. Census of India, 1981, *Maharashtra Part-IX (ii), Special Tables for Scheduled Castes* Tables 4-6, pp. 960 & 1284.

9

THE STRUCTURE OF STAGNANCY
Sweepers in Ahmedabad District

TAKASHI SHINODA

Sweeping and scavenging have been regarded as menial jobs and workers doing these jobs have been put under social discrimination in most of the countries. In India, social discrimination against scavengers and sweepers has been woven into the caste system which has assigned these works to particular *jatis* of the Scheduled Castes (SCs) as their 'traditional' occupations. They have been regarded as the most polluted community and have been discriminated against in their religious, social, and economic life, not only by the *Savarna Hindus* but also by other SCs.

The origin of scavenging work dates back to the Mughal period when dry latrines[1] were introduced in the courts. At this stage, the number of scavengers was very small since the latrines were confined to the courts only. The number of dry latrines increased remarkably during the British rule with the increased use among urban dwellers and growth of urban population. Accordingly, the demand for scavenging also increased, which was mostly met by that segment of sweepers who found the scavenging work beneficial as a source of additional income. Later on, scavengers formed the lower stratum of this community in the gradual process of division of labour among them. Migration of scavengers took place in a massive scale from Punjab, Gujarat, and the United Provinces to Bengal, Deccan and many parts of south India, where the society lacked indigenous scavengers. Notably, sweeping also became the dominant occupation of this community with the development of cities and towns in the past two hundred years, though sweeping has a much longer history than scavenging. Thus, the concentration of this community in the sweeping and scavenging works is of recent origin.

At the time of Independence, dry latrines were very common in urban India, and a lot of workers were engaged in scavenging under extremely poor working conditions. After Independence, the Central Government set-up the Malkani Committee (India, 1960), the Pandya Committee (India, 1969), the Basu Task Force (India, 1990-91), and the National Scheme (India, 1991-92) for inquiring into the service and working conditions of sweepers and scavengers in various parts of India. Some state governments such as Saurashtra (Saurashtra, 1956), Bombay (Bombay, 1958), Haryana (Haryana, 1972), and Karnataka (Karnataka, 1976) also appointed independent committees on the service and working conditions of sweepers and scavengers in their own states. Their reports point out the problems and difficulties in improving the service, working, and living conditions of sweepers and scavengers.

Scavenging includes several processes such as collection of human excreta from dry latrines, its transportation to pail depots or dumping grounds, and the final treatment of human excreta in the dumping grounds. Several Committees recommended the introduction of wheel barrows, scrapers, rubber gloves, and other tools and equipments to improve the working conditions (Bombay, 1958; India, 1960; India, 1969; India, 1990-91). However, both the local bodies and the scavengers themselves tended to be indifferent to such changes. Consequently, it took a long time to curb the terrible but common practice of carrying human excreta in a bamboo basket on the head.

Customary rights of the scavengers, called *gharaki* in Gujarat and *jagirdari dastoori*, *virat,* etc., in other parts of India, are another barrier for their improvement (India, 1968). The origin of these rights date back to the Mughal period. The rights continued to prevail among the scavengers with the increase of dry latrines during British rule. The rights—hereditary, salable, and transferable—were of two kinds: one for cleaning dry latrines in certain private households exclusively and the other for the sale and disposal of human excreta collected by private scavengers. This system of customary rights brought about a vicious circle between low emoluments and poor service, leading to the deterioration of overall hygienic conditions in each level of labour process. It also encouraged the holders of the customary rights to lease out the work to non-holders within their community at a nominal wage. Since the scavengers tended to cling to their hereditary rights because of their poor mobility for other jobs, it was difficult for the local bodies to municipalize the scavenging service, even with compensation.

The turning point arrived in the mid-60s with the launch of *the Bhangi Kasht Mukti Karyakram* (Jairamdas, 1969). The *Harijan Sevak Sangh* took the initiative in starting the scheme, with the cooperation of the Central Government and some State Governments to abolish dry latrines by October 2, 1969, the centenary year of Mahatma Gandhi. The scheme was effective in curbing the number of dry latrines and mitigating the hardship of scavengers, to some extent. Again, in the 80s, several low cost sanitation programmes were started in some states, with the financial assistance of the World Bank, UNDP, and the Central Government, to spread cheap substituted latrines in urban and rural areas. As a result, the number of dry latrines declined slowly but steadily, and many scavengers were absorbed as sweepers in the local bodies. Improvements were remarkable where NGOs worked in association with the State governments.

The estimated number of dry latrines in urban and rural India was 72 lakhs and 25 lakhs, respectively, in 1983. The number has declined by 40 per cent in urban India and by 12 per cent in rural India between 1973-74 and 1983. Dry latrines were owned by 18 per cent of urban households and 2 per cent of rural households in 1983. Though the number of sanitary workers slightly increased from 8.02 lakh in 1961 to 8.55 lakh in 1981, the percentage share of scavengers among sanitary workers has declined considerably with the spread of substitute latrines and the development of sewerage systems in large cities. Accordingly, the central issues have also shifted from the abolition of dry latrines to the improvement of service and working conditions of sanitary workers and their rehabilitation (India, 1991-92).

The major employers of sweepers are the local bodies and the Central and State governments. Besides, a considerable number of sweepers are working on contract basis in factories, business firms, private residential complexes, and other institutional organizations. We hardly know the actual number of such workers in the private sector and their service conditions. However, a series of census data on the Scheduled Castes suggest that sweepers are widely spread out, both in public and private sectors. Sweepers employed by Central and the State governments are 'fortunate' in terms of their service and working conditions, while those in the private sector suffer most because of poor service and working conditions and lack of legal protection, such as the Minimum Wage Act.

The service and working conditions of workers employed by the local bodies have considerable variations. The level of wages and various allowances, the availability of trade unions, and financial institutions are in favour of large local bodies, while the workers in small local bodies suffer from low wages, unstable service conditions, and low accessibility to trade unions and financial institutions.

As a part of my research work on the status of sweepers in India, I undertook a socio-economic survey of sweepers employed by eight local bodies in Ahmedabad district, during three months from July to September 1991. This paper is an attempt to assess the impact of the institutional development on the socio-economic conditions of sweepers and their occupational mobility, based on the survey which covered 288 sweeper households.[2] As a relevant form of institutional development, the paper deals with impact of trade union activities and the availability of institutional finance. The paper also examines occupation, education, income, and liability of the sweeper households.

Ahmedabad city, the biggest centre of trade and industry in Gujarat, is located in Ahmedabad city taluka. Dehgam, Sanand, Viramgam, and Dholka are the headquarters of four out of six talukas of Ahmedabad district. Bareja and Bavala are small towns in the Dehgam and Dholka talukas respectively. Sola is located on the outskirts of Ahmedabad city. According to the administrative division of local bodies by population, Ahmedabad is classified as a municipal corporation (3 lakh and above), Dehgam, Viramgam, and Dholka as municipalities (25,000 to 300,000), Sanand, Bareja, Bavala as nagar panchayats (10,000 to 25,000), and Sola as a Gram Panchayat (less than 10,000). Thus, the local bodies surveyed cover four administrative divisions. However, the population size of the three municipalities does not differ much from that of the three Nagar Panchayats and we notice a similarity in the various socio-economic indices of the sweepers in the two administrative divisions. For simplification, Sola, the single Gram Panchayat surveyed, has been clubbed with Nagar Panchayats. The Ahmedabad Municipal Corporation is under the regulation of the Bombay Municipal Corporation Act, 1947, the municipalities are controlled by the Gujarat Municipalities Act, 1963, and the Nagar Panchayats and Gram Panchayat by the Gram/Nagar/Taluka/District Panchayats Act, 1961.

Majority of the sweepers surveyed belong to the community classified as the Bhangis in the Indian censuses. The 1981 census divides SCs in Gujarat into thirty groups, out of which the Vankars (traditionally weavers), Chamars (tanners) and Bhangis (sweepers and scavengers) are 43.1 per cent, 27.2 per cent and 12.6 per cent respectively being the three most populous castes. There is considerable variation in the level of political, social, and economic development among the SCs in Gujarat. The Vankars and Chamars constitute an advanced group, while the Bhangis remain one of the most backward groups. [As for the title of SC communities, I follow the census classification, but only when I compare these communities in this paper. Of course, I am aware that the title of the Bhangis is disliked by Bhangis themselves owing to its negative connotation (hemp, drunken, ex-communicated, etc.). Some of them prefer such titles as Mehtar, Valmiki, or even sweepers. In other contexts, I replace the title of the Bhangis with such expressions as sweepers or the community.]

Occupation

According to the 1981 census, the share of main workers among the urban Bhangi population in Gujarat is 40.4 per cent among males and 18.7 per cent among females, while the share of marginal workers is 0.6 per cent among males and 0.9 per cent among females (Tables 9.1 and 9.2). The work participation ratio (WPR) of the Bhangi males is almost the same as that of other SCs; however, the work participation ratio of the Bhangi females is higher than that of other SCs in Gujarat.

TABLE 9.1 : Industrial Distribution of the Bhangi Male Main Workers in Gujarat State and Ahmedabad District, 1981

	Gujarat		Ahmedabad District	
Industry	Rural	Urban	Rural	Urban
I. Cultivators	128	3	53	0
II. Agri. Labourers	556	26	697	15
III. Animal Husbandry	10	3	17	3
IV. Mining & Quarrying	2	4	0	2
V. Manufacturing				
(a) Household Industry	95	3	47	2
(b) Other than (a)	42	72	47	68
VI. Construction	7	19	6	25
VII. Trade and Commerce	8	30	9	39
VIII. Transport & Communication	34	142	31	130
IX. Other Services	118	698	93	716
Total	1000	1000	1000	1000
No. of Main Workers	495	404	484	399
No. of Marginal Workers	12	6	16	2
Population	86,529	70,876	7,449	21,790

Source: Government of India, Census of India 1981, Series-5, Gujarat, Part IX (i), Special Tables for Scheduled Castes, 1988, pp. 10-15, 214-219.

The survey-based WPR of the Bhangi males is considerably lower than the ratio of the urban Bhangi males of Gujarat because of

TABLE 9.2: Industrial Distribution of the Bhangi Female Main Workers in Gujarat State and Ahmedabad District, 1981

Industry	Gujarat		Ahmedabad District	
	Rural	Urban	Rural	Urban
I. Cultivators	58	2	7	0
II. Agri. Labourers	728	17	898	14
III. Animal Husbandry	4	1	3	1
IV. Mining & Quarrying	1	1	1	0
V. Manufacturing				
(a) Household Industry	82	3	30	1
(b) Other than (a)	15	15	13	19
VI. Construction	5	10	1	23
VII. Trade and Commerce	3	5	1	6
VIII. Transport & Communication	4	35	2	24
IX. Other Services	100	911	44	914
Total	1000	1000	1000	1000
No. of Main Workers	155	187	216	181
No. of Marginal Workers	110	9	91	4
Population	82,737	66,889	7,003	18,701

Source: Government of India, Census of India 1981, Series-5, Gujarat, Part IX (i), Special Tables for Scheduled Castes, 1988, pp. 10-15, 214-219.

their pursuit of higher education as well as the difficulty in obtaining a job in the age group of 20-29 (Table 9.3). Many Bhangi youths of this age group are unemployed. This is owing to either their search for a better job or being waitlisted for temporary or permanent jobs. WPR reaches a peak in the age group of 45-49. The survey based WPR of the Bhangi females is fairly higher than that of other SCs of Gujarat, thus supplementing the relatively lower WPR of the Bhangi males (Table 9.4). This is particularly so in the Ahmedabad Municipal Corporation which has an equitable employment policy

TABLE 9.3: Distribution of Male Workers in Sample Households and Their Work Participation Ratios by Age Group and Type of Local Body

(Number)

Age Group	Municipal Corp.	Munici-pality	Nagar Panchayat	Gram Panchayat	Total
10-14	—	—	1	—	1 (0.9)
15-19	4	9	4	1	18 (11.2)
20-24	37	20	10	2	69 (48.3)
25-29	21	12	9	—	42 (62.7)
30-34	33	15	8	—	56 (80.7)
35-39	25	11	9	1	46 (88.5)
40-44	26	7	6	2	41 (91.1)
45-49	25	6	2	1	34 (91.9)
50-54	21	6	3	—	30 (78.9)
55-59	7	3	2	—	12 (75.0)
60+	3	—	—	—	3 (13.6)
Total	202	89	54	7	353 (36.5)

Note: Figures in parentheses show the work participation ratio.

Source: Household Survey of the Bhangi Community, 1992.

for both sexes. WPR of females in the age group below 20 is lower than that of the males. Prevalence of education, housework before marriage, and child care after marriage are the major reasons for the late entry of the females in the work force. Thus, approximately 50 per cent of the female workers belong to the age group of 40 and above, while the share of the male workers of the same age group is 34 per cent only. There is a considerable difference in the work participation pattern of the male workers among the local bodies. In the municipal corporation, 30 per cent of the workers surveyed were in the age group below 30, while in the municipalities and nagar panchayats 46 per cent and 45 per cent of the workers respectively were in the same age group. We notice a similar tendency among the female workers, too. The employment policy of local bodies towards

TABLE 9.4: Distribution of Female Workers in Sample Households and Their Work Participation Ratios by Age Group

Age group	Number of Workers	Work Participation Ratio (%)
15-19	5	4.1
20-24	18	16.1
25-29	37	52.1
30-34	37	68.5
35-39	37	75.5
40-44	38	80.9
45-49	39	88.6
50-54	24	85.7
55-59	16	84.2
60+	6	25.0
Total	257	30.2

Source: Household Survey of the Bhangi Community, 1992.

sweepers is one of the decisive factors in shaping this work participation pattern.

Interestingly, there is not much difference between the male and female workers in terms of their working status. The share of permanent workers among all categories of workers is 64 per cent among males, and 61 per cent among females. The rest of the workers are clubbed under the title of temporary workers. However, the service and working conditions of the temporary workers vary a great deal. Some are engaged in sweeping and scavenging on a contract basis with a nominal emolument, while some others, who are put in a waiting list as candidates (*ummedvar*) for permanent workers, enjoy similar service and working conditions as permanent workers.

The distribution of permanent workers according to their age group shows a keen contrast with that of the temporary workers. Temporary workers are dominant in the age group below 30 in both sexes though the female temporary workers are more widely distributed in different age groups than the male workers. The distribution of workers by working status and age group suggests a common pattern of mobility among the Bhangis from temporary to permanent status, which is confirmed by the survey result on the previous working status of the workers (Table 9.5). A major trend is the change of working status for both sexes.

TABLE 9.5: Distribution of Workers by Working Status of Their Present and Previous Occupations and Sex

(Number, %)

Working Status	Present occupation		Previous occupation	
	Male	Female	Male	Female
Permanent	220	161	29	8
	(59.3)	(62.2)	(12.1)	(5.3)
Temporary	151	98	210	142
	(40.7)	(37.8)	(87.9)	(94.7)
Total	371	259	239	150
	(100.0)	(100.0)	(100.0)	(100.0)

Source: Household Survey of the Bhangi Community, 1992.

The occupational structure of the Bhangi workers does not suggest any signs of diversification. In the present survey 80 per cent of the male workers and 93 per cent of the female workers are classified as sweepers (Tables 9.6 and 9.7). According to the type of work, sweepers can be divided into dry sweepers and wet sweepers. Dry sweepers are engaged in removal, transportation, and disposal of solid wastes, while wet sweepers handle liquid wastes. The former clean roads, housing complexes, factories, hospitals, other buildings, and public and private waterborne toilets, and remove carcasses. The latter clean gutters and sewers, and remove liquid wastes from cess pools, septic tanks, and so on. Those who remove human excreta from dry latrines are called scavengers. Out of the different works which fall under the head of sweeping, a major

TABLE 9.6: Distribution of Male Workers in Sample Households by Occupation and Type of Local Body

(Number, %)

Occupation	Municipal Corp.	Municipa-lity	Nagar & Gram Panchayat	Total
Sweepers	196	81	48	325
(incl. Mukadams)	(81.3)	(84.4)	(70.6)	(80.2)
Clerks & Teachers	6	7	2	15
	(2.5)	(7.3)	(2.9)	(3.7)
Other Workers	39	8	18	65
	(16.2)	(8.3)	(26.5)	(16.1)
Total	241	96	68	405
	(100.0)	(100.0)	(100.0)	(100.0)

Source: Household Survey of the Bhangi Community, 1992.

TABLE 9.7: Distribution of Female Workers in Sample Households by Occupation and Type of Local Body

(Number, %)

Occupation	Municipal Corp.	Municipa-lity	Nagar & Gram Panchayat	Total
Sweepers	157	53	53	263
(incl. Mukadams)	(95.2)	(91.4)	(86.9)	(92.6)
Clerks & Teachers	6	1	—	4
	(1.8)	(1.7)	—	(1.4)
Other Workers	5	4	8	17
	(3.0)	(6.9)	(13.1)	(6.0)
Total	165	58	61	284
	(100.0)	(100.0)	(100.0)	(100.0)

Source: Household Survey of the Bhangi Community, 1992.

proportion of the workers, particularly females, is occupied in road sweeping. [In this paper, workers involved in various activities related to sweeping are put under the head of sweepers for simplicity of analysis.] Occupations other than sweeping consist of clerical, teaching, technical, and other miscellaneous works. Only 15 per cent of male workers and 5 per cent of female workers are employed in these occupations. Though all these works are so-called 'clean' works, the only prestigious ones are the clerical and teaching occupations.

TABLE 9.8: Occupational Distribution of the Respondent's Father, Mother, Grandfather and Grandmother

(Number of Persons, %)

Occupation	Father	Mother	Grand-father	Grand-mother	Total
Sweepers	254	200	146	101	701
	(90.7)	(95.2)	(93.6)	(95.3)	(93.2)
Mukadams	5	3	2	1	11
	(1.8)	(91.4)	(91.3)	(0.9)	(1.5)
Technical Workers	8	2	3	—	13
	(2.9)	(1.0)	(1.9)	—	(1.7)
Clerical Workers	4	2	2	—	8
	(1.4)	(1.0)	(1.3)		(1.1)
Teachers	—	—	—	1	1
				(0.9)	(0.1)
Singers	—	1	—	—	1
		(0.4)			(0.1)
Miscellaneous Workers	9	2	3	3	17
	(3.2)	(1.0)	(1.9)	(2.9)	(2.3)
Total	280	210	156	106	752
	(100.0)	(100.0)	(100.0)	(100.0)	(100.0)

Source: Household Survey of the Bhangi Community, 1992.

The occupational immobility of the community is not confined to the present generation. The last reported occupation of the respondents' father, mother, paternal grandfather and paternal grand-mother clearly indicates that there has not been any visible improvement in the occupational mobility of the Bhangis as a whole over three generations (Table 9.8). This occupational immobility is the very factor which restrains the socio-economic development of the community.

Education

Education plays a strategic role in socio-economic development. With a drastic change in the educational structure in recent years, the key issue of the education has shifted from eradication of illiteracy to upgrading of educational structure in most of the communities except the Scheduled Tribes and some other backward communities. The educational structure of the urban Bhangis surveyed indicates that the enrollment ratio at the primary and middle school level has been shooting up in both sexes though illiteracy is still dominant among the adult females. Since schooling has spread rapidly, illiteracy is expected to be minimized sooner or later. An important feature of their educational structure, in comparison with other SCs is that they have fewer number of graduates. Graduation is a minimum qualification for a 'white collar' job, which may contribute to the upliftment of the community as a whole. There are several factors which discourage a rise in the number of graduates among the Bhangis, such as poor financial position, tough competition with other SCs for the reserved seats in higher educational institutions and government services, and social discrimination against the employment of the Bhangi graduates. Out of 14 graduate in the household survey, 11 were still unemployed.

The census data indicate that the Vankars and Chamars are the dominant castes among the SCs of Gujarat, in terms of the number and the share of graduates for both sexes. The share of the Chamars has considerably increased between the 1961 and 1981 censuses, while the share of the Vankars has remained stable. On the contrary the share of the Bhangis has decreased over the last 20 years, in spite of the increase in the number of graduates among them. The census data also confirm the backwardness of the Bhangis in higher education.

Since most of the occupations in which the Bhangis are engaged do not require any educational qualifications, the educational pattern of workers by occupation does not suggest much variation (Tables 9.9 and 9.10). The educational variation among sweepers is very wide, ranging from illiterates to graduates. The educational structure of thc Bhangis is, to a considerable extent, reflected through the educational distribution of sweepers, since sweeping is the major occupation of the Bhangis. Interestingly, the *mukadam*, who is the supervisor of the sweepers, is not better-educated than his fellow sweepers. Thus, the education of the Bhangis are quite irrelevant, atleast, to their occupation. As long as sweeping remains the dominant occupation of the Bhangis, they may lack the motivation to achieve higher educational qualifications. Their occupations, other than sweeping, are professional, technical or other miscellaneous occupations. Professional occupations include that of teachers, clerks, and compounders. Technical occupations include mechanics, while other miscellaneous occupations cover peons, watchmen, door boys, ward boys, petrol pump operators, mill workers, and agricultural and general workers. Out of these only teachers and clerks need higher educational qualifications.

TABLE 9.9: Distribution of Male Workers in Sample Households by Occupation and Education

(Number, %)

Occupation	Illiterate	<Primary	Primary	Middle	Second-ary	Graduate	Total
1	2	3	4	5	6	7	8
Sweepers	53	74	85	53	21	2	288
	(18.4)	(25.7)	(29.5)	(14.8)	(7.3)	(0.7)	(100.0)
	[94.6]	[83.1]	[79.4]	[86.9]	[77.8]	[100.0]	[84.2]
Mukadams	2	5	6	1	2	—	16
	(12.5)	(31.3)	(37.5)	(6.3)	(12.5)	—	(100.0)
	[3.6]	[5.6]	[5.6]	[1.6]	[7.4]	—	[4.7]
Peons	—	4	5	5	—	—	14
	(28.6)	(35.7)	(35.7)	—	—	—	(100.0)

(Contd.)

TABLE 9.9 *(Contd.)*

1	2	3	4	5	6	7	8
	—	[4.5]	[4.7]	[8.2]	—	—	[4.1]
Clerks	—	—	—	—	1	—	1
	—	—	—	—	(100.0)	—	(100.0)
	—	—	—	—	[3.7]	—	[0.3]
Compounders	—	—	1	—	—	—	1
		—	(100.0)	—	—	—	(100.0)
		—	[0.9]	—	—	—	[0.3]
Mechanics	1	—	4	—	—	—	5
	(20.0)	—	(80.0)	—	—	—	(100.0)
	[1.8]	—	[3.7]	—	—	—	[1.5]
Watchmen	—	—	—	1	—	—	1
	—	—	—	(100.0)	—	—	(100.0)
	—	—	—	[1.6]	—	—	[0.3]
Ward Boys	—	1	—	1	—	—	2
	—	(50.0)	—	(50.0)	—	—	(100.0)
	—	[1.1]	—	[3.7]	—	—	[0.6]
Petrol Pump	—	1	—	—	—	—	1
Operators	—	(100.0)	—	—	—	—	(100.0)
	—	[1.1]	—	—	—	—	[0.3]
Other	—	4	5	—	1	—	10
Labourers	—	(40.0)	(50.0)	—	(10.0)	—	(100.0)
	—	[4.5]	[4.7]	—	[3.7]	—	[2.9]
Total	56	89	107	61	27	2	342
	(16.4)	(26.0)	(31.3)	(17.8)	(7.9)	(0.6)	(100.0)
	[100.0]	[100.0]	[100.0]	[100.0]	[100.0]	[100.0]	[100.0]

Source: Household Survey of the Bhangi Community, 1992.

The association between the working status and education is interesting. It is noteworthy that the share of temporary workers in higher education is slightly greater than that of permanent workers, not only for both sexes but also for both occupational groups,

TABLE 9.10: Distribution of Female Workers in Sample Households by Occupation and Education

(Number, %)

Occupation	Illiterate	<Primary	Primary	Middle	Secondary	Graduate	Total
Sweepers	140	43	43	4	6	1	237
	(59.1)	(18.1)	(18.1)	(1.7)	(2.5)	(0.4)	(100.0)
	[94.6]	[95.6]	[91.5]	[100.0]	[100.0]	[100.0]	[94.4]
Compounders	—	1	—	—	—	—	1
		(100.0)					(100.0)
		[2.2]					[0.4]
Domestic Workers	2	—	2	—	—	—	4
	(50.0)		(50.0)				(100.0)
	[1.4]		[4.3]				[1.6]
Other Labourers	6	1	2	—	—	—	9
	(66.7)	(11.1)	(22.2)				(100.0)
	[4.1]	[2.2]	[4.3]				[3.6]
Total	148	45	47	4	6	1	251
	(59.0)	(17.9)	(18.7)	(1.6)	(2.4)	(0.4)	(100.0)
	[100.0]	[100.0]	[100.0]	[100.0]	[100.0]	[100.0]	[100.0]

Source: Household Survey of the Bhangi Community, 1992.

sweepers and non-sweepers (Tables 9.11 and 9.12). This is because temporary workers are concentrated among the younger generation that has a close association with middle or higher level of education. Another important finding is that the occupation of three graduates is confined to sweeping. One female graduate is a permanent sweeper and two male graduates are temporary sweepers. An intensive interview with them revealed that they have succumbed to social as well as family pressure and taken up the broom after several failed efforts to get a 'clean' government job. The rest of the eleven unemployed graduates are also involved in the struggle to find a 'clean' job. Though the number is relatively small, these angry and rebellious youth may contribute to the social development of the community in the future.

TABLE 9.11: Distribution of Male Workers in Sample Households by Working Status and Education

(Number, %)

Education	Permanent Workers	Temporary Workers	Total
Illiterate	39	18	57
	(68.4)	(31.6)	(100.0)
	[18.4]	[13.6]	[16.6]
Read & Write	58	31	89
	(65.2)	(34.8)	(100.0)
	[27.4]	[23.5]	[25.9]
Primary	68	39	107
	(63.6)	(36.4)	(100.0)
	[32.1]	[29.5]	[31.1]
Middle	33	28	61
	(54.1)	(45.9)	(100.0)
	[15.6]	[21.2]	[17.7]
Secondary	14	14	28
	(50.0)	(50.0)	(100.0)
	[6.6]	[10.6]	[8.1]
Graduate	—	2	2
	—	(100.0)	(100.0)
	—	[1.5]	[0.6]
Total	212	132	344
	(61.6)	(38.4)	(100.0)
	[100.0]	[100.0]	[100.0]

Source: Household Survey of the Bhangi Community, 1992.

Income

Income level and its distribution pattern in a community is generally associated with the level of economic development of the community as a whole within the socio-economic structure. The income

TABLE 9.12: Distribution of Female Workers in Sample Households by Working Status and Education

(Number, %)

Education	Permanent Workers	Temporary Workers	Total
Illiterate	100	49	149
	(67.1)	(32.9)	(100.0)
	[61.7]	[54.4]	[59.1]
Read & Write	29	16	45
	(64.4)	(35.6)	(100.0)
	[17.9]	[17.8]	[17.9]
Primary	27	20	47
	(57.4)	(42.6)	(100.0)
	[16.7]	[22.2]	[18.7]
Middle	2	2	4
	(50.0)	(50.0)	(100.0)
	[1.2]	[2.2]	[1.6]
Secondary	3	3	6
	(50.0)	(50.0)	(100.0)
	[1.9]	[3.3]	[2.4]
Graduate	1	—	1
	(100.0)	—	(100.0)
	[0.6]	—	[0.4]
Total	162	90	252
	(64.3)	(35.7)	(100.0)
	[100.0]	[100.0]	[100.0]

Source: Household Survey of the Bhangi Community, 1992.

distribution pattern of the sweeper households particularly attracts our attention as they are at the lowest of the social hierarchy. The household survey reveals that nearly 55 per cent of the households enjoy an annual household income of more than Rs. 20,000 (Table 9.13). This income group has nothing to do with poverty in economic

TABLE 9.13: Distribution of Sample Households by Annual Income and Type of Local Body

(Number of Households, %)

Annual Income (Rs.)	Municipal Corp.	Munici-pality	Nagar Panchayat	Gram Panchayat	Total
Less than 5000	6	5	3	—	14
	(42.9)	(35.7)	(21.4)	—	(100.0)
	[3.6]	[7.0]	[6.7]	—	[6.9]
5000-10000	9	6	5	2	22
	(40.9)	(27.3)	(22.7)	(9.1)	(100.0)
	[5.4]	[8.5]	[11.1]	[33.3]	[7.6]
10001-20000	41	32	21	1	95
	(43.2)	(33.7)	(22.1)	(1.1)	(100.0)
	[24.7]	[45.1]	[46.7]	[16.7]	[33.3]
20001-30000	33	17	6	2	58
	(56.9)	(29.3)	(10.3)	(3.4)	(100.0)
	[19.9]	[23.9]	[13.3]	[33.3]	[20.1]
30001-50000	65	11	6	1	83
	(78.3)	(13.3)	(7.2)	(1.2)	(100.0)
	[39.2]	[15.5]	[13.3]	[16.7]	[28.8]
50001+	12	—	4	—	16
	(75.0)		(25.0)		(100.0)
	[7.2]		[8.9]		[5.6]
Total	166	71	45	6	288
	(57.6)	(24.7)	(15.6)	(2.1)	(100.0)
	[100.0]	[100.0]	[100.0]	[100.0]	[100.0

Source: Household Survey of the Bhangi Community, 1992.

terms and is better off than other labour classes of urban Gujarat. The income level of households seems to be positively correlated with the number of permanent sweepers (or workers) in a household. One permanent sweeper in a household may get Rs.10,000 to 15,000 as annual income, and in the case of two permanent sweepers the figure may range from Rs.20,000 to 30,000. Thus, a household income group of Rs.10,000 to 20,000 tends to have one permanent sweeper, while the income group of less than Rs.10,000 indicates not to have a permanent sweeper in the household. The former is weak in financial position and the latter generally falls into the category of urban poor. With well developed legal protection and active trade unions, the household income of the municipal sweepers is higher than those of other local bodies. There is hardly any difference in the income distribution pattern of households between the municipalities and Nagar Panchayats owing to the similar conditions of legal protection and trade unions.

Per capita income, in the context of the present survey, is a useful criterion to demarcate the urban poor from others and to assess the distribution of the actual strength of economic power of the households. Since per capita income is worked out by dividing the annual income of a household by the number of family members, let us first examine the distribution of household by family size (Table 9.14). The family size varies from two to eighteen persons.

TABLE 9.14: Distribution of Sample Households by Family Size

(Number of Households, Persons, %)

Family size	Households			Persons		
	Number	%	Cum. %	Number	%	Cum. %
1	2	3	4	5	6	7
2	6	2.1	2.1	12	0.7	0.7
3	12	4.2	6.3	36	2.0	2.6
4	34	11.8	18.1	136	7.5	10.1
5	62	21.5	39.6	310	17.1	27.2
6	60	20.8	60.4	360	19.8	47.0
7	50	17.4	77.8	350	19.3	66.2
8	24	8.3	86.1	192	10.6	76.8
9	19	6.6	92.7	171	9.4	86.2
10	6	2.1	94.8	60	3.3	89.5
11	7	2.4	97.2	77	4.2	93.7
12	3	1.1	98.3	36	2.0	95.7

(Contd.)

TABLE 9.14 *(Contd.)*

1	2	3	4	5	6	7
13	2	0.7	99.0	26	1.4	97.1
17	2	0.7	99.7	34	1.9	99.0
18	1	0.3	100.0	18	1.0	100.0
Total	288	100.0	100.0	1818	100.0	100.0

Source: Household Survey of the Bhangi Community, 1992.

Out of 288 households and 1,818 persons surveyed, 64 households and 614 persons were with family size of eight persons and above. The average family size of the sweeper households surveyed is 6.3, which is larger than the average family size of urban Gujarat by 1.2 persons. Thus, the distributed per capita income is lower than it appears to be. In the light of the criterion of the Planning Commission for the rural poor during the Seventh Five Year Plan, the urban poor may be referred to a group whose per capita annual income does not reach Rs.1,500. Given this criterion, 9.4 per cent of households fall in the category of the urban poor (Table 9.15). Here

TABLE 9.15: Distribution of Sample Households by Annual Per Capita Income and Type of Local Body

(Number of Households, %)

Per Capita Income (Rs.)	Municipal Corp.	Munici-pality	Nagar Panchayat	Gram Panchayat	Total
1	2	3	4	5	6
<1500	13	7	7	—	27
	(48.1)	(25.9)	(25.9)		(100.0)
	[7.8]	[9.9]	[15.6]		[9.4]
1500-2500	21	15	6	2	44
	(47.7)	(34.1)	(13.6)	(4.5)	(100.0)
	[12.7]	[21.1]	[3.3]	[33.3]	[15.3]
2501-4000	41	26	21	2	90
	(45.6)	(28.9)	(23.3)	(2.2)	(100.0)
	[24.7]	[36.6]	[46.7]	[33.3]	[31.3]

(Contd.)

TABLE 9.15 *(Contd.)*

1	2	3	4	5	6
4001-6000	50	16	3	1	70
	(71.4)	(22.9)	(4.3)	(1.4)	(100.0)
	[30.1]	[22.5]	[6.7]	[16.7]	[24.3]
6001-8000	29	4	6	—	39
	(74.4)	(10.3)	(15.4)		(100.0)
	[17.5]	[5.6]	[13.3]		[13.5]
>8001	12	3	2	1	18
	(66.7)	(16.7)	(11.1)	(5.6)	(100.0)
	[7.2]	[4.2]	[4.4]	[16.7]	[6.3]
Total	166	71	45	6	288
	(57.6)	(24.7)	(15.6)	(2.1)	(100.0)
	[100.0]	[100.0]	[100.0]	[100.0]	[100.0]

Source: Household Survey of the Bhangi Community, 1992.

again, the percentage of the urban poor in the Municipal Corporation is relatively smaller than those in other local bodies. Also there is not much difference in the distribution pattern of per capita income between the municipalities and Nagar Panchayats.

Trade unions have a specific importance for the sweepers. Since a considerable number of sweepers are employed in the organized sector, trade unions play a major role in shaping the service, working, and living conditions of the sweepers. The activities of the major trade unions in the Ahmedabad Municipal Corporations, for example, have covered various fields such as the increase in basic wages and allowances, introduction of a compensatory appointment and relaxation of its conditions, the expansion of quota for permanent sweepers, constant supply of equipment, construction of the sweepers' quarters, and so on. The trade unions have also vigorously fought in labour courts to solve the disputed cases of individual workers. Though the trade union emphasised more on the increase of pay and quota, rather than improving the working conditions, their overall contribution was noteworthy in improving the material benefits of the sweepers. Trade unions were working at the time of the survey in two municipalities, Dholka, and Viramgam, and in one Nagar Panchayat, Bavala, besides in Ahmedabad. There were no trade unions for sweepers in the rest of the local bodies (Dehgam, Bareja, Sanand and Sola). These local bodies with no trade unions were inclined not only to minimize the number of permanent sweepers with the substitution of temporary sweepers, and often violate the Minimum Wage Act.

Availability of institutional finance is closely associated with the activities of the trade unions. It is generally the trade union, which sets up a cooperative financial institution, the most important institutional financial source for sweepers, in co-operation with a local body. Again, sweepers who have no trade union affiliation are alienated from this major source of finance and are forced to depend upon private institutions, with a very high interest rate

Liability

Liability is another criterion of assessing the financial position of the sweepers, since it constitutes a crucial indicator to measure economic and social backwardness. Most of the concerned studies refer to the heavy burden of liability among the sweepers, which is attributed to their low income and/or high expenditure on religious and social occasions, and on gambling and liquor.

The household survey reveals that 187 households out of 288 are eligible for institutional loans (Table 9.16). A major source of institutional liability is the credit society, accounting for 82.9 per cent of the total cases of institutional liability. Banks follow credit societies accounting for 13.4 per cent. There are rare cases where advance has been taken against the provident fund. Though advance taken against the provident fund is not a liability, we counted it as one of the sources of liability.

Institutional liability is very common in the Municipal Corporation, accounting for 72.3 per cent of the surveyed households, but is less common in the municipalities with a share of 47.9 per cent of the households. The share of the nagar panchayats

TABLE 9.16: Distribution of the Sources of Institutional Liability by Type of Local Body

(Number of Households, %)

Source of Liability	Municipal Corp.	Munici-pality	Nagar Panchayat	Total
Credit Society	99	27	29	155
	(82.5)	(79.4)	(87.9)	(82.9)
Bank	18	4	3	25
	(15.0)	(11.8)	(9.1)	(13.4)
Provident Fund	3	3	1	7
	(2.5)	(8.8)	(3.0)	(3.7)
Total	120	34	33	187
	(100.0)	(100.0)	(100.0)	(100.0)
	[64.2]	[18.2]	[17.6]	[100.0]

Source: Household Survey of the Bhangi Community, 1992.

falls in between. The average amount of institutional liability is Rs.8,474. It varies from Rs.9,770 in the Municipal Corporation to Rs.6,917 in the municipalities and Rs.5,715 in the Nagar Panchayats. In the case of the Ahmedabad Municipal Corporation, permanent sweepers are allowed to borrow up to Rs.10,000 at a time from their credit society. It is the role of the Ahmedabad Municipal Corporation to recover the amount with interest on behalf of the credit society by deducting Rs.250 from their monthly salary for the period of five years, if the amount borrowed is Rs.10,000. Thus, the total amount of recovery would be Rs.15,000, which is favourable to borrowers in a country with a high inflation rate.

Nothing is wrong in incurring a liability, if a considerable portion of it is used for actual needs or productive purposes. However, the survey reveals to the contrary (Table 9.17). The dominant reason for liability is consumption only. The major reason for institutional liability, as expected, is marriage, which accounted for 45 per cent of the total cases of institutional liability. Marriage is said to be a heavy burden on the finances of the sweepers, and the survey also confirms the statement. The average expense for the marriage of a boy are around Rs.10,000, while the expenses for a girl are around Rs.15,000. Since the average monthly income of the Bhangi households surveyed is about Rs.2,000, expenses for a marriage is equal to the household income of five months for a boy, and eight months for a girl. The amount may not appear to be heavy in comparison with their income level; however, their average family size and financial backwardness should be taken into consideration to assess the impact of marriage expenses on their finances. The family size generally corresponds to the frequency of marriage and a fresh liability is quite burdensome to the households whose financial position is already weak. The second major reason for liability is household expenditure. Reasons such as sickness and pregnancy can be clubbed with household expenditure in a broad sense. The share of this category simply implies the prevalence of financial weakness and lack of savings among the sweeper households. Notably, 8.7 per cent of institutional liability is used for settling private loans. Construction and repair of houses has a steady share in both institutional and private loans.

TABLE 9.17: Distribution of the Reasons for Institutional Loans

Reasons	Frequency	Percentage
Marriage	81	44.0
Religious events	9	4.9
Household expenditure	33	17.9
Sickness	4	2.2
Delivery	2	1.1
House construction	17	9.2
House repair	14	7.6
Settling other debts	16	8.7
Others	8	4.4
Total	184	100.0

Source: Household Survey of the Bhangi Community, 1992.

Generally speaking, the terms and conditions of institutional loans are better than private loans. However, there are several limitations in institutional loans, such as the unfamiliar procedure of application for the lower classes, intervention by middle men, and a relatively longer waiting period. Also, a large segment of the society is actually ill informed about the use of institutional loans.

On the contrary, private money-lenders are easy to approach and quick in the supply of money, despite charging a higher interest rate. The main sources of private loans are *mahajans* (professional money-lenders) and private loan institutions (traditional saving clubs) (Table 9.18). Relatives contributed 15 per cent of the total cases of private liability reported. Since, the private liability of small amounts was totally unreported, the actual number of cases of private loans would surpass that of institutional loans. The average amount of a private loan is Rs.5,479 which is lower than the average amount of an institutional loan by Rs.3,000. It varies from Rs.6,465 in the Municipal Corporation to Rs.5,150 in the municipalities, and Rs.4,187 in the Nagar Panchayats. Here again, the average amount of the Municipal Corporation surpasses the amount of other local

TABLE 9.18: Distribution of the Sources of Private Loans by Type of Local Body

(Number of Households, %)

Source of Liability	Municipal Corp.	Munici-pality	Nagar Panchayat	Total
Relatives	7	4	7	18
	(14.9)	(10.5)	(21.9)	(15.4)
Mahajan	30	30	24	84
	(63.8)	(79.0)	(75.0)	(71.8)
Private Institution	10	4	1	15
	(21.3)	(10.5)	(3.1)	(12.8)
Total	47	28	32	117
	(100.0)	(100.0)	(100.0)	(100.0)
	[40.2]	[32.5]	[27.3]	[100.0]

Source: Household Survey of the Bhangi Community, 1992.

bodies. However, the frequency of private loans is much less than that of the institutional loans in the Municipal Corporation, while in the municipalities and Nagar Panchayats, the sweeper households make frequent use of private loans as institutional loans are not easily accessible. The interest rate of private loans varies from 2 to 15 per cent per month. The average interest rate per month comes to 5.95 per cent, which is equal to the simple interest rate of 71.4 per cent per annum. Since it takes more than one year to repay the amount in most of the cases, the prevalence of private loans tends to further deteriorate the financial basis of the sweeper households.

The major reason for private loans differs from that of institutional loans. Household expenditure in a broad sense shares nearly 44 per cent of the total cases of private loans (Table 9.19). Day-to-day maintenance of a family is the major reason for private loans. Marriage comes second in the frequency of reasons (with its share slightly less than 30 per cent), followed by construction and repair of houses. Again there are several cases of private loans for settling other private debts to escape from the immediate threat and social pressure.

TABLE 9.19: Distribution of the Reasons for Private Loans

Reasons	Frequency	Percentage
Marriage	33	28.2
Religious events	1	0.9
Household expenditure	37	31.6
Sickness	11	9.4
Delivery	3	2.6
House construction	12	10.3
House repair	3	2.6
Settling other debts	3	2.6
Others	14	11.8
Total	117	100.0

Source: Household Survey of the Bhangi Community, 1992.

Conclusions

The major findings in this study may be summarized as follows. As regards the institutional climate, there is a considerable gap between the large and small local bodies. The level of wages and various allowances, the availability of trade unions, and financial institutions are in favour of the large local bodies, while the workers in the small local bodies suffer from low wages, unstable service conditions and less accessibility to trade unions and financial institutions.

The argument that the local bodies should raise the level of wages of the sweepers to encourage their socio-economic development holds good for the sweepers employed by small local bodies. However, it is less applicable to the sweepers employed by large local bodies. It is a serious issue that those employed by large local bodies still remain backward in spite of having relatively better institutional climate and service conditions.

The sweepers have been downtrodden for quite long and their consciousness is thus moulded. Any improvement of the institutional climate and their service and working conditions may surely provide them a material basis for their socio-economic development. However, actual development may take place in the wake of a massive movement to overcome their internal weaknesses and social contradictions.

NOTES

1. A type of a latrine which scavengers have to remove human excreta manually everyday from the lower chamber of the latrine. The latrine is also called a receptacle latrine or service latrine.
2. I selected 166 households from the Ahmedabad Municipal Corporation (AMC), 71 households from the three municipalities (Dehgam, Viramgam and Dholka), 45 households from the three nagar panchayats (Sanand, Bareja and Bavala), and 6 households from Sola Gram Panchayat. Except the Sola Gram Panchayat, sample households were selected from those having at least one permanent or temporary sweeper employed by the local bodies. As for the AMC, I selected the three sweepers' quarters from the east zone, and two from the west zone. As for the other local bodies, I took the sample households

from the main colony of sweepers, where majority of the sweepers resided. I have not applied the random sampling method rigidly for the selection of households, owing to some difficulty in contacting the respondents or owing to the congested structure of the colonies. Since my survey has covered around 30 per cent of the sweeper households in the municipalities and nearly 50 per cent of those in the nagar panchayats, I feel that the survey results give us a fairly comprehensive picture of the sweepers in these local bodies.

REFERENCES.

Census of India, Gujarat, Tables on Scheduled Castes and Scheduled Tribes, New Delhi, 1944.

Census of India, Special Tables for Scheduled Castes, New Delhi, 1988.

Desai, I.P., *Untouchability in Rural Gujarat,* Bombay : Popular Prakashan, 1976.

Gandhi, M.K., *The Removal of Untouchability,* Ahmedabad: Navjivan Publishing House, 1954.

Jairamdas, J., *Bhangi Kasht Mukti and Bhangi Mukti,* New Delhi : National Committee for Gandhi Centenary, 1969.

Kothari, V.N., *A Study of Economic Profiles of the Scheduled Castes in Gujarat,* Baroda: M.S. University of Baroda, 1976.

Patel, B.B., *Report on the Implementation of Minimum Wages for Sweepers in Village Panchayats in Saurashtra,* Ahmedabad: Gandhi Labour Institute, 1990.

Patel, Ishwarbhai, *Safai-Marg Darshika : A Guide Book on Sanitation,* New Delhi: Harijan Sevak Sangh, 1970.

Pathak, Bindeshwar, *Road to Freedom: A Sociological Study on the Abolition of Scavenging in India,* New Delhi: Motilal Banarsidass, 1991.

Pfaffenberger, B., 1980. 'Social Communication in Dravidian Ritual', *Journal of Anthropological Research,* 36: 196-219.

Pfaffenberger, B., 1982. *Caste in Tamil Culture: The Religious Foundations Sudra Domination in Tamil Sri Lanka,* 'Syracuse: Maxwell School of Citizenship and Public Affairs, Syracuse University.

Pfaffenberger, B., *Report of the Task Force for Tackling the Problems of Scavengers and Suggesting Measures to Abolish Scavenging with Particular Emphasis on Their Rehabilitation.* New Delhi : Planning Commission, 1990-91.

Raheja, G., *The Poison in the Gift: Ritual, Prestation and the Dominant Caste in A North Indian Village.* Chicago: Chicago University Press, 1988.

Raj, A.P.M.J., The Social Bases of Obedience of the Untouchables in India. Ph.D. dissertation, Chicago: Chicago University, 1987.

Rao, S., The Feeble Voices: A Study of Dominance and Resistance in a South Indian Village, Ph.D. Dissertation, Rochester: University of Rochester, 1993.

Reddy, N.S., *Transition in Caste Structure in Andhra Pradesh with Particular Reference to Depressed Castes*, Ph.D. Dissertation, Lucknow: Lucknow University, 1952.

Report of the Committee on Improvement of Living and Working Conditions of Sweepers and Scavengers, Banglore: Government of Karnataka, 1976.

Report of the Scavengers' Living Conditions Enquiry Committee, Bombay : Government of Bombay, 1958.

Report of the Scavenging Conditions Enquiry Committee, New Delhi : Ministry of Home Affairs, 1960.

Report of the National Scheme of Liberation and Rehabilitation of Scavengers and Their Dependents, New Delhi : Ministry of Welfare 1991-92.

Report of the Committee to Study the Working and Service Conditions of Sweepers and Scavengers, New Delhi: National Commission on Labour, 1969.

Saurashtra Safai Kamdaro Angeni Rivyu Samitino (Vyas Samiti) Aheval, Government of Saurashtra (in Gujarati), 1956.

Scott, J.S., *Weapons of the Weak*, New Haven: Yale University Press, 1985.

Shah, Ghanshyam, *Politics of Scheduled Castes and Tribes : Adivasi and Harijan Leaders of Gujarat*, Bombay : Vora & Co. Publishers, 1975.

Sharma, Rama, *Bhangi Scavengers in Indian Society : Marginality, Identity and Politicization of the Community*, New Delhi: M.D. Publications, 1995.

Shinoda, Takashi, *Traditional Occupations and Jajmani Relationships in West India With Special Reference to Survey Villages in the Ahmedabad District* (in Japanese), Kiyou, No. 27, Daito Bunka University, 1989.

Shinoda, Takashi, "Castes, Occupations and Backwardness in Rural Gujarat" (in Japanese), in F. Oshikawa (ed.), *Socio-Economic Development and Castes in India*, IDE Research Series No. 391, Tokyo: Institute of Developing Economies, 1990.

Shinoda, Takashi, *Indono Seisonin Kasuto Kenkyu : A Study on the Status of Sweepers in India*, Tokyo: Syunjusya, 1995 (in Japanese).

Shinoda, Takashi, "Socio-Economic Conditions of Sweepers Employed by Local Bodies in Ahmedabad District", in S. Taniuguchi, H. Yanagisawa, T. Shinoda, and F. Oshikawa (eds.), *Economic Changes and Social Transformation in Modern and Contemporary South Asia*, Tokyo: Hitotsubashi University, 1994.

Shyamlal, *The Bhangi: A Sweeper Caste Its Socio-Economic Portraits with Special Reference to Jodhpur City*, Bombay: Popular Prakashan, 1992.

Singh, T.R., *The Madiga: A Study in Social Structure and Change*, Lucknow: Ethnographic and Folk Culture Society, 1969.

Thurston, E.,*Castes and Tribes of Southern India*, Volume-7, Madras: Government Press, 1909.

Trawick, M., 'Untouchability and the Fear of Death in a Tamil Song', in Lutz A. Catherine and Lila Abu-Lughod, eds. *Language and Politics of Emotions*, Cambridge: University of Cambridge Press, 1990.

Trawick, M., 'Wandering Lost: A Landless Labourer's Sense of Place and Self,' in Arjun Appadurai, Frank J. Koram and Margaret A. Mill eds. *Gender, Genre and Power in South Asian Expressive Tradition*, Philadelphia: University of Pennsylvania Press, 1991.

Vincentnathan, L., Harijan Sub-culture and Self-esteem Management in a South Indian community, Ph.D. Dissertation, Wisconsin: Wisconsin University, 1987.

10

UNTOUCHABILITY AND ATROCITIES

P.S. KRISHNAN

The people belonging to the castes, to which "untouhability" has been ascribed by the elite of Indian society, have cast aside the various appellations imposed on them and have given expression to their self-assertion by calling themselves 'Dalit', which means the oppressed people. This is in line with Dr. B.R. Ambedkar's way of looking at the social reality. He insisted that they be called 'untouchables' so that there is no obfuscation of reality. Prior to that they were called by their various local or regional caste names, as though there was nothing in common between them or by abominable "common" names like *Chandala* and *Dhed*, or by the common term "lower castes".

Imposed Names

More recently, Western scholars and colonial administrators, affected by obfuscation's of the elite, have invented curious terms like "Depressed classes" and "Exterior Castes", the latter reflecting the upper caste perception of them as outcastes. Gandhiji's name for them was Harijan, comparable to Emperor Meiji's Buraku-i for Japan's 'untouchables', at the time of the Meiji Restoration in 1868, in substitution of the name then in vogue, etc., which was semantically in the same class as *Chandala*. This name was rejected by Dr. Ambedkar on the ground that it did not bring out the real condition of the people to whom the term was applied. Ambedkar was particular about using the name "untouchables", apparently for two related reasons—to rouse the self-respect of the victims of "untouchability" and to sting the conscience of those individuals of upper castes, who were capable to feeling the qualms of a social conscience, and in any case deprive the practitioners of "untouchability" of the luxury of an easy salve for their conscience.

The Government of India Act, 1935, as well as the Constitution of India, 1950, have, as expected, preferred to use an absolutely neutral term "Scheduled Castes", which neither conceals nor reveals anything about the castes in the schedules referred to. One Governmental document adopts the term, that the victims of "untouchability" have, in the spirit of Ambedkar, given to themselves. In formulating the portion relating to the Scheduled Castes in the approach to the eighth plan document, I deliberately used the term Dalit and the Planning Commission accepted it and hitherto is the only instance of such a usage in an official document. Interestingly about a century back Swami Vivekananda referred to the "untouchables" as the "Suppressed".

Of Dalit, Vidrohi-Dalit, Sah-Dalit and Vishal Dalit

It is appropriate that a people's sentiments and, reflective of it, the name they choose for themselves, are respected. But I feel that time has come for the Dalits to consider giving another dimension to the term Dalit by expanding it as Vidrohi-Dalit—the oppressed in revolt. For, revolt is what the Dalits have been engaged in over the last two centuries. They have been up in revolt, first sporadically, like spring fires here and there, and later, with the appearance of Ambedkar on the scene, like a mighty colossus striding across time and space, like a wildfire engulfing the whole country. It is the historic task of the Dalits to revive this revolt and transform it into a mighty avalanche that relentlessly sweeps aside the injustice of centuries and annihilate caste, as Ambedkar had envisaged.

The term Dalit, Vidrohi-Dalit, are significant not only in the semantic sense but also as vital clues to the state of the people whose sufferings and agonies are unparalleled in history and geography and to the beastly phenomena of "untouchability" and "atrocities" so unique to India.

In this paper, the focus is primarily on the constitutional category of the Scheduled Castes, i.e., Dalits, for they are the main victims of "untouchability" and "atrocities". But I shall also seek to turn the light on their brothers in millennial suffering, the Scheduled Tribes, and that larger section of the other Backward Classes or socially Backward Classes, who too are, in different ways, the targets of atrocities, and who may be encompassed respectively by the terms Sah-Dalit (co-oppressed) and Vishal Dalit (the oppressed in the wider sense of the term which would be inclusive of the Dalit, Vidrohi-Dalit and Sah-Dalit too).

Brief Historical Backdrop

The people who today comprise the Dalit, with their labour and the agricultural surplus they produced, created history. But they were not historiographers. The consumers and controllers of their labour and agricultural surplus, who had leisure and the monopoly of education, recorded history. In spite of the selective and distorted historiography of the past, which some modern historiographers are trying against heavy odds to partly correct, it is possible to discern in the dim corridors of India's pre-historical and historical past, the link between the growth of the country's agricultural civilisation and, in the peculiar climatic conditions of India, the emergence, from the common stratum of India's population of Agricultural Labour Castes (ALCs), who now constitute the bulk of the Dalit population in the country. In fact, India's remarkable agricultural civilisation and economy was built on them, so it is today. According to quantitative data that I have collated from different sources, the rural Dalit shoulder more than 5 times as much of the burden of agricultural labour than the non-Dalits which is an important socio-economic feature of the Indian caste system.

Significant Existential Features of Dalit Plight

This historical backdrop was essential for a clear understanding of the age-old phenomenon of "untouchability", an integral part and essential feature of the Indian caste system, and of the recent phenomenon of atrocities. It is also necessary to briefly consider significant features of Dalit existence today, rooted in the history of the emergence of agricultural labour castes in India.

As mentioned in the preceding section, the most significant aspect of Dalit existence is that, most of the numerically large Dalit castes of each region of India and in each of its regions (except the north-eastern states of India), are agricultural labour castes. No wonder then, that about two-thirds of the bonded labourers of India are from Dalit castes, most of the remaining one-third or nearly one-fifth of the total being from the Sah-Dalit tribes. This is the second significant feature of Dalit existence.

The third socio-economic feature of Dalit existence today is their poor share in India's agricultural landholding and still poorer share in its irrigated landholding. This is no accident. It is the deliberate outcome of the working of the Indian caste system through history. There are parts of India where formal laws prohibited ownership of land by "untouchable" castes or cultivation of land by them on their own account. Elsewhere, the Indian caste system, with greater effectiveness than a mere formal law did, could make land out of bounds for them, except as agricultural labourers, or as agrestic slaves or serfs or as in Bengal, as *Bar gador* or crop-sharing tenants-at-will.

Yet, the Dalits tenaciously clung to some land, with varying success, in different regions. Their holdings have been augmented by the allotment of government wastelands to them in the past half century, partly following Dalit agitations and movements for land, e.g., the *Banjar* (waste) land movement in Andhra Pradesh. With all this, their landholdings constitute only two-fifths of their population proportion and only a little more area under irrigation. This share dwindles further in the area irrigated by the more dependable sources of irrigation, *viz.*, by canals and tubewells, reducing most Dalit landholders, some of whom are only sharecroppers, to chronic economic dependency, and forcing them, into the demeaning and highly vulnerable position of agricultural wage labourers.

A fourth feature is that Dalits, mainly their womenfolk and girl children (the latter ought to be in full-time formal educational institutions) have been left out to "enjoy" a near-monopoly of civic sanitation work or *safai* work, usually referred to as "scavenging", practically in all parts of India. Another occupation, left by force almost entirely to the Dalits in most parts of India, is leather work, consisting of flaying and country-tanning and manufacture of footwear in the unorganised sector. This forced near-monopoly of an activity despised under the Indian caste system and performed under conditions of extreme squalor, is the fifth important feature of Dalit existence today, with its roots in the depths of India's past. Corresponding to the above two features, which like the other features of Dalit existence discussed here, are national in the sense that they are phenomena of all-India occurrence, various other despised and/or arduous forms of labour at different regional levels are forced on the Dalits. For example, in some regions of India, Dalit women are forced to function as traditional *dais* and attend on cases of child birth in other communities as a matter of social obligation.

A sixth feature is the continued severe educational lag of the Dalits, expressed even at the entry point of the educational ladder, in comparison with the literacy rate for the non-Dalit, non-ST population. The disparity increases as one goes up the educational ladder. This is partly the result of their economic deprivation and partly the effect of the denial of education to them until the doors of the school were forced open.

A seventh feature is the residential segregation of Dalits in localities known in different parts of the country by different names, some of which are pejorative in keeping with one of the distinct socio-linguistic characteristics of Indian languages. They are typically at a lower level than non-Dalit localities, more distant from the village, road, distant enough (sometimes symbolically but all the same significantly by no more than an intervening lane), to indicate humiliating segregation, but near enough for Dalit labour to be at the beck and call of landowners of dominant upper or middle castes of the village or region.

Each of these features is important for understanding the terms on which Dalits have been existing and still exist, and for understanding in particular "untouchability" and atrocities, either as causative factors or as effects or as both. This enumeration of features is not exhaustive. There are others, some national in spread and some regional, like continued denial of their due share of class II/Group B and Class I/Group A posts to Dalits in the services of the Government of India and state organisations. But my focus is on those features which are of explanatory value in the context of "untouchability" and "atrocities".

Untouchability

The term 'Untouchability' should not be taken too literally. It is a "culture" code word—note the irony in the description of so uncultured a practice—coined at the beginning of this country to collectively describe a complex of cruel and humiliating discriminatory practices and disabilities, which may or may not include prohibition of physical contact to which members of Dalit castes were and still are subjected by the rest of society.

Some common forms that "untouchability" takes can be seen in the formulations of sections 3, 4, 5, 6, and 7A of the Protection of Civil Rights (PCR) Act, 1955, which was re-enacted in 1976 to re-name and amend the Untouchability (Offences) Act, 1955. But even the enumerations in the PCR Act are not exhaustive. It is not possible to exhaustively catalogue all instances of behaviour which come within the ambit of "untouchability".

"Untouchability" may be regarded both as an important feature of Dalit existence, and also as a mechanism whereby, as an integral part of the Indian caste system, the Dalits have been kept in line through the centuries. How could a larger segment of India's population be kept down as agricultural labour, *safai karamchari* or leather working castes, deprived of the right to own or hold land or cultivate it on own account, slaving the long day in the slushy field and existing in hovels in squalid conditions through centuries? The answer is the instrumentality of "untouchability". For its ghoulish purpose, it is an extremely effective and efficient mechanism, extremely versatile, extraordinarily protean, changing its form and expression to suit the exigencies of the situation in each area and at each period. Its injunctions and mandates and prohibitions have been vested with sanction that is religious or pseudo-religious, depending on how one views the *Manu Smriti* and other *Smritis* and the rest of the literature in which they are contained. It is thus not only a disciplinary instrument of behaviour control but also a powerful weapon, forged in both senses of the term, to secure unquestioning conformity from the Dalits.

Legal Measures

Article 17 of the Constitution of India boldly proclaimed "untouchability" abolished, and its practice in any form, forbidden. The enforcement of any disability arising out of "untouchability" shall be an offence punishable in accordance with the law. But the law to punish such offences took five years to arrive, giving a first taste of the degree of urgency attached by the Indian elite, ensconced in governance, to the furtherance of this crucial moral-constitutional imperative. The Untouchability (Offences) Act was enacted in 1955.

Ever since it came into force on 1 June 1955, it was felt that the Act was not serving its purpose and the punishments provided in it were few and inadequate. Therefore, 17 years later the Untouchability (Offences) Amendment and Miscellaneous Provisions Bill, 1972, was introduced in the Lok Sabha. It was passed four years later, in 1976, with comprehensive amendments proposed by the Joint Select Committee of the Parliament, and with certain other modifications. The chronology needs no further comment, regarding the sense of urgency behind the exercise.

One of the innovations of the Act was that every year the Central Government is required to place on the table of each House of the Parliament, a report on the measures taken by itself and by the State Governments in pursuance of the mandate contained in Section 15A(2) and (3). So far 12 reports have been laid on the table of both the Houses, for the years (1) 1977; (2) 1978; (3) 1979; (4) 1980; (5) 1981 and 1982; (6) 1983; (7) 1984; (8) 1985; (9) 1986; (10) 1987 and 1988; (11) 1989 and 1990; and the last in March-April 1992.

Qualitative Changes

Before proceeding to analyse the quantitative data contained in these Annual Reports, I would like to mention the present scenario in respect of the prevalence of "untouchability" in qualitative terms from my experience during my visits to a larger number of villages in different states in the past few decades and from my interaction with students studying in different universities and colleges or residing in hostels.

(i) Untouchability in its classic expressions known all over India, as exemplified by *Mahad* in 1927, continues to exist in many part of India. The Act and the machinery thereunder are not able to reach out to most of the victims in the villages or to alter the situation there significantly.

(ii) Some of the classic expressions of untouchability have ceased to be practised in some parts of the country.

(iii) Some of the classic forms of untouchability have been modified in some parts of the country.

(iv) New forms of untouchability have appeared in rural as well as urban areas in many parts of the country, in keeping with new developments. For example, village tea shops are a recent phenomenon in many villages. With this has arisen a variety of discriminatory practices such as no separate seating, separate glasses, usually old, dirty and cracked or chipped.

(v) In many metropolitan areas, "untouchability" has seemingly attenuated, but is practised with sophisticated concealment in a variety of ingenious ways, revealing creativity worthy of a better cause. In many modern offices, Dalits have to suffer snide remarks and quiet and neat acts of discrimination.

(vi) Wherever punishments as per the Act have been inflicted and proven offenders sentenced to imprisonment by Magistrates, I have found salutary effects in the villages, where the offence took place and surrounding villages, at least for sometime, as I found in Medak District of Andhra

Pradesh in 1988.

Quantitative Data on Convictions

I have listed these six trends and features as qualitative data not capable of being captured. Now coming to the quantitative data which can be subjected to evaluatory analysis on a number of parameters, one of the important requirements for the effective enforcement of any penal law is that the crime should normally be accompanied by punishment. Crime divorced from punishment is an invitation to licence. Table 10.1 shows the percentage of convictions and acquittals in total cases in the court in the year and the ratio of convictions to acquittals for India as a whole.

TABLE 10.1: Convictions and Acquittals to Total Cases Disposed of by Courts under the PCR Act

Year	Percentage of Convictions	Percentage of Acquittals	Acquittals Ratio
1977	27.4	72.6	1:3
1978	19.7	80.3	1:4
1979	22.9	77.1	1:3
1980	30.7	6.3	1:2
1981	17.5	82.5	1:5
1982	10.9	89.1	1:8
1983	Not Available	—	—
1984	14.2	86.8	1:6
1985	12.2	87.8	1:7
1986	19.6	80.4	1:4
1987	15.4	84.6	1:5
1988	12.8	87.2	1:7
1989	21.7	78.3	1:4
1990	12.3	87.7	1:7

Not only has the proportion of convictions never exceeded half of the acquittals, but compared to the earlier years, say 1977 to 1980, the proportion of convictions has flagged and fallen in subsequent years. The results achieved in some states show that other states could have done better in the matter of convictions and improved the All-India average in most of the years. Further, in that State in 1977 to 1980 and again in 1984 and 1986, convictions were more than or nearly equal to acquittals. From 1977 to 1979 and in 1984 Madhya Pradesh accounted for a third to a fifth of India's total convictions. Maharashtra had been doing relatively well till before 1987. In eight of those years its conviction rate has been better than India's. In 1980 and 1984, convictions exceeded or were fairly close to acquittals, and it contributed close to a fourth to a third of India's convictions and in 1981 close to one-half. Tamil Nadu did well in the early years with convictions exceeding acquittals in 1977 and nearly equalising acquittals in 1979 and contributing one-half and one-third respectively of India's convictions in those two years. But in other years, though it generally made a fair contribution to the total convictions of India, its acquittals have far outstripped convictions, leaving Tamil Nadu's proportion of convictions to total disposals behind India's average. Kerala had 100 per cent convictions consecutively in 1987 and 1988 and had more convictions than acquittals in 1979. In recent years, Uttar Pradesh has been doing better with convictions exceeding acquittals or fairly comparable to the latter in 1986 to 1989 and 100 per cent convictions in 1988 and contributing a fifth to three-fifths of the convictions in India in these three years. Bihar registered an honourable presence in 1990 with close to one-half of India's total convictions.

The causative factors behind the uneven inter-state and inter-year performances need further investigation. But they are at this stage enough to show that results overall are far below the sporadically established potential. An analysis of other performances of quantitative data would reveal similar gaps in the implementation of this important socio-moral legislation based on a categorical imperative of the Indian Constitution.

But enforcement of the PCR Act in terms of cases registered, disposed of at different stages and levels from the police to the court, and convictions, is not adequate. The mandate in Section 15A(1) and Section 15A(3) respectively on the State and Central Governments needs to be fulfilled in a far more effective objective-oriented manner. For example, very few states have taken seriously the establishment of Special Courts as per clause (iii) of Section 15A(2), preferably Mobile Special Courts, as advised by the Government of India in the early 80s with an offer of cost-sharing. Madhya Pradesh has created four mobile Special Courts with 10 to 12 districts each and has decided to create special magistrates in 37 districts, which cannot be covered effectively by these four courts. Andhra Pradesh has at present seventeen Mobile Special Courts and proposes to create five more. (But I have found some of these Mobile Special Courts being sometimes deprived of their means of mobility). Karnataka has two Mobile Special Courts, Orissa has decided to set up three, Rajasthan has six non-mobile Exclusive Special Courts, Tamil Nadu has four. Some states have resorted to the practice of "specifying" existing courts and calling them special; Uttar Pradesh has recently discovered that this is not enough.

Delay for want of quick trials through exclusive special courts and Mobile Special Courts results in the state, unintentionally though but not unwittingly, promoting acquittals, leaving enough time for complainants and witnesses to be reduced to silence. Many other comprehensive socio-economic measures are required to secure the economic liberation of the Dalit rural masses, so that they can afford to register complaints against the rampant practices of "untouchability", which are yet to see the light of law, and dare to tender evidence.

Atrocities

As mentioned earlier, the Dalits have in the main been the providers of labour which created the ancient Indian agricultural civilisation that has continued to this day. In order to force the Dalits and the Sah-Dalit tribes of the plains to remain permanently tied down as helots providing agricultural and other labour, members of these castes and plains tribes were denied the right of owning land or cultivating it on their own account. The system of caste had been devised to destroy their morale and capacity to organise resistance.

Independence has not made any substantial difference to the

situation except to add new classes, new processes and new styles of operation and the peculiar phenomenon of atrocities to curb the spirit of freedom that was lit in the Dalit by people like Mahatma Phule and Narayana Guru.

For many centuries the Indian caste system was able to operate as a perfect instrument to keep the "untouchable" castes and plains tribes under total subjugation as providers of labour for agriculture and other purposes. But the revolutionary movements of the last one and a half centuries have instilled a new sense of awareness in them. Under its influence they refused to accept their status as pre-ordained. This was given another dimension by the movement for land reforms, for reduction of crippling burdens on sharecropping tenants and for improvements in agricultural wages like the Telengana and Tebhaga movements and the agricultural labourers' strikes in places like Thanjavur.

It became necessary for the dominant classes drawn from Different Upper Castes (DUCs) later on, some of the Different Middle Castes (DMCs) too, in different parts of the country to force new instruments of control. This is how atrocities, as we know them, made their debut in the '60s. As the resistance of the Dalits has grown, the frequency and brutal ferocity of atrocities have grown apace.

Wages, Bondage and Atrocities

Many of the cases of atrocities arise from agricultural wage issues, with Dalit agricultural labourers demanding, not the statutory minimum wages—which are low by objective standards—but something between them and their prevalent wages. And the larger landholders or DUCs/DMCs employing wage-labourers refuse to pay even such mid-level wages. In some of those cases, in addition to wages are the issue of assertion of and organisation for rights by Dalits. Examples of such wage-related atrocities are:

Kilavenmani in Tamil Nadu, where 42 Dalits, mostly women, children and elders were killed on 25-12-1968. But their fiery ordeal has not gone in vain as I found when I made a social pilgrimage to this great village, nearly 20 years later on 4-2-1988.

Belchi in Bihar, where 11 Dalits along with 2 OBCs, coming within the category of Vishal Dalit, were killed on 27-5-1977.

Pipra in Bihar, where 14 Dalits were killed and 26 houses burnt on the night between 26-2-1980 and 27-2-1980.

Nonki-Nagawa in Bihar, where 19 Dalits were killed on the night between 11-8-1988 and 12-8-1988.

Gurha Slathian in Jammu in 1985.

Some of the atrocities against Dalits are connected with bonded labour. A recent gruesome example is the brutal killing in 1992, of 3 Dalit persons of a particularly weak and helpless community known as *Bacchda*, in Mandsaur district of Madhya Pradesh, on the ground that some young men of this community refused to render bonded labour in agriculture and wanted to work for somewhat higher wages than that the market offered. The market, even under the regime of liberalisation, is the place of worship of the metropolitan and rural elite of DUCs and DMCs; the "untouchable" is prohibited from entering its portals. Another recorded ferocious example of atrocities related to bonded labour in stone-quarrying, is the case of Chikkabasavanahalli, Bangalore district, a village right at the doorstep of the city of Bangalore, in 1976. I remember the marks of whiplash on her back, that Nagamma showed my team.

Land and Atrocities

Connected with the state of absolute or relative landlessness of the Dalit is their land hunger. In the thousands of villages that I have visited in the past few decades, the most prominent in the Dalit response to the question, "what do you want?", is a chorus, *Bhoomi* or *Zamin*. This reflects their aspiration for or efforts to get or retain small chunks of government owned land, i.e., lands not owned by any private individual, known by different regional revenue terms like gair *mazarua khas*, *poromboke*, "assessed waste" etc., some of them illegally encroached upon by well-to-do persons belonging to DUCs/DMCs of the village, sometimes *benami*. These demands have triggered off some of the atrocities, even though the Dalit efforts have been according to the law or revenue rules and National Policy. Some examples are:

Vijaynagar, Sriganganagar district of Rajasthan where landlords attacked three Dalit families and gang-raped two Dalit women, in June 1983, as penalty for complaining about land grabbing by landlords.

Bichgaon, Alwar district of Rajasthan, where seven Dalits including two women were massacred on 20-1-1984, the issue being possession of a paltry 4.5 bighas of land each allotted to three Dalits, ten years earlier.

Golana, Kheda district in Gujarat, where four Dalits were killed and 20 injured on 25-1-1986 in connection with land granted by the government to Dalit agricultural labourers, who were also released bonded labourers. This and the formation of a cooperative by them to secure for themselves economic and social self-reliance was resented by the local DMCs.

Bodh Gaya, Bihar, where on 8-8-1979 two Dalits were killed and one grievously injured by the Mahant's henchmen in a long drawn out case of Dalit efforts to secure lands held *benami*, violating the law for nearly three decades.

Chinpur, Gaya district, Bihar where two Dalits were killed on 10-12-1978 in connection with a mere 4 *bigha* 5 *kathe* of land, also a long drawn out matter since 1965.

Civic Facilities and Atrocities

Some of the atrocities are related to lack of facilities essential or access to in Dalit localities. A few illustrations are:

Kachur, Rewa district in Madhya Pradesh. The entire Dalit village was burnt down and three Dalits killed by a "brave" 300 strong mob, under the immediate 'provocation' of installation of a new hand-pump in the water starved Dalit basti.

Konalam, N. Arcot district, Tamil Nadu in 1982 and Patchalmada Kuda in Nizamabad District, Andhra Pradesh in 1989, witnessed the hold-up of the dead bodies of two aged women on the pathway, on account of disputes regarding pathway to the segregated burial ground of the Dalits.

Divalpur, Kurukshetra district, Haryana, women and children were beaten up in connection with plots or house sites for Dalits.

In a larger number of cases, untouchability related events graduated into atrocities, they include: Kafalta, Almora District, Uttar Pradesh on 9-5-1980; Jetalpur, Kheda District, Gujarat in 1981; Dervrali, Sikar District, Rajasthan in December 1983 (a village also came to notice in connection with an incident of *sati*); Kachur, Rewa District, Madhya Pradesh on 25-6-1985; a number of villages in South Arcot and adjoining districts of Tamil Nadu in 1987-88; Udamgal-Khanapur, Raichur District, Karnataka on 6-2-1988; Nathdwara, Udaipur District, Rajasthan on 23-6-1988 and again from July 1988 to 1-11-1988; Masari, Alwar District, Rajasthan on 9-7-1989; Panwari, Agra District, Uttar Pradesh, where seven Dalits were killed and 210 injured, and Kumher in Rajasthan in 1992.

Self-Assertion and Atrocities

A new phenomenon is atrocities arising from no specific cause other than Dálit assertion of self-respect. A typical example is the case of Tsunduru, Guntur District, Andhra Pradesh, where on 6-8-1991, a ghastly massacre of eight Dalits took place, most of them well educated.

One would have to go deeper into the incident to know what Tsunduru means in the gory history of Dalit martyrdom for equality. But within this limited space, one can only point out that Tsunduru was not the result, of wage demands or disputes, nor was there any dispute or claim regarding cultivable government wastelands, since there is none in this intensively cultivated and irrigated village. Generally, in this area imposition of overt types of "untouchability" based discrimination of the type envisaged in the PCR Act, does not exist any more.

What the Dalits of Tsunduru have brought forth prominently is their expectation and demand to be treated as equals at the individual and social group level, irrespective of their economic position as members of agricultural labour families. These demands and the fact of the DUCs of the village being unprepared to reconcile itself to this, is at the root of the Tsunduru atrocity. The present generation of Tsunduru youth, typical of Dalit youth in the Central Districts of Andhra Pradesh, are fired by an *Ekalavya* thirst for education. Their sensitivity for self-respect has been honed by their exposure to the Ambedkar philosophy, coming after the past few generations of Dalits, to human treatment for the first time in the centuries of their history, from Christian missionaries who undertook relief work during the Guntur famine in the 19th century; the nationalist movement; the adoption of the anti-untouchablity plank in the second quarter of the 20th century; and the Communist movement during the mid-20th century. Each of these have increasingly sharpened their perception of and aspiration for equality. Tsunduru is a pointer to the future.

Atrocities on Other Dalits

The situation of the Sah-Dalit tribes is marked, among others, by loss of their lands to individuals who delay the laws, aided by state inaction or inadequate action, and on account of larger government projects, of which the cost is borne by the Sah-Dalit tribes and the benefits go to others. This goes hand in hand with the deprivation of their age-old traditional rights in the tribal areas. To this is added the increasing burden of agricultural and migrant labour. All these are reflected in the pattern of atrocities on them. Some examples are:

Banjhi, Sahibganj District, Bihar, where 15 Sah-Dalits including Anthony Murmu, ex-M.P. were killed on 19-4-1985. One can also include Indravalli, Andhra Pradesh in 1978. Padaria, Bihar, where six Sah-Dalit women were mass-raped.

The other Vashal Dalit, the labouring, landless, resourceless sections of other Backward Classes, whose traditional occupations are under pressure from the market, technology and finance, none of which is accessible to them, are also vulnerable to atrocities, whether from DUCs or DMCs. This is illustrated by:

Kansara, Jehanabad District, Bihar where 10 landless Kahar, including six women and two children, were gunned down on 8-7-1986.

Rani Diara, Bhagalpur, Bihar, where sixteen fishermen were killed in November 1988.

Parasbigha, Bihar, where thirteen were killed on 6-2-1980.

Taufir Tola, Munger, Bihar, where a massacre of sharecropper

Binds took place on 11-11-1985, at the hands of landowners, both being OBCs.

Official statistics are suggestive. The number of incidents of crimes against Dalits by others is in the range of 16,000 to 18,000 per year in recent years, up from less than 10,000 per year before 1976. They include about 550 incidents of murders and 800 of rapes per year. The corresponding figures for Sah-Dalit are about 3,500 incidents per year in recent years, including more than 100 murders and 200-250 rapes per year.

Conclusion: Beyond "Untouchability" and "Atrocities"

How do we go beyond the age-old prime marker of Dalit existence, reinforced by the modern marker "untouchability" and "atrocities"? Without going into details one can here indicate a few directions:

(1) Serious implementation of the elaborate guidelines of the Government of India of 10-3-1980, consistently in all cases.

(2) Serious implementation of the S.C. and S.T. (Preventation of Atrocities) Act, 1989, including establishment of exclusive special courts with exclusive special judicial and investigative and prosecuting officers, all carefully selected for proven sensitivity to social justice and caste-based bias.

(3) Amendments to the SC and ST (POA) Act to cure it of some of its serious deficiencies. These steps on the part of the Central and State Governments should help to achieve the goal of effective prevention, and quick punishment in most cases, instead of exceptions at present like the Belchi-Pipra convictions which only prove the rule that successful prosecution of cases of atrocities is possible. This is also true of cases of "untouchability".

(4) Meaningful economic development and economic liberation of Dalits *inter alia* to bring to an end the present explosive juxtaposition of Dalit agricultural labour castes and landowners belonging to dominant upper middle castes and to enhance their ability to resist "untouchability" based discrimination. Blueprints and pilot experiences

encompassing a wide range of measures required, are available. We also have the experience of "untouchable" castes ceasing to be "untouchable" through a combination of growth or built up awareness, education, economic liberation and mobilisation.

(5) A peaceful democratic mass movement, consistent and persistent, which will let no case of atrocity anywhere in the country remain unnoticed by the nation, i.e., the state and society.

This should be spearheaded by the Dalits, and take in its embrace, Sah-Dalits and other backward Vishal Dalits and also Mahila Dalits, who are victims of another brand of atrocities. It should include humane and liberal non-Dalits also. This mass movement should also direct itself against discriminatory practices in areas of chronic forms of "untouchability". The direction for this is contained in the threefold formulation of Dr. Ambedkar—educate, agitate, and organise.

The issue is not only one of liberating the Dalits from the agony of what has been a painful marker of their identity; it is also in the moral context, one of cleansing the soul of India of the evil of caste and caste-based oppression that has besmirched it. At a material level it is one of preserving the integrity of India and ensuring that its dreams of prosperity are not turned into ashes.

[*Note* : This paper was earlier published in *Social Action* 43, 1993 and subsequently in the volume *Emerging Dalit Identity: The Reassertion of the Subalterns*, (ed.) Walter Fernandes, Delhi: Indian Social Institute, 1996.]

11

THE WORKING OF THE SCHEDULED CASTES AND SCHEDULED TRIBES (PREVENTION OF ATROCITIES) ACT, 1989 IN GUJARAT

P.V. Rathod and Vijay Kumar

Atrocities against Scheduled Castes and Scheduled Tribes continue unabated despite several provisions in the Constitution of India to safeguard and protect their interests. The main reason for this is the persistence of the age-old practice of untouchability in our caste-ridden society. Under Article 17 of the Constitution, untouchability is abolished and its practice is forbidden. The provisions under the Act relate to removal of disabilities and discrimination against SCs and STs, restriction of access to any public place, abolition of untouchability, etc. Prior to this there was no such central provision on the subject. However, between 1950 to 1955 some states had passed laws on this subject. The Untouchability (Offences) Act, 1955, enacted by Parliament made untouchability a cognizable offence punishable under the law. But there was a general feeling that the legislation had failed to fully serve its purpose. It was also felt that the punishments awarded under the Act were neither a deterrent nor adequate. Hence, the Act was amended in 1976 and renamed Protection of Civil Rights Act, 1955, and it came into force on 19 November, 1976. Under this Act, the preaching and practice of untouchability for the enforcement of any disability arising therefrom and for matters connected therewith have been made congnizable and non-compoundable offences and the terms of imprisonment have been enhanced. State Governments have been empowered to impose collective fines on the inhabitants of any area found committing and abetting untouchability offences.

Despite several measures to improve the socio-economic conditions of the members of Scheduled Castes and Scheduled Tribes, these communities are still being harassed, exploited, and subjected to humiliations by higher caste groups. There are several brutal instances of murder, rape and destructions of property. One of the major reasons for such crises is the awareness which has now spread amongst the weaker sections. Their assertion of their legitimate rights is strongly resented by the dominant and powerful sections of society. The Scheduled Castes and Scheduled Tribes, on account of their poverty, ignorance, illiteracy and age-old backwardness have been fighting an unequal battle with vested interests of the society. They lack the courage and wherewithal's to fight legal battles in courts to secure justice. It is common knowledge that the present judicial machinery is over-burdened with cases even during normal times. Therefore, it can hardly be expected to pay attention and give adequate time to mitigate the sufferings of these vulnerable communities, though it is a matter of priority.

It was against this backdrop that a central legislation, Scheduled Castes and the Scheduled Tribes (Protection of Atrocities) Act, 1989, was enacted which came into force on 30 January, 1990.

The enactment aims to prevent the offences of atrocities against the members of Scheduled Castes and the Scheduled Tribes; provides for special courts for the trial of such offences; for the relief and rehabilitation of the victims of such offences, and for matters connected therewith or incidental thereto. Section 3 of the Act specifies the list of offences and the punishment for commission of such atrocities.

State governments are expected to institute in each district a special court for speedy trial of offences under the Act. For every special court, State governments "will specify a public prosecutor or appoint an advocate who has been in practice as an advocate for not less than seven years, as a special public prosecutor for the purpose of conducting cases in court". State governments can confer by notification in the official gazette on any of its officers, powers exercisable by a police officer under the criminal procedure, viz., the powers of arrest, investigation and prosecution of persons before any special court. The law and order machinery of the state government can declare an area as atrocity-prone area, and take appropriate preventive action for checking atrocities in that area.

For effective implementation of the legislation, State governments have to take certain measures which includes:

1. Provision of adequate facilities including legal aid to persons subjected to atrocities to enable them to avail themselves of justice.
2. Provision for travelling and maintenance expenses to witnesses, including the victims of atrocities, during investigation and trial offences.
3. Appointment of officers for initiating or exercising supervision over prosecutions for the contravention of the provisions.
4. Setting up of a committee at such appropriate levels as the State government may think fit, to assist that government in the formulation or implementation of such measures.
5. Provision for a periodic survey of the working of the provisions, with a view to suggesting measures for its better implementation.
6. Identification of the areas where the members of the Scheduled Castes and Scheduled Tribes are likely to be subjected to atrocities, and adoption of such measures so as to ensure safety for them.

The Government of Gujarat has taken administrative measures for the implementation of the Scheduled Castes and Scheduled Tribes (Prevention of Atrocities) Act, 1989, as envisaged therein. According to the notification of the Legal Department, Government of Gujarat, No. APT-3390 G.K./02/H1, dated 31 January, 1992, the government, in exercise of the powers conferred by Section 15 of the Act, has designated each of the senior-most additional public prosecutors as special public prosecutors for the purpose of conducting cases of atrocities in special courts. There are 18 such courts and 18 special public prosecutors in Gujarat for the purpose.

The Government of Gujarat has also adopted the rules framed by the Government of India under the SCs and STs (Prevention of Atrocities) Act, 1989, *vide* the Government of India notification, dated 31 March, 1995, under Section 23(1) of the said Act, the norms for relief amount to be paid to the victims of atrocity. The State government has already taken action regarding provision of economic rehabilitation to victims of atrocities. Monetary relief and other measures as envisaged under Section 21 of the Act are given to victims of atrocities in Gujarat.

A high level committee under the chairmanship of the Chief Minister and a sub-committee under the chairmanship of the Minister of Social Welfare have been set-up to review cases of atrocities. Besides this three vigilance officers and vigilance inspectors have been appointed in Ahmedabad, Rajkot and Vadodara. Each has jurisdiction over six districts. Their functions are is constantly watch over the tension between SCs and others in areas which are prone to violence. Further, the State government has entrusted the responsibilities to investigate cases of atrocities and give protection to affected persons to an officer of the rank of (Director General of Police) DIG, designated as DIG, Harijan Cell, functioning at Ahmedabad under DG & IG of police. Cases of atrocities are also reviewed every month and quarter by the Secretary, Social Welfare Department. The State Government has created cells at the district level, headed by the Deputy Superintendent of Police, for investigating crimes against SCs and STs on 31 October, 1991.

Further, there is a scheme for extending free legal aid in civil and criminal cases to SCs and STs (annual income should not exceed Rs. 12,000) under the legal aid scheme.

A Brief Analysis of Case Studies in Gujarat

Information about the on the spot enquiries into the incidents of atrocities made by the Director for SCs/STs, Ahmedabad, for over a decade and a half has been obtained. The statistical information regarding number of IPC crimes against members of Scheduled Castes and Scheduled Tribes from 1981 to 1995 in Gujarat is provided in Tables 11.1 and 11.2. Moreover, brief notes in respect of some important cases are also given below.

TABLE 11.1: Atrocities against SCs in Gujarat (1981-1995)

Year	Natures of Crime					Total
	Murder	Grievous Hurt	Rape	Other	Arson IPC	
1981 to 1985	82	316	34	2,230	252	2,914
1986 to 1990	76	322	78	2,889	71	3,436
1991 to 1995	117	383	100	7,272	103	7,995
Total	275	1,021	212	12,391	426	14,345

TABLE 11.2: Atrocities Against STs in Gujarat (1981-1995)

Year	Natures of Crime					Total
	Murder	Grievous Hurt	Rape	Other	Arson IPC	
1981 to 1985	38	114	34	327	16	529
1986 to 1990	53	129	92	421	16	711
1991 to 1995	86	193	150	1,359	17	1,805
Total	177	436	276	2,107	49	3,045

The above Tables show a rising trend in atrocities committed against Scheduled Castes and Scheduled Tribes in Gujarat during 1981 to 1995. However, the cases of murder of SCs have declined, from 82 to 76 during 1981-85 to 1986-90, though they rose to 177 during 1991-95. The same is true of cases of arson.

It may be observed from the Tables that the total number of crimes against Scheduled Castes in Gujarat was on the continuous rise. Fortunately, the number of cases of crimes relating to the Scheduled Tribes did not show such rise during the period from 1981 to 1995.

Case 1: Rape of Smt. Budhiben Indiyabhai Bhil Garasia of Village Antras, Taluka Naswadi, District Vadodara, Gujarat State

Antras village is entirely inhabited by tribals consisting of 30 Bhil families. It is situated on the bank of Narmada river in the Naswadi taluka of Vadodara district. In this village there are two groups. Some of the tribal families of one group have shifted voluntarily to Sonali village on account of the Narmada Yojna. Another group of families have vowed not to leave their ancestral homes and have resolved to stay in the village. The victim Smt. Budhiben Indiyabhai Bhil Garasia belongs to the second group.

On the afternoon of 19 April, 1993, Shri M.N. Patel, Assistant Engineer, Kavadia colony, was engaged in shifting work of houses in Antras village. At that time "Narmada Bachao" supporters alleged to have attacked government officials and beat them up. The Assistant Engineer lodged a complaint at the Kavadia colony police station and gave the list of accused, including Smt. Budhiben. On the basis of this complaint, on 24 April, 1993, policemen loaded in two jeeps came at mid-night, forced opened the door and took away Budhiben and her son-in-law. The police first beat her up and then took to a spot, where two policemen and one Sajaya, who had come along, raped her. At 4.00 a.m. they reached Naswadi police station and took her thumb impression on a peace of paper. Being illiterate, Budhiben did not know what it contained. Budhiben was then presented before the court on the basis of the complaint. The Magistrate did not ask any question about the rape, and she was lodged in Vadodara jail.

As per medical report no external or internal injury was found on the body. Budhiben identified the accused police constable and others but they were not arrested. After the strenuous efforts of Narmada Bachao supporters, the High Court appointed Mr. K.V. Joseph, DIG computer-cum-state crime record department, Gandhinagar, to inquire into the case. The special IGP, Ahmedabad, has directed that the final report be presented as a case of false complaint made maliciously with the intention to discredit and defame persons named in the FIR.

Case 2: Atrocities against SCs by Police officials in Jamnagar City, Gujarat, in March 1996

There were two immediate causes of the incident. First, the Jamnagar Municipal Corporation decided to broaden the road where the statue of Dr. Baba Saheb Ambedkar stood. The second provocation was that in the presence of the Mayor, his party workers tore away the oil portrait of Dr. Baba Saheb Ambedkar from the general council hall.

The SC leaders and people had no objections to changing of place of the statue of Baba Saheb, but they suggested three alternative sites. Without their knowledge, corporation officials removed the surroundings compound wall of the statue. Of the three places, one was accepted by the Municipal Commissioner, but Shri Avinash Bhatt, the Mayor, refused to accept the proposal on the ground that the Municipal Corporation had the authority to shift the statue anywhere as per its choice. The Mayor was not ready to discuss this issue with the Dalit Samaj (community).

1. Due to such attitude of the Mayor, Dalit Samaj sat on a *Dharna* on 14 February, 1996, and submitted a memorandum.
2. On 16 February, a *Sarvadharm* (all religions) rally was conducted. And on 19 February, 1996, a *Bhim garjana* (thunder) rally was planned.

Permission for the rally had been requested by the Dalit Samaj, but the authorities did not respond. Section 144 was promulgated in the mid-night of 18 February, 1996, without the knowledge of the people. When the rally took place the next morning, the police officials made a lathi charge, fired tear gas shells and subsequently opened fire in the air to disperse the peacefully gathered Dalit crowd. Thirty to forty persons were injured, some of them seriously. The police filed cases against SCs, arrested some of them and sent them the jail. According to the statement of victims some of those not even present on that occasion were also arrested by the police.

Findings

1. Police officials and other government authorities did not hear them properly.
2. The injured persons were kept in the hospital custody for nine days, and proper treatment was not given.
3. The police got four days remand for the arrested SC persons, remanded the arrested SC persons to custody for four days whereas caste Hindu accused were released on bail on the same or very next day.
4. It was found that the injured SC persons had not received any financial relief from the Social Welfare Department. Both the officers, *viz.*, District Backward Class Welfare Officer, Jamnagar, and Vigilance Officer, Social Welfare Department, Rajkot, visited SC localities during this incident.

It is learnt that the corporation and other government officials ultimately decided to resolve the matter amicably and a compromise was reached on the issue.

Case 3: Ahir Savagery on Chamars of Village Chavand in Amreli District

According to a news item which appeared in the *Times of India* (Ahmedabad) on 4 July, 1996, the Chamars (SCs) of village Chavand, taluka Lathi, of Amreli district were victimised and assaulted by Ahirs on 29 June, 1996.

On enquiry, it was learnt that on 14 March, 1996, some Ahir caste Hindus had visited the Chamar locality to hire farm labours. However, the residents declined to take up work, since in the past the Ahirs had not paid daily wages at the prevalent rate, and in some cases the SC agricultural labourers had been refused the wage amount. The Ahirs got angry and beat up some SCs, who filed a complaint with the police. Though the Ahirs tried to arrive at a compromise, the SCs did not agree. Another cause of the incident of assault of SCs by Ahirs appeared to be the molestation by an Ahir youth of a SC girl, studying in 10th standard. Moreover, the Ahir youth put a vulgar demand before the brother of the girl, that he send the girl to his house. Visibily upset with this incident, the girl's father visited the Ahir youth's house and slapped the youth in the presence of other Ahirs. Somehow a compromise was reached by both the parties. But some strong-headed Ahirs, smarting from the two incidents, decided to teach the SCs a lesson. The Ahirs held secret meetings to finalise the ways and means to attack the SC mohalla. Accordingly, on the night of 29 June, 1996, at about 10 p.m., a mob of 60 to 75 persons, mostly belonging to the Ahir community, attacked the SC locality with swords, lathis, stones, iron pipes and other deadly weapons. Six SC persons, both male and female, were seriously injured. Meanwhile, one Police Sub-Inspector (PSI), Mr. Jadeja, who was on his round duty heard a wireless message of this incident, rushed to the spot and controlled the situation.

The PSI, had no fire some rounds from his service revolver to disperse the mob. The injured SC victims were first given medical treatment at the primary health centre at Lathi, and then sent to the Amreli Civil Hospital for further treatment. Of the six injured SCs victims, four were referred to the V. V. Hospital, in Ahmedabad for better treatment.

Ultimately, the police filed a case under Indian Panel Code (IPC) 326, 325, 324, 323, 143, 147, 148, 149, 506 and Section 3(16)(10) of the SCs and the STs (Prevention of Atrocities) Act, 1989, against six of the accused who could be recognised by the victims there and then, at the spot of incident as the other attackers fled taking advantage of the darkness of night. Later the PSI added IPC 307 in this case as one victim, Shri Manji Parmar, had been very seriously injured by the accused. The police also added Section 3(5) of the Act. Subsequently, the police arrested Sardar Laxman Ahir on 30 June, 1996, and other four on 5 July, 1996. One accused Shri Ravat Babu Ahir, who was injured (as reported by police) during the incident, got himself admitted in a hospital at Jamnagar for treatment.

The District Backward Class Welfare Office, Amreli, gave an application to the police requesting arrest of the others involved in the attack on SCs. Accordingly, the PSI, Lathi, arrested 22 more accused in this case.

It was found that the police, particularly PSI, Lathi, Mr. Jadeja, took speedy steps and did commendable work in the wake of this incident. Due to the immediate help of the PSI, none was killed by the armed mob of Ahirs. The District Superintendent of Police (DSP), Deputy S.P. and other police officials also performed their duties promptly and efficiently. Police action in this particular case appeared to be unbiased.

The DSP, Amreli, posted 40 armed police constables in the SC locality of the village Chavand, from 30 June, 1996. One CPI and two PSIs were also posted in the village for effective police *bandobast*.

Other officers, such as the Collector, Amreli, DSP, deputy S.P. District Backward Class Welfare Officer, Project Officer, Amreli, Mamlatdar, Lathi, also visited the village the next day and assessed the situation. They made arrangements for ensuring peace in the area.

A small incident of stone throwing took place (as reported by the SCs) in the SCs locality on 7 July, 1996. Disturbed by this, the SCs left village Chavand and migrated to Amreli. The district officers as well as the Home Minister visited the scene of the incident and met and heard the SC people. The SCs who had migrated did not want to return to their village, they wanted to be rehabilitated in Amreli itself on security grounds. All the district officers tried their best to persuade them to come back to Chavand, but the migrant SCs did not agree.

The SC migrants as well as some of the Dalit leaders wanted that the Section 3(15) of the SC and ST (Prevention of Atrocities) Act, 1989 should be applied in this case so as to help the victims properly. The DSP Amreli, was of the view that the SC people's migration to Amreli on 7 July, 1996, could not be justified as only one unknown person threw a stone on the SC locality and no major incident took place after 29 June, 1996.

The village Chavand was visited for on the spot inquiry by the Research Officer of the Director, National Commissioner for SCs and STs, Government of India, Ahmedabad on 22-23 July, 1996.

The position of the case as of then was that the accused were released on bail. The victims were not given any financial assistance as per the rules, since the police could not submit a charge-sheet. The District Backward Class Welfare Office, Amreli, is the granting authority for financial assistance in such atrocity cases, but in the absence of a charge-sheet, he could not grant any payment to the victims. The police did not add Section 3(15) of the SCs and the STs (Prevention of Atrocities) Act, 1989 in this case.

Case 4: A Scheduled Caste Farmer Killed at Vani Village of Viramgam Taluka, Ahmedabad District

The farms of the victim and accused were adjacent to each others. Shri Rambhai Parmar wanted to construct a compound wall to protect his crops, but the accused was against this. Shri Rambhai started the construction on 2 July, 1996. This was opposed by Shri Rameshbhai who threatened to kill Rambhai. The accused, Rameshbhai and Shri Hasmukhbhai Nondoda Patel fired two rounds from their country-made revolver on 4 July, 1996. Shri Rambhai Parmar was injured seriously and admitted to the Viramgam Hospital. On the same day he was transferred to V.S. Hospital, Ahmedabad, for better treatment.

(i) The police filed a case under IPC 307, 342, 114, Arms Act 25(I), AB and Section 3(10) of the SCs and STs (Prevention of Atrocities) Act, 1989. The main accused, Shri Rameshbhai B. Nandoda and Shri Hasmukhbhai Haribhai Nandoda Patel were arrested and sent to judicial custody. The Sub-Inspector of Police, Viramgam, went to inquire into the matter, but as per rules, the offence committed under the Act should be investigated by a police officer not, below the rank of Deputy Superintendent of Police.

(ii) It was observed that the police officials deliberately applied the Section 3(N) of the SCs and STs (Prevention of Atrocities) Act, 1989 instead of Section 3(ii)(v) and (x).

The District Superintendent of Police, Ahmedabad (Rural), posted four police constables in Vankar Vas to protect SC persons.

The District Backward Class Welfare Officer, Ahmedabad, could not release the financial assistance of Rs. 25,000 because the charge-sheet was yet to be submitted by the police.

According to the people of Vani village, because the accused and their supporters were influential, strong-headed and notorious persons in the village, the victims did not dare to register complaints against them.

The main accused, Shri Rameshbhai Bhavanbhai Nandoda Patel and Shri Hasmukhbhai Hirabhai Nandoda Patel were arrested by the police after two days, i.e., on 7 July, 1996, and all accused were recommended to the judicial custody at Viramgam. The case is still pending in court.

Case 5: Alleged Rape of Geetaben Rathawa of Rangpur Ashram, Taluka Chhota Udepur, District Vadodara

A news-item captioned, "Harivallabh issue sparks a row in Chhota Udepur" appeared in the daily *Times of India* (Ahmedabad), dated 7 June, 1996. Moreover, some non-government organisations working for women's welfare in Gujarat also raised hue and cry against Shri Harivallabh Parikh, a worker and the *sanchalak* (organiser) of the Anand Niketan Ashram, Rangpur, who has been working among tribals for more than two and a half decades. Shri Parikh was charged with sexually assaulting tribal girls for the past several years.

In the present case of rape, Geetaben D. Rathawa of village Nani Sankal, taluka Chhota Udepur, district Baroda, was one of the trainees in the tailoring class being conducted by the Rangpur Ashram for girls. In all, 40 tribal girls joined the class in December, 1994. All the trainees were provided free food, cloth and accommodation.

Mr. Harivallabh Parikh, the *sanchalak* of the ashram used to give pocket money to the girls. It is alleged that Mr. Dalpat Vankar, Secretary, Lok Adalat, and Mrs. Noori, a worker of the ashram used to talk and induce girls in vulgar language so that girls may be attracted to Mr. Parikh for sexual enjoyment. Mr. Parikh used to take a bath with the help of young and good-looking girls daily. It is believed that he was guilty of "group custodian rape". It is further alleged that he used to have intercourse with almost all the girls of the tailoring class as well as the other girls of the Rangpur Ashram. If any girl ever dared to protest, he would give threats and sometimes even beat her up. The poor tribal girls never dared to oppose any of Mr. Parikh's sexual demands as many of them were married and in the interest of their family life, they could not utter anything against Mr. Parikh.

Geetaben Rathawa was also one of the victims of Mr. Parikh. She painfully narrated how Mr. Harivallabh Parikh repeatedly had intercourse with almost all the girls of the tailoring class including herself. This continued for long with Geetaben. She said that after 15 days of her admission, she was taken by Mrs. Noori before Mr. Parikh to give him personal service including bathing and sexual intercourse. She further narrated that in the beginning, being a young unmarried girl, she refused to submit herself to Mr. Parikh, but she was raped forcefully and had to sleep with him the whole night. This torture continued till she got pregnant.

Mr. Parikh took her along with him to visit places in Madhya Pradesh in February 1996. Mr. Parikh wanted to meet Baba Amte. When he stayed overnight at Nandugarh, he raped her as well as Kum. Jaya who also accompanied him. At Dhar Mr. Parikh was caught red-handed by a lady police officer for misbehaving in a public place. During his tours, Mr. Parikh took Geetaben Rathawa to various places: Ambaji, Kavadia, Ahmedabad, Surendranagar, etc., where he continued to rape her. She was also taken to Bombay where Mr. Parikh got himself operated for some disease in his leg. Geeta was required to stay with Mr. Parikh for his personal service. During this period she was in her advanced stage of pregnancy, but Mr. Parikh could not be bothered. On the contrary, he asked the Ashram employees to arrange for her abortion. She was taken to the community health centre at Chhota Udepur. But Geetaben did not agree to the abortion or any other medical treatment for termination of the pregnancy. Mr. Parikh, became angry and got upset.

Thereafter, it was reported, a story was fabricated about one Mr. Raimal who had affairs with Geeta and got her pregnant. But Geeta vehemently refused this story. Then she was not allowed to go anywhere, even to her parents' house during the Diwali or Holi festivals.

To save himself from this scandal, Mr. Parikh arranged for strict security steps around the ashram. The sordid stories of Mr. Parikh's Ashram were well known in the area, but because of his close links with the police, nobody had ever dared to touch him. Mr. Parikh was alleged to have sold out one tribal girl of Dharoli village to a foreigner. He was guilty of group custodian rape and of all the other girls, namely, Sumitra, Urmila, Sharmistha, Dariyaben, Shushila, Shurati, Kailas, who have been the victims of his sexual lust.

On 14 May, 1996, Mr. Parikh took Geeta to a distant village, Khadkwada, along with some other Ashram inmates to attend the marriage ceremony of a tribal girl, Kusum (also an Ashram inmate, very close to Mr. Parikh), where she developed labour pain. Because of her critical condition, Mr. Parikh left along with other ashram inmates. During the return journey in a truck, Geeta got very severe labium pains and on reaching the Chhota Udepur petrol pump, she prematurely delivered (a still-born girl), while she was unconscious. Someone informed the Chhota Udepur hospital about this case, and the staff admitted Geeta for treatment. The dead child of Geeta's was then cremated by the hospital authorities and the police was informed of this case.

Geeta in her statement to the police said, under threat from Mr. Parikh, that one Mr. Ramesh Tadvi was the father of her child. On 16 May, 1996, her mother arrived at the community health centre, Chhota-Udepur, and took her daughter to her village.

Ultimately, Geeta submitted a written complaint to the judicial magistrate first class at Udepur through an advocate Mr. Ramesh. She was again admitted to hospital by the police for treatment on 25 May, 1996, where she stayed for about 20 to 25 days.

Geeta Rathwada has been severely victimised by Mr. Parikh and has suffered a lot at his hands. She wants justice. Mr. Parikh must be arrested and punished. She has approached the Gujarat High Court through a pleader, Mr. K.B. Pandy, on 6 June, 1996, and filed a special criminal application, No. 648 of 1996.

The Vigilance Officer, Vadodara, of the Social Welfare Department visited the area and met the victim and other related persons and sent his report to the higher authorities at Gandhinagar. He also granted a sum of Rs. 25,000 to Geeta, as per rules of this department, in Gujarat in such type of atrocity cases.

The case has been registered in Kwant police station under I-110/96 of IPC 376, 114 and of the SCs and the STs (Prevention of Atrocities) Act, 1989, Section 3(1)(xi) 12. It is an unhappy story about police inaction in this case. It is believed that the police did not take prompt action intentionally, since Mr. Parikh was a well-known figure and highly influential in political circles as well. The police did not arrest him for long, which allowed Mr. Parikh to abscond and did not even get medically examined. Due to the inactivity of the police, Mr. Parikh fled the Rangpur Ashram and got himself admitted in a private hospital in Baroda to avoid possible arrest.

But the Honourable Justice of the High Court of Gujarat, Ahmedabad, has directed Mr. Parikh to appear before the Special Inspector General of Police, CID Branch. The Special I.G.P. has also been directed to record Mr. Parikh's statement and, if necessary, have him medically examined by a panel of three doctors and submit his report by 13 June, 1996. As per the directions of the High Court, CID Gujarat, took over the investigation of this case on 8 June, 1996. The Deputy Superintendent, CID (Crime), was put in charge of the probe. Subsequently, Mr. Harivallabh Parikh was arrested was remanded to judicial custody by the Chief Judicial Magistrate of Chhota Udepur. At present the case is pending before the court.

The above cases speak for themselves. They highlight the condition of the deprived sections of society and starkly show that the available legal measures have not reduced atrocities against them. The National Commission for Scheduled Castes and Scheduled Tribes, the National Police Commission and various committees have made several recommendations for a more rigorous implementation of the Scheduled Castes and Scheduled Tribes (Prevention of Atrocities) Act, 1989. On the basis of these recommendations and our own observations, we make the following suggestions:

1. It is essential that special cells for inquiring into and investigation of atrocity cases be established. The

Government of India order regarding the establishment of independent special courts for atrocity cases should be fully implemented. In this connection it may be stated that at present the Government of Gujarat has specified certain session courts and nominated some public prosecutors for dealing with atrocity cases, but this arrangement has not been beneficial to the victims of atrocity cases.

2. It is necessary that serious cases of atrocities be looked into by higher officers in the Directorate of Social Welfare, Gujarat. Moreover, follow-up action relating to court cases should be taken regularly.
3. Surveys on the working of the SCs and STs (Prevention of Atrocities) Act, 1989, should be conducted periodically in sensitive areas of the state.
4. It is very important, particularly for lower-level functionaries of the police, revenue, forest and excise departments to have adequate orientation in tribal life and culture. This will help them tackle sensitive situations tactfully and avoid use of force. Such an orientation should form an important part of their training at the entry point, which should be repeated, through a refresher course. No training should be considered as complete unless it is certified that such orientation has been achieved on the basis of performance of the trainee.
5. Local officers like Taluka Development Officer (TDO), Mamlatdar, Range Officer, etc., should show adequate interest and act promptly and tactfully and make all efforts to defuse tension before it reaches a flash point.
6. Forest laws must take into account the stark reality of the dependence of tribal people on forests for their livelihood.
7. SCs, apart from being subjected to economic exploitation by powerful caste Hindus in their village, also suffer from social disabilities. It is, therefore, essential that lower-level functionaries who come into day-to-day contact with them identify themselves with the cause of their upliftment. This is particularly important in the case of the police. The police must not only defend the SCs, but their demeanour and

attitude should be a deterrent to potential perpetrators of atrocities. This will go a long way in not only creating faith in the law and order machinery but also drastically reducing the incidence of atrocity.

8. Prompt action is called for from the Collector and District Superintendent of Police when atrocities take place. All efforts should be made to settle the dispute amicably between the communities involved in the village/areas, no outside agency should be allowed to fish in trouble waters for political gains.
9. There should be an effective inbuilt mechanism in the day-to-day functioning of the police for collection of intelligence regarding possible violence against SCs and STs. This should be given priority in the duties of all concerned at all levels so that the administration is not cought off guard.
10. The National Police Commission has in its report pointed out that several complaints have been levelled against the police, such as refusal to register complaints; delayed arrival at the scene of the incident; half-hearted action in investigation; treating high castes softly, while treating the SCs brutally; and failing to make arrests of high caste persons on mollified consideration. It is essential that the police identify itself with the SCs and STs, the oppressed ones, and not with vested interests, powerful caste Hindus in the village. This will result in a dramatic reduction in the number of atrocities and be effective in creating faith of the SCs and STs in the law and order machinery. The government functionaries in the forest, revenue and excise departments, who come in regular contact with SCs and STs must also perform a similar role. It will indeed be the beginning of a new era in the history of upliftment of backward classes if such transformations take place. Effective remedial steps should also be taken in such cases.
11. There should be a clear-cut incentive-cum-disincentive policy. It should operate in such a manner that officers who do their duty to the SCs in an exemplary manner should be rewarded and the careers of those who fail in this receive a

significant set-back.

A few civil servants who are committed to the cause of the downtrodden should be given protection against vested interests, when the occasion arises. The government should specially recognise the services of such civil servants, and refrain from transferring them suddenly on the request of affected vested interests. Further, such officers should be posted in sensitive areas with adequate discretionary powers.

12. SCs are generally relegated to the outskirts of village devoid of the facilities and conveniences available to the rest of the population. One way of bringing dignity to that part of the village, and thereby the SCs, is to get all Collectors and SPs and their sub-divisional subordinates to spend a substantial part of their time there, when on tours to villages. Work pertaining to the general advancement and problems of the village should be transacted from these localities. Similar instructions may be given to the officers of the major development departments and of local bodies. This will have a far-reaching psychological impact.

13. A few units of Special Striking Force, highly mobile and well-equipped may be located in strategic areas, in such a manner that it will give confidence to the SCs and other weaker sections, and deter potential perpetrators of atrocities.

14. The efficacy of punitive action depends not only on its quantum, but also its speed. Therefore, the police machinery should be streamlined to complete investigations promptly and be free from lacunae and defects. The prosecuting machinery should be strengthened to effectively resist granting of bail and to ensure prompt conviction and deterrent punishment.

15. The lacunae pointed out in the SCs and STs (Prevention of Atrocities) Act, namely offences relating to non-payment of minimum wages, theft of cattle, fraud in maintenance of loan accounts, and prevention from access to burial or cremation grounds, may also be brought within the ambit of

the Act.

16. Demarcation of the boundaries of land allotted to SCs and STs or owned by them should be carried out properly under the supervision of a senior officers. Land records should be updated at the earliest. Steps should be taken to ensure use of community land by SCs and STs, including that of grazing cattle.
17. A scrutiny of existing provisions regarding transfer of land of SCs and STs should be done urgently and the various loopholes plugged.
18. Confrontation between landlords and SCs and STs labourers on wage issues usually results in violence and atrocities. Women agriculture labourers form a larger proportion of the victims. The creation of an effective machinery for enforcing minimum wage and its periodic revision and monitoring is, therefore, essential. Similar steps should be taken for the payment of minimum wages in other occupations like leather works, tanning, flaying and curing hides, scavenging and sweeping, where the majority of those employed belong to SCs. Further, to improve their bargaining power, additional employment opportunities should be created, throughout the year, by implementation of various employment generation schemes by the government.
19. There is a mismatch between government forest policy and the ground reality. The government must accept the fact that forests are major source of livelihood of the tribal people, and reshape its forest policy accordingly. The place of tribals in forests, their special skills, handicrafts, customs and traditions, and approach to forest conservation, should be made an integral part of the training of forest officials.
20. The following precautionary and preventive steps should be taken to identify potential areas of tensions and atrocities; regular collection of intelligence solving disputes in the initial in a fair manner; reviewing gun licences in sensitive areas, sending promptly police protection where necessary, arresting musclemen/gang leaders under various preventive sections of Criminal Procedure Code (CRPC) and other

legislation's, immediate giving police protection to victims of atrocity to instill a sense of security and confidence.

21. Measures envisaged in the rehabilitation scheme for victims of atrocities should be taken without any delay. Prompt action will go a long way in mitigating their sufferings.
22. Widespread publicity should be given through the media to the offences and punishments covered by the SCs and STs (Prevention of Atrocities) Act. A sympathetic attitude of the media and its alertness goes a long way in building the confidence level of the weaker sections.
23. The translation of the SCs and STs (Prevention of Atrocities) Act, into regional languages should be completed without any delay and adequate copies should be printed for wide distribution at each and every police station.

12

RESERVATION
An Insufficient Condition for Social Transformation

S.C. Behar

The transition from a feudal society to a democratic polity is necessarily a painful, slow and arduous process. Colonial India was characterised by a predominance of feudal relationships, attitudes and organisation. These forces were supported by an oligarchic state. Power was primarily in the hands of small elite groups comprising representatives of the imperial government and its local allies, who, with some honourable exceptions, were, to paraphrase Macaulay, English in taste, behaviour, intellect, and morals.

Leaders of the freedom struggle were aware of the conditions of, and were able to identify themselves, to an extent, with the rural masses. This is why they succeeded in mobilising common people for the cause they espoused. Their appreciation of the social realities, however, was partial; it enabled them to anticipate only certain kinds of difficulties inherent in the transition process. Leaders like Gandhiji and Dr. Baba Saheb Ambedkar were able to effectively highlight the existing inequalities, injustice and extreme forms of social discrimination, economic exploitation, and inhuman customs and practices. Though Gandhiji called untouchability a sin against God and humanity, and initiated a number of measures to abolish the practice, it continued unabated in its revolting cruelty, intolerable indignity, and insufferable humiliation.

Gandhiji's crusade against untouchability touched only the fringe of the Indian orthodoxy. Although the new expression "Harijan" or God's people, was coined to signify transformation in their social status, in reality there was hardly any significant change. Many other measures like their entry into temples, also proved, in the long run, to be only symbolic gestures.

These measures seldom touched the core of the problem, which was deeply rooted in the socio-economic structure and derived sustenance and strength from religious beliefs. The leaders of our freedom struggle, apart from Gandhiji, had perhaps a limited purpose of mobilising people against the foreign rule. This limitation, some how, pushed to the back the social priorities, and inhibited their understanding of the complexity of the caste system and *Varnashram*.

Throwing away the shackles of foreign power was probably the only item on the agenda of the leaders of the freedom struggle. Visionaries like Mahatma Gandhi and Jawaharlal Nehru tried to include social and economic issues, but these remained on the margins and never became the focus of attention. To what extent this was to do with the basic character of the 'elite' leading our freedom struggle, is a matter of deeper analysis and we shall not venture here into that. Certainly there was an unstated assumption that freedom from foreign rule, and the consequent achievement of political power held the key to other desirable changes in the country. There was probably a naïve belief that through political power socio-economic transformation could be achieved.

This perception is manifested in the fundamental approach and the basic framework of the Constitution for the development of disadvantaged groups: the Scheduled Castes, Scheduled Tribes and socially and educationally backward classes. Since political power was seen as the vantage point for initiating socio-economic changes, the emphasis was on developing a system of power-sharing by disadvantaged groups. The policy of reservation is an integral part of this attempt to provide a share in political and administrative power.

The privileging of political power over social and economic structure also resulted in a disproportionately deep and blind faith in the legal and constitutional framework. This explains the attempt to incorporate in the Constitution, the Fundamental Rights (Articles 12 to 35), the Directive Principles of State Policy (Articles 36 to 51), special provisions relating to certain classes (Articles 330-342), and special directive (Articles 350,350A, 350B and 351), all reflect this vision of the Constitution-markers. This overemphasis on constitutional and legal measures to achieve economic change and social transformation persisted in the formulation of a policy framework, its approach and strategy. This is why in the past five decades, the problems of social discrimination and economic exploitation have been sought to be tackled primarily through legal, constitutional and administrative measures. Social issues and economic malaise have rarely been confronted squarely.

There has been little evidence of policy measures and programmes clearly directed towards bringing about structural changes in the society and the economy. In an agrarian economy, measures of land reforms are absolutely necessary for unleashing forces of socio-economic change. After the successful step of abolition of intermediaries and proprietary rights, the progress in land reforms has been hesitant, halting and unsatisfactory, except in a few states. As a result, the agrarian structure has not changed appreciably and the economic interrelations continue to be in a *status quo*. A large number of labourers do not even get subsistence wages and are fully beholden to the landowners. The industrial scenario is equally dismal from the point of view of equity and social justice. The social structure also largely persists, with only marginal and cosmetic changes. This brief assessment indicates how reliance on political and administrative measures alone has failed to bring about the kind of structural changes that are inherent in the progress towards an ideal society. In the Constitution, a fair share for disadvantaged groups in political power and control over administrative apparatus was sought to be achieved by a policy of positive discrimination, more specially, by providing for reservations in Parliament and in public services. Seats in Parliament and state legislatures were reserved for Scheduled Castes and Scheduled Tribes, under Articles 330 and 332 of the Constitution. Although this provision was initially for a limited period (10 years), by consequent constitutional amendments, the provision continues to exist.

Since seats in Parliament and the legislatures are filled

periodically by elections, the SCs and STs have been finding adequate numerical representation in these bodies. Initially, representatives of these communities lacked the articulation and skills to use their position, power and authority. Over the years there has been a distinct improvement in this regard.

Members of Parliament and legislative assemblies belonging to Scheduled Caste and Scheduled Tribe have increasingly shown signs of maturity and the ability to work together as pressure groups for the advancement of their interests. While opinions may vary about their efficacy in this regard, there will be near unanimity on the fact that, generally speaking, they have become much more adept at using political power. It is, however, doubtful whether this power is commensurate with their numerical strength. Moreover, their participation in the proceedings of legislatures and Parliament, as also in the decision-making process continues to be inadequate and marginal. Since there is no constitutional reservation for SCs and STs in the ministries, their representation both at the union and state level, has been varying from symbolic to substantial, depending upon the political expediency of the hour. Observers of our political scenario believe that the provision of reservation in the seats of Parliament and legislatures has definitely accelerated the political education of these disadvantaged groups. They have come to increasingly realise their significance in the power game and their capacity to tilt the balance decisively in favour of one of the competing groups. Factions within the ruling parties, therefore, give due regard to the needs and views of the representatives of Scheduled Castes and Scheduled Tribes. Political parties also appreciate the crucial role, these groups can play in Parliament and state legislatures, and therefore, their election manifestos and promises and pre-electoral decisions are calculated to influence the voters of these groups in their favour.

Generally, a number of decisions, policy measures and programmes of various state governments also focus on the development of the Scheduled Castes and Scheduled Tribes. To this extent, the policy of reserving seats in the legislatures has proved advantageous. Following this broad approach, representation by reservation to SCs and STs has been provided in other elective bodies, like Panchayats at different levels, municipalities and municipal corporations. While they have acquired numerical representation and gained political awareness, their participation and role in the decision-making process still remains marginal. Article 335 provides for reservation for Scheduled Castes and Scheduled Tribes in government services.

Table 12.1 indicates the progress in filling up posts reserved for Scheduled Castes and Scheduled Tribes in Central government services from 1977 to 1987. For Group A and B posts, representation continues to be low. This is generally attributed to the non-availability of qualified candidates for technical posts. In the case of Group C and D posts, SCs have relatively high proportion, while the representation of Scheduled Tribes remains deplorably poor. Even the low level of representation in ministerial posts cannot be justified on any ground. The usual excuse of non-availability of suitable candidates in sufficient numbers is a lame one.

TABLE 12.1: Reservation in Central Government Services, 1977 to 1987

Group of Posts	SC		ST		Increase	
	1977	1987	1977	1987	SC	ST
A	4.16	8.25	0.77	2.05	4.07	1.28
B	6.07	10.40	0.77	1.92	4.33	1.15
C	11.84	14.46	2.78	4.23	2.62	1.45
D	19.07	20.09	4.35	4.35	1.02	1.49

Note: 1977 and 1987 figures refer to 1 January.
Source: Twenty-Eighth Report of the Commissioner for Scheduled Castes and Scheduled Tribes, 1986-87.

Table 12.2 gives the extent of reservation prescribed for Scheduled Castes and Scheduled Tribes in various states and the percentage of actual representation. The data have been classified groupwise in Table 12.3. It will be seen that there is only one state in which for Group A and B posts, Scheduled Castes have full representation. Reserved posts filled to the extent of 50 per cent or less for SCs are found in 21 states and union territories for group A; in 16 states and UTs for Group B, in 7 for group C, and 3 for group

D. Reserved posts for STs have been filled to the extent of 50 per cent or less in 15 states and union territories, for Group A, in 16 states and UTs for Group B, in 12 Group C, and 8 for Group D.

TABLE 12.2: Statewise Reservation for SCs and STs

State	Reservation Prescribed per cent		Actual Representation (per cent)							
			Group A		Group B		Group C		Group D	
	SC	ST	SC	ST	SC	ST	SC	ST	SC	ST
Punjab	25	—	9.23	—	12.39	—	9.56	—	14.38	—
Haryana	20	—	5.60	—	4.70	—	8.0	—	26.20	—
Tamil Nadu	18	—	7.00	0.40	14.30	0.10	13.70	0.10	16.60	0.40
Uttar	18$	02	—	—	—	—	—	—	—	—
Pradesh	25$	02	—	—	—	—	—	—	—	—
	30	02	7.40	0.45	7.11	0.37	13.66	0.42	17.58	0.50
Rajasthan	16	12	17.90	2.78	9.80	8.70	9.02	7.71	22.65	11.43
Madhya	15#	18	2.13	1.94	5.31	2.44	9.17	9.45	11.75	8.67
Pradesh	16@	20								
Himachal	15#	7.5	5.40	3.90	7.80	3.70	12.00	3.40	20.50	5.80
Pradesh	22@	05								
Andhra Pradesh	15	06	3.99	0.70	5.52	0.80	19.40	0.94	15.81	2.68
Karnataka	15	03	12.23	1.79	8.06	1.49	11.20	1.57	18.58	3.28
Orissa	15	23	1.41	0.88	2.87	1.56	8.64	5.62	21.29	12.02
Tripura	15	29	4.40	5.69	6.65	7.73	9.59	19.20	16.26	19.21
West Bengal	15	05	4.63	0.92	6.01	0.82	9.50	2.08	16.21	4.05
Maharashtra	13	07	6.90	2.29	7.91	2.28	3.83	5.02	21.30	7.45
Jammu & Kashmir	08	—	2.08	—	—	—	3.08	—	4.29	—
Kerala	08	02	8.41	8.41	8.41	8.41	9.00	9.00	13.40	13.49
Gujarat	07	14	9.64	5.91	11.49	4.00	17.68	8.98	41.62	17.78
Manipur	02	31	0.81	13.83	0.91	17.96	1.46	29.18	1.36	26.4
Andaman & Nicobar Islands		15#	7.5	0.90	0.45	0.92	0.03	3.37	—	3.70

(Contd.)

TABLE 12.2 *(Contd.)*

1	2	3	4	5	6	7	8	9	10	11
Arunachal Pradesh	—	80	2.37	12.58	3.44	25.02	3.76	25.30	4.39	5.95
Chandigarh	15# 14@	7.5	3.60	—	2.50	—	11.52	0.22	27.65	0.60
Dadra & Nagar Haveli	15 02@	7.5	7.14	—	6.89	6.89	5.97	33.14	8.23	9.42
Delhi	15	7.5	7.3	0.9	9.2	2.1	10.63	1.19	13.3	3.4
Laksha-dweep	15#	7.5	3.70	44.44	4.16	47.91	0.63	59.88	0.37	89.00
Goa, Daman & Diu	15 02@	7.5	2.17	0.32	2.91	0.48	1.95	0.36	2.95	0.73
Mizoram	—	45	4.40	73.20	1.55	87.41	0.54	90.12	2.17	88.54
Pondichery	15#	7.5	3.95	—	11.56	0.80	9.33	0.42	14.78	1.23

#Group A & B, $ Group C, @ D.
Source: *Ibid.*

TABLE 12.3: Group of Posts by Extent of Reservation

Reserved Posts filled (per cent)	Group A		Group B		Group C		Group D	
	SC	ST	SC	ST	SC	ST	SC	ST
to 50	21	15	16	16	7	12	3	8
50 to 90	4	2	7	3	14	7	8	7
100 & above	1	2	1	2	5	4	14	8

Source: *Ibid.*

It is clear that in the case of both Central and State Governments, a large percentage of the reserved posts remain vacant. The situation in respect of tribals would even be worse if one was to exclude from the consideration the predominantly tribal states of the North-East.

Such continued low representation leads to the following

conclusions. First, serious effort is lacking in filling up reserved posts. It is done more as a routine exercise than with a sincere desire and commitment to fill the posts. Second, there has been no systematic manpower planning and corresponding efforts to provide education to the children of Scheduled Castes and Scheduled Tribes in such a manner that they become eligible and qualified for all the posts usually available. If systematic manpower planning and matching educational arrangements had been undertaken, the question of non-availability of suitable candidates from these deprived groups would not have arisen. This also serves to highlight the need to pay greater attention to the education of these communities.

Third, despite the availability of educational opportunities, the socio-economic conditions of Scheduled Castes and Scheduled Tribes do not allow a sufficient number of boys and girls to pursue education and obtain the qualifications for appointment in government jobs. This highlights the need to have a critical review of the existing policy of scholarships and stipends, which appears to be symbolic and ritual, rather than substantial and effective for neutralising the disability created by socio-economic hardships.

It is common knowledge that the amount of scholarship given cannot enable a child to meet all kinds of education related expenditure. The government will have to clearly commit to a policy of meeting all expenses of educating SC and ST boys and girls to ensure their adequate educational development. Both the direct and indirect costs of education should be met by society/government to encourage education amongst these communities. For effective implementation of this policy, it will also be necessary to ensure that the quantum of scholarship and other compensatory measures are not fixed only periodically, but are linked to the actual cost by including the provision for automatic increase to adjust for inflation.

Fourth, the representation of these communities in Group D and C posts is much better than that in Group B and A posts, reflecting the caste hierarchy and social discrimination in the pattern of representation. Persons of these communities are getting better representations only for low paid jobs. It is very disturbing to find that reservation, instead of upsetting and disturbing the caste hierarchy, is only perpetuating it. As a modest measure to counter this trend, reservation in promotion has also been prescribed from the year 1974. The figures in the Tables indicate that despite this, representation in the higher services continues to be low. At the same time, reservation has given rise to grievance among the non-Scheduled Caste, non-Scheduled Tribe employees. Many of them feel that promoting a junior not because of pure merit, but because of the accident of birth, is unjust to them. They forget the advantage they have enjoyed historically by the accident of birth, which has given them such an edge over the disadvantaged communities. In any case, the fact remains that reservation in promotions has given rise to a sense of grievance and heartburn without corresponding and proportionate benefits to the deprived groups. There is a need to take a fresh look at this policy and to redesign it in such a manner that representation in higher services improves within a framework that does not cause widespread dissatisfaction.

Table 12.4 gives the number and percentage of Scheduled Caste and Scheduled Tribe persons working in different categories of government jobs in Madhya Pradesh in each of the three years 1988-89 and 1990. The following conclusions emerge:

1. The improvement in the percentage of representation over these three years is negligible. In Group A positions, the percentage for Scheduled Tribes has risen from 1.41 per cent in 1988 to only 1.49 per cent in 1990. For the Scheduled Castes, the increase is only from 2.70 to 3.06 per cent. Even in Group B and C positions, the increase in percentage for both Scheduled Castes and Scheduled Tribes is very nominal, not exceeding 1 per cent.
2. In Group D, in case of Scheduled Tribes, there is an increase of more than 3 per cent, but in case of Scheduled Castes it is less than 1 per cent. However, the representation in Group D for Scheduled Castes in the year 1990 is close to the total percentage of reservation prescribed for them.
3. The representation prescribed in Madhya Pradesh for Scheduled Castes in Group A and B posts, is 15 per cent and in Group C and D posts, 16 per cent. The corresponding figures for Scheduled Tribes are 18 per cent and 20 per cent,

respectively. The representation for Scheduled Tribes in Group A has never exceeded 1.49 per cent, while for Scheduled Castes the highest is 3.06 per cent. For Group B posts, while the position is better, the gap continues to be very wide. Even in Group C positions, the percentage continues to be far below of that prescribed. In case of Group D, the position is not as dismal, though for Scheduled Tribes, there is still a considerable gap.

4. The inter-group disparity in percentage of actual posts filled continues to be very significant and noticeable. In the case of tribals, there is a gradual increase in representation from Group A to Group B, a sudden jump in Group C, and again a marginal increase in Group D. The picture in respect of Scheduled Castes is similar. The all India pattern and better representation in lower groups is also reflected in Madhya Pradesh.

TABLE 12.4: Representation of SCs and STs in M.P. Government Services

Year	Total No.	SC	Percentage	ST	Percentage
1	2	3	4	5	6
		Group A			
Prescribed % of reservation		15		18	
1988	5,600	151	2.70	79	1.41
1989	5,816	169	2.90	85	1.46
1990	5,789	177	3.06	86	1.49
		Group B			
Prescribed % of reservation		15		18	
1988	36,475	2,607	7.15	1,574	4.31
1989	36,539	2,644	7.24	1,751	4.79
1990	36,519	2,649	7.25	1,807	4.95

(Contd.)

TABLE 12.4 *(Contd.)*

1	2	3	4	5	6
		Group C			
Prescribed % of reservation		16		20	
1988	540,829	52,998	9.80	56,810	10.50
1989	546,102	56,311	10.31	63,242	11.58
1990	551,669	57,281	10.38	65,402	11.86
		Group D			
Prescribed % of reservation		16		20	
1988	72,634	9,944	13.70	7,610	10.48
1989	70,801	9,957	14.06	9,390	13.26
1990	7,788	10,449	14.56	9,873	13.75

It is clear from the analysis of these four Tables that the instrument of reservation has failed to provide adequate represen-tation in government services to Scheduled Castes and Scheduled Tribes. This measure has not been able to make a significant dent in the stratified Indian social structure, which seems to be resistant to change, even though it has influenced the policy of reservation itself. As a consequence, the distortions of a stratified and fractured social order are reflected in the pattern of representation in government services.

Despite this failure as a tool of social change, positive discrimination continues to be the most popular measure for recti-fying the injustice meted out to disadvantaged groups for centuries. It has, therefore, grown in scope. It is no longer confined only to government services or even public sector undertakings. In some states, reservation for Scheduled Caste and Scheduled Tribes has been made obligatory even in the non-governmental organisations receiving grants from the government. In addition to the broad objective of providing an equitable share for SCs and STs in administrative power, the specific purpose of reservation in services is also to ensure that programmes and policies targeted at them are properly implemented and the interests of these disadvantaged groups are adequately and consistently protected.

There are other more significant assumptions behind the reservation policy. It is believed that a fair share in political and administrative set-up will accelerate social mobility, and lead to economic development of the Scheduled Castes and Scheduled Tribes. A review of the current situation indicates that these objectives have been achieved only partially. Social mobility as well as economic prosperity have been limited to particular families that have been able to take advantage of reservations, whether in educational institutions, in services, or in legislatures and Parliament. Accrual of benefits to the community at large is still a distant goal. On the other hand, further subdivision and intragroup inequality seem to be growing. The benefits of reservation are being cornered by only some tribal groups and Scheduled Castes. This should make such tribes and castes ineligible for reservation, as they are now advanced enough to compete on equal terms with the non-Scheduled Caste, non-Scheduled Tribe population. This, however, cannot be done, among other things, because of political considerations. The ruling elite is unwilling to invite the wrath of the advanced SCs and STs. The rationalisation for not undertaking and evolving dependable, valid and reliable methods of measurement to assess a need for reservation for a family or a social group has wider implications. Once it accepted that development of some Scheduled Tribes and Scheduled Castes cannot be systematically assessed, this will apply with greater force in the context of Scheduled Castes and Scheduled Tribes in general, implying thereby that at no stage can it be demonstrated that they have advanced enough to be equal to other, and to the stage where reservations have become unnecessary. Conceding this stand, therefore, will mean continuation of reservations in perpetuity, which was neither the intention of the Constitution makers, nor is the demand of any political group or party. Therefore, the challenge has to be met by social scientists, practical administrators and statesmen who have to evolve and achieve a broad consensus on the parameters by which the development of a Scheduled Caste or a Scheduled Tribe will be assessed. This should be high on the agenda for future action, because once this is publicly known and accepted, and implemented by deleting some tribes and castes from the concerned scheduled people at large will believe that the policy of reservation will gradually come to an end. This is important not for appeasing the hawks among the non-Scheduled Caste and non-Scheduled Tribe middle class, aspiring for government jobs, but to provide the benefits of the policy of reservation to those Scheduled Castes and Scheduled Tribes who really deserve such assistance, because of their continued backwardness.

In other words the absence of such periodic review to make those Scheduled Tribes and Scheduled Castes that advance beyond a point, ineligible for reservation, defeats the very objective and spirit of reservations.

Another distortion in the implementation of the reservation policy is the cornering of benefits by the same families. It has been very vehemently argued by many anti-reservationists that there is no justification for giving benefits of reservation to the children of those who have already attained a high socio-economic status, e.g. the children of MLAs, MPs, senior civil servants, or senior officers of the armed forces, who enjoy privileges akin to those available to children of other similarly highly placed persons in society. Such children do not suffer from any deprivation and disadvantage. Keeping in view the force in this line of argument, it will be more reasonable to modify the policy in such a manner that children of parents who have already taken advantage of the benefits of reservation shall not get it except for a position in a higher legislature. This will mean that children of MLAs, can take benefit of reservations only for contesting for a seat in the Parliament and not in the state legislature. In the case of government services, it will mean that children can take benefit of reservations only for a post higher in category than the one in which anyone of the parents is working. For instance, sons/daughters of a SC/ST employees holding a Group B post, Group C or Groups D posts. Similarly, children of persons working in a Group D post cannot take advantage of reservations for a Group D posts but will be eligible for such benefits for a post in Group C and above.

There could be some difficulties in the implementation of this modified policy, but none of them are insurmountable. Such modifications in the reservation policy, again, is in the larger interest of disadvantaged groups and, therefore, should be immediately acted upon.

An important assumption behind providing reservations is that persons who occupy positions of power and authority by taking benefit of reservations, will accelerate the development of the entire community in several ways. One of them is by serving as an example worthy of emulation by others in the disadvantaged groups. When people see that one amongst them has been able to achieve a certain position they may be inspired and feel that such a feat is within their reach as well.

Such measures probably boost the morale and confidence of the children of those benefited, although no systematic studies are available. It is also hoped that persons who reach high positions will continue to remember the disadvantages and deprivation they suffered from and therefore will be more motivated to work for changing the situation and ameliorating the lost of their brethren. This does not seem to have happened as a general rule. The picture probably is a mixed one. It has been generally found that many persons belonging to SCs/STs who reach positions of eminence, cut off their ties from their community and in several cases, even from their extended families. In other words, they are co-opted by the elite groups of society. In cases where they get properly absorbed by, and adapt successfully to privileged groups, there can be cause for satisfaction that at least some families have moved upward in the social ladder. However, it is seen that in a larger number of cases such persons and families cannot adjust to the elite society they are thrown into. To emphasise this is no to argue against reservations, but to suggest that measures to boost their confidence and enable them to adjust to the changed environment should be a necessary part of the larger policy of reservation. There can be several ways of achieving this. The best, however, would be to make them feel proud of their achievement and to enable them to maintain a high level of sensitivity towards the disadvantages, and suffering that they themselves have been able to successfully overcome.

If instead of feeling embarrassed about their origin and their lack of acquaintance with etiquette and manners, all of which are superficial and skindeep, they should be made to realise that their inner behaviour and psychological makeup is no different from that of any other group. If they can inculcate a sense of pride in their simple ways and their achievements, they will be better adjusted, and they can be expected to continue to work for their brethren with greater zeal, dedication and perseverance.

There is clearly a need for appropriate counselling and guidance in this regard for all those who succeed in securing a reserved post in higher categories. Preventing alienation from the group of origin, continued identification with that group, and a smooth, easy and natural adjustment with colleagues in the services are important components of a package which could make the policy of reservation fruitful and beneficial to its individual beneficiaries, as well as to the communities from which they come.

There is an important distinction in the public eye between the reservation of seats in state legislatures and Parliament, on the one hand, and government services, on the other. For contesting an election, no qualifications have been prescribed and, therefore, merit does not seem to be a criterion for the elective posts, whether the candidates are from SCs and STs or from the general population. In respect of government services, however, merit is generally perceived to be the most important criterion and, therefore, repeatedly the argument of dilution of standards of efficiency and merit is advanced against the policy of reservation. In this, strength is derived from Article 335 of the Constitution. While it provides for taking into consideration the claims of members of the Scheduled Castes and Scheduled Tribes for appointment in government services, the articles also point to the need to consider the maintenance of efficiency of administration. The issue of merit is also raised in the context to reservations in educational institutions.

In this whole debate on merit, certain misconceptions are widespread. Most importantly, it is ignored that merit is defined by those who are in a position to decide policies, the framework of evaluation, and the system of judging merit. The amazing knowledge of tribals about plants, animals and stars, and their unusual and rare skills which enable them to survive in the most difficult conditions are not acknowledged by all those who advocate the cause of merit and argue against reservations on this ground.

13

COMPETITION AND CONFLICT AMONG THE DALITS
Madiga Dandora Movement in Andhra Pradesh

G. VENKATA SIVA REDDY

Orgainsed struggles by Dalits to fight against oppression and for their emancipation are not of recent occurrence in Indian Society. They have organised protest as well as reformative movements in both Pre and Post-Independence era.[1] As a result of such movements by depressed castes, our Indian Constitution (Under the various Articles 15, 16, 17, 29, 38, 46, 330, 332, 334 and 335) has guaranteed protection for them and thus, has provided reservation facilities for their welfare and development. The reservations are provided as a combined package for all the sub-castes among the Scheduled Castes according to their total population in a particular State. All of them were clubbed together to take advantage of the facilities, as there was then much homogeneity in their socio-economic conditions, irrespective of their traditional occupations. The reservations for the SCs have been in force for about 5 decades. Though they were not fully utilised for a long period, gradually the SCs became conscious of their rights to utilise the facilities. As a result there is a growing competition among the various castes of Dalits for the benefits of reservations. It is, therefore, relevant now to ask questions, like, have the reservations really helped the SCs for their mobility and development? If so, to what extent? Who are the actual people benefited among the Dalits? Whether all the castes in SCs have received equal benefits in proportion to their population or not? If there are differences, which castes have reaped more benefits and which one have not? These questions are important and need to be examined, because the Policy of Protective Discrimination was introduced basically to provide justice to the SCs and to eradicate caste inequalities. But it appears that the SC reservation have reached among the SCs in an unequal manner resulting in differential development among them. Uma Ramaswamy writes, "... The very success of the policy has brought in its wake a new set of problems. While, on the one hand, protectionism attempts to moderate the inequality between the Scheduled Castes and the rest, on the other hand it has engendered inequality among the Scheduled Castes themselves. The exploitation of benefits by some sections of these castes has pushed to the fore the differences rather than the uniformities among them".[2] Such differences surely contribute caste animosities among them and the less benefited segments would raise their voice for Justice and equality. This is what exactly has happened in the case of Madigas in Andhra Pradesh (AP) and they have successfully organised the 'Dandora Movement', demanding their just share in SC reservation system.

Caste Composition, Education and Occupational Position of SCs in Andhra Pradesh

The Madigas are numerically the largest caste among the 60 Scheduled Castes in A.P. The other major castes among the SCs in A.P. are Mala and Adi-Andhra. The people of Madiga and Mala castes together form more than 80% of the total SC population and the Adi-Andhra comprises nearly 8%, while the remaining 56 castes constitute a meagre portion of the SCs in the State. Table 13.1 shows the figures of division among the SCs population in the State.

The State of Andhra Pradesh has three regions: Telangana, the coastal Andhra and Rayalaseema. The Telangana region forms part of north-west region of the state with ten districts, which were under the erstwhile State of Hyderabad before its merger with A.P.

TABLE 13.1: Main SCs Population in 1971 and 1981

Caste	1971 census	1981 census
1. Madiga	25.18 (lakhs)	37.38 (lakhs)
	43.55%	46.94%
2. Mala	21.15 (lakhs)	32.64 (lakhs)
	36.6%	40.99%
3. Adi-Andhra	6.15 (lakhs)	7.14 (lakhs)
	10.67%	8.96 %
4. Others	4.85 (lakhs)	1.34 (lakhs)
	8.47%	1.67%

The coastal Andhra consists of 9 districts, spread into western coasts of A.P., which covers the fertile Krishna-Godavari delta area. The Rayalaseema is a backward dry tract, which covers 4 districts in the southern part of A.P. The coastal Andhra and Rayalaseema were in erstwhile Madras State and under the British Rule. The Madigas and Malas are spread in all three regions of A.P. while the Adi-Andhra, another caste, which emerged on the scene only after 1921, is considered to be an SC in Coastal Andhra and Rayalaseema regions only. The people of Madiga caste in Telangana region form the largest proportion (61%), when compared to the other two regions. The Malas form the major SC group in the coastal region (43.1%).

In the Telugu speaking areas of Madras Presidency, the Malas and Madigas were the only castes to be classified as depressed, in 1901 and 1911.[3] In the year 1921, when the untouchables in Madras demanded to recognise them with a new name as Adi-Dravidas or the original Dravidas), the Madras government agreed to change it. As a result, many of them identified themselves as Adi-Dravidas to better their position with a new identity. The Telugu Untouchables in the Madras Presidency also changed their caste-name to "Adi-Andhra", by prefixing 'Adi' to their linguistic regional group-name. The Adi-Andhras figured as a caste group in the census of 1931, resulting in a decrease of Malas and Madigas, the Telugu Untouchables (Table 13.2). After 1931, several small segments of scheduled castes have grown in number.[4]

TABLE 13.2: Population of (Telugu) Untouchable castes (in the areas of Madras Presidency) 1921-31

(in Thousands)

Caste	1921	1931
Madiga	737	612
Mala	1,493	838
Adi-Andhra	—	665

The Madiga's traditional occupation was tanning leather and to work as village servants, known as *Tettivadu*. As village servants, they used to be involved in several socially polluting functions, like making footwear, carrying the dead cattle, attending to cremation activity, guarding the graveyard, informing the people (taking massages of death and such related news etc.). They were also involved in preparing leather tools for agricultural and irrigation purposes and were attached labourers to high caste — rich peasants, under the *Jajmani* system. They also used to perform *tum-te-tuming* to make announcements in the village. They used to beat 'dappulu', which is called 'Dandora'. Besides their traditional occupations, most of the Madigas were also agricultural labourers. The traditional occupation of Mala's was weaving. But most of them were involved in agriculture. As they were not holders of land, they were engaged in the lands as labourers.

The Malas and Madigas used to live in separate segments of the village. Though, of late, both are found in the same locality, after the provision of the house sites for SCs and with the construction of SC colonies by the government. But here also they have occupied separate streets or segments for each of them.

These two major untouchable castes have never maintained any social relations right from the remembered past. In rural Andhra, the two castes do not draw water from the same well. N.S. Reddy found in his study that they do not even worship each other's deities in some parts of the Circars.[5] Though both are untouchable castes, there is no interdining practice between them. The Malas consider the Madigas inferior to them. Thus reflecting the caste hierarchy among the SCs.

The Madigas have mostly remained in their traditional

occupations or in agricultural labour work. As a result, they were unable to enter in non-polluting occupations. But, the position of Malas was different. Their traditional occupation was not a polluting one. Again they slowly switched over to other occupations from agricultural work, since, unlike Madigas, they were free and were not attached to any *Jajmani* system. The Malas in villages have not only been independent in choosing their occupations, but have also maintained distance from the other polluting occupations.[6]

Another factor which contributed to the advancement of Malas was their preponderant position in the prosperous coastal area, where several social reform movements like, Brahmo Samaj and the activity of certain Philanthropist like Maharaja of Pitapuram etc., took place in the early part of the century. The upliftment of the Scheduled Castes through education, inter-marriage and eradication of degrading customs was an important programme of Brahmo-inspired social reform.[7] This has however helped the Malas to get educated and enter other fields than the Madigas, whose population was less in that region. Again the Malas took advantage of schools and other welfare activities started by Christian missionaries.[8] These activities have not only contributed to the development of their education but also made them more conscious that led to the emergence of many leaders among them. This is quite clear from the book of Sri Nirikshina Rao, which listed about 130 Scheduled Caste leaders and reformers and of them, only less than a dozen were Madigas.[9]

Consequent to their advantageous social position among SCs, the Malas are more benefited in their education. They are ahead of all other SCs. It is quite clear from Table 13.3.[10]

Table 13.4 shows the figures relating to the post-metric scholarships allotted to SC students during 1974-84. It is clear from the table that the Malas have benefited more with one half of the total scholarships in each region of the state. But the share of the Madigas was only in between 20 and 30 per cent.

The inequalities are also found between these castes in their political and governmental positions. An analysis prepared by a co-ordination committee of all Arudathiya Sangam or Madiga organisations brings out the differences in Table 13.5.[12]

TABLE 13.3: Literacy Level Among the Mala and Madiga (1961-1971)

	1961		1971	
	Mala	Madiga	Mala	Madiga
Total Population	17,45,466	21,47,879	21,13,393	23,14,948
Literates	1,15,031	78,123	1,09,484	73,566
Educational level %	6.6	3.6	5.2	2.9
Primary	55,653	28,715	1,40,956	72,950
%	3.2	1.3	6.7	2.9
Matric	5,624	2,249	19,164	8,692
%	0.3	0.1	0.9	0.3
Graduates and above	387	107	3,300	520
%	0.02	0.01	0.15	0.02
Total literates %	10.1	5.1	12.9	6.2

TABLE 13.4: Post Matric Scholarships to Scheduled Caste Students by Region (1974-84)[11]

	Circars	Rayalaseema	Telangana	All Andhra
1	2	3	4	5
Mala	90,605	30,493	65,469	1,86,567
	52.4	48.0	52.9	51.8
Madiga	39,512	17,319	48,424	1,05,255
	22.9	27.3	39.1	29.2
Mala Dasu	2,500	365	550	3,415
	1.4	0.06	0.4	0.9
Madiga Dasu	1,239	366	315	1,920
	0.74	0.6	0.3	0.5
Relli	2,626	426	40	2,666
	1.5	0.7	0.03	0.7
Mochi	342	426	880	1,648
	0.2	0.7	0.7	0.5
Dhor	55	9	153	217
	0.03	0.01	0.1	0.1

(Contd.)

TABLE 13.4 *(Contd.)*

1	2	3	4	5
Adi Andhra	34,074	8,318	1,342	43,734
	19.7	13.1	1.1	12.1
Adi Dravida	—	916	—	916
	—	1.4	—	0.3
Others	1,910	5,264	6,588	13,762
	1.1	8.3	5.3	3.8
Total	1,72,863	63,476	1,23,761	3,60,100

TABLE 13.5: Employees in the State Government & Government Undertakings

	Malas	Madigas
1. Political field :		
a) Z.P. Chairman	2	1
b) Chairmen of Mandal Parishad	102	57
c) Members of Lok Sabha	5	1
d) Members of Rajya Sabha	1	0
e) Members of Legislative Assembly	23	16
f) Chairmen of Municipalities	10	6
2. Services:		
a) I.A.S. (State Secretary rank)	11	0
b) I.P.S. (in the State)	15	7
c) I.A.S. (in other states)	20	7
d) I.P.S. (in other states)	10	3
e) Allied Central Services	20	5
f) Medical, Health Dept.	17	5
g) Social Welfare Dept.	4	1
h) High Court Judges	1	0
i) High Court Advocates	20	5
j) District Munsif Magistrates	12	3
k) Govt. Pleaders	10	0
l) Commercial Taxes Dept.	16	3
m) A.P.S.R.T.C.	20	4

(Contd.)

TABLE 13.5 *(Contd.)*

Total No. of employees in (Gazetted & Non-Gazetted)	No. of S.C. Employees loyees (Gaz. & Non Gaz.)	No. of Employees belonging to Mala Caste	No. of Employees belonging to Madiga caste
5,76,892	83,539	62,655	20,884

It is now clear that the Malas are far ahead of Madigas in their education and occupational position. Though the Madigas are more numerous they have remained backward in utilising the benefits of reservation. There were some organisations like the Arudathiya Sangam, Andhra Pradesh Madiga Congress and State Madiga Sangam[13] etc., formed during 1970s and 80s, which tried to fight for the justice of their caste brethren.

Beginning of the Movement

The Madiga Dandora movement has evoked tremendous response from the Madigas, in a short span of two years, as it has penetrated in rural 'Madigawadas' and mobilised their support to various Dandora rallies and meetings. The Madiga Dandora was led by *Madiga Reservation Porata Samithi* (MRPS), which was first started by about 20 Madiga youths on 27 July, 1994, in Eadumudi Village of Prakasam District.[14] The reason behind the formation was that they realised the general discontent among the Madigas was mainly about the injustice done to them in receiving benefits out of reservations.

It is important to note that the MRPS has not demanded any further enhancement in the quota of reservations, nor did they raise any fresh demand for any separate quota for the Madigas. They have simply demanded their just share in the present quota of reservations, according to their population.

Disparity among SCs

As a result of the MRPS' organisational strength and dynamism the A.P. Government was compelled to appoint a one-man commission, with Justice Ramachandra Raju, on 10-9-1996, to study the implementation of reservations among SCs and its impact on their development in education and employment fields. The Commission confirmed the existence of disparities among the SCs in availing of reservations in the fields of education and employment and has recommended for classification of SCs to avail the reservation facilities according to their population.

The Commission has divided the SCs into four groups on the basis of their backwardness and composition of their population, based on 1981 census.[15] As there are many minor caste groups, the Commission has felt that the classification of reservations for all 60 caste categories would be a difficult one. The following table explains the division of SC groups and their population.

TABLE 13.6 : Sub-divisions among the Main SCs and their Population

Group	Sub-Castes	Population	% to total SCs
(a) Relli	12	133,689	1.67
(b) Madiga	18	3,737,609	46.94
(c) Mala	25	3,263,655	40.99
(d) Adi-Andhra	5	713,824	8.96

The above table clearly shows that the Madigas with its sub-castes, constitute majority of SC population. But they are less benefited through the reservations in the educational and employment fields. The Commission has brought out the disparities among them, as shown in Table 13.7.

It is clear from Table 13.7 that the Madiga group is far behind in their educational level compared to the Malas. Unfortunately the Rellis have not got any share. Let us now examine the SCs employment position in Table 13.8.[16]

Table 13.8 clearly reveals that the Madiga group has not got a reasonable share equivalent to their population even in public employment, while the Mala group has bagged a lion's share in reservations. The Adi-Andhras have however achieved positions

TABLE 13.7: Enrollment of the Main SCs in Higher Education Institutions

Category	Mala	Madiga	Adi-Andhra	Relli
1. J.N.T. University	98	43	15	—
(Engineering admissions 1992-96)	59%	26%	10%	
2. Osmania University	65	27	1	
(Engineering admissions 1992-97)	48.5%	20%	3%	
3. Science Courses in	314	183	7	
Three Universities	65%	68%	1.4%	
4. Arts groups in	600	331	14	—
Three Universities	71.5%	39.5%	1.6%	
5. Residential	6790	3880	214	42
(Upto Intermediate) (1996-97)	62%	35%	2%	0.4%

TABLE 13.8: Employment of the Main SCs in Government

Category (Employment)	Mala	Madiga	Adi-Andhra	Relli
1. Employees in Central and	5896	3756	1112	83
public undertakings	51.96%	32.86%	9.73%	0.72%
2. State Govt. Sector	735	369	33	2
	61.8%	31%	2.77%	0.25%
3. Employment in Dist. Officers	10703	7282	2402	577
(in 15 Dists.)	50%	34%	11.23%	26%
3. Secretariat (in 19 Depts.)	169	70	20	—
	63%	26%	7.5%	
4. Heads of Dept. (in 66 Depts.)	2101	1216	149	43
	59.5%	34.4%	4%	1.2%

equal to their numerical strength in some sectors and in the remaining, they have atleast shown their presence. But the position of Rellis is distressing. The Commission has therefore recommended the Relli group as very backward and also placed them in 'A' group, allotting one per cent of reservation.

Thus, the Commission has recommended the categorisation of caste groups and the allocation of the 15 per cent quota of reservations, according to their relative backwardness and population they are as follows:

TABLE 13.9: Caste Groups Allocation of Reservation

Sl.No.	Caste group	Category	Percentage of reservations
1.	Relli	A	1
2.	Madiga	B	7
3.	Mala	C	6
4.	Adi-Andhra	D	1

Before the Commission submitted its report, the MRPS, as a last resort, organised a *Maha Padyatra*, covering 1062 kms., from the Chief Minister's village Naravaripalle in Chittoor District to Hyderabad, where a massive rally of Madigas and a large-scale meeting took place.

Meanwhile the Commission submitted its report to the Government on 28-5-1997. When the *Maha Padayatra* ended at Hyderabad on 6-6-1997, the Dandora leaders threatened not to disperse from the capital until the government concedes their demand. The government immediately responded to the Commission's recommendations and released a G.O. classifying the reservations among the SCs in education and employment sectors only. They are yet to achieve such classification in economic and political sectors.

This was, however, a significant achievement of 'Dandora' Movement, since the MRPS basically wanted to get their justified share in SC reservations. It is now interesting to know that though there were organised attempts made earlier in 1970s and 80s by many Madiga organisations like Arundhatiya Sangam, Andhra Pradesh Madiga Congress[17] etc., with similar types of demands nothing could be achieved. Then what made the MRPS led 'Dandora' movement to succeed?

Strategy and Leadership

The success of MPRS in organising the movement mainly depended on its strategy, leadership and ideology. The MRPS has never allowed the established SC political leaders to join hands with them. Though they did not object to like-minded SC politicians' support, but the movement was largely non-political. Another point is that the leaders of MRPS have never tried to hurt the feelings of their Mala caste brethren, while expressing the injustice done to the Madigas. In the meetings or in rallies, they had always raised the issue of Madigas only, but never ventilated antagonistic feelings. They used to say in their meetings:

> We are not against our Mala brothers. We are asking only our reasonable share in SC reservations. This is like asking the reasonable division of property among brothers in a family.[18]

The reaction of Malas was however set against the demands of the 'Dandora'. They complained that the MRPS was creating differences among the SCs. They are opposed to any move to modify the existing policy. As a result, they have formed an organisation called 'Mala Mahanadu' and have started demanding the government to withdraw the G.O. issued classifying the SC reservaton.[19]

The *Mala Mahanadu* and *Mala Samkshema Sangam* have filed writ petitions challenging the G.O. classifying SC reservations in the High Court. The Court has granted an interim order on 21-7-1997 suspending the G.O. The MRPS has immediately announced that they would seek justice by making an appeal to the division bench of the High Court (*Vaartha*, 21-7-1997). The High Court has suspended the SC classification G.O., on technical reasons. Now the issue is pending before the Supreme Court of India.

It is also argued that they have got more benefits out of reservations because of their 'merit'. When such opinions are expressed, the Madigas answer them in a fitting manner. This is quite clear from a 'Dandora' poem,[20] which reads as follows :

My head is bloody but I fight
With my bare trunk I realise my right
I am the original one
My life is a fight through out,
For me, it is as easy as beating a 'dappu'
Look,
Till yesterday, he clamoured for 'Merit and Merit'
And we criticised his fictitious merit
Now you too clamour for Merit and Merit
I stare at you as we saw him
Difference is not in me but in you
Now, my fight is
Whatever you have ... I too should have equally,
My share is mine.... Let me have my share
I do not want to rob you of your due
My fight is only for my right
I can live no longer with you with internal squabbles
Now
All 'dappulu' sound vehemently to perform 'Dandora'.

The MRPS leaders have however made it clear that the classification of SC reservations would in no way harm the reasonable share of Malas. They argued, "The Madigas receive their rightful share with the classification of reservations. The Malas may not get any more additional advantage but they do not loose their justified share".[21]

Another notable feature of the 'Dandora' movement was the successful attempt made by the leaders by way of raising self-respect and dignified social identity of the Madigas. The Mandora leaders have not followed the traditional 'Sanskritisation' model, to mobilise their people—like adopting the high caste symbols and culture, nor have they adopted any new symbols or slogans. Their method of organising the Madigas was that of identifying and glorifying their own traditional caste symbols norms and values. They have adopted the technique of using their caste symbols like 'Dappulu' in their public rallies and using the terms like 'Madiga and Dandora' to refer to their movement. And such symbols and caste terms, which were earlier seen with ridicule, are now proudly used in their public rallies and meetings. Firstly, the term 'Dandora' itself refers to one of their traditional occupation of beating the tom-tom (tum-te-tuming) called *dappulu* to make an announcement in the village. The Madigas have acquired the skill of performing 'dappulu' and used it beat them in all village fairs and temple processions. The beating of 'dappulu' has thus been a skilled professional activity, identified with the Madigas. The 'dappu' was one of their caste symbols and it was commonly found in most of the Madiga houses. They have adopted and used it now to express their voice protesting against the injustice done to them as well as to demand their rights.

The MRPS leaders have clearly tried to glorify their caste in their public meetings. They have expressed that the Madiga caste has a long history and had its origins with the sage, Jambavantha. Arundhati, the wife of Sage Vashista, was also of their caste. They have even said that the Madigas activity of tanning of leather was not a polluted function, but had a lot of advantages, which helped the high castes in their agriculture.

The Dandora leaders have shown and made the Madigas politically conscious enough to express their caste identity with all pride and without any hesitation, though earlier, they were not inclined to disclose their caste identity fearing ill-treatment in society. The term 'Madiga' itself was considered abusive. Now the Dandora has made them realise that use of their caste name, 'Madiga', is not a defile one. In fact, they are proud of using the caste name and they even started calling and publicising their caste (surname) along with their own names by suffixing it. Thus the names of 'Dandora' leaders read like Krishna Madiga, Krupakar Madiga and Srinivas Madiga etc., and many other leaders have also followed the same path.

Similar is the case with the slogans adopted and raised by Dandora leaders to mobilise the Madigas in their public rallies and meetings. The Slogans[22] raised are like,

Madiga *Nijayathi* (honesty) Zindabad;
Madiga *Karyadakshata* (Dedication) Zindabad;
Madiga *Prema* (Love) Zindabad;
Madiga *Shakthi* (Power) Zindabad, etc.

The strategy of Dandora leaders with such efforts and slogans has however served two purposes. First, it has helped the Madigas to gain self-respect and make them conscious by realising that their caste identity and occupations are in no way polluted. Among other things, this has contributed to their mobilisation for the movement. Second, the usage of their caste-name and symbols in public by the Dandora leaders has clearly brought out a message to the higher castes, that they can no longer abuse the Madigas by calling them by their caste names and also the Madigas would no longer be subjugated.

The leadership of Dandora hails from lower middle class Madiga families and they are all young and educated. They are not identified with any political party and thus, organised the movement without any political affiliations.

Conclusion

The MRPS, following the above strategy, has successfully organised the movement. They were successful in raising the caste consciousness and mobilising Madigas for the movement. The Dandora has proved that if the demands of the oppressed are properly represented it would certainly make any movement successful. Such an organisation and committed leadership is needed today for the emancipation of the backward Dalits, which would bring out its own ideology to unite them all, to fight against the inequalities.

The Dandora leaders have made it clear that their fight was not only for 'the Madigas' alone, but for seeking justice to other backward SCs, like Rellis etc. They want justice to be done to all those who are placed in the 'bottom layer' (lower stratum) of all the low and high castes. They have also promised to support any such movements among different castes. They believe that the reservations should first be provided to those who are in the 'lower stratum' so that 'development from below' can be realised.[23] They are aware of class-divisions in every caste, but have sought to tackle the issue on 'caste' lines.

The Dalits among themselves are divided both on Caste and 'Class' lines and these certainly act as a basis of exploitation and oppression. The Dalits have first preferred to get Justice within the Caste System. This has however been proved in the case of Madiga Dandora. It is now pertinent to note the words of Rajni Kothari, who wrote:[24]

> The Dalit's expectation and strategy seems to be designed to challenge the dominant castes by means of education, employment and special rights, in a struggle against the system that begins with the challenging injustices within it, thinking of the struggle against imperialism and other such things as a second order importance.

The Dandora leaders are now concentrating on getting classification in political reservations too. Though they are aware of the limitations of SC political representatives in helping their caste brethren, but still they demand for their due share in every field, because due to combined SC reservations, the Madigas are given a back seat in politics too. Of the 39 SC M.L.A.s in A.P. there are 28 Malas and 11 Madigas. There are only two Madiga M.P.s as against 4 Malas in A.P. This clearly brings out that there is justification for the Dandora to organise the movement, taking the caste as a basis in their fight against inequality and thus seeking equal benefits for the people of Madiga caste.

The movement has brought out another important revelation. The SC reservations have created not only a 'class' division among the SCs but also the 'Caste' cleavages among them, resulting in the emergence of conflicts among them to avail the benefits earmarked for their development. Therefore, the policy of SC reservations and its impact on the development of SCs need to be carefully studied in the light of present circumstances, and the necessary modifications should be incorporated to provide protection and justice to the backward and needy Dalits. Then only the inequalities and tensions among the Dalits can be resolved.

Another contribution of the Dandora movement is that its success has influenced the backward Scheduled Tribes to organise *Thudum* movement, demanding classification of ST reservations.[25] The backward tribes like Gonds, Koyas, Thoti, Erukula etc., have now started demanding justice for them in the ST reservations. They have expressed that the Lambadis and Banjaras have benefited more out of the ST reservations, while the other tribes remained backward. Thus, they want to get their just share.

Acknowledgements

This article is a revised version of a paper presented to the Golden Jubilee Conference of the Indian Political Science Association, held at Palai (Kerala) during 25-27 July, 1997.

The author is thankful to Prof. Ghanshyam Shah, Dr. B. Padmanabha Reddy, Mr. A. Chandra Sekhar and Dr. P. Sudhakar for their useful comments on an earlier draft of the paper.

NOTES

1. Ghanshyam Shah, *Anti-Untouchability Movements in Removal of Untouchability* (ed.) Vimal P. Shah, *Seminar Papers*, Gujarat University, Ahmedabad, December 1979.
2. Uma Ramaswamy, 'Protection and Inequality among Backward Groups', *Economic and Political Weekly*, Vol. XXI, No. 9, March, 1986.
3. *Ibid.*
4. Census of India, 1931, Vol. XIV, Madras, Part-1, p. 349. Cited in Indu Rajagopal, *The Tyranny of Caste: The Non-Brahmin Movement and Political Development in South India*, Delhi: Vikas Publishing House Pvt. Ltd., 1985, pp. 119-20.
5. N.S. Reddy, Transition in caste structure in A.P. with special reference to Depressed Classes, unpublished Ph.D. Thesis, University of Lucknow, 1954, Quoted from Uma Ramaswamy, *ibid.*, 1986.
6. Nallapati Sivanaraiah, "Andhra Pradesh Restramulo Arundhatheeyula

Sthithigathulu—Rastra prabhuthvam vari Reservational Amaluvidhanam—Sameekshavashyakatha" (Telugu), *Telugu Anubanda Patrika*, Telugu Academy, Vol.2, No. 5, August, 1996, p.17.

7. Uma Ramaswamy, *op.cit.*, 1986.
8. Nallapati Sivanaraiah, *op.cit.*, 1996, p. 17.
9. Uma Ramaswamy, *op.cit.*, 1986.
10. Census of India 1961, Andhra Pradesh, Part V-A; 1971, Part V-A. Taken from Uma Ramaswamy, *op.cit.*, 1986.
11. Department of Social Welfare, quoted from Uma Ramaswamy, *op.cit.*, 1986.
12. Nallapati Sivanaraiah, *op.cit.*, 1996, pp. 21-22.
13. *Eenadu*, Saturday, June 19, 1982, p. 4.
14. Interview of Krishna Madiga: *Vaartha*, 4 July 1997.
15. Quoted from B. Venkat's article: "Vargikarana Samuchitam—Vyshayalu Hanikaram" (Telugu), *Prajashakthi*, 24 June, 1997.
16. *Ibid.*
17. Uma Ramaswamy, *op.cit.*, 1986.
18. Meeting of Dandora at Ambedkar Bhavan, Anantapur, 11 April, 1996, *Vaartha*, 17 May, 1996.
19. *Vaartha*, 19 June, 1997, 24 June, 1997, 16 July, 1997.
20. Raavinuthala Prema Kishore, *Andhra Jyothi*, 14 July, 1996, quoted from Nallapati Sivanaraiah.
21. Kolakaluri Enoch, 'Dandora Ambedkar Abheestam' (Telugu), *Andhra Jyothi*, 16 July, 1996.
22. *Dandora Meetings*, Anantapur, 11 April, 1996 and 25 October, 1996.
23. Interview of Krishna Madiga, *Vaartha*, 5 July, 1997.
24. Rajni Kothari, "Rise of the Dalits and the Renewed Debate on Caste", *Economic and Political Weekly*, 25 June, 1994.
25. *Vaartha*, 7 June 1997.

14

ADMINISTRATION AND THE POOR

S.R. SANKARAN

With his abiding concern for the principles of justice, equality, liberty and fraternity, so eloquently enshrined in the Preamble to the Constitution, Babasaheb Ambedkar fought against the inhuman inequality in Indian society. I wish to deliberate here on some of the aspects of the administration in relation to the poor people of the country. Dr. Ambedkar in his final address to the Constituent Assembly, wherein he drew attention to the emerging contradictions—political equality in the midst of socio-economic in equality— in the society of free India and emphasised:

> We must remove this contradiction at the earliest possible moment; or else those who suffer from inequality will blow up the structure of political democracy, which this Assembly has laboriously built up.

The Indian Constitution is a testament with a mission to secure to all its citizens, justice— social, economic and political — liberty of thought, expression, belief, faith and worship, equality of status and opportunity, and fraternity assuring the dignity of the individual and unity and integrity of the nation. It sets out the fundamental rights of citizens, especially equality, protection of life and liberty, non-discrimination, abolition of untouchability, and prohibition of forced labour. The Directive Principles of state policy envisage a social order in which justice, social, economic and political, will inform all institutions of national life, minimising the inequalities of income, status and opportunities with the right to adequate means of livelihood; equitable control and ownership of the material resources of the community; protection of the interests of the weaker sections of the people, particularly Scheduled Castes and Scheduled Tribes, from social injustice and all forms of exploitation. The Constitution is an instrument heavily weighed in favour of the weaker sections of the Indian society. Almost all the issues for which the poor struggle in their daily lives find a place in the Indian Constitution, whether it is equality, freedom, human dignity, discrimination, social and economic justice, right to livelihood, to work, living wage, or protection from exploitation. The Indian Constitution is, thus, a quest for a just and equitable society, the responsibility for achieving which is enjoined on the state and the agencies of the state, i.e., the administration.

Historical experience, starting with the abolition of slavery by the Indian Slavery Act, 1843, down to the proscription of bonded labour 130 years later by the Bonded Labour System (Abolition) Act, 1976, highlights the leading role of the state and its institutions in the process of social transformation.[1] Subsequent to the enactment of the Constitution, a variety of institutions were set up for the protection and promotion of values, such as liberty, freedom and rule of law. The imperative need for economic and social justice was recognised through a number of public policy responses with a direct bearing on the condition of masses in relation to the distribution of property and means of livelihood. A series of laws, more importantly, a series of social legislation, emerged in line with the spirit of the Constitution. Enactments on land reforms, protection of civil rights, abolition of bonded labour, represented the institutionalised pursuit of justice.

The civil service, which forms an important part of the institutions of the state, plays a crucial part in the administration of the country. It has to carry out tasks in terms of the constitutional mandate and the legal framework. A stable body of experienced and competent permanent officials in diverse fields, it constitutes an elite corps, with the vast authority vested in it to be exercised in public interest for achieving public policy objectives.

About two billion people in the world, one in every five, are said to be in absolute poverty, which is defined as the inability to attain a minimum standard of living, infringing on the very basic sustenance of life. There is extensive literature on the measurement of poverty and its magnitude, nature and content. Conventionally, poverty in aggregate terms has been measured with reference to a poverty line, which distinguishes the poor from the non-poor.[2] It has been estimated on the basis of the 43rd Round of the National Sample Survey (1987-88) that about 237.6 million people in India, around 40 per cent of the people, were below the poverty line. Of these 195.9 million were living in rural areas and 41.7 million in urban areas. An expert group set up in 1993, placed the figure at 312.7 million – 83.3 million in urban areas and 229.4 million in rural areas. On the basis of the results of the 50th Round of the National Sample Survey, it has been recently assessed that the proportion of people below the poverty line has declined to 18.96 per cent by the year 1993-94, though the findings are yet to be validated. While there are limitations in regard to the concept of poverty line and the undimensional measurement of poverty, the fact that a large segment of the population of the country, about 200 to 250 million people, is living below the margin of subsistence is not very much in doubt. It should also be borne in mind that the poverty line is based on an annual household expenditure of Rs. 11,000 at 1991-1992 prices, which itself provides only for a bare subsistence.[3]

Poverty is multidimensional and multisectoral in nature, having originated from a diverse range of conditions. The poor exist in both urban and rural areas of the country, though about 80 per cent of them are found in the latter. The poor are not homogeneous. The rural poor consist of economically and socially heterogeneous groups, such as tenants, share-croppers, agricultural labourers, artisans, fishermen and other workers in the unorganised sector. Rural poverty is, in fact, directly related to land ownership and control over land. The poor have very little command over or access to resources, assets, income or credit. They depend heavily on their labour, and there is little else they can derive their income from. Added to this are various forms of unfree labour including bonded labour, migrant labour and child labour. There is also the gender dimension to poverty—poor women having to shoulder the double burden of being women and poor.

The urban poor consists largely of overflow of the rural poor, engaged mainly in casual and uncertain occupations such as street vending, construction, rickshaw-pulling, etc. There is little more than token space in urban areas for the poor pushed out from villages by poverty and social degradation. Most of them live in unhygienic conditions in unending insecurity, never sure when they will be displaced by local authorities or other powerful groups.

Poor people are typically unorganised, hard to reach, inarticulate, often invisible, particularly, women and children, and even their residential locations in rural areas are in the periphery. They have very little access to education and are largely illiterate. In fact, there is a close interrelationship between poverty and illiteracy, the number of poor and the number of illiterates are not very different. Powerless and placed at the lower rungs of society, lacking the ability to articulate their own problems, highly vulnerable to manipulation by more resourceful and powerful sections of the society, an ideology of inferiority, submission and dependence has been internalised by the poor. Self-reliance and creative self-engagement are difficult to emerge. The problem of poverty is further aggravated by social deprivations and discrimination. The close intertwining of social oppression and economic exploitation can be seen in the case of Scheduled Castes who constitute a major segment of the poor.

Since a majority of the poor live in rural areas, the rural setting has a predominant impact on the poverty situation. The issue of land is of fundamental importance to the rural poor. The distribution and redistribution of land in favour of the poor, frees them from exploitation, strengthens labour and credit markets, provides a source of sustenance, and confers economic and social status. In short, it empowers the poor within the rural structure.

One of the major efforts undertaken by the government soon after Independence was land reforms. The objectives of land reforms included the elimination of exploitative relations in land, achieving the goal of land to the tiller, improvement in agricultural production and productivity, widening the land base of rural poor and facilitating their land based development, and infusing a measure of equality into local institutions. The programmes taken up in line with these objectives were the abolition of intermediaries in land, imposition of ceiling on agricultural landholdings, regulation of tenancy, distribution of government, *bhoodan*, gram sabha and *gair mazrua* lands, provision of house sites and homesteads and protection of the lands of weaker sections such as Scheduled Castes and Scheduled Tribes. It is estimated that taken together, all these efforts have resulted in reordering rights and relationships in about 10 per cent of the cultivated area of the country. In states such as Kerala and West Bengal, about 25 per cent of the rural households benefited in one way or the other by land reforms.

While it is not the case that all landless poor in the country can be accommodated as owner-cultivators, the restructuring of land relations is a matter of great significance to the rural poor. The protection, preservation and enlargement of the control and command over the land is one of the crucial issues in relation to poverty in the rural areas. The effective implementation of land reforms and the allotment of government lands ensuring undisturbed possession can secure a substantial improvement in the conditions of living of rural poor. Simultaneously, pre-emptive steps are required for the prevention of erosion of control of the poor over their lands. There are increasing instances of lands being lost by the poor, particularly the Scheduled Tribes.

The deep yearning for equality and land among the rural poor is not something new. They reflect the attitudes and values which have grown in them in the course of their interaction with the material reality, which has deprived them of both equality and land. To them ownership of land denotes one's social status and equality means equality in the ownership of land.[4]

While land is perhaps the most obvious asset to redistribute, it has to be borne in mind that the economic opportunities in India depend on a much wider range of endowments. The distribution of employment, environmental, resources, educational facilities, and affordable credit arrangements are examples of other influential factors. As Amartya Sen has shown, the opportunities for redistribution of these diverse endowments have to be considered along with the scope for land distribution, if the conditions of the poorer sections of the people are to significantly improve.

Poverty is closely related to employment or unemployment. The marginalised groups of poor in rural areas consist of landless labourers, located precariously on the brink of subsistence, depending on uncertain employment and wages. The number of agricultural labourers is estimated at 110 million, about 75 per cent of the total rural labour force. Nearly half of them belong to Scheduled Castes and Scheduled Tribes. They suffer from socio-economic deprivation and form the core of the labouring classes. It is also worth noting that the number of agricultural labourers is increasing in the last few decades at a rate faster than the population growth rate. For the large mass of agricultural and other labourers who have only their labour power to sell, wages and wage systems have enormous relevance.

In India, the state and its administrative agencies have the powers to legislate and regulate the wages for many sections including agricultural labour. But the detailed analysis made by the National Commission on Rural Labour (1991), showed that no specific principles have been followed by the Central or the State governments in fixing the minimum wages.[5] This has led to a situation of highly depressed minimum wages for the rural labour, based on dual standards, one for the organised and another for the unorganised sector. In many states, the notified minimum wage is far lower than the amount needed even to cross the poverty line, not to speak of the living wage referred to in the directive principles of the Constitution. In any event, the minimum wage fixed by the government is itself only a distant dream for most agricultural workers, as the actual ruling wage remains far below the minimum for most parts of the year, and the basic problem is that of securing employment itself irrespective of the wage levels. Only in Kerala and West Bengal legislations exists which lay down, among other things, security of employment, payment of wages, as well as provision for welfare and social security of agricultural workers. With regard to rural unorganised labour, particularly the agricultural labourers, the law is weak and its implementation almost non-existent. There is little doubt that the administrative agencies at the policy-making and implementation levels have not carried out their functions in an effective manner.

One of the most exploited sections of the labour forces is child labour. The Indian Constitution prohibits the employment of children below 14 years of age in factories and other hazardous occupations. The Constitution also provides for free and compulsory education up to 14 years of age. These two constitutional requirements have to be seen together as the recognition of the right of the child to be in school and not at the workplace.[6] But India has one of the largest number of child workers, variously estimated at 17.5 million, 44 million or even 72 million. More distressing is the fact that the number of child workers in the country is increasing. While child workers are found in a variety of occupations such as construction, hotel industry, domestic labour, stone breaking, carpet weaving, match factories, slate industry and gem polishing, the largest number are in fact engaged in agriculture and related occupations. Corresponding to the number of child labourers, there are about 72 million out of school children in India, notwithstanding the constitutional commitment and high enrollment figures.

It is unfortunate that there has been a woeful lack of understanding of the problem of child labour at all levels of the administration. Child labour has been viewed as social inevitability, a harsh reality or a necessary evil. There has been an inability, and in fact an unwillingness to perceive this as an extremely illegitimate practice in a modern society, with highly damaging implications for the future generations of the nation. The paradox of large-scale employment of children coexisting with equally large-scale adult unemployment and another one of child workers never growing into adult labour even with the passage of years, have never been sought to be interrogated by the administrative agencies of the state. As pointed out by Myron Weiner, India is a significant exception to the global trend towards the removal of children from the labour force and ensuring education as a legal entitlement. While there have been limited efforts recently in the form of child labour projects for those engaged in hazardous occupations, there is no well-defined policy or concerted effort in terms of implementation. The conclusion drawn by Myron Weiner (1991) seems inescapable:

> One is left with the pessimistic conclusion that barring a conceptual change in the thinking of those who make and implement policy and a new direction in policy by the Indian Government, the number of children in the labour force will not significantly decline, conditions for working children will not significantly improve, school retention rates will not significantly increase, and literacy rates will continue to grow at a slow pace and leave a large part of the Indian population illiterate well into the middle of the twenty-first century. With illiteracy and child labour declining worldwide, India's global share of illiterates and child labourers will continue to increase.

Bonded labour which was widely prevalent in all parts of the country until recently, is still in existence in many parts of the country, in spite of official denials. Utsa Patnaik (1985) describes it thus:

> Indian is a country of survival and adaptation to new function of social forms which elsewhere have become extinct. The various forms of subordination of one class of human beings by another have not been swept away here by any revolutionary upheaval; on the contrary, their characteristics have accumulated and mutated sometimes under the impact of capitalism to produce an extraordinary amalgam of the modern and the archaic. While subordination and bondage are characteristics of many aspects of social life, agrestic servitude has formed historically the most important component. A consideration of the history of agrestic subordination of one class by another inevitably becomes the history of the evolution of the class of agricultural labourers in India.

In many regions in India, hereditary servitude, institutionalised as bondage, was the condition of a large proportion of agricultural labour. Instead of labourers cultivating the land belonging to them, it was often a case of labourers cultivating the land to which they belonged. Despite the generalised emergence and occurrence of wage labour, representing a formal freedom, extreme poverty and staggering levels of inequality in village life still persist, becoming fetters on the creation of a completely free workforce. Freedom and unfreedom of agricultural labourers are influenced by agricultural growth and production conditions in agriculture and the material conditions of their lives; economic dominance of a small group of landlords, caste discrimination and practice of untouchability, severe discrimination against women, usury and indebtedness, widespread illiteracy and terribly slow rate of spread of primary and secondary education among the poor and in general, slow penetration of scientific temper in the lives of the people. The structure of surplus labour, unemployment and underemployment, inequitable distribution of land and assets, low wages, distress migration and unjust social institutions result in an environment which perpetuates the system of bonded labour. An important fact is that bonded labour represents an unequal exchange system, the virtual absence of bargaining power, and an unequal relationship between the creditor and the debtor.

Surprisingly, in British India, in the early 19th century, magistrates were authorised to apprehend and return to their master any bonded labourers who had absconded.[7] It is to be noted that when the British government initiated measures to abolish slavery, the Indian *zamindars* strongly voiced their opposition. Following the publication of the draft Anti-Slavery Act in 1843, some *zamindars* and *talukdars* submitted in a memorandum to the government:

> It would tend to be the ruin of all India, specially that of the respectable part of population of Sylhet. From time immemorial, slaves of both the sexes were engaged in the services of respectable men and performed drudgeries of various descriptions. According to the *Shastras* and the customs of the country, the slaves were alienable by sale purchase or

fight. If the proposed Act is passed into law, the slaves would consider themselves men of respectability and would refuse to perform duties which were habitually assigned to them.[8]

Abject poverty compels the agricultural labourer resort to loans in kind or cash, often for subsistence meeting expenses of marriage, medical expenses, or customary needs, usually from a landlord. In turn, the labourer undertakes to work for the creditor in order to pay off the debt. Because of the low wage he receives and the fact that he has to work as captive labour and has no freedom to work for anyone other than the creditor, his chances of repaying the debt are remote or virtually non-existent. With usurious interest leading to bondage for life and for the next generation, the bondedness becomes hereditary and permanent.[9] As poignantly described by the Ministry of Labour, Government of India:

> A poor peasant or agricultural worker takes a small loan. His dues accumulate very fast under exorbitantly high rates of interest. Soon he finds it impossible to extinguish his debts; he is dispossessed of his property, but he still continues in his debts. He thus begins to work for his creditor under absurdly low wages and hopes to repay the debts by the fruits of his labour; but the cruel logic of usury defeats him. His children and grandchildren also begin to work for nominal wages to liquidate the debt. The entire future of the family gets mortgaged to a small loan taken in the remote past. The debt becomes the destiny. Bonded labour ceases to be a free economic agent. He is reduced to an appendage of feudal property. The debt dehumanises him, he lives like a subhuman. Indeed he lives like a thing.

There are numerous variants of the bonded labour system in the country—the *Vetti*, *Bhagela* and *Jeetham* in Andhra Pradesh, *Hali* of South Gujarat and Madhya Pradesh, *Kolta* of Uttar Kashi, Dehra Dun and Jaunsar Bawar, *Padiyal* of Tamil Nadu, Adiyar of Kerala, Sagri of Rajasthan, as well as *Kamia*, *Bhaoli*, *Kishani* and

Harwaha of Bihar. No doubt many of these orthodox forms of agrestic bondage have undergone changes over a period of time, but they have not been eliminated altogether. There are also large number of bonded labourers in brick kilns, stone quarries, limestone mines, match factories, carpet weaving, irrigation works, and a variety of other occupations. The distinction between child labour, migrant labour, contract labour and bonded labour is indeed, in practice, very thin.

Article 23 of the Constitution prohibits forced labour and declares it a punishable offence. It took a quarter of a century for the Bonded Labour System (Abolition) Ordinance, 1975, to be promulgated and the Bonded Labour System (Abolition) Act, 1976, to be enacted. The scope of legal provisions has been strengthened and widened by the rulings of the Supreme Court in various cases, such as the Asiad case and the Bandhua Mukthi Morcha case. Further, it has been declared by the Supreme Court that the denial of minimum wages is itself enough evidence of the existence of forced labour. No doubt the efficacy of legislation alone is bound to be limited in the absence of attempts to tackle the structural causes of bondage. This has been further diluted by the fact that intervention by state agencies around legislation has been found, barring exceptions, to be formal, rigid and unimaginative. The identification of bonded labour has been largely left to the lower echelons of bureaucracy, with little or no supervision and guidance. There has been a lack of understanding of the role and responsibility of the executive magistrates in whom the judicial powers have been specially vested under the Bonded Labour System (Abolition) Act. Nor have the vast powers given to district magistrates been made full use of. Rehabilitation measures for the released bonded labourers have also been ineffective, as the crucial fact that the world of freedom is associated with uncertainty, whereas the world of bondage is linked with apparent security, has not been adequately appreciated. Any socio-economic legislation is bound to be reduced to a dead letter if appropriate follow-up action is not taken on the economic and social fronts by the administration.

The Scheduled Castes and Scheduled Tribes constitute a very

large segment of the poorer sections of society. The establishment of an egalitarian social order with equity for all sections of the society, free from any form of discrimination whatsoever is the cherished goal of our nation as enshrined in the Constitution. As pointed out by Upendra Baxi,[10] the founding fathers realised the intrinsic culpability of iniquitous forces embedded in the social systems, economic institutions and political organisations, both old and new, in relation to certain vulnerable sections of the society, and therefore considered it necessary to provide for specific safeguards in the Constitution in their favour. The nature of the safeguards for the Scheduled Castes is somewhat different from those for the members of Scheduled Tribes in view of the differences in their socio-economic conditions. Those for the former relate to the removal of disabilities cast on them by nefarious tradition, and provisions for positive discrimination in their favour to enable them to acquire a dignified position due to them in national life. The major concern about members of Scheduled Tribes has been to ensure that they do not lose control over common resources in the process of change and development, and that while they are enabled to take full advantage of new advances in knowledge, the best in their tradition is not lost.

Caste is a specifically Indian expression of institutionalised inequality and indignity. The meaning of caste for those who suffer it, is power on one side, and vulnerability on the other; privilege and oppression; honour and denigration; plenty and want; reward and deprivation. Socially, the most significant marker of Scheduled Castes is untouchability, which is the denial of human dignity in its most extreme form. Untouchability is part and parcel of the caste structure; more than this, it is an economically exploitative system, worse than slavery. In economic terms, Scheduled Castes constitute the largest segment of the most exploited class of wage labourers in the most important sector of the economy, i.e., agriculture. Scheduled Castes represent the unfreedom of Indian society in its most acute form.

Scheduled Castes, who number 13.82 crores, constitute about one-sixth of the population of the country. A large majority of them are agricultural labourers living below the poverty line, and their conditions of life are worse than that of other poverty groups. The literacy rate among Scheduled Castes in 1991 was only 37.41 per cent against the national average of 52.21 per cent. There is a clear nexus between the economic plight of Scheduled Castes and the atrocities and social disabilities which they are subjected to. Despite this extremely adverse situation, Scheduled Castes contribute significantly to the growth of productive systems of the country as wage labourers, leather workers, artisans, weavers, fisherman and scavengers.

Initially, the developmental approach to Scheduled Castes took the form of a few schemes of an ameliorative nature. A systematic institutionalised effort in planning was introduced in the late 1978 in the nature of the Special Component Plan (SCP) for Scheduled Castes.[11] In 1980, the special central assistance was also introduced as supplement to the special component plan, which intended to secure the rapid socio-economic development of Scheduled Castes. It seeks to ensure and secure the flow of resources, both material and financial, for the integrated development of Scheduled Castes. It is intended to be a plan for the development of Scheduled Castes in relation to their resource endowments and needs in all areas of social and economic activity including agriculture, animal husbandry, poultry, fisheries, education including scholarship; hostels and mid-day meals, provision of drinking water, electrification of Scheduled Caste localities, development of sericulture, minor irrigation, including construction and energisation of irrigation wells, programmes for specially vulnerable groups, housing and house-sites, link roads, self-employment schemes, social forestry, allotment and development of lands and allotment of shops and stalls in public places.[12]

Over a period of time, however, except in some states, the special component plans have become mechanical and routine disaggregation exercises, rather than meaningful plans for Scheduled Caste development. Their implementation has been uninspiring. In view of the fact that Scheduled Castes constitute the largest single group among the population below the poverty line, the share of the special component plan should not be a mere equivalent of their protection in the population, as is happening in most of cases, but should constitute a much larger chunk of the developmental outlay. The blame for the unimaginative and stereotyped formulation and implementation of plans in this respect rests largely with the administrative agencies.

Notwithstanding the shortcomings in planning and implementation, it should be observed that State intervention in this area includes an array of constitutional and legal provisions, positive discrimination through reservations in public appointments and in elected bodies, budgetary and planning support through the special component plan, and according priority to anti-poverty programmes. The Protection of Civil Rights Act, 1955, and the Scheduled Castes and Scheduled Tribes (Prevention of Atrocities) Act, 1989, are special legislations for social protection. This impressive range of enactment and administrative arrangements can and should be made effective use of, along with legal support and steps to improve the response of law and order machinery, mass literacy, restructuring of the special component plan strategy,[13] health and education measures, programmes for their liberation from traditional unclean occupations, to strengthen state intervention in favour of Scheduled Castes.

Scheduled Tribes, who comprise about 8 per cent of the population, also constitute a large segment of the poor and need special attention on the part of the administration. Apart from specific constitutional provisions including the Fifth and Sixth Schedules and the long history of protective regulations, particularly regarding land, a special thrust was given to developmental efforts through the mechanism of the Tribal Sub-Plan, introduced in 1974-1975, during the Fifth Five-Year Plan. The Tribal Sub-Plan strategy envisaged the development of tribal areas in comprehensive terms, with all activities relevant to tribals forming part of the sub-plan. It is based on demarcation of areas with a high concentration of tribals, administrative, financial and functional integration of all developmental schemes in the sub-plan area, and all necessary measures to eliminate any exploitative relationships.

For the tribal population, there has always been a close association with a territory. The tribal economy centres largely around land and land based resources; but land is more than a source of livelihood for them. In tribal areas, the programme of building assets should be so designed that the control of people over their resource base continues, while its potential and productivity improve.

As tribal communities live within forests or in close proximity to them, forest policy, and forest laws and traditional rights in forest produce, specially minor forest produce, become extremely relevant to their daily life. The problem of displacement affects the tribal population more than others. A sensitive administration has to take into account all these factors in the formulation and implementation of programmes for tribal development.

It is a sad commentary on the administration that in 1986, Madhya Pradesh High Court was called upon to decide whether the tribals of Chainpura village could lawfully collect the droppings (dung) from their own cattle, which were allowed to graze in the reserved forest, under a licence granted by the government. The Government of Madhya Pradesh argued that this excrement became state property under Section 2(4)(b) of the Indian Forest Act. It was left to the Madhya Pradesh High Court to pronounce that the dung excreted by the cattle of licensed graziers is not minor forest produce, nor are the graziers to be deprived of their natural right to dung.[14]

The concern for widespread poverty in the country had been a part of the country's struggle for freedom. Beginning with Dadabhai Naoroji, whose treatise 'Poverty in India' was presented in 1876, successive national leaders placed the issue of poverty in the forefront. As pointed out by V.S. Vyas and Pradeep Bhargava, (1995), the national consensus on the goal of poverty alleviation is an important positive factor in India, which has not been the case in most developing countries. At the commencement of the planning era, in 1951, it was expected that the developmental process itself will be able to take care of the needs of the poor. The First Five-Year Plan (1951-56) witnessed the introduction of the Community Development Programme and the National Extension Service. The Second and the Third Five-Year Plans continued the same approach with some additions and modifications. In the fifties and sixties, state-sponsored redistribution of land and the parallel movement of

Bhoodan were perhaps the most important measures for improving the living conditions of the poor, though reliance was placed largely on the process of growth itself to resolve the problem of poverty. It was in the early seventies, during the Fourth Five-Year Plan (1969-74), that a direct attack on poverty was initiated and anti-poverty measures or Poverty Alleviation Programmes (PAP), directly and exclusively aimed at the poor, were introduced. This has been continued in one form or the other in the successive plans.

No doubt that there is a vast potential for reducing poverty through an overall growth process, that is positively biased in favour of the poor. But the nature of growth has been such as to limit the percolation of its benefits to the poor. Poverty alleviation has, therefore, come to be regarded as something that can no longer be left to the processes of growth and the operation of the trickle-down effect. On the contrary, poverty alleviation has been accepted as an explicit objective, and the development policy is now structured to achieve this objective. State intervention in poverty alleviation thus includes programmes for access to land and water for the poor, asset and skill development and access to institutional credit, creation of employment opportunities and ensuring minimum wages, securing of basic needs covering food, public distribution system, shelter and other requirements for identified rural poor, and arrangements for social security. Poverty alleviation programmes refer to the specific programmes of employment and asset creation to improve the conditions of the rural poor, undertaken in recent years. Self-employment programmes envisage the provision of income earning asset, provide skills or human resource development, or a combination of both. The wage employment schemes seek to create opportunities of employment in public works, simultaneously creating social assets as well as assets in favour of the poor. The Small Farmers Development Agency (SFDA) and the Marginal Farmers and Landless Labour (MFAL) schemes, which can be considered to be the earliest of the poverty alleviation programmes, were started in the year 1970-71, in order to assist these identified categories of the rural poor through appropriate programmes of inputs, services, credit and subsidy. The Integrated Rural Development Programme (IRDP) replaced these schemes in 1978 and was extended to the entire country in 1980. To provide greater thrust to self-employment, the programme of Training of Rural Youth in Self-Employment (TRYSEM) and Development of Women and Children in Rural Areas (DWCRA) were introduced as part of the IRDP. While these were in the nature of self-employment and skill development in rural areas, a series of wage employment schemes or public works programmes also emerged, starting from the Rural Manpower Programme of 1960-61, Crash Scheme of Rural Employment (CSRE) in 1971, Rural Works Programme in 1970-71, and the Pilot Intensive Rural Employment Programme (PIREP) in 1972. The Drought Prone Area Programme (DPAP), was also started as an employment programme in 1973-74. The Food For Work Programme emerged in 1977 and the National Rural Employment Programme (NREP) commenced in 1980. The Rural Landless Employment Guarantee Programme (RLEGP) was introduced in 1983. In 1989-90, the Jawahar Rozgar Yojana (JRY) replaced the earlier schemes. The Employment Assurance Scheme was started on 2 October, 1993 to provide atleast 100 days of assured unskilled manual work to the rural poor. This is expected to be extended to the entire country. The Prime Minister's Rozgar Yojana (PMRY) is another scheme to provide employment to one million youth in urban and rural areas during the period 1993 to 1997. In order to cater to the urban areas, programmes such as Scheme for Urban Micro Enterprises (SUME), Scheme for Urban Wage Employment (SUWE), Scheme of Housing and Shelter Upgradation were evolved over a period of time.

The Integrated Rural Development Programme (IRDP) aims at raising the economic viability of poor households in self-employment oriented activities. In concept, this was to be done by strengthening the asset base and raising productivity by technology and skill upgradation combined with efforts at improving the access to credit input and output markets. The objectives of the Jawahar Rozgar Yojana (JRY) include the generation of gainful wage employment leading to sustained employment by strengthening rural infrastructure, creation of community and social assets as well assets in favour of the poor, securing a positive impact on wage levels, and achieving an overall improvement in the quality of life in rural areas, JRY also made a distinct departure from the earlier approach in decentralising the implementation by transferring the resources and decision-making to panchayats to a large extent. A programme of land development and construction of irrigation wells in the landholdings of the rural poor was taken up under the Million Wells Programme. The construction of houses for Scheduled Castes, Scheduled Tribes, freed bonded labourers, and other poor was also initiated under the Indira Awas Yojana. More than a million wells and about three million houses have been constructed under these programmes since their inception.

It is significant to note that a large amount of resources has been committed by the country to the rural employment programme. This is in recognition of the fact that in an essentially agricultural economy, with a growing population, there is large-scale unemployment and underemployment and, therefore, the leeway should be made up through public expenditure. However, public works are designed to offer employment at different places at different times in a given year and across the years. This implies that they do not offer employment on a continuing basis to the same group of individuals; by their very nature they can offer only temporary income support and are essentially oriented to providing slack season supplementary employment. But even this makes a critical difference to survival in an economy, where one-third of the households substantially depend on wage employment for their livelihood without any firm social security arrangements.

Maharashtra has the unique distinction of being the only state in India where an Employment Guarantee Scheme (EGS) with a statutory right to work is being implemented for more than two decades. The guaranteed employment on unskilled manual work has created, in Amartya Sen's expressive phrase, "an entitlement in favour of the rural poor". It has decreased rural unemployment rates; raised average earnings of the poor; reduced fluctuations in wages by providing strong support. The severity of poverty has thus been significantly reduced by the Employment Guarantee Scheme; employment is an antidote to poverty. The acceptance of the concepts of right to work and employment guarantee will provide a framework in which the state and its agencies will fulfil their obligation to provide employment, and the poor will receive a corresponding entitlement, even if it is manual work at a minimum wage. The programme of work guarantee will be self-regulating as only the poor are likely to turn up for manual work; the programme will need no targeting and can be universal. It will ensure minimum levels of living for poor who are prepared to work. There will be a built-in flexibility as the size of the programme will vary with the demand and allocation will increase due to guarantee. The poor will demand work as a matter of right. If the projects are well-chosen, they will lead to permanent employment, creating adequate workplaces including subsequent and multiplier effects.

In order to provide social security to poor households and in fulfilment of the Directive Principles enshrined in Article 41 and Article 42 of the Constitution, the National Social Assistance Scheme was introduced in August 1995. The scheme includes old-age pensions; family benefits in cases of death; and maternity benefits to the women of households below the poverty line. This is perhaps the first time that a nationwide social security scheme has been attempted in India. Apart from these programmes, there are schemes such as the Integrated Child Development Services (ICDS), Indira Mahila Yojana (IMY), as well as a number of state specific programmes, including those relating to housing, which benefit the poor in some way or the other. I should also refer in this context to the recent decision of the Government of India to address the concerns of the poor and provide in a time bound manner (by the year 2000) basic minimum services to the people including 100 per cent coverage of provision of safe drinking water; 100 per cent coverage of primary health centres; universalisation of primary education; public housing assistance to all shelterless families; extension of the mid-day meal scheme; road connectivity to all villages and habitations; and streamlining public distribution system targeted at families below the poverty line.[15]

Given the strategic role of economic growth in poverty reduction, the critical importance of sound macro-economic (fiscal, monetary, foreign exchange) and sectoral (agriculture, industry and trade) policies are self-evident. Macro-economic analysis should look into with great care at policies which are relevant to the poor, such as employment, food prices, land tenure, health and education. There has to be positive discrimination in favour of the poorer sections of the society which have been traditionally or historically discriminated against. The choice of macro-economic policies and poverty alleviation programmes should be such that they are mutually reinforcing and complementary. Economics in a poor country, as Professor Sukhamoy Chakravarty observed, is a moral issue.

As Amartya Sen has pointed out, the enormous expansion of food production makes it possible to guarantee adequate food for all. For a substantial part of humanity, the health problems connected with food consumption have ceased to be the result of having too little, instead they stem from having too much. One part of humanity desperately searches for food to eat, another part counts calories and looks for ways of slimming! Persistence of hunger is related to extreme inequality within the society. In simple terms, food security has two aspects availability of food and accessibility to food stocks. A household can feel food secure if food which is culturally acceptable with appropriate nutritional value is available in the system; households have the capacity to buy; have freedom to choose from the available food stock; there is no institutional bar to access the available food; and within the household, all members specially women and children have access. The critical role played by a well-organised public distribution system for essential foodgrains in a densely populated low income economy in insulating the poor from the rise in food grain prices should be appreciated by policy-makers in the administration. The State should make an explicit guarantee of the right of the poor to food security. Food security is an important component not only of survival, but also of basic dignity and well-being of the poor. The running of the public distribution system is entirely in the hands of the administration. The success of schemes in Andhra Pradesh and Kerala show that an efficient and imaginative administrative machinery could ensure that the benefits reach the poor.

There has been in recent years a good deal of debate on the allied issues of structural reforms, liberalisation, globalisation and marketisation. The poor have neither the skills nor assets to respond to market signals, hence, markets have little relevance for them. As rightly observed by Amartya Sen and Jean Dreze, the policy debate in India has to be shifted away from the narrow concentration on the issues of liberalisation towards taking adequate note of the tremendous social and economic deprivations that blight living conditions in India. While the case for economic reforms may prefer the diagnosis that India has excessive government interference in several fields, it ignores the fact that India has also had insufficient and inefficient state intervention in many areas including basic education, health care, social security, land reforms and promotion of social change. The central issue is the expansion of social opportunities for the people. The role of the government and administrative agencies in programmes of poverty alleviation is thus crucial.

Our efforts at poverty alleviation have expanded exponentially in recent years; there has been a phenomenal increase in the allocation of resources and manpower. But there has been a sharp decline in the competence with which programmes are conceived, formulated and implemented. It was assumed that a set of technocratically evolved projects and policies and some marginal social welfare measures could be designed, and these could be delivered from the top with some consultation with the people. While in some cases, dedicated administrators were able to deliver the inputs to the poor, it was not universally so. An essential prerequisite of an effective poverty eradication strategy is human development, which guarantees the right of poor to participate in decisions that affect their lives. Poverty cannot be eradicated without the participation of the poor themselves.

For most of human history, the plight of the poor has been often excluded from the consciousness of those who have the power to administer. Government contacts with the poor has largely been limited to collecting taxes, ensuring law and order and providing some limited welfare services. Administrations have been largely unresponsive to or even unaware of either the aspirations of the poor or conditions that perpetuate their poverty. The poor on their part remained distrustful of governments which had done so little to serve their interests.[16] The poor often happen to be on the wrong side of the law for the simple reason that the laws themselves may be incongruous or incompatible with their perceptions about the issues involved. The poor in general have very little knowledge of law or legal rights. In relation to the poor, many of the laws, rules and regulations have in practice been found to be oppressive and disabling rather than enabling and liberating.[17]

Though I have been avoiding the use of the term "bureaucracy", it is used in the literature on public administration to refer to the administrative characteristics of centralisation of authority, heavy emphasis on rules and tortuous procedures, narrow outlook, red tape, high-handed and autocratic behaviour, lack of adaptiveness, restriction on communication, fear of innovation, and maintenance of *status quo*, which, in practice means the maintenance and safeguarding of the existing property and social relations. The administrative behaviour of public functionaries entrusted with the governmental activities including the task of social development and public welfare, has been motivated largely by the need for status-oriented power and by an aversion to social programmes for the poor. A lack of concern for the problems of the poor and various types of bias against the poor appear inherent in the administrative structure. While no uniform model is possible, there has to be a pro-poor agenda for the administration and self-critical awareness of the shortcomings and the biases in order to make sensitive and conscious efforts to overcome them.

There are laws which are enabling, empowering and facilitating mechanisms, which give sanction and authority to the various public functionaries. They should be used as tools in favour of the poor to enhance the space for them. Legislations such as the Minimum Wages Act, Bonded Labour Abolition Act, Protection of Civil Rights Act, Prevention of Atrocities Act, Child Labour (Prohibition and Regulation) Act and various land reforms enactments are instances of powerful legal weapons in the hands of administrators. The effective and imaginative implementation of laws in favour of the poor will itself go a long way in securing their rights. While the battle against poverty and social evils cannot be won by laws alone, it cannot be fought without them either.

In Indian society, the civil servant has respectability and social standing. In the long run, what will count are the human qualities of the individual civil servant. Administration is not a uniform monolith; individual administrators matter and to a very significant extent. The professional skill of the administrator will be of little use unless it is grounded in ethical values and moral standards. Equally important will be the collective ethos of the civil services. The civil services should be guided by a code of ethics and become an ethical mission motivated by a value system and a tradition of humanism. It is essential that the administration develop into a confident and professional group with values and attitudes appropriate to the building of a just and humane society.

The role of the government, the administration and the administrators will continue to be considerable and crucial for quite sometime in the improvement of the conditions of the poor. Where they have been compassionate and motivated, civil servants have been a source of great strength to the Indian poor. There is a vast difference that the pro-poor civil servants can make in terms of advocacy of a proper policy, allocation of resources, and earnest and effective implementation of programmes for the poor. The protection and support that the poor need in a society, that is shot with social and economic inequalities can be guaranteed by impartial and fearless civil servants. There are a large number of cases where great changes have been brought about by a dedicated and motivated team of administrators. In can recall a number of instances such as the abolition of the exploitative Gorakhpuri labour system; enactment of the law to abolish the bonded labour system; leadership role in the literacy mission; curbing of female infanticide; *Jal Hai Jan Hai* scheme[18] in Bihar; restoration of communal harmony; the eradication of the guinea worm disease; protection of Scheduled Castes and Scheduled Tribes, formulation of poverty alleviation and social assistance programmes; and in Mussoorie, the rehabilitation and restoration of the human dignity of rickshaw pullers.[19]

The injustice suffered by the poor in India mainly relates to property, and wages on the one hand, and body and person, on the other. The poor in different strata and occupations face varying degrees of oppression and atrocities with different degrees of intensity. The poor lose their land and even where title over land has been conferred, they have been prevented from occupying and cultivating the land. There are severe problems faced by them in enjoying the fruits of their own labour; the problems of sharecroppers in North Bihar are well known. The poor in the villages have often been in permissive possession of house sites or homesteads with a constant threat of eviction. In urban areas, the problem is of living space itself; the term "slum clearance or encroachment removal" is often an euphemism for uprooting powerless urban migrants from their homes and shifting them to low value sites usually at the periphery, leading to their virtual economic extinction. The victims of custodial violence or illegal, detention are mostly people from the poor and backward sections of society, with little financial or political power to back them.

A sensitive administrator can ensure justice and fair play. The least that the administration can do is prevent injustice to the poor in the society and in the various arenas of administration, such as public offices, police stations etc. The upholding and protection of human rights, not merely in the sense of preventing their violation but also in the positive sense of enhancing the human rights of Dalits, women, the poor and oppressed, is a fundamental duty of any modern administration. In all issues that concern the poor, sensitisation and motivation, high-level review and monitoring, a simple redressal mechanism, close supervision, a regular flow of information and more than anything else, accessibility to the poor will bring a lot of relief to them. The fact that millions of people suffer from deprivation should engender indignation, shock and disquiet in our minds. Reports of starvation deaths in Kalahandi, Koraput or Bolangir should not remain news items; but provoke administrators to initiate immediate action to prevent their recurrence.

At the last fringes of our society subsists an enormous mass of the unseen, and unheard. These are the aged, physically handicapped, orphaned, abandoned and abused children, women in distress, the mentally ill, leprosy patients, destitutes, beggars, poor undertrials and displaced persons. It is the moral responsibility of the administration to reach them all. If the administration, particularly the district administration, does not reach them, no one else will. This calls for the highest degree of humanism.

The prevalence of the evil and inhuman practice of untouchability in many parts of the country and the perpetration of atrocities on the weaker sections constitute a blot on any civilised society and a challenge to sensitive administrators. It will be a true and lasting tribute to the memory of Babasaheb Ambedkar, if we could take up and accomplish the mission of abolition of untouchability in the country. This, in my view, is well within the capabilities of our administrators.

Unlike in the past, there are a variety of programmes and policies which are available to present day administrators. Modern technology has opened up many possibilities and has provided new instruments. There is a scheme or a programme for every identifiable group of the poor, be they landless poor, or landed poor, women, children, bonded or free, wage labourer or self-employed, urban or rural, old or young. The potential for administrative interventions is immense.

As long as a significant number of poor exist in the society, equality will mean social justice, and social justice will necessarily imply equality. Many years ago, on 25th December, 1927, while leading the Scheduled Caste people to assert their right to take the water from the Chowdwar tank in Mahad in Maharashtra[20], Babasaheb Ambedkar observed:

> It is not as if drinking the water of Chowdwar lake will make us immortal. We have survived well enough all these days without drinking it. We are going to the tank to assert that we too are human beings like others. It must be clear that this meeting has been called to set up norms of equality.

None of us really knows the final answer to this complex question of poverty. But all of us, and particularly those who are part of the administration, engaged in the governance of this country for many decades to come, have some power and capability to lessen, even if it be in a small measure, the intensity of the suffering of the poor. In the words of Pandit Jawaharlal Nehru:

> It is our passionate desire to serve our people and remove the many burdens they have carried for generations past. Gandhiji said on one occasion that it was his supreme ambition to wipe every tear from every eye. That was an ambition beyond even his power to realise, for many millions of eyes have shed tears in India and perhaps it will never be possible to stop completely this unending flow of human sorrow. But it is certainly possible for us to lessen human want and misery and suffering.

NOTES

1. Slavery was prevalent in many parts of India even until the early part of the 19th century. There are various forms of bondage which emerged over a period of time. Bonded labour continued into the twentieth century and the enactment of the Bonded Labour (Abolition) Act was in fulfilment of the Twenty-Point Programme, announced soon after the declaration of emergency in 1975.
2. The measurement of poverty in India has been the subject of study by academicians, planners and experts. The concept of "poverty line" which has been adopted, is anchored essentially in the nutrition requirements of 2,400 calories in rural areas and 2,100 calories in urban areas and the monetary equivalent of expenditure required by the household to secure this energy intake. The population below the poverty line is estimated by applying the updated poverty line to the corresponding National Sample Survey distribution of households by levels of consumption expenditure. For a closer understanding, the *Report of the Expert Group on Estimation of Proportion and Number of Poor* (Lakdawala Group), Planning Commission, 1993, may be seen.
3. This has been referred to in the Economic Survey of the Government of India for the year 1995-1996. The results have been treated as preliminary.
4. This is a very perceptive observation made by S.P. Tiwari, in his article on Santhal Parganas in the collection of articles edited by Utsa Patnaik and Manjari Dingwancy (1985). It is the common experience of most field officers that the one request universally made by the rural poor is for a piece of land.

5. The criteria, if any, adopted by the Centre and State Government in fixing the statutory minimum wage have been examined in depth by the Study Group on Wages, set up by the National Commission on Rural Labour (1991). Strangely, even the Government of India was unable to explain the basis for the minimum wages fixed by them.
6. Article 24 of the Constitution prohibits the employment of children below 14 years in any factory or mine or in any hazardous employment. This forms part of the chapter on fundamental rights. Article 45 which is part of the Directive Principles requires the state to endeavour to provide free and compulsory education for all children until they complete the age of 14 years.
7. This has been referred to by Jan Breman in his work on South Gujarat. The magistrates were authorised to apprehend and return to their master any bonded labourer who had absconded.
8. Sylhet district went to Pakistan at the time of partition and is now in Bangladesh. It is interesting to note that in 1978, when the work on bonded labour was being done effectively for sometime in Andhra Pradesh, the landlords of a district made a representation in a similar vein to the then Chief Minister that if the Act was strictly enforced, agricultural operations will come to a standstill and agricultural production will suffer (Author's experience).
9. As Secretary of the Social Welfare Department in Andhra Pradesh, during 1976-1978, I personally came across second-generation bonded labourers, who were working to repay a loan taken by their grandfathers.
10. The reference is to the foreword written by Upendra Baxi to the book, *Dalits Betrayed* by Dr. B.D. Sharma (1994).
11. The Special Component Plan owes its origin to the initiative and imagination of Shri P.S. Krishnan, Joint Secretary in the Ministry of Welfare and later Secretary of the Ministry. The Tribal Sub-Plan largely owes its origin to the initiative of Dr. B.D. Sharma, then Joint Secretary in the Ministry of Welfare and later Commissioner for Scheduled Castes and Scheduled Tribes. I am mentioning this to emphasise that the work of individual administrators and their leadership does have a far reaching significance.
12. I have in mind the formulation of the Special Component Plan for Scheduled Castes in Andhra Pradesh, when discussion were held with each administrative department and its role in the development of Scheduled Castes delineated. This was reviewed at the district level, Kerala also adopted a decentralised model.
13. The restructuring of the Special Component Plan will involve the initial setting aside of resources for the development of Scheduled Castes. A plan for Scheduled Castes will have to be drawn up taking into account their needs, which is then incorporated into the State or Central Plan. This is in contrast with the present practice of first drawing up the state plan and then making the Special Component Plan. It is reported that Uttar Pradesh and

Maharashtra have restructured the Special Component Plan in this manner, but details are not readily available.

14. A very curious and pathetic case, it shows the unconcern for the poor on the part of all wings of the state. This has been referred to in the *Twenty-eighth Report of the Commissioner of Scheduled Castes and Scheduled Tribes* and reported in 1986 *Madhya Pradesh Law Journal*, pp. 704-107.
15. The adoption of seven specific items as what has been termed as Basic Minimum Services programme was announced in the budget speech of the Union Finance Minister (1996-97). [Alas! This announcement has remained rhetorical. Ed.]
16. While working as Chief Secretary in Tripura, I had a number of occasions to stay in tribal villages: On one occasion, a group of tribals who came to see me, long after everyone else had left, made only one request to save them from the departments of forest, revenue and police! This showed the negative image of administration in the minds of the poor. I must add that this pushed us to make strenuous efforts to prove that the administration existed for their benefit and good.
17. The compilation and documentation of the laws, regulations, rules, orders and practices which disable the poor has been undertaken by the National Academy of Administration under the guidance of Dr. N.C. Saxena.
18. Funds available under the Million Wells Scheme of Jawahar Rozgar Yojana were effectively utilised to provide irrigation wells for the tribal lands in Dumka in Santhal Parganas. This was done by involving the people and eliminating contractors or middlemen.
19. I am personally aware of the initiative taken, and troubles undergone by Deputy Director, LBSNAA, Harsh Mander, and the probationers of the Academy in this matter. The human aspect is most important. The issue is not abolition of rickshaws, but providing the people dependent on this means of living with an alternative and a more dignfied way of life.
20. The Chowdwar tank was a public tank from which Scheduled Caste persons could not take water as they were prohibited from doing so by the upper-caste inhabitants. Babasaheb Ambedkar led a satyagraha to assert the civil rights of Scheduled Caste people in December 1927.

REFERENCES

Breman, Jan, *Patronage and Exploitation: Changing Agrarian Relations in South Gujarat*, New Delhi: Manohar Publications, 1979.

Breman, Jan, *Of Peasants, Migrants and Paupers: Rural Labour Circulation and Capitalist Production in West India*, New Delhi: Oxford University Press: 1985.

Chambers, Robert, *Rural Development: Putting the Last First*, London : Longman Scientific and Technical, 1983.

Dreze, Jean and Sen, Amartya, *Hunger and Public Action*, New Delhi: Oxford University Press, 1989.

Dreze, Jean and Sen, Amartya, *India, Economic Development and Social Opportunity*, New Delhi: Oxford University Press, 1995.

Government of India, Ministry of Labour, *Report of the National Commission on Rural Labour*, New Delhi: Government of India, 1991.

Government of India, Ministry of Finance, *Economic Survey*, 1995-96.

Korten, David, and Alfonso, Felipe, *Beauracracy and the Poor: Closing the Gap*, New Delhi: McGraw Hill, 1981.

Krishna Iyer, V.R. *Dr. Ambedkar and the Dalit Future*, Delhi: B.R. Publishing Corporation, 1990.

Mishra, Lakshmidhar, *Anguish of the Deprived*, New Delhi: Har Anand Publications, 1995.

Ramachandran, V.K., *Wage Labour and Unfreedom in Agriculture*, Oxford: Clarendon Press, 1990.

Sharma, B.D., *Dalits Betrayed*, Har Anand Publications, New Delhi: 1994.

Patnaik Usha, and Dingwaney Manjari, *Chains of Servitude: Bondage and Slavery in India*, Delhi: Sangam Books, 1985.

Vyas, V.S. and Bhargava Pradeep, "Public Intervention for Poverty Alleviation: An Overview", *Economic and Political Weekly*, October, 14-21, 1995.

Weiner, Myron, *The Child and the State in India*, New Delhi: Oxford University Press, 1991.

15

EQUALITY THROUGH LEGISLATION
Social Consequences of Gradual Change

NANDU RAM

The idea of equality among unequals or social equality has been the most contentious yet highly cherished goal of every human society in the world. In modern time, it was perhaps first proclaimed in the French society through the French National Assembly Proclamations of 1789. Thereafter, its articulations and adoption spread to the other European and American societies wherein it attained legal sanction. At the epistemological level, various inherent aspects of equality, such as equality of conditions, justice or social justice, freedom, liberty, fraternity, etc. have systematically been analysed by a host of scholars the world over. In our own society, the idea of social equality was conceived, substantially practised and propagated by the Gautama Buddha, more than 2500 years ago. Equality was subsequently revered at the level of spiritual transcendence through the *Bhakti* movements, but sparsely paved the way for conceiving and propagating the idea of social equality among all human beings during the medieval period. This obviously became the stepping foundation for articulation of social equality during the period of enlightenment and social reform in the late nineteenth century, in which a number of reforms enacted by the British rulers in India also contributed substantially. Yet, with the looming effect of such reforms, the idea of equality or social equality was strenuously articulated afresh by Ambedkar in the social, economic and political spheres during the early decades of the twentieth century. This got elaborately incorporated later in the Constitution of the Indian republic. Besides granting legal equality to all citizens, the Indian Constitution has also ensured social equality among them by making special provisions for the most unequal groups of citizens, like Scheduled Castes (Dalits as they call themselves) and Tribes, minorities, and other socially and educationally backward classes or castes of citizens.

Notwithstanding the oft repeated discussions and debates on the constitutional provisions and related legislative measures, with their benefits accruing to the Scheduled Castes or Dalits, the focus in this paper is on their viability for promoting the latter's strivings for attaining the goals of social justice, equality, liberty and fraternity enshrined in the Preamble to the Constitution. While pointing out certain limitations of these provisions and measures, specially their implementations, the emphasis here is on both their protective and developmental aspects, without undermining entirely their welfare aspect. Finally, in the light of a number of movements organised by Dalits in recent times for achieving socio-economic progress and a distinct social identity, certain ways and means are argued out to effectively administer the existing provisions and measures for realising the goals of their proper and sustainable progress and development in the country.

Existing Provisions and Measures

Before analysing roles of the constitutional provisions and related legislative measures in bringing gradual socio-economic change among the Dalits, it may be in order to briefly spell them out. Besides the general provisions like right to equality and promotion of welfare of people, equal justice, etc. enshrined in the section on Fundamental Rights of the citizens in the Constitution which are equally applicable to the Dalits, the specific provisions and related legislative measures have been enacted in their favour under Article 15(4) of the same Section and various other Articles included in the

Section on the Directive Principles of State Policy. These provisions and measures which are also sometimes termed social legislations can broadly be categorised into three types. In the first type are a number of constitutional provisions safeguarding representations of Dalits in educational institutions (Article 46), in both Central and State government jobs (Article 335), and in Parliament and State Assemblies (Articles 330 and 332 respectively). Being representative in nature in terms of ensuring representation of Dalits in these spheres, these provisions have been made in a way for their educational, economic and political welfare. Hence, these are welfare measures, stipulated under the specific policy commonly known as reservation policy. In academic as well as non-academic writings, the policy has been rephrased as the policy of protective discrimination, compensatory discrimination, reverse discrimination, affirmative action, concessions, privileges, special provisions, special treatment, and preferential treatment (for details, see Galanter, 1991:2-3) each one having different connotation. Our intention here is not to go into the etymology and contextual usages of these terms; rather to affirm that from the Dalits' perspective, it may better be accepted as the policy of compensation to discriminations of past as well as of present time meted to them.

In the second category are certain protective measures like prohibition of discriminations, or social and religious disabilities (Article 15), abolition of untouchability (Article 17), ban on forced or bonded labour (Article 23) or *begar*, and throwing open public places such as temples, roads, tea stalls, etc. (Article 15, 2). Based on Article 17 and combination of other relevant Articles of the Constitution, two special Acts—Untouchability (Offences) Act, 1955, amended later in 1976 as Protection of Civil Rights Act, and the Scheduled Castes and Scheduled Tribes (Prevention of Atrocities) Act, 1989, have also been legislated to protect their life, honour and property. These provisions in essence protect physical, social and culturai or religious interests of the Dalits. Finally, in the third category are developmental measures—mostly legislative measures like, providing grants-in-aid and other facilities for constructing houses, digging wells for drinking and irrigation purposes, starting small enterprises, etc. These measures have been enacted under Article 15(4) and Article 46 of the Constitution and are meant, on the one hand, to lessen excessive dependence of Dalits on the reservation policy, and on the other, to enable them to achieve socio-economic development in their own geographical location, if they do not fulfil even the minimum prerequisites for deriving benefits of the said policy.

We may hasten to clarify here that though such classification of the existing provisions and measures adopted in favour of Dalits is relevant only for analytical purpose, the latter overlap a great deal in their actual spirit and implications. For instance, while the welfare measures safeguard interests of Dalits by facilitating their access to avenues like education, government jobs and political power which might not be easily possible otherwise, these also protect them from discriminations and injustices practised earlier of preventing them from entering into these avenues or spheres. Also, the net results of these measures directly promote socio-economic interest and development of those Dalits who are immediate beneficiaries, but indirectly encourage even others to get benefited from these. Same is true with the other types of provisions and measures. All the three types of provisions and measures are thus interrelated and that is why these were generally known as welfare measures, a little prior to independence of the country. Such usage of welfare measures in generic sense (inclusive of all the three types of provisions and measures) has remained in vogue in the government, as is evident from the very nomenclature of the ministry at the central level till recently which is associated with safeguarding interests mainly of the Dalits.

All the three types of provisions and measures are, anyway, equally significant for welfare, protection and development of the Dalits. Our intention here is not to view them in a hierarchical manner in which one type of provisions and measures may be rated more important than the other. Yet, their significance can be valued on the basis of contextual need and priorities of the beneficiaries. This can also be inferred from the government's emphasis in making financial allocations on each provision for safeguarding interests of the Dalits. But the fact of the matter is that the welfare measures or provisions made under the reservation policy have gained much more importance over other provisions and measures right from the very beginning, perhaps due to the simple reason that these were much sought after by the Dalit leadership even prior to independence. The policy enjoyed applause from the leadership and also people at large, but has invited, since the nineteen-seventies, lot of criticisms on the ground that its various provisions and measures have been misused by the beneficiaries. The counter-criticisms have equally been heralded by the beneficiaries and prospective beneficiaries against the prejudicial and apathetic attitudes and acts of the implementing machineries.

Without entering into such controversy here, it may be said that various provisions and measures made under the reservation policy ought to be accepted as prerequisites for social formation of middle class, or more appropriately a new middle class, among the Dalits (Ram, 1988). The necessity of such a class is to be seen in relation to the nature of historical formation and role of the middle class *per se* along with its growing importance in the contemporary Indian society. In contrast, the new middle class of Dalits is relatively much newer and is a creation of the constitutional provisions and measures. Such a class of Dalits is vivisected in its role of acting as catalytic agent for bringing social change and mobility among the Dalit masses, and its efforts for getting structurally accommodated in the Indian middle class. It is in this sense their social formation and role of change setters are to be taken whether they are termed Harijan elite (Sachchidananda, 1977) or Scheduled Caste classes *vis-a-vis* neo-Brahmins (Parvathamma, 1989: 128-144).

Retrospectively, going by needs and priorities of Dalits, the welfare measures or reservation facilities, for instance, may not directly be relevant to those Dalits living in rural areas whose immediate problems of physical protection and socio-economic development need to be resolved first by strengthening and vigorously implementing the protective and developmental measures. Once they are brought out of the fray through protecting them from their socio-religious discriminations, economic exploitation, atrocious social conditions and also through facilitating their socio-economic development, they may be better equipped to make proper and effective use of the welfare measures. Yet, some such measures may be necessary to facilitate them achieve somewhat better elementary education, specially of the type which is imparted in the elite educational institutions solely located in urban areas.

The basic philosophy and objectives of all the three types of provisions and measures are, however, not only to provide safeguards to the Dalits but their basic spirit is said to bring them to the 'mainstream' or at par with others, though the very notion of mainstream is not free from problematic in terms of its nature and social composition. For instance, the notion of mainstream is supposedly constituted of philosophical foundation, socio-cultural practices and literary tradition(s) of the *dwijas*—twice born castes (Oommen, 1990:43-66). Filtering down to the grassroot level, the mainstream is then to be constituted by both the landowning and even landless upper castes in villages, which is now often contested by the Dalits and backward castes (Kapadia, 1995; Ilaiah, 1996).

Moreover, the very notion of mainstream is an inference drawn by academic and non-academic interpreters of the people's perception. In no case it is endorsed by Indian Constitution, either in its letter or spirit, while making provisions and measures for the Dalits and other vulnerable sections of people in the country. Anyway, the main objective of these provisions and measures is to reduce and not increase the caste consciousness (Beteille, 1992:54). But this itself is highly contestable at both ideological (principle) and substantive levels. It may, however, be suggested that the latent objective of these provisions and measures is also to enable the Dalits to act as active agents to the national progress, which they have been doing even otherwise for centuries together.

Not going into further details of the aims and objectives of these provisions and measures when we look at their viability in regard to translating the spirit of the Preamble to the Constitution in favour of Dalits, we find that these are capable of meeting some, if not all, of their requirements. Yet, at the implementation level the situation is not very satisfactory. This is not to deny the fact that these have definitely brought considerable amount of socio-economic change among Dalits through all these years. Some of the provisions and measures have protected them, though more in principle than in practice, from social discriminations, economic bondage and exploitation, and from their miserable life conditions. These have also helped them in their access to the educational endeavour, public sector employment and political power. But more than that these have raised their aspirations and expectations high and dry with tremendous amount of socio-political awareness and consciousness among them. Consequently, the slow and sluggish implementation of these provisions and measures have frustrated their aspirations for achieving social mobility *vis-a-vis* equality, for whose fulfilment they have frequently opted for recourse to movements.

These provisions and measures are, however, viewed by non-Dalits as privileges or concessions doled out to the Dalits and tribals at the cost of others. Hence, these are considered highly discriminatory both in letter and spirit. Even these are said to have created new types of discriminations which are termed protective or reverse discriminations, as stated earlier, in distributing available opportunities and resources to the citizens or mass of the people in the country. These are also perceived as discriminations by the non-Dalits against them, and, in their view, these go against the very spirit of the Constitution which treats all citizens equal and does not discriminate them on the basis of caste, creed, colour, sex, region, etc. But from the Dalits' point of view, these provisions and measures are in a way some sorts of compensations to the loss incurred to them on account of their exploitations and resultant backwardness at the hands of others for centuries, as stated earlier. Due to their multiple forms of deprivations and discriminations in the past which also continue in many ways even today, they are at present not equally equipped for competing with the privileged people. Competitions for various available opportunities are also not all fair and non-discriminatory. Hence, Dalits' access to such opportunities through compensatory discriminations or reservation. Even some sections of Dalits go to the extent in saying that benefits of the constitutional provisions and legislative measures are their rights and not doles from the state or society. These are, in a way, very modest forms of their shares in the existing opportunities and resources in the country. Such stand-points may obliquely be construed as their strong reactions to the magnitudes of on-going resentment of non-Dalits to the referred provisions and measures for the Dalits.

Such stand-points, specially of the middle level castes, is epistemologically contested on the ground that:

> It is difficult to see how the idea that castes and communities have rights to proportionate shares in public employment can be made compatible with the working of a modern society, committed to economic development and liberal democracy. It is true that caste continues to operate in many spheres of social life; but it does not do so any longer as a matter of right. The continued existence of caste is one thing; its legitimacy is different thing altogther. The attempt to invest the caste system with legitimacy by claiming that its constituent units have rights and entitlements is bound to be defeated in the end; but in the meantime, it can cause enormous harm to society and its institutions (Beteille, 1992:53-54).

Our intention is neither to counterpose questions nor to enter into any debate at his stage. Instead, we simply wish to remind that if the individual continues to be subordinate to the group, namely caste, if caste exists not as a material edifice to be 'physically dismantled and destroyed' but 'in the consciousness of the people—in their deep sense of division and separation on the one hand and of rank and inequality on the other' (*Ibid.*: 54, see also, p.49) and if merit is largely attributed to the birth in a family not completely distanced from a caste or community, then it is simply unfounded to argue that it loses its legitimacy in claiming for certain rights or shares.

Anyway, it may be mentioned here that such continued opposition has often resulted in temporal, though perhaps artificial or hidden, threat of the state (government and judiciary) to terminate, at any given point, the special provisions and legislative measures, more so the provisions relating to the policy of political reservation enacted even for Dalits. But the claims of Dalits for ever continuation of these provisions and measures are not altogether unfounded on the ground that they represent a large chunk of the toiling masses and largely bear the brunt and share discontent of non-Dalits who are also by now disillusioned from the possible benefits of numerous developmental schemes implemented in the country from time to time.

The Constitution makers in their wisdom, however, did not remain contend with incorporating social equality as a mere rhetoric. Nor were they satisfied with the provisions of 'equality before law' and 'equal opportunity to all'. Instead, they had recognised the contemporary socio-economic disparities of glaring nature between Dalits (besides tribals, other socially and educationally backward classes, and other weaker sections of population) and rest of the people in the country. Hence, they made special provisions in the Constitution, followed by certain legislative measures for realising social equality between Dalits and non-Dalits. These provisions and measures are no doubt capable of creating certain type of equality between people of both categories, provided these are properly and rigorously implemented with their full length and breadth.

These provisions and measures are, however, means and not ends in themselves. These are means or strategies to promote interests of Dalits and to prepare them to come at par and compete with others. In net analysis, these are meant to help them achieve social, economic and political justice; enjoy liberty of thought and expression; pursue religious belief, faith and worship; endow with equality of opportunity and of status; and promote fraternity in terms of fellow-feelings. These definitely have made some headways but have largely failed on many counts. This is so as these have been adopted with both immediate and proximate aims of enabling Dalits' access to a few available opportunities, and thereby evolving a new social order in the country. The state with its different organs exhibits its secular credentials, though the functionaries of these organs play their roles not entirely devoid of their primordial social and cultural predispostions. In fact, the conceptions of a value-neutral state, equality or social equality, equal opportunity, etc. are totally alien to the highly divided and hierarchised society in India. This is easily evident from the lack of vigour in full and proper implementation of the various provisions and measures by those who are in the helm of the affairs.

The sluggish implementation of these provisions and measures is also due to a number of inherent contradictions built in them as these are interpreted differently and some of these, specially those related to the policy of reservation, are frequently challenged in the courts of law. Perhaps there is a lack of political will on the part of the state and its implementing machinery. The often repeated argument given by respective departments of the governments is that there is lack of suitability of majority of the Dalits for getting benefits of the provisions and measures existing in their favour. The frames of reference of such argument are obviously with regard to provisions and measures related to the reservation policy and developmental grants-in-aid to the Dalits and not to the removal of their socio-religious disabilities, physical protection, etc. As stated earlier, Dalits on their part invariably blame the implementing machinery for its general apathy, prejudiced attitudes and actions, and, over and above, its manoeuvrability of existing provisions and measures. Hence, a breach of trusts and commitments lurk on both sides. Even then, the tiny section of Dalits and tribals with whatsoever limited amount of social equality they have achieved, have tried to get better adjusted in the existing social order, instead of evolving a new one with the joint efforts of those of similar class of non-Dalits.

Yet, the gradual changes brought through these provisions and measures are much appreciated by others, though not so much by the Dalits. The former view them longitudinally, whereas the latter locate them in their growing aspirations and expectations. Thus, there seems to be an increasing gap between the gradual change and high aspirations and expectations of Dalits which need to be properly analysed and bridged within the shortest possible time, lest they become completely alienated and intensify their movements, even violent ones, for achieving their goals.

Equality Through Welfare Measures

Equality to all citizens guaranteed in the Indian Constitution is an ideal to be pursued by the state, society and individual in regard to substantive issues and contexts. More specifically, equality guaranteed through the Articles included in the Fundamental Rights (Part III) of the citizens, with exception of Article 16(4), is termed 'formal equality', whereas equality guaranteed through the Articles included in the Directive Principles of State Policy (Part IV), along with Article 16(4) of the previous Part, is called 'substantive equality'. The former type of equality is also known as 'horizontal equality' by treating unequal citizens on equal footing, whereas the latter is termed 'vertical equality' as it enables unequals to compete for equality with others. In regard to equality and reservation policy, it is argued:

> The relation of equality and compensatory discrimination is viewed very differently what we may call the vertical perspective. In this view, the present is seen as a transition from a past of inequality to a desired future of substantive equality; the purpose of compensatory discrimination is to promote equalisation by offsetting historically accumulated inequalities. Thus, compensatory discrimination does not detract from equality in the interest of present fairness; rather, it is seen as requisite to the fulfilment of the nation's long-range goal of substantial redistribution and equalisation. Not only present claims, but historical deprivations and national aspirations are relevant (Galanter, 1991: 379-80).

In the given perspective, the above mentioned aspirations and expectations of Dalits need some elaborations here *vis-a-vis* their realisation with the help of the welfare measures, inclusive of all the three types of measures. Their aspirations are to be seen in the light of their strong urge for achieving equality with others in all spheres of life. Since the very idea of equality is difficult to conceptualise besides its being absolute and relative, it varies from time to time and context to context. The different types and levels of aspirations of Dalits for achieving social equality are also to be seen as absolute and variant. For instance, the meaning of equality *vis-a-vis* aspirations and expectations for the middle class Dalits may be seen in terms of their being equal to non-Dalits of the similar class or socio-economic background. But equality for a poor Dalit may mean enhancement in his/her economic status at par with others, first in the locality—be it a village or slum, then in the region and finally outside the region, through availing of benefits of the provisions of equality before law, equality of opportunity and more so through the special opportunities provided in the Constitution. Similarly, an illiterate Dalit may aspire to be educated at par with others and a powerless one would definitely look at equality in terms of enjoying power similar to the powerful ones. In sum, the Dalit masses aspire to cross both the poverty and pollution lines as a first step and then desire to be social equal with others, though in the process they may or may not look at those who would remain below them or their unequal (Moffott, 1979).

One may argue that such aspirations of Dalits are utopian and may not get translated into reality because of the inner social contradictions, unmanageable population size in the country, paucity of the resources available for the purpose, and sluggish imple-mentation of the constitutional provisions and legislative measures adopted in their favour. True, these reasons are very valid and cannot be easily wished away. But what is required at this stage is to instill the civic sense in the society according to which the welfarism does not remain in the ambit of the state, but also spreads, both at the individual and society levels. The individual has to grapple with the idea of welfare of others and the society needs to prepare and promote such individuals to achieve the status of a civic or civil society. In fact, welfarism at all the three levels of individuals, state and society needs to be engrossed with the principle and practice of social justice and equality. Besides, the general process of social and economic development in the country is to be streamlined and adhered strictly to the principles of equality and to the special opportunity in favour of the Dalits, in spite of the newly introduced economic liberalisation in the name of reform or structural adjustment in the economy.

This also goes quite in the order of the constitutional spirit and the growing high aspirations and expectations of Dalits who generally look at the special provisions and measures as fully competent for realising social justice and equality, provided these are properly and fully implemented as stated earlier. It is quite evident that the quantum of the welfare measures or provisions under the reservation policy has been implemented hardly to the tune of 50 per cent of the quota reserved for them, except in the case of representation of Dalits in Parliament and State Assemblies. But, there problem is of a different nature wherein Dalit leadership is largely subordinated to the non-Dalit elite. Same is true of the protective and developmental measures whose implementations and resultant consequences need a thorough evaluation at this stage. In such a situation, aspirations and expectations of Dalits to achieve social justice and equality of any variety through the 'welfare measures' (all the tree types of provisions and measures) appear to be a day-dream and can get easily frustrated specially in the event of the aforesaid inadequate and improper implementations of these measures and in a relatively more hostile atmosphere prevailing all around.

Limits of Gradual Change

Generally speaking, out of the two types of changes—gradual and fast or rapid—on the basis of their pace or rate, the former is brought by the state agencies through the implementation of various policies and programmes, whereas the latter is initiated and taken to the logical end by the people and their organisations. This, however, does not mean that the former type of changes are always conservative or *status-quoist*. Instead, these may also be radical though their pace may be slow either due to less progressive nature of the state and its agencies with inadequate resources at its disposal or due to its continued links with and accommodativeness of traditional institutions and forces. The radical changes, on the other hand, bring overall transformation in the society through altering structures and functions of existing institutions. These changes are brought, exclusively by active role of the people and their organisations, with a clear goal of evolving a new type of society or social order in place of the existing one which in their reckoning is conservative, hence, outdated. Needless to say that in both the cases the goal of change is generally well set and it is the means which makes them gradual or fast.

The nature and goal of social change in India was, in a way, set soon after it got political independence and adopted a new Constitution for the republic. The specific goal was to evolve an egalitarian social order based on equality, liberty, fraternity and social justice. Besides, it also aimed at creating a citizen or an individual with considerable amount of rationality, civic sense and modern outlook or world-view. Towards this end, a number of policies and programmes have been adopted since the very beginning to achieve planned social change, though the underlying institutions of traditions have not altogether been curbed and undermined. Moreover, no specific time frame has been set to achieve the goal of planned or induced changes and thereby evolve a new social order in the country; rather, it has been left to the passage of time. Hence, bearing the gradual nature of change in mind it has been envisaged to achieve this change as early as possible, through the stipulated plans for every succeeding five years, with active participation of the people.

The constitutional provisions and legislative measures adopted in favour of Dalits and tribals have generated a gradual change. However, these have not yet produced the desired results due to reasons stated above. The implementation of special provisions and measures is not only confined to the more publicised welfare measures or measures under the reservation policy as categorised above but is equally applicable to the protective and developmental measures. Whatever results have they produced so far are viewed in the longitudinal fashion, wherein the present socio-economic status of Dalits (and tribals) is compared with that in the past which appears to be much improved. But the increasing disparities between Dalits (and tribals) and non-Dalits (and non-tribals) are overlooked, and their growing aspirations and expectations are ignored.

Around 50 per cent of the quantum of 'welfare measures' is still unfulfilled. The cases of implementation of the protective and developmental measures are in no way better than that of the welfare measures. In fact, their implementation has remained even worse during all these years as is evident from the rising cases of atrocities or physical violence committed against the Dalits and tribals, and their growing poverty and unemployment specially in the rural areas. This type of gradual change has produced, in recent years, three kinds of results. One, it has produced limited positive results by bringing some improvement in socio-economic status and power position of the Dalits and tribals. Two, this has raised their aspirations and expectations, specially in view of the principles of equality enshrined in the Constitution, their adoption and avowed implementation by the state. And finally, due to the vast gap between the first and second types of results there is a growing discontent among the Dalits (and tribals). This may be taken as part of the general discontent among people in the country, though nature of the former is both quantitatively and qualitatively different from the latter.

Dalit Movements for Equality

Dalit movements, howsoever loosely structured or organised at the micro level with parochial issues, are directed ultimately towards achievement of social justice and equality. These movements can broadly be classified into two categories in regard to their objectives. The first type of movements aim to get the welfare (reservation) and protective measures fully implemented. Dalit movements strive for their full and proper implementation to achieve equality at both the local and national level. Dalits agitate for social justice and equality to be fully accorded to them particularly in regard to their proportional access to the available resources, including politico-administrative power and social prestige. The underlying objective of their movements is to play an active and equal role in the overall governance of the state and society rather than being passive recipients of the state patronage and thereby facing hostility and antagonism of others. The second type of movements are for eradication of their social discriminations, economic exploitation and political vulnerability due to which they face grievous atrocities of the upper and middle level castes in rural areas. They fight back these atrocities through their collective movements which have attracted not much serious attention in social science research.

The Dalits' urge for achieving socio-economic development, social justice, equality and, in a word, equal social status can also be seen from their agitations for acquiring a more dignified and respectful social identity (Ram, 1995:29-34). It is true that the welfare measures have helped some Dalits in achieving better socio-economic status and power positions, as stated earlier. Some of them have also adopted the course of 'passing and percolation' which, at one level, is denial of their Dalit identity. But at the crucial levels of availing benefits of the welfare measures and their close interaction with non-Dalits, they are repeatedly reminded of their Dalit identity. Hence, their 'dual or marginal identity'. In fact, their agitations for identity can be seen at two levels: one, they are inclined to retain their traditional identity widely known at the local and regional levels. But they also insist on the accordance of a respectable status in social hierarchy consisting of both caste system and class structure (Pimpley and Sharma, 1985). Presently, this may perhaps be difficult due to a number of embedded social contradictions and graded inequality in the social system itself, operating both in theory and practice at the local level. Two, a more articulate and visible choice of Dalits is to switch over to an altogether new social identity as they perceive their traditional identity socially downgrading and coming in their way of achieving social equality and social justice. The best example is the recently owned identity of their being Dalits.

Then, the question is as to what extent their urge for new social identity is nourished by the prevailing constitutional provisions and legislative measures. We have mentioned above that the most important contribution the welfare measures have made to the Dalits is that these have enabled them to become socially and politically more conscious and aware of their place in society. They have also become more conscious of their exploitation and social degradation. These measures, along with an overall change in the existing socio-political scenario in the country, have made them confident of retaining in some contexts their traditional social identity with a new outlook and/or claiming for new social identity of their choice in other contexts. In the latter case, they have partially succeeded in internalising the new identity and convinced others to recognise that. The examples of Jatavs (Chamars) of Agra, U.P. (Lynch, 1974) and of Mahars—Buddhist, Dalits of Maharashtra (Zelliot, 1996) may be cited here. Moreover, while claiming a new social identity the latter seem strictly to adhere to the constitutional norms of equality outside caste, race, creed, colour and so forth. Their claimed social identity or identities are thus secular in nature and do not connote the sense of their being associated with any caste or community. Also, these are not sectarian but are very much within the framework of the national identity. Therefore, such social identities need to be protected and nourished by incorporating in full their claims for benefits of the welfare and developmental measures and thus transforming vertical equality into a horizontal one.

Conclusion

It is thus clear that the prime objective of Dalits is to embrace social equality at all levels and in all spheres of their social life. The existing constitutional provisions and legislative measures have helped them achieve some socio-economic change, but the nature and pace of such change is gradual. In many cases, the special provisions and measures have been interpreted as being against interests of the non-Dalits and have not thus far been properly implemented. In turn, this has frustrated their high aspirations and expectations for achieving social justice and equality with others. Their aspirations and expectations, in accordance with the principles and spirit of the Constitution, need to be managed at the level of formulation and implementation of certain policies and programmes in addition to the existing ones. In fact, the existing policies and programmes need to be fully and properly implemented for their more cohesive and balanced socio-economic development and integration with others.

The existing provisions and measures adopted in favour of Dalits have invited a host of criticisms from the various sections of society. Their slow and sluggish implementation has not made much headway towards social equality between Dalits and non-Dalits. Most of the Dalits in the country are poor and illiterate. The majority of them are disenchanted about the possible benefits of the special provisions and measures adopted in their favour. Dalits in different parts of the country have already adopted the course of movements of various hues for achieving social equality, liberty and fraternity, and for getting social justice accorded to them. There is every likelihood that in coming years they would intensify such movements for achieving their goals. Such a situation can be averted by fully and properly implementing various policies and programmes through a strong political will, unquestioned commitment of the personnel and the society.

REFERENCES

Beteille, Andre, *The Backward Classes in Contemporary India*, Delhi : Oxford University Press, 1992.

Galanter, Marc, *Competing Equalities: Law and the Backward Classes in India*, Delhi: Oxford University Press, 1991.

Ilaiah, Kancha, *Why I am not a Hindu*, Calcutta: Samya, 1996.

Kapadia, Karen, *Siva and Her Sisters: Gender, Caste and Class in Rural South India*, Oxford: Westview Press, 1995.

Lynch, O.M., *The Politics of Untouchability*, New Delhi: Nationals, 1974.

Moffatt, Michael, *An Untouchable Community in South India: Structure and Concensus*, Princeton: Princeton University Press, 1979.

Oommen, T.K., 'Insiders and Outsiders in India: Primordial Collectivism and Cultural Pluralism', in his *State and Society: Studies in Nation-Building*, New Delhi: Sage Publications, 1990.

Parvathamma, C., *Scheduled Castes at the Cross Roads*, New Delhi: Ashish Publishing House, 1989.

Pimpley, P.N. and S.K. Sharma (eds.), *Struggle for Status*, Delhi: B.R. Publishing Corporation, 1985.

Ram, Nandu, *The Mobile Scheduled Castes: Rise of a New Middle Class*, Delhi: Hindustan Publishing Corporation, 1988.

——, *Beyond Ambedkar: Essays on Dalits in India*, New Delhi: Har-Anand Publications, 1995.

Sachchidananda, *The Harijan Elite*, Faridabad: Thompson Press, 1977.

Zelliot, Elenor, *From Untouchable to Dalit: Essays on the Ambedkar Movement*, New Delhi:Manohar, 1996.

INDEX